THE FIRST KINGDOM

MAX ADAMS is the author of an acclaimed sequence of histories of Early Medieval Britain: *The King in the North*, *In the Land of Giants* and *Ælfred's Britain*. His other books include *Admiral Collingwood* and the bestselling *The Wisdom of Trees*. He has lived and worked in County Durham, in the North-East of England, since 1993.

MAX ADAMS

THE FIRST KINGDOM

HEAD
ZEUS

An Apollo Book

First published in the UK in 2021 by Head of Zeus Ltd
This paperback edition first published in 2021 by Head of Zeus Ltd
An Apollo book

9 7 5 3 1 2 4 6 8

A catalogue record for this book is available
from the British Library.

ISBN (PB): 9781788543484
ISBN (E): 9781788543460

Typeset by Adrian McLaughlin
Maps [inside cover and on pages xiii to xviii] by Jeff Edwards

Printed and bound in Great Britain by
CPI Group (UK) Ltd, Croydon CR0 4YY

Head of Zeus Ltd
First Floor East
5–8 Hardwick Street
London EC1R 4RG

WWW.HEADOFZEUS.COM

*For the Friends of Bernice,
on the occasion of her 10th birthday*

Hardly a pure science, history is closer to animal husbandry than it is to mathematics in that it involves selective breeding. The principal difference between the husbandryman and the historian is that the former breeds sheep or cows or such, and the latter breeds (assumed) facts. The husbandryman uses his skills to enrich the future, the historian uses his to enrich the past. Both are usually up to their ankles in bullshit.

TOM ROBBINS, *Another Roadside Attraction*, 1971

The fact is that the academic mind is so flexible that it can reconcile almost anything with almost anything else.

SIMMS-WILLIAMS, *The Settlement of England in Bede and the Chronicle*, 1983

Contents

List of maps and figures

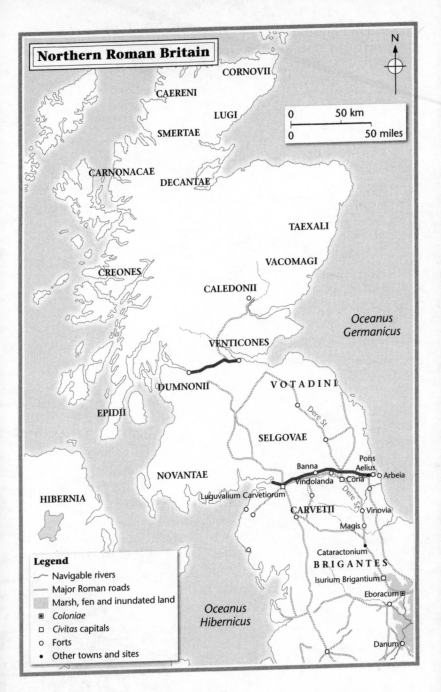

Northern Roman Britain

N

| 0 | 50 km |
| 0 | 50 miles |

CORNOVII

CAERENI

LUGI

SMERTAE

CARNONACAE

DECANTAE

TAEXALI

VACOMAGI

CREONES

CALEDONII

Oceanus Germanicus

VENTICONES

DUMNONII

V O T A D I N I

EPIDII

Dere St.

SELGOVAE

Banna
Pons
Aelius
NOVANTAE
Vindolanda   Coria   Arbeia

Luguvalium Carvetiorum

Dere St.

HIBERNIA

CARVETII

Vinovia

Magis

Cataractonium

B R I G A N T E S

Isurium Brigantium

Oceanus Hibernicus

Eboracum

Danum

Legend

〜 Navigable rivers
— Major Roman roads
  Marsh, fen and inundated land
⊡ *Coloniae*
□ *Civitas* capitals
○ Forts
● Other towns and sites

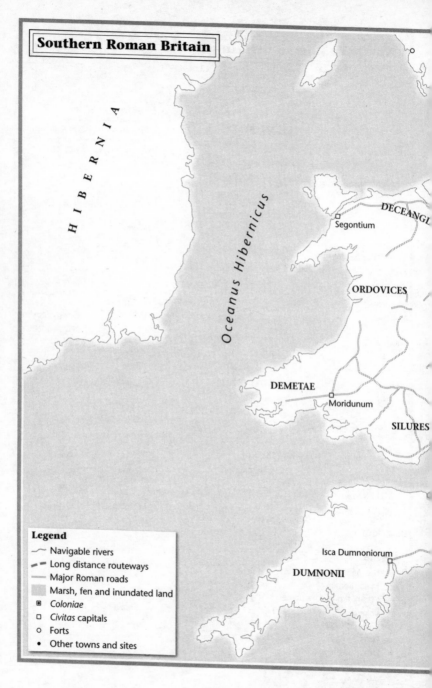

Southern Roman Britain

HIBERNIA

Oceanus Hibernicus

DECEANGL

Segontium

ORDOVICES

DEMETAE

Moridunum

SILURES

Isca Dumnoniorum

DUMNONII

Legend

— Navigable rivers
– – Long distance routeways
— Major Roman roads
Marsh, fen and inundated land
▣ *Coloniae*
□ *Civitas* capitals
○ Forts
• Other towns and sites

N

Cataractonium
BRIGANTES
Isurium Brigantium
Derventio
Eboracum
PARISI
Petuaria
Oceanus Germanicus
Danum
eva
Lindum
Derventio Coritanorum
Branodunum
CORNOVII
Viroconium Cornoviorum
Watling Street
CORIELTAUVI
Durobrivae
Garrianonum
Venta Icenorum
Ratae Corieltauvorum
Stonea Grange
ICENI
Salinae
Fosse Way
CATUVELLAUNI
TRINOVANTES
agnis
Gt Chesterford
Walton Castle
Ariconium
Akemann Street
Braughing
Camulodunum
Glevum
DOBUNNI
Icknield Way
Verulamium
Othona
Corinium Dobunnorum
Venta Silurum
Cunetio
ATREBATES
Londinium
Durobrivae
Regulbium
Aquae Sulis
Calleva Atrebatum
Durovernum Cantiacorum
Rutupiae
BELGAE
Ridgeway
Dubris
Durotrigam Lendiniensis
REGNI
CANTIACI
Fretum Gallicum
DUROTRIGES
Venta Belgarum
Portus Adurni
Anderida
Durnovaria
Noviomagus Regensium

Oceanus Britannicus

| 0 | 50 km |
| 0 | 50 miles |

XV

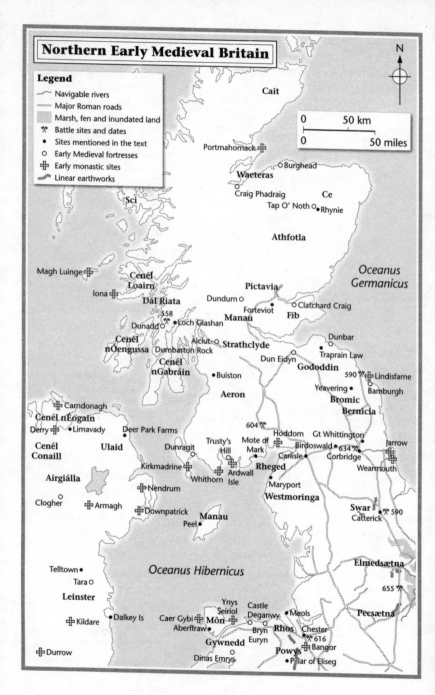

Northern Early Medieval Britain

Legend

⎯ Navigable rivers
▓ Major Roman roads
▓ Marsh, fen and inundated land
⚔ Battle sites and dates
• Sites mentioned in the text
○ Early Medieval fortresses
✠ Early monastic sites
〰 Linear earthworks

N

0 ___ 50 km
0 ___ 50 miles

Cait

✠ Portmahomack

○ Burghead

Waeteras

• Craig Phadraig

Ce

Tap O' Noth • Rhynie

Sci

Athfotla

Oceanus Germanicus

✠ Magh Luinge

Cenél Loairn

✠ Iona

Dál Riata

Pictavia

Dundurn ○

Forteviot ○ Clatchard Craig

Manau

Fib

558 ⚔

Dunadd ○ ⚔ • Loch Glashan

Cenél nOengussa

Alclut ○ **Strathclyde**

Dumbarton Rock

Cenél nGabráin

Dunbar ○

Traprain Law

Dun Eidyn ○

Gododdin

• Buiston

Aeron

Yeavering •

Bromic

Bernicia

590 ⚔ ✠ Lindisfarne

• Bamburgh

✠ Carndonagh

Cenél nEógain

Derry ✠ • Limavady

Cenél Conaill

Ulaid

• Deer Park Farms

604 ⚔

Hoddom Gt Whittington

Dunragit •

Trusty's Hill

Mote of Mark ✠

Birdoswald • 634 ⚔

Carlisle • Corbridge

Rheged

Jarrow ✠

Airgiálla

Kirkmadrine ✠

Whithorn ✠ Ardwall Isle

Maryport •

Westmoringa

Wearmouth

Clogher •

✠ Armagh

✠ Nendrum

✠ Downpatrick

Manau

Peel •

Swar ⚔ 590

Catterick

Elmedsætna

Telltown •

Tara ○

Oceanus Hibernicus

655 ⚔

Leinster

✠ Kildare

• Dalkey Is

Ynys Seiriol

Caer Gybi ✠ **Môn** ✠

Aberffraw •

Pecsætna

Castle Deganwy ○

• Meols

Bryn Euryn

Rhos

Chester ○

Gywnedd

Powys ✠ Bangor

✠ Durrow

Dinas Emrys •

• Pillar of Eliseg

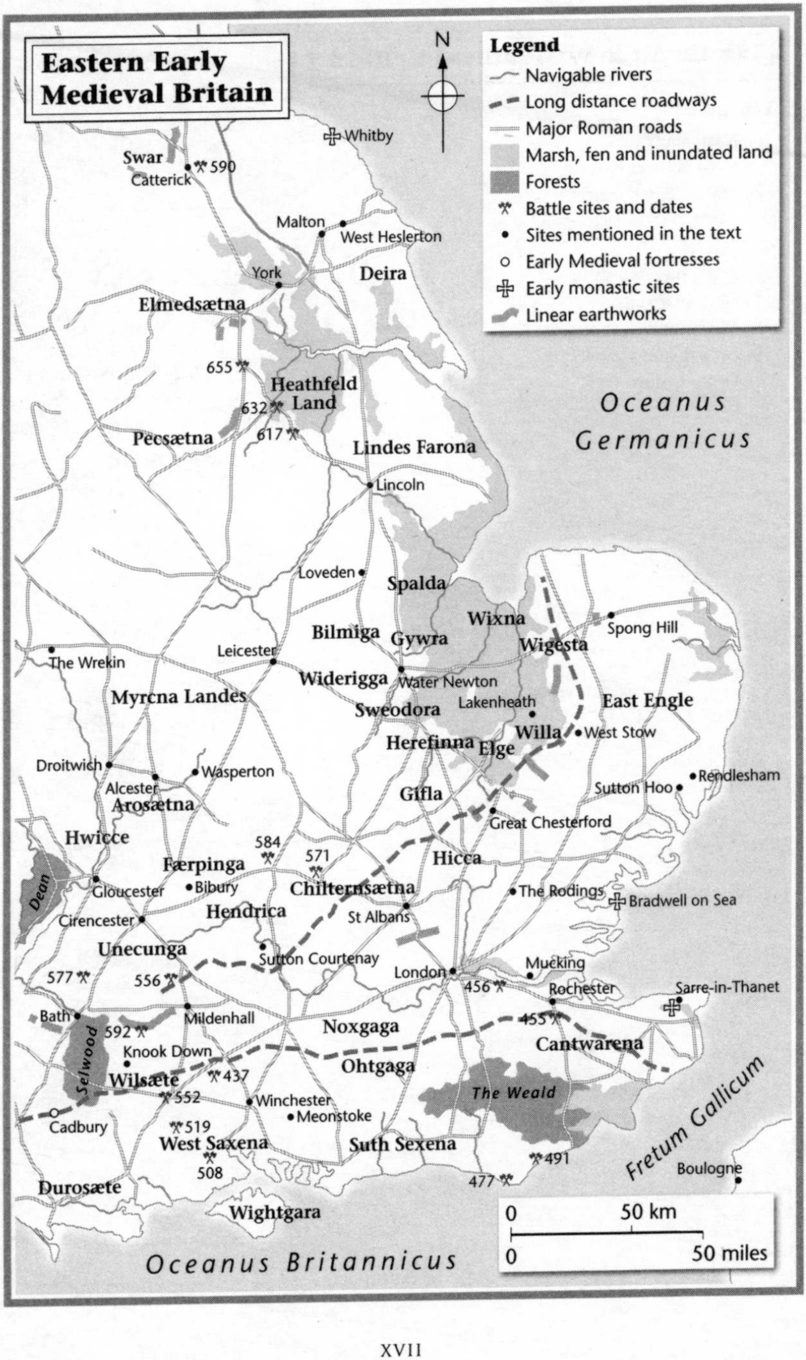
Eastern Early
Medieval Britain
N
Legend
Navigable rivers
Long distance roadways
Major Roman roads
Marsh, fen and inundated land
Forests
Battle sites and dates
Sites mentioned in the text
Early Medieval fortresses
Early monastic sites
Linear earthworks
Whitby
Swar
590
Catterick
Malton
West Heslerton
York
Deira
Elmedsætna
655
Heathfeld
Land
632
617
Pecsætna
Lindes Farona
Oceanus
Germanicus
Lincoln
Loveden
Spalda
Wixna
Spong Hill
Bilmiga
Gywra
Wigesta
The Wrekin
Leicester
Widerigga
Water Newton
Myrcna Landes
Lakenheath
East Engle
Sweodora
Willa
West Stow
Herefinna
Elge
Droitwich
Wasperton
Alcester
Rendlesham
Sutton Hoo
Arosætna
Gifla
Great Chesterford
Hwicce
584
571
Hicca
Færpinga
Dean
Gloucester
Bibury
Chilternsætna
The Rodings
Bradwell on Sea
Hendrica
St Albans
Cirencester
Unecunga
Sutton Courtenay
Mucking
London
577
556
456
Rochester
Sarre-in-Thanet
Bath
Mildenhall
592
Noxgaga
455
Cantwarena
Knook Down
Selwood
Ohtgaga
437
Wilsæte
The Weald
552
Winchester
Cadbury
Meonstoke
Fretum Gallicum
519
West Saxena
Suth Sexena
491
508
Boulogne
477
Durosæte
0
50 km
Wightgara
0
50 miles
Oceanus Britannicus

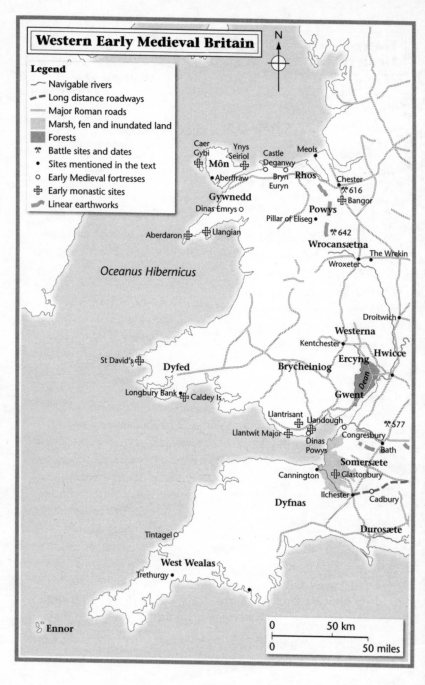

Western Early Medieval Britain

N

Legend

~~~ Navigable rivers
- - Long distance roadways
····· Major Roman roads
░ Marsh, fen and inundated land
▓ Forests
✳ Battle sites and dates
• Sites mentioned in the text
○ Early Medieval fortresses
⊞ Early monastic sites
▨ Linear earthworks

Caer Gybi
Ynys Seiriol
Môn
Aberffraw
Castle Deganwy
Meols
Bryn Euryn
Rhos
Chester
✳ 616
⊞ Bangor
Gywnedd
Dinas Emrys ○
Pillar of Eliseg •
Powys
✳ 642
Wrocansætna
The Wrekin
Aberdaron ⊞ ⊞ Llangian
Wroxeter

Oceanus Hibernicus

Droitwich •
Westerna
Kentchester •
Ercyng
Hwicce
St David's ⊞ **Dyfed**
Brycheiniog
Gwent
Dean
Longbury Bank •⊞ Caldey Is.
Llantrisant ⊞ Llandough
✳ 577
Llantwit Major ⊞
Congresbury ○
Gwent
Dinas Powys ○
Bath
Somersæte
Cannington •
⊞ Glastonbury
Ilchester •
Cadbury ○
Dyfnas
Durosæte
Tintagel ○

West Wealas
Trethurgy •

≋ **Ennor**

0   50 km
0   50 miles

Author's note and acknowledgements

The pioneers of Early Medieval archaeology who rescued 'paper cup culture', as it was derisively called up until the 1960s, are the giants to whose shoulders any fool rushing into murky Dark Age waters clings. I was lucky enough to be taught by many of them and have been strongly influenced by others: Philip Rahtz, the indefatigable excavator and mentor of so many students; Rosemary Cramp and Tania Dickinson, who gave Anglo-Saxon studies a sharp cutting edge; Leslie Alcock and Charles Thomas, who found the landscapes and sites in which the narrative could be set; Thomas Charles-Edwards, the great scholar of the Celtic West; John Morris, who carved the idol for following iconoclasts to tear down; Brian Hope-Taylor and Philip Barker, who worked out how to do Dark Age archaeology, and Dominic Powlesland, who worked out how to do it on a bigger scale; Richard Morris and John Blair, who gave us a credible landscape for Christianity's rise; Nick Higham, who saw how to read its politics; and Margaret Gelling, the pioneer of Early English place-name studies. There are many others: I am constantly reminded of the staggering scholarship that lies behind comprehensible modern English translations of primary sources, without which linguistic klutzes like me would still be swimming in unlit pools.

I apologize in advance for any inadvertent failure to attribute ideas that I might pass off as original. All errors of fact are my own. I have other personal debts to acknowledge. The Royal Literary Fund helped me to keep my head above water when I had no other visible means of support. Colleagues in the north-east – especially Colm O'Brien (who kindly read an early version of the manuscript for this book), Diana Whaley, Hermann Moisl, Brian Roberts and the splendidly unherdable cats of the Bernician Studies Group (Bernice's godparents, so to speak) – have indulged my experimental Dark Age recipes, corrected my wilder trajectories and honed my thinking. Many friends and colleagues in Ireland have enriched my knowledge and comprehension: Brian Lacey, Seán Beattie, Neil McGrory, Martin Hopkins, Brian Lafferty, Rosemary Moulden, Dessie McCallion and all those others who have contributed to Lands of Éogain projects over the last nine years. I want also to thank Dominic Powlesland for kindly providing me with the latest West Heslerton plan; Nick Cooper of the University of Leicester Archaeology Unit; my friend Lynne Ballew; and, not least, my publisher Richard Milbank and all those kind colleagues at Head of Zeus who produce such fine books.

Authors see only flaws in their work. The American poet Anne Bradstreet described the relationship perfectly, in about 1647:

I cast thee by as one unfit for light,
Thy Visage was so irksome in my sight;
Yet being mine own, at length affection would
Thy blemishes amend, if so I could:
I wash'd thy face, but more defects I saw,
And rubbing off a spot, still made a flaw.
I stretched thy joynts to make thee even feet,
Yet still thou run'st more hobling then is meet.

Enough said.

MAX ADAMS,
Dunadd,
June 2020

PART I

THE END OF HISTORY

Without doubt Britain... was a land that the
state could ill-afford to lose, so plentiful are its
harvests, so numerous are the pasturelands in
which it rejoices, so many are the metals of which
seams run through it, so much wealth comes
from its taxes.

EUMENIUS, *Panegyric to Constantius* 11.1[1]

I

Late Romans

Fragments – Salisbury Plain – villagers – *civitates* –
Gildas – ultra-Roman Britons – the fall – *Britannia*'s
regions – the edges of the empire – Stonea Grange

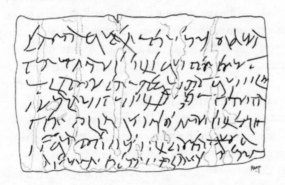

*The sheet (of lead) which is given to Mercury, that he exact
vengeance for the gloves which have been lost; that he take
blood and health from the person who has stolen them; that
he provide what we ask the god Mercury [...] as quickly as
possible for the person who has taken these gloves.*[1]

Modern translation from the Latin, of an inscribed
third-century lead tablet from the temple of Mercury
excavated at Uley West Hill, Gloucestershire, in 1978.

A Roman Briton scrawls a curse on the thief who has run off with a pair of her gloves. Paying her coin to the temple priests or their lackeys, she mutters one last imprecation to the patron spirit of the shrine, pins the curse that bears her hopes for revenge onto a wooden post – a sort of staff noticeboard for the gods – and goes about her business trusting that some ill fate will overtake her enemy. We do not know her name, or that of the thief. We know nothing of the circumstances in which the gloves were stolen – or lost; nor of the success or failure of the curse.

There is no time machine: we cannot go back and interrogate our forebears. The past lies in fragments like celluloid clippings heaped on a cutting-room floor. Join those clips together in some fashion and you find yourself watching a grainy, jump-cut, apparently plotless story following nonsensical characters, with snatches of forgotten songs from a half-familiar, half-strange soundtrack playing over and over in your ear. You pull the sellotaped frames apart, join them together again in a different sequence; spool them onto a reel; thread the lead into a projector and watch the credits roll again... and again. One might just as well try to reconstruct the idea of a tree from its leaves, or an ocean wave from a dripping tap. So much is lost; truth is a chimera.

From the two centuries of Britain's history that followed the collapse of the Western Roman empire around 400, the fragments left for us to hold up to the light are tiny. It is an impossible task to string them together in a coherent sequence to tell the history of those turbulent, enigmatic times; of how the first kingdoms of Early Medieval Britain came into being. And yet, the accumulated pile of these fragments, gathered together over the last decades of research, is now mountainous; and if the original storyline cannot be reassembled, it is now possible to furnish the set on which that lost drama was performed; to populate it with a cast drawn from a carnival scene painted by some imaginative observer of human nature, like Brueghel or Lowry.

The props at our disposal include such wonders as thatched cottages that look like tents; fantastical beasts carved in wood and gold; the humdrum equipment of farm and weaving shed;

grass-covered mounds beneath whose smooth turf are buried ocean-going ships fit for a king; and a landscape littered with myriad names for hill and field, wood and wold, creek and fen. A cast of extras – citizens of those troubled times – can be observed as they go about their sometimes eccentric business, digging holes in once-fine mosaic floors to make blacksmiths' forges; sending across the known world for an amphora of their favourite brand of olive oil; cursing thieves or rivals in love; venerating headless walking corpses or arguing over whose flowers produced the nectar collected by their precious honey bees.

Even in freeze-frame it is hard to tear one's eyes away from a drama whose beginning is lost in obscurity but whose dénouement was recorded centuries later by a towering intellect of the Early Medieval world, the Venerable Bede. This erudite and curious monk of Jarrow, on the muddy banks of the River Tyne, who knew almost all that could be known of the world in his own time, set out to chronicle how Anglo-Saxon kings had been chosen by God to bring about a single, universal church and people. He wrote of impious, foolish native Britons who, rejecting the civilizing influence of the Christian Roman empire, spurned both God and their rightful rulers and descended into civil strife and tyranny. He recounted how the chiefs of invading pagan Germanic peoples made war with, and conquered, those Britons; how they forged new, powerful kingdoms; how they, in turn, were converted by two Christian missions, one from Iona, the other from Rome, half a century or more before his own time. Bede's story is persuasive – in truth it is the only credible narrative to survive from the crucible of Early Medieval Britain.* We may now doubt his motives and some of his sources; and even Bede had little to say of the century and a half between the last written notices of imperial *Britannia* and the arrival from Rome of St Augustine, on the Isle of Thanet,

---

* By Early Medieval I mean those centuries between Rome's nominal fall in about 410 up until the Norman Conquest of 1066. The more popular term 'Dark Ages' can only really be used of the period between 400 and 600. Most academics dislike the term.

in 597: he covered that century and a half in just nineteen lines out of 300 pages in a modern English edition of his *Historia Ecclesiastica Gentis Anglorum*.* But if the truth of this story, how the first Christian kingdoms came into being, cannot be verified, one might still hope to lay bare the whirring, clicking mechanisms that breathed life into his drama, its actors and their tragi-comic tale. The closing episodes of this book will be familiar to those who have read *The King in the North*. Here, though, they are cast in another light: seen not from Bede's retrospectively assured eighth-century perspective but from the horizon of a new age of experimental institutions and social relations, whose witnesses have left us precious little testimony. *The First Kingdom* is, necessarily, a contemplative history.

It might start with an early-morning balloon flight over the chalk downs of Salisbury Plain: rising above mist that still clings to the villages, woods, neatly hedged fields and riverside meadows of the Wylye valley above Heytesbury. Ahead lies a great expanse of grassland, pockmarked with shell holes and veined with chalky tank tracks showing creamy white against the matt green that fills the view to the north. Looking down, you might see tiny red flags hanging limp from their poles – a reminder to keep your distance, for this land belongs to the British army. In the distance the squat, square stone tower of a medieval parish church, enfolded by its graveyard flock of tombs and memorials, stands proud of a tight cluster of houses and barns: a timeless scene.

A closer look at the hamlet of Imber, whose Old English name – meaning 'Imma's pond' – is a clue to its longevity on this otherwise dry plateau, would reveal that all is not what it seems.† It is

---

* Bede died in 735, a few years after the completion of his masterwork, the *Ecclesiastical History of the English People*, which survives in both early manuscripts and innumerable modern editions.
† All place-name references, unless otherwise stated, come from Watts 2004.

a ghost village. No one lives here, although the pond that dams a tiny seasonal stream can still be traced in outline; the buildings that survive intact are kept weathertight with tin roofs; once a year, in September, the church is filled with a congregation for a service to celebrate the feast day of its patron, St Giles. On that day the guns on the ranges fall silent and only church bells, hymns and prayers can be heard.

Imber, unquiet symbol of a twentieth-century world in turmoil, is first mentioned in a charter of King Edgar in 968.[2] It enjoyed its most populous days in the early fourteenth century before the ravages of the Black Death culled a third or more of Britain's, and Europe's, population. In 1943 the few families still living here were evicted in order to accommodate a benign invasion of American troops; they have never been allowed to return. Now the manor house, Bell Inn and post office stand empty, unless some military exercise involves their capture from the imagined armies of another state.

Other long-abandoned villages fringe the Wiltshire downlands, their histories much more obscure. Less than half an hour's drifting balloon flight south of Imber, on a gentle sun-facing slope at the head of a waterless combe, the land's surface has been etched into a series of grassy terraces that betray the presence of a once thriving community, set among square fields within sight of Neolithic long barrows, Bronze Age farm embankments and a small Iron Age hillfort. Knook Down was inhabited long before Imber – the name *Cnucc* is Brythonic, the indigenous precursor to medieval Welsh, and means, simply, 'hill'. On Knook Down two adjacent hamlets co-existed more than 1,500 years ago, connected by a trackway hollowed from the passage of numberless cattle. Neither has been excavated using modern archaeological methods but nineteenth-century antiquarians, first alerted to their great age by the efforts of moles shovelling coins and pottery to the surface, tested for remains with their spades. They found domestic hearths, painted stucco, the foundations of corn-drying kilns and jewellery belonging, according to the testimony of the coins, to another period of military domination: the second to fourth centuries of the Common Era (CE) when Britain was a coveted province of ancient Europe's greatest empire.[3]

The Roman countryside of Britain is littered, in the popular imagination, with the remains of villas: the stately homes of retired army officers, absentee Gaulish civil servants, the stewards and bailiffs of distant emperors and of a wealthy toga-wearing native bourgeoisie. Three centuries or so of occupation seem to have spawned the construction of about 2,500 of these exclusive dwellings, many of them the centres of extensive farming estates. But archaeological research over many years has shown that these show homes of the wealthy and status-conscious were quite atypical of Roman Britain's housing stock.[4] Some 100,000 rural settlements belonging to the period of Roman rule are now known from across Britain, many of them from areas where no villa stood. Tenant farmers and their unfree dependants – labourers, potters, weavers, woodsmen and herders – lived, for the most part, either in isolated farmsteads with their extended families or in clusters of dwellings, paddocks and farm outbuildings, like those on Salisbury Plain, that look for all the world like villages with main streets, back lanes and outhouses surrounded by small fields and extensive areas of open pasture beyond. Knook Down may have been quite unexceptional in its day.

At least another eleven, perhaps more, abandoned Roman-period villages survive as earthworks on the dry Wiltshire downlands, owing their continued existence as visible monuments to a history of exploitation by ox herders and shepherds rather than ploughmen, and to modern military land management. None of them has been substantially excavated – a reflection of archaeologists' preoccupation with the juicier ruins of imperial Britain: villas, forts, towns and the two massive walls of Hadrian and Antoninus Pius. It is a pity. What stories lie in wait for us to tell of the lives of ordinary Britons, those resentful subjects or glad citizens of Rome?

At Charlton* Down, on the far north-eastern edge of Salisbury

---

* Old English *Ceorl-tun*: the settlement of ceorls or free farmers.

Lumps and bumps preserved on the military firing ranges betray
the site of a large and busy Roman period British village.

Plain, at least 200 house compounds can be identified from their
grassy earthworks, covering no less than 26 hectares – the size of a
substantial Roman town. Settlers here built themselves a reservoir
both to store precious water – a clue to Charlton's densely crowded
habitation – and also, one suspects, to attract wildfowl for trapping
and shooting. Streets can be identified, weaving their way through
a hugger-mugger of close-set houses, yards and workshops. Filled
with busy people and the sights, smells and sounds of farm and
family industry, Charlton must have been a buzzing, productive
community – larger, more industrious and more populous than any
settlement, anywhere in Britain during the 300 years after Rome's
fall. Even Bede's own prodigiously large monastic community at
Jarrow was modest by comparison.

Houses built here during the three and a half centuries of the
Roman occupation were of the common native form – circular,

constructed of low stone or wattle panel walls with thatched or turfed conical roofs – and life revolved around them: cooking, weaning infants, grooming, mending and fabricating, spinning yarns of one sort or another. Children chased each other through back lanes; parents scolded while they strung looms, sheared sheep or curdled milk, hammered horseshoes and cured meat for winter. Ducks quacked, pigs grunted, oxen bellowed and snorted; steam rose from fresh dung heaps. From the domestic hearth, life's crucible, women saw everything and knew everything. Fruit trees blossomed in springtime and bore apples, plums or medlars in autumn; vegetable plots fed with manure from pigs, sheep and goats grew beans, cabbages, lentils, carrots, herbs and onions (the latter a Roman culinary contribution). In the fields hazy blue flowers of a flax crop cultivated for linen and linseed oil grew in rotation with barley or bread wheat. Out on the broad undulating plain, flocks of brown sheep grazed. After spring lambing, ewes and wethers were plucked or sheared in early summer, then fanned out across the grasslands with their herders to fatten during the warm months, before being brought down to the sheltered combes as winter's frosts bit and snow lay in deep drifts on higher ground. Autumn and winter were times for threshing, weaving and coppicing trees, for storing and securing harvest surplus; for fettling tools and storytelling around the fire. A preoccupation with fate and the unknowable future, with fertility and death, impelled people to offer gifts, promises and incantations to their spiritual pantheon – a mix of Roman, native and perhaps more exotic eastern cult figures.

Herders, traders, charlatans, officials and tax gatherers came and went; gossip judged the lives of friends, enemies, potential partners and relatives. Periodic fairs, feasts and assemblies, like a cross between a county show and a tribal council, saw disputes resolved, marriages contracted, horses traded and political alliances forged and broken. News of distant events must occasionally have found its way here – great armies clashing on other frontiers; emperors falling to usurpers; barbarian hordes crossing the Rhine; Irish pirates stealing families and livestock from coastal and river communities; a fall in the value of the meagre stash of coins and trinkets buried in the back yard. Closer to home, a civic riot in the nearest town, the appointment of a new governor with a reputation for brutality or corruption, the construction of town walls – all may have been of no more than passing interest to the downland folk chatting as they took their pails down to the village pond for water.

Almost no rural settlement – hamlet, farm or villa – has ever produced signs of having been defended by a wall or rampart at any time during the period of Roman rule;* not even in the last decades when Britain was 'fertile in usurpers' and said to have been prey to raiders on all sides.[5] For the most part, *Britannia* must have been, or was seen to be, a secure land – with its fair share of criminals, prisons, vigilantes and fearsome guard dogs, to be sure – but essentially ordered and conspicuously productive.

Did the villages of the chalk plains sustain themselves and grow so large by exploiting the downs for their pasture, or were they sufficiently hooked up to the outside world to act as production centres for pottery and metal goods, perhaps especially for textiles, destined for the marketplace? Did the collapse of the Roman market economy in the third century seal their fate? One day archaeologists will be able to answer that question. Salisbury Plain, substantially cleared of its woods a thousand years and more before the Common Era by Bronze Age pastoralists, was also intensively cultivated throughout later prehistory and right through the Roman period. The large population that thrived here speaks for itself. So do the empty, silent terraces and sunken ways that the balloonist spies today. But, until the villages are excavated, we cannot say why, nor can we say when or how, their inhabitants left, never to return. Rarely do archaeologists have the luxury of knowing, as they do at Imber, that a settlement was deserted in its entirety in a single event, precisely dated.

---

* Castle Dikes, in the Vale of Mowbray south of Ripon in North Yorkshire, is an exception, enclosed by substantial earthworks some time after the second century and destroyed before the end of the third.

Pompeii, Herculaneum and the extraordinarily well-preserved Bronze Age houses at Must Farm in the Peterborough fens are rare, tragic paradigms for sudden, catastrophic abandonment. More often, settlements decline gradually, imperceptibly, until, perhaps, just a few time-expired families are found clinging to an unsustainable lifestyle – like the last folk on the remote island of St Kilda in 1930. Perhaps one final, failed harvest or an outbreak of some cattle disease killed the village off. We do not know how the plains villages died.

Even more than Imber, Knook Down's low-relief earthworks echo only faintly the lives of the people who were born, who lived and died there across the centuries. Readers and contemplative balloonists hoping to evoke the smells, sounds and human interactions of life in such communities would do well to turn to much better known, if more recent, histories like that of the Pyrenean village of Montaillou, whose Cathar inhabitants' lives, centred on the 'foghana' or kitchen, were recorded by the prurient proto-ethnologists of the early fourteenth-century Inquisition.[6] No collection of material remains can compete with the richness of human relations, of venality, tragedy and tales of survival recorded in the testimonies of the heroic Béatrice de Planissoles, her friends, enemies, servants and acquaintances; and yet, they are all we have.

It is impossible to be certain how the villagers of the plains saw themselves. Very likely they were united by a strong sense of belonging to family and household and to their wider clan; conscious, too, of their status, displayed by a brooch worn at the shoulder, distinctively patterned tablet-woven cuffs and hems on their clothes and by hairstyle and family resemblance. Anthropologists suspect that personal prestige reflected age and marital status and one's position within a household as much as it did that household's social standing. But did they think of themselves as belonging to a people or culture – to a sept or *pagus*, a division of one of the *civitates* or administrative tribal units imposed or recognized by the conquering governors of the Roman provinces? Did they think of themselves as Britons?

With two very peripheral exceptions,* none of these villages shows signs of having a grand, lordly house at its centre – a villa, aisled hall, communal round house or fort – so we cannot say if the downlanders belonged to great landed estates or if they lived lives, in some senses, beyond the margins of regional power. Judging by the limited range of finds retrieved so far, they enjoyed access to the trappings of what was then modern technology: coinage, tools, fashions, food and decorative arts. But what name they gave themselves or were known by as communities, and as part of a larger ethnic or territorial group, is beyond knowledge. The name of just one of these so-called *pagi* survives for Roman Britain, scratched into the wooden backing of a wax writing tablet that records a legal dispute over a small parcel of Kentish woodland.[7] The *Dibussi* belonged to the *civitas* of the *Cantiaci* whose tribal capital, *Durovernum*, became Canterbury; but that single instance of their name merely hints at a sense of belonging.

Names that tell of geographical identity, and of affiliation, in the centuries after Rome – like the *Meanware* of Hampshire's Meon valley, the *Hroðingas*† of Essex or the *Magonsæte* of the Wye valley – survive from no earlier than the seventh century.‡ By that time the descendants of the downlanders probably belonged to the *Wilsæte*, the dwellers of the Wylye valley whose name, via the small town of Wilton, was inherited by the county of Wiltshire.§ Their entry into the annals of Early Medieval history comes from the year 552, when a supposed victory by the warlord Cynric over his rivals at *Searoburh*¶ led to 'Anglo-Saxon' domination of the plains. They would eventually enjoy the dubious benefits of absorption into a greater Wessex.

* At Pit Mead, in the Wylye valley and Netheravon in the Wiltshire Avon valley.
† Pronounced Rothingas with the 'th' as in 'then', represented by ð: the Old English character called 'eth'.
‡ See Chapter 8.
§ The name first occurs in an entry in the *Anglo-Saxon Chronicle* for 800.
¶ The hillfort of Old Sarum, 2 miles north of Salisbury. Entry under 552 in the *Anglo-Saxon Chronicle*.

Whether the downlanders of the later Roman centuries felt themselves to be an oppressed native minority or proud members of a pan-European civilization we cannot say, although Britons had been citizens of the empire, with all legal privileges, since the reign of Caracalla (198–217). They spoke a local or regional Brythonic dialect, perhaps alongside what is known as Late Spoken Latin; a few, especially those involved in trade, were literate.

The imperial administrators of the Claudian invasion of 43 CE were quick to impose a sense of proper Mediterranean order on their newly conquered territories. They needed to know where things and people were: minerals, timber and good farmland; navigable rivers, passable mountains and impassable bogs and fens; potential pockets of native resistance. They needed to establish which native leaders boasted control over which peoples, so that they could devolve power, exact tribute and pacify or subdue the uncivilized barbarians. So their geographers identified a number of tribes inhabiting broad swathes of this new land: among them *Trinovantes* and *Iceni* in the east, *Brigantes* in the hill country of the Pennines, *Durotriges* and *Dumnonii* in the south-west. Colonial administrators are rarely subtle enough to detect the sort of nuance that matters to people; imagine drawing boundaries around the territories of those who call themselves Geordies or Makems, or trying to distinguish on the ground where Brum stops and Black Country starts. No tax gatherer's accounts survive to give us the local names used by *Britannia*'s indigenes.

Over many generations, scholars of Roman Britain have sought to define the tribal territories, the *civitates*, of *Britannia* and draw plausible boundaries around them on maps of the conquest. Recent thinking has come to the view, generally, that the tribal heartlands were in fact quite discrete: power and influence were focused on a number of central places – perhaps twenty of them – with large peripheral areas of less determinate affiliation; not frontier or marcher lands so much as regions of weaker tribal identity, where the idea of *not* belonging may have been as potent as belonging. Dwellers of border lands everywhere know that feeling.

What are now Hampshire and Wiltshire were thought by

Roman geographers to be the lands of the *Belgae*, a confederation of sometime Gaulish settlers. Historically immigrant or not, the leaders of the *Belgae* were defeated in sometimes bloody battle by the legions and came to terms with Rome, whose military governors established for them a *civitas* capital: the meeting place (*venta*) of the *Belgae*. Here the natives would see what Roman power and privilege looked like; what civilization looked like. It was always part of the colonial project that those who embraced Rome *became* Roman.

If the downland villagers were supposed administratively to belong to their nearest *civitas* capital, then they must look to *Venta Belgarum*, Winchester, three days' journey to the south-east. There, many of the amenities of a Mediterranean town might be enjoyed, or at least gawped at: public baths, a forum with its basilica or court house, formal shrines and a temple of the imperial cult; stone- and brick-built townhouses of considerable architectural pretensions. In later centuries the town was furnished with impressive walls, perhaps more a display of civic pride and urban exclusivity than a response to an otherwise imperceptible military threat. Winchester may also have boasted a *gynaeceum*, an imperial weaving works, if the *Venta* whose factory superintendent was mentioned in a late Roman list of state offices – the *Notitia Dignitatum* – can be identified with Winchester.[8]

Gynaecea, named from the Greek practice of segregating women in weaving and spinning chambers, produced woollen cloth for the military and the imperial court as a provincial tax in kind or render: a levy imposed on the conquered province to pay for the cost of invading it. Some of the downland women and, very probably, unfree men and women from villages and farms closer to *Venta*, may have undertaken piece work for the factory in their own homes. The factory premises in fourth-century *Venta*, as yet unidentified by excavation, may have been substantially staffed by runaways or convicts under a superintendent, like a Victorian workhouse. It might not be too fanciful to suggest that a *gynaeceum* was set up at *Venta* precisely because of the abundant wool-producing potential of the downland shepherds and their flocks. Distinctive British woven products included hooded capes – *byrri* – and very pricey, much-sought-after rugs called *tapetia* that sold well on the other side of the *Fretum Gallicum*, the Channel.

A cult temple and town at *Aquae Sulis*, where celebrated hot baths attracted wealth and the wealthy from across the region, may have been a more magnetic draw for downlanders' produce and for social interaction with a Romanized world. Bath was well connected: to the estuary of the Severn (*Sabrina fluvium*) by virtue of the navigable Bristol Avon and by one of the great roads of Britain, the Fosse Way, which connected distant Exeter (*Isca*, the *civitas* capital of the *Dumnonii*) with a provincial capital and military veterans' *colonia** at Lincoln (*Lindum*), in a more or less dead-straight line running north-east across the province. Lincoln, in turn, was joined to the important thoroughfare of the River Trent (*Trisantona fluvium*) and thence to North Sea coastal trade, by a marvellous canal, the Foss Dyke – a gift, or imposition, of the empire. Another road, known as Akemann Street in later centuries, connected *Aquae Sulis* directly with the provincial capital at *Londinium* via the *civitas* capital of the *Dobunni* (*Corinium Dobunnorum*: modern Cirencester) and *Verulamium* (modern St Albans).

The temple and bath complex at *Aquae Sulis* have been the focus of much excavation and study. The native British goddess Sulis, equated by Romans with their Minerva, was a popular cult figure whose steamy, healing hot springs prompted them for both offerings – coins and small gifts in great profusion – and supplications, like that of the outraged glove theft victim of Uley whose surviving plaque heads this chapter. No fewer than 130 messages to the goddess, scratched onto small metal sheets, have been retrieved from the spring, some of the most authentic vernacular voices to survive from Roman Britain – including the only surviving written contemporary example of Brythonic script. Many of the messages or supplications are the fist-shaking curses

---

* A settlement of army veterans constructed next to a large fortress. See Chapter 2.

of a jilted lover or burgled householder, revealing not just the tawdry detail of urban or suburban crime and lust or infidelity but also the personal possessions that mattered: a *birra* belonging to one Docilianus; a tunic and horse blanket; linen, pewter vessels, cups, mirrors, rings and even a mule.[9]

During the third century CE, it seems, the whole establishment was enclosed by imposing stone walls, like many other small and large towns in *Britannia*. The bathers, acolytes and supplicants at *Aquae Sulis* sound as though they belong to a class that archae-ologists, tongue in cheek, call ultra-Roman Britons – those whose families had done rather well out of being incorporated into the European superstate and who regarded themselves as thoroughly Roman; thoroughly civilized. Latinized and urbane, they lived in stone houses in a well-mannered landscape which, by the fourth century, was studded with substantial rural settlements, small towns, fancy villas and many metalled roads. These citizens kept slaves, signed their letters and bills of sale with Romanized patronyms, wore togas to the basilica and attended the theatre. They may have maintained both a small place in town and somewhere less modest in the country, rather like the moneyed gentlefolk of the eighteenth-century English shires or the dacha-owning aristocracy of Tolstoy's Russia. By the end of the fourth century, when Britain seems to have succumbed to a pan-European economic and political malaise, many of those ultra-Roman Britons had adopted the fashionable trappings and rituals of Christianity. With the appropriate material and social mores, they epitomized the homogeneous culture of a colonizing Mediterranean superpower. They were its ultimate success story.

Two, perhaps four, generations after the last Latin curse tablet was thrown into the spring at Bath along with a few worn coins for luck, a British cleric, known to us as Gildas, looked back on the heyday of Roman Britain as if through the wrong end of a telescope. In a coruscating written Latin sermon of admonition addressed to contemporary kings and clergy, he lamented the sins and failings of those ultra-Roman Britons; how, through ingratitude and complacency, they had expelled Rome's governors, cast aside its laws and protections, abjured the Christian God and, in consequence, paid a devastating price. Civil wars, plague, apostasy, unrest and the invasion of pagan barbarians from all points of the compass had reduced the glories of *Britannia* to ashes. Gildas wrote that, in the aftermath, the flames of anarchy spread from sea to sea, laying waste a productive countryside that became fertile only for the roots of tyranny. Towns lay in ruins and unburied bodies festered in the streets, carrion for beast and bird. Gildas's Britain still had its watchers, its governors; but they were bowed under great burdens. The old world had been swept away.

Gildas, and Bede, saw history as a providential text: how faith and obedience were repaid with peace and wealth while sin, weakness and ignorance brought down the wrath of God delivered by foolish or predatory sinners and faithless barbarians. The Old Testament was their *vade mecum*. Like Gildas, modern historians want to understand how a productive, ordered, taxed, administered and highly functional, populous society was apparently so rapidly laid low and, after many tribulations, in later centuries rebuilt in a new fashion. They look for clues in excavated remains, in Gildas's testimony, in the earliest Anglo-Saxon, British and Irish law codes, in the scraps collected centuries later by a self-appointed historian of the Britons known as Nennius and in the opening entries of the *Anglo-Saxon Chronicle*. They visualize these processes as a British social and political journey across two centuries, from the starting point of a centrally directed, Latinized military state, via its collapse and disappearance into a seeming historical black hole, to its re-emergence as a patchwork of small, dynamic warrior kingdoms suffused with the vitality of a creatively intellectual church. One might reasonably ask whether, between 400 and 600, we should be describing an evolution or a revolution. Somewhere in a sheaf of possible narratives one might try to clutch at a straw bearing the name of Arthur.

An anthropologist, sifting though fragments of excavated remains and social spaces and comparing the institutions, languages and cultural rules of Roman Britain with those of Early Medieval Wales, Scotland and England, must address a complementary set of problems. How did people's lives change through those tumultuous centuries? What were the principal social units in which lives were lived, and by what social rules did they function and evolve? Why do modern Britons speak and name their settlements in Welsh, Gaelic and English, rather than in Latin? How did native Britons interact with invading or immigrant Germans or Gauls or Irish? Why did burial customs alter so radically, from inhumation to cremation, from unfurnished to furnished,* then back to unfurnished graves? The richest seams for anthropological researchers to tap are the means by which the late Roman population and their fifth- and sixth-century successors used display – in buildings, personal adornments, burial ceremonies and trappings – to express and reinforce ideas about identity, belonging and status. But even if, armed with the physical knowledge of every artefact and a map of every settlement, anthropologists were able one day to say what ordinary people got up to during those lost generations, they will never know what thoughts ran through their minds as they stared into the dying embers of their fires.

Geographers, whose work is increasingly important in the search for a route map to guide the modern traveller through these obscure centuries, want to know how ideas about, and physical forms of, territoriality changed or did not change. Some see in the tribal kingdoms of the seventh century a sort of continuity, over half a millennium, from late Iron Age confederations like the *Dobunni* and *Cantiaci* to Early Medieval kingdoms such as *Hwicce* and more familiar counties like Kent. But they are also able to detect much more subtle and nuanced developments in the mosaic of smaller political, social and cultural entities – perhaps 200 of them can be identified – whose roots tap deeply into Britain's diverse landscapes and whose identities surface tantalizingly

---

* Furnished: that is, accompanied by one or more of a range of grave goods and personal possessions such as knives, rings, food remains, jewellery or weaponry.

in early names and legal documents: the *Arosætna* of Worcestershire's River Arrow, the *Pecsætna* of the Derbyshire Peaks and the *Myrcna* – the Mercians, or dwellers in the marches. Many of these names are preserved in a remarkable but enigmatic seventh-century list, known as Tribal Hidage – the first political map of a new age.* Even so, crucial pieces of the geographical puzzle are missing: we see snapshots, not movies, and grainy snapshots at that.

Field archaeologists record, with increasing confidence, transitions in space and time at all scales, from the remodelling and repair of individual artefacts and buildings to broad trends in settlement pattern and form: fine dinner plates broken and not replaced but mended, held together with copper wire; villas inhabited long into the fifth century but not as they had once been; town centres repurposed as industrial workshops; the spread of new house types and exotic burial rites. They map distributions and trends in material trappings, from jewellery and belt fittings to weaponry and architecture; track the movement of pottery from Anatolian kiln to Welsh hillfort; describe inventories of tools and reconstruct craft techniques; track the daily lives of women and men as they move through house and farmyard.

Archaeology's greatest challenge is one of imagination. It has succeeded beyond expectation in extracting and describing sequences from material processes: how walls collapse; how ditches fill with silt, how organic materials can be dated and used to describe environmental change, diet, disease and injury. But it cannot get to grips with empty space and time: the unknown months, weeks, years or centuries missing from that inscrutable gap between the last fastidious scrubbing of a mosaic floor and the grassy field that now covers it. The excavator, given sufficient resources, could say a great deal about what the downlanders of Salisbury Plain got up to in their daily lives; but rarely why, when or how they left. And the story of the end of Roman Britain is, above all, one of abandonment – or so it seems.

* See Chapter 8.

*

A broad consensus has emerged over the last three decades that the population of Britain in the first four centuries CE numbered, at its peak, well in excess of 2 million. But the most detailed and ambitious analysis goes further, estimating that with perhaps 250,000 people living in towns, ranging in size from *Londinium* down to roadside settlements smaller than Knook Down, 100,000 or so military personnel living in and around garrisons, and more than 3 million civilians inhabiting the farms and villages of the countryside, the total population could have been in the order of 3.5 million.[10] If this is wrong, it is unlikely to be wildly so. Aerial photography and LiDAR* finds reported under the Portable Antiquities Scheme† and the published reports of excavations carried out in advance of building works have hugely expanded the known inventory of Roman-period settlements across Britain – and many more remain undetected, if suspected, beneath existing farms, villages and towns.

No serious scholar believes that anything like those numbers can be proposed for Bede's day, or any time until after the Norman conquest – even supposing that many settlements and burial sites of the second half of the first millennium lie as yet uncounted. By the implication of Gildas's testimony, there was a substantial fall in birth rates or an equally large rise in death rates – or both – by the time he wrote his letter of admonition, *De Excidio et Conquestu Britanniae*,‡ sometime during the half-century between 490 and

---

* LiDAR: Light Radar, an aerial laser scanning technique that reveals, even through woodland cover, very subtle undulations on the Earth's surface; undulations that may be invisible to the naked eye or in ground survey.

† Set up in 1997 to promote a voluntary code of conduct for metal detector users and others in England and Wales to record and report artefact finds to a central database: https://finds.org.uk/.

‡ Conventionally translated as *On the Ruin and Conquest of Britain*, although *excidio* is very strong, meaning something more like 'extirpation' than 'ruin'. Lynne Ballew, personal communication. The standard English translation is by Winterbottom 1978.

540. It is profoundly frustrating that we cannot accurately date Gildas or his letter;[11] that we cannot say how rapid was the reduction in population. The negative evidence of abandonment is an unreliable witness, at least in part because it does not tell us where people went or, if they died in famine or massacre, where they lie.

The most reliable existing picture of the Early Medieval environment – the evidence of tell-tale pollen profiles covering those centuries, taken from boggy places and lakes right across Britain and Ireland – presents something of a paradox. A thorough recent investigation of all the available evidence suggests that, broadly speaking, the British landscape underwent a metamorphosis in the first few centuries after Rome's fall, during which the same amount of land, particularly pasture, remained under some form of management but was less intensively exploited.[12] A small and very patchy rise in tree pollen may be accounted for by the partial neglect of coppiced woodlands. So the well-rehearsed story, inspired by early excavations and the pages of Gildas and Bede, of widespread reforestation and the abandonment of arable fields – tell-tale signs of a deserted and unmanaged countryside – will not wash. Cattle and sheep, perhaps also horses, were no longer bred and fattened to feed the voracious centralized military economy of an empire, but for the subsistence of their communities. This paints a picture of gradual population decline, lower productivity, less agricultural surplus: a fall in the birth rate, very possibly. A catastrophe? Apparently not. Geographers seem increasingly confident that they can identify field and estate boundaries meaningfully retained and maintained into the second half of the first millennium.[13]

To understand the apparently drastic political and cultural realignment that turned Roman Britain into Anglo-Saxon England, Welsh Wales and Pictish Scotland, some weighty contradictions must be reconciled. On one side is a long-established narrative of deserted dwellings and of dramatic discontinuity in Romano-British towns; the end of imperial coinage, of villa life and industrial-scale pottery production; the withdrawal of the Roman military; a swathe of new – apparently alien – settlements and burials; and the widespread displacement of not one but two languages. On the other, increasingly visible, if subtle, signs of continuity are being recognized in environment and landscape – communities abandoning villas, for example, only to set up new dwellings a few hundred yards away; the survival of an indigenous pottery industry; the apparent re-emergence of tribal entities that look very like Iron Age predecessors. Tackling these apparent irreconcilables means taking a long, hard look at the fragile limits of our knowledge and capabilities: that line of metaphysical unconformity where forum pavement meets ploughsoil; where timber door post cuts through forgotten grave; where boundary ditch and fence lose their identity and are lost to memory. In an archaeological sense, at least, this is the edge of chaos.

Britain, even after 400 years of colonial rule or, in the far north and west, periodic trade, temporary occupation and military interference, was an island of highly diverse regional traditions with contrasting experiences of the Roman project. That regionality has a firm basis in landscape and climate. Divide Britain into four quarters and, very roughly, you get a mild and wet south-west, a cool and wet north-west, a cool and dry north-east and a mild, dry south-east. The further west and north you go, the older the rocks; the hillier the land; the poorer the soils. The most easily navigable rivers lie in the south and east. In March and September Britain enjoys days and nights of equal length; the sun rises due east and sets due west. At the summer solstice the sun rises and sets more northerly, in winter more southerly; and these effects are exaggerated by increased latitude. The Lizard, mainland Britain's most southerly point, lies at about 50 degrees north; Dunnet Head, the most northerly point on the British mainland, at nearly 59 degrees. In the north, summer growing seasons are shorter, but the days are longer. Tides are affected in a monthly cycle by both sun and moon, and by local currents, landforms and estuaries whose idiosyncrasies, blessings and perils have always been the subject of precious local knowledge. Moons and seasons give rise to natural

cycles on which many ceremonies, festivals and agricultural practices hinged.

The land's capacity to yield grass for pasture and meadow or
arable crops like wheat, oats and barley is dependent on a few
key soil characteristics: depth; clay and sand content; acidity;
how well it holds and drains rainwater; its average temperature
and natural mineral content. Broad river valleys enriched by
glacial and alluvial silts – the so-called fertile corelands – are well
drained, with abundant water and deep soils. They were favoured
by early farming communities who ploughed, de-stoned, weeded,
fertilized and aerated them, effectively warming them to lengthen
the natural growing season.[14] These plains – *maghs*, *maes* and
straths, to use the native terms – fostered core areas of human
settlement, already well established by the time that Julius Caesar
led his exploratory invasion in 55 BCE. Rivers brought seasonal
floods and their life-giving fertile silts; they abounded with fish,
molluscs and waterfowl. Surrounding hills, long cleared of their
forests, provided ample summer grazing lands for sheep and oxen:
the former for wool and for their skins; the latter, primarily, for pulling ploughs and waggons. Goats supplied households with milk;
pigs, fattened quickly in autumn, were slaughtered and cured for
winter protein. Stud bulls and horses were coveted possessions of
the wealthy and powerful.

In such fertile and productive territories political cohesion and
identity fostered the evolution of what one might loosely term
petty kingdoms or tribal fiefdoms. Some of these can be tentatively
identified in the drainage basins of rivers like the Tay and Clyde,
Tyne, Tees and Thames, Severn and Avon; perhaps also around
the Moray and Solway Firths, the Mersey, Wye and Solent, Nene,
Ouse, Cam, Lea and upper Trent. These fertile corelands, far from
being divided by their navigable rivers, were united by a shared
geography and dependence on their waters for food and travel.
They became prime targets for the colonizing emperors of Rome.
South of the early second-century Hadrianic frontier, these are
the lands where villas were built during the occupation; where
indigenous noble families bought into the imperial project, lived in

swanky stone townhouses, erected Latin memorials to their loved ones and gave their children an expensive classical education. Gildas was the product of such a family; so was St Patrick.

Rome's military planners were quick to see how Britain's tribal corelands might be both politically neutered and economically exploited, by linking the highest navigable points on the major rivers with a network of roads, controlled by forts at strategic junctions.* This brilliant strategy fostered a sophisticated topological network beyond the imaginations of Rome's provincial subjects. It turned *Britannia* into a densely connected, high-speed landscape that enabled Rome to extract its mineral treasures, control its natives and promote trade, markets and wealth: to create the *Pax Romana*.

More mountainous or intractable lands – the acidic hills of Wales, the Pennines, the Highlands; the heavy clays and dry chalklands; the East Anglian Fens and seasonally flooded Vale of York; the peat hags of the west and north – were not so densely inhabited. These less centralized landscapes were harder and less rewarding to explore and exploit. Sometimes, so far as the armies of Rome were concerned, the game was not worth the candle; it was enough to establish a thin network of forts and roads; to monitor native politics and show the flag. Occasionally, the cohorts patrolling and subduing these more debatable lands found themselves on the wrong end of a good spanking.

Some special places attracted the attention of the Roman state by virtue of their mineral resources: salt springs in the West Midlands and briny fens in East Anglia; the lead ores of the Pennines and Mendip hills; the ironstones and timber of high forests of the Weald and of Dean; tin from Cornwall; copper and gold from Wales.

The pattern and type of settlements seen across this mosaic of human-natural landscapes were distinct, highly adapted to their cultural and natural milieu, but essentially conservative. In less fertile hill country, where building stone, turf and heather are

---

* The rivers marked as navigable on the maps in this book are based on certain and likely navigations derived from Hill 1984 and Cole 2013.

abundant local materials, one finds brochs, duns and crannogs,* Cornish 'rounds', Cheviot 'scooped settlements', farmsteads of stone and turf-walled roundhouses, very often set in circular or rectangular compounds and often dispersed rather than clustered into villages. These discrete family or extended family units, related socially and by family ties with neighbours, knew and expressed solidarity with the broad groups to which they belonged and distinguished themselves equally consciously from groups to which they did not belong.

Many communities in such challenging environments practised transhumance – living at close quarters in the valleys during the colder months; migrating to upland pastures for the summer. Some of the richest material culture of the late Iron Age onwards comes from élite summer dwellings – the crannogs – strung out along the shallow waters of lochs and lakes in what are now Scotland and Wales, and from the celebrated lake villages of the Somerset levels. Pile-built houses, connected to land by wooden causeways and constructed entirely of organic materials that were later abandoned to the cool, anaerobic sediments of their waters, have yielded astonishing records of their inhabitants' lives – tools and cookware, craft techniques and diets, parasites and bedding. They confirm that a lack of fine glassware, posh pottery and stone houses is not necessarily evidence of material poverty, but of the sophisticated management of nature's abundant resources.

A map of Roman Britain shows a stark contrast between what might be called zones of Romanization – with their roads, forts, villas, small towns, *coloniae* and *civitates* – and zones of control and enforcement, where such wonders are either not found or are rare. A rough line can be drawn round inner *Britannia*, circumscribing the lands east of the Yorkshire Ouse, south and east of the Trent, east of the rivers Parrett, Wye and Severn (but excluding the

---

* Large houses on artificial islands in shallow lochs accessed by causeways. The organic richness of the often waterlogged archaeological remains has greatly enlarged understanding of the material culture of Early Medieval rural élites.

Pile-built luxury: the reconstructed crannog on Loch Tay, Perthshire.

Weald of Kent and Sussex). Here the imperial project succeeded in making Romans of Britons. For the rest of the island – that is, the majority of the land of Britain – Rome was a peripheral, if unignorable, force in their lives: sometimes an unwelcome military, judicial and fiscal presence; sometimes a source of useful relations and wealth or material goods. Archaeologists excavating the settlements of these lands very often rely on the occasional presence of 'Roman' artefacts to date occupation phases; otherwise, there seems to have been a broad continuum in architecture, economy and social practice from the late Iron Age right through into the Early Medieval centuries.

Between the very Roman and the distinctly native lay liminal communities, sometime clients and allies of the emperor, whose dynamic and evolving interactions with their more conservative neighbours, and with the empire, allowed them to negotiate a deliberately ambiguous set of relations and identities. Some of them profited from their relations with Rome while maintaining a credible foot in the native camp.

In what is now Northumberland, a big-skied swathe of contrasts between fertile volcanic hills, peat hags, wide glacial valleys and tractable coastal plains, Rome found allies in the tribes they called *Selgovae* and *Votadini*. For a brief period, during the ambitious military programmes of the first and second centuries CE, these tribes were subject peoples. But the bulk of Britain's fertile lands and ample minerals lay to the south and, after the second quarter of the second century, the Hadrianic Wall frontier zone was established as the primary line of military control. After that, several of the tribes to the north negotiated an advantageous 'client' status. A very large number of settlements, visible as earthworks and stone ramparts in the pasture lands of the Cheviot Hills tell, like their southern downland counterparts, of prosperity during the Roman centuries.

At Greave's Ash, high up in the Breamish valley (*Bromic* in the earliest sources), sit two linked hamlets of roundhouses with carefully managed stock enclosures and trackways interconnected with dozens of farms and hilltop enclosures sitting in arable fields and improved pastures. The climate is oddly favourable: southeast facing slopes enjoy early sun and long days in summer; the soils are volcanic and nutrient rich, well drained and easily tilled by chisel plough and hoe. Embanked compounds containing the circular stone footings of multiple houses and storage and craft huts – probably extended family units – sit in landscapes of managed pasture and tilled fields bounded by hedgebanks, all sure signs of substantial investment in the landscape; of a thriving population. The high meadows of the Cheviots make good grazing. The Breamish valley drains to the east where a natural routeway out of the hills is linked to the natural harbour at Berwick and to the forts and towns of Hadrian's Wall by a Roman road known as the Devil's Causeway. There is a good case to suggest that the hill farmers here provided surplus livestock, wool and grain to the forts on the Wall.[15] They may have traded craft items with the town and possible *civitas* capital at *Coria* (Corbridge, in the Tyne valley). As barbarians by definition, their traders may have been forced to queue at the entrance to the empire. Intriguing concentrations of finds from the Northumberland village of Great Whittington, just a mile or so north of the Wall, suggest that here was a sort of caravanserai where drovers, traders, petitioners, embassies and wannabe citizens had to bivouac and prove their bona fides before being allowed in.[16]

A few miles north of Greave's Ash the indomitable twin-domed hillfort of Yeavering Bell looms imperiously over Glendale and the Milfield plain beyond. Here, an Iron Age fortress and summer camp were the focus of regional power and of a tribal cult. Yeavering's chieftains seem to have retained their power and identity through the Roman centuries and beyond: below the Bell, on a broad whaleback shelf above the river, lies the Bernician royal township of Yeavering – Bede's *Ad Gefrin*. Here, revealed in a brilliant campaign of excavation in the 1950s and 1960s, royal feasting, an immense cattle corral and a cult of the dead proclaimed tribal identity and territorial power.[17] *Gefrin* and the Breamish valley retained their coherence as units of land and production across the centuries of the empire, into an age of Northumbrian kingship and regional power. The Breamish valley was granted *in toto* as a small shire, from the portfolio of one of those kings to the monks of Lindisfarne in the seventh century. In the cold, tumbling waters of the River Glen the first Northumbrians were baptized by missionaries from Rome in 627.[18] Yeavering Bell itself has not been substantially excavated but at another great hillfort of the *Votadini*, Traprain Law in East Lothian, successive archaeological campaigns have revealed a substantial reinforcing of the ramparts at the end of the fourth century and yielded a colossal hoard of fifth-century Roman silver weighing 53 lb. Most of the pieces had been hacked into handy sizes, as if weighed in for scrap. The consensus is that the hoard was payment to a client chieftain for services rendered or anticipated: services that were either not delivered or were insufficient to save Roman Britain from its fate.

Even within the corelands of the new province, Britain's highly regionalized geographies presented Rome with unexpected challenges. The densely wooded Weald in what is now Kent and

Sussex was rich in timber and iron ore, but largely impenetrable. It may have produced riches for the empire, but it remained as empty of towns, villas and forts as the remotest parts of Wales, the north and the south-west. A wild country of delvers and charcoal burners, it seems never to have become truly Romanized.

Even more mysterious and daunting for outsiders, the Fens around the Wash, then a vast wetland basin protected from the North Sea by a low-lying but habitable band of silt, extended some 25 miles inland from the modern coastline. This was a land of small island communities separated, or connected, by slowly meandering rivers, some of them tidal and brackish and increasingly prone to flooding. The fenland marshes and seasonally flooded meadows were rich in grazing and wildlife, abundant in seasonal foods and raw materials: wild ducks and geese; fish and eels; sedges, reeds, salt and peat. But, in a land that floated somehow between water and sky, with no visible landmarks and many a pitfall for the unwary, imposing the monolithic culture of the empire was an immense challenge.

Fenland communities were 'other', in culture and outlook, managing their landscape and its resources in a distinctively communal fashion. Malaria may have been an endemic driver of infant and adult mortality, while the fens and the rivers that fed them were a physical and cultural buffer between East Anglia and the Midlands. Long into the Early Medieval period the Fens were regarded by outsiders with a mixture of awe, fear and disgust; but for those who knew them they were an incomparably productive and wondrous resource. For Roman governors – perhaps including Hadrian himself – the Fens offered opportunities: to drain, to tame, to exploit and conquer; to civilize.

On a small island close to what is now March, connected east and west to drier, higher ground by a causeway, lie the remains of a defended Iron Age enclosure, no more than 13 ft above modern sea level but dominating an otherwise flat horizon of rectangular, peaty black fields bounded by innumerable drains and dykes. This may have been the last redoubt of Boudicca's Icenian army in 60 or 61 CE.

A new, carefully planned and laid out settlement, now known by the name of the nearby farm at Stonea Grange, was established just to the north of this enclosure before the middle of the second century CE.[19] It was no mere hamlet. A grid of small streets divided square plots 50 Roman feet* across, containing houses and workshops, the buildings of industrious and productive craftspeople. A temple stood in isolation on the opposite side of the Fen Causeway, within a distinctive square enclosure. Looking down onto its own piazza, and facing directly onto the causeway, stood an enormous three- or four-storey square building of faced limestone – transported by barge from a quarry some 25 miles away near Peterborough. It boasted glazed, round-arched windows and an apsidal chamber flanked by corridors and domestic ranges, served by its own separate boiler room and hypocaust.[†] Extraordinarily rich remains from a construction trench or drainage 'sump', used as a rubbish pit by its builders, testify to the everyday: a wooden spade whose iron tip was encrusted with mortar; planks and bundles of withies; a pair of much-repaired size 9½ shoes. Such an uncompromising show of architectural and logistical superiority was designed to impose, to dominate, to inspire awe. It can hardly have failed to impress.

The tower house must have been visible from miles around, piercing that two- dimensional landscape like the later steeples and churches of the medieval Fenland parishes. Defying the relentless purging winds of the flat marshes, the tragic ululations of curlews and mocking calls of the oystercatcher, this was a wild land tamed, both physically and metaphorically. There has been speculation that Stonea's complex, and the estate at whose centre it seems to have stood, was a personal project undertaken at the behest of far-off emperors, comparable as an expression of hubristic egotism to Victorian opera houses in the Amazon.

---

* The so-called *pedes monetales*, equal to 11.65 in or 29.57 cm. Jackson and Potter 1996, 136.
† An underfloor heating system. Warm air was fed from a furnace into cavities supported by columns of tiles and up through flues within the walls.

Whatever the economic foundations of that architectural fist of masonry – as an inland port-of-trade for wool, lamb, oysters, eels and wildfowl, perhaps salt – it did not last. In about 250 CE the tower house was dismantled, less than 100 years after its construction – its loss of official status and patronage perhaps a result of well-testified fenland flooding or of some off-stage political crisis. The materials were systematically robbed, the whole plot later redeveloped on a much more modest scale. But the settlement at Stonea survived into the fourth century, recovered some of its prosperity and continued beyond the end of empire. Its boundary ditches, pits and wells were still open when the first sherds of 'Anglo-Saxon' style pottery were discarded from houses whose builders might equally have been natives or incomers. Even so, there is some unseen discontinuity here: social, economic, perhaps cultural changes whose nuances are lost but which parallel empire-wide fortunes.

What is so striking about Stonea and, indeed, the hundreds of rural stately piles that we know as villas, is that in essence they are expressions not of rural, but of urban display. Rome's towns and cities were more than mere marketplaces, courts and administrative centres. In their formal layout and architecture they advertised the success of the Roman cultural project and the social and political ambitions of its curial classes.* The *civitas* capitals of the conquered provinces offered competing tribal élites, dispossessed of their weapons and opportunities for martial glory, access to such civilizing grandeur, while the smaller roadside towns and trading centres scattered across the province imprinted Rome's cultural and economic efficiency like a festoon of beads strung out on the necklace of its metalled highways. Country houses, built in sprawling imitation of their civic counterparts, ensured that the fruits of cultivated urbanity and *Romanitas* were exhibited (if not distributed) as widely and as visibly as possible across the conquered province.

---

* The *curiales* were leading merchants, businessmen and landowners with civic responsibilities and dignities.

The waxing and waning fortunes of Romano-British towns, archetypes of Mediterranean civil order and cultural self-satisfaction, have always been a litmus test of Roman achievement and failure. Towns are dynamic, ever-changing; their archaeological remains ought to be expressive and reflective of those dynamics. Some now lie buried beneath fields of corn or meadow grass; others became the provincial towns of medieval England or the great cities of Britain's own empire. In their soggy or desiccated remains the story of the end of Roman Britain is written.

2

The ruin

Dark matters – *Pax Romana* – the troubles –
messy humans – the fortunes of towns –
the weakening state – adaptations

D N VALENTIN IANVS P F AVG

Gold solidus of Emperor Valentinian III, from 441–450,
minted in Constantinople. Very few of these coins ever
reached Britain: the Portable Antiquities Scheme lists a
single copper coin from his reign.

After conquest and exploitation, Roman Britain's third and final act, a passage from consolidation to crisis, is stutteringly illuminated by a strobe lamp of periodic notices in Continental sources. Their general theme is of military crisis and usurpation, before a dramatic curtain fall in the first decade of the fifth century. Cut to Gildas, writing sometime in the later fifth or early sixth century, recording a woeful picture of abandoned cities, civil war and invasion by the impious tribes of *Germania*. Bede copied him, and more remote chroniclers of the Britons and of the Eastern empire in Constantinople concurred: when Rome left *Britannia*, anarchy ensued.

Before the late twentieth century, archaeologists peering into keyhole excavations in our densely populated cities, and even in those more accessible Roman towns, like Silchester, where no medieval or modern development constrained the size of their trenches, struggled to find evidence for a single Romano-British town functioning as a genuinely urban settlement into the fifth century. Early Medieval Britain had no towns before the late ninth century. Towards the end of the seventh century St Cuthbert, on a visit to Carlisle (Latin *Luguvalium*; Brythonic *Caer Luel*), was shown a remarkable Roman fountain built into the city's still standing walls; but it was no more than a tourist attraction; a curiosity.[1] Bede claimed that in his day (674–735) London, the former provincial capital of *Britannia*, was an emporium where many nations came to trade; but the *Lundenwic* of the eighth century was in reality a shanty town trading post half a mile upriver from the apparently deserted Roman city. Its muddy shore, where boats drew up to load or disgorge their wares, is buried beneath the Strand; its traders plied their business at Aldwych: literally, the 'old port'.

Both archaeological obscurity and the narrative voice-overs tolling *Britannia*'s funeral bells appear persuasive of demise. But, from the late 1970s onwards, signs of the casualty's weak but unmistakeable pulse began to be detected, in part because archaeologists began to look for them in earnest. At Wroxeter, in what is now Shropshire, on the east bank of the River Severn where it is joined by the River Tern, Philip Barker's painstaking excavations revealed traces of substantial buildings erected at the Roman town of *Viroconium Cornoviorum* in the fifth century; of classical design but in perishable timber, not monumental stone.[2] At *Verulamium*, the Roman precursor to St Albans, excavations showed that stone buildings constructed in the late fourth century were maintained and remodelled over several generations.[3] At Silchester, the former *civitas* capital *Calleva Atrebatum*, decades-long investigations have now produced similar evidence, including the remains of a putative early church just to the south-east of the forum.[4]

From the floor of a late Roman house at Caistor, just south of Norwich, a much-cited 1930s excavation retrieved the remains of at least thirty inhabitants who 'had come to a violent end in the early years of the fifth century'; but recent analysis of the very unsatisfactory contemporary excavation records suggests that the bodies concerned had not lain rotting in the streets, as the most lurid accounts would have it, but had probably been dumped as a collection of bones unearthed from a nearby cemetery by later ploughing.[5] Archaeologists have forced a hard-headed re-examination of Gildas, Bede and the Continental Cassandras who pronounced *Britannia* dead in 410.

In the rich but challenging seams that lie deeply stratified beneath modern towns and cities, the large open trenches enjoyed by greenfield archaeologists are unviable. Ephemeral timber footings exposed in plan are often invisible in the narrow profiles of deep, complex excavations; and the latest imperial coins to reach Britain, generally of Honorius (395–423) and minted no later than about 400, give only *termini post quos* – dates *after* which something happened, rather than dates *when* things happened. The coins of Honorius's successors are deafening in their silence; life in fifth-century Roman towns is well camouflaged.

Widespread deposits of so-called 'dark earth', lying above the latest layers of obvious Romano-British occupation in many towns, and on top of which 'foreign' or 'squatter' occupation later left its mark, may provide just the confirmation of chaotic unconformity that the abruptness of the historical lacuna seems to indicate. But they may be telling us something else entirely.* The accumulation of huge quantities of soil, detritus and rubble in the back streets of once thriving towns is often touted as evidence for abandonment – almost as a marker for the end of civilization; but from another point of view dark earth is anything but: it is a sure sign of activity, of human agency in late Roman towns. It is easy to focus on the solid, easily identified material culture of Britain's Romanized élite: the fine tablewares, the bath suites and mosaics that fall into disrepair in the decades either side of 400 – perhaps quickly, perhaps not. Their absence does not mean that society ceased to function. A more complex and nuanced picture is slowly emerging: one of townscapes repurposed as the fiefdoms of petty lordship.

Britain, and especially the southern and eastern kingdoms of the late Iron Age,† had been exposed to knowledge of Roman culture and military capabilities long before Julius Caesar's short-lived expedition of 55–54 BCE. In turn, Rome's geographers knew enough about Britain to understand its basic geography; they knew of its wealth in cattle, furs, gold, lead, copper and tin; of its fine hunting dogs and of the – in their minds – primitive peoples who might be usefully yoked to the Roman juggernaut. Their sometimes ludicrous descriptions of savage natives belong to a tradition of colonial powers dehumanizing or diminishing the cultures of their intended conquests. In fact, British societies were sophisticated, socially complex and culturally rich; very much connected to the outside world.

The Claudian invasion of 43 CE was a largely political enterprise targeted, to begin with, at the lands of the *Trinovantes* and *Iceni* of East Anglia and Essex, the ground already prepared by 'understandings' with potential allies and client kings. Some of the natives were not as enthusiastic in their embrace of the Claudian project as the conquerors had hoped. The *Iceni* rose in

* See Chapter 6, p. 184.
† Roughly 100 BCE to the middle of the first century CE.

rebellion against the legions in 47 CE and again in 60 under their celebrated leader Boudicca, inflicting devastating humiliation on imperial forces and on the flat-pack towns of the new province. Savage and long-lasting reprisals left East Anglia shorn of state investment and only partially integrated with the town and villa landscapes of Essex and the Midlands.

Even so, military victories over barbarians reflected prestige on commanders-in-chief while booty, slaves, minerals and grain made the economic case for conquest. The *Pax Romana* was a universal benefit bestowed on lucky peoples. A conquering and exploratory phase, by no means without its setbacks and brutalities, was shadowed by a military administration underpinned with infra-structure: tribes disarmed, fortresses slighted, lands confiscated and recalcitrant subject peoples relocated. Towns were imposed on these tribal lands as centralizing, civilizing hot spots; direct state taxation and economic control of key resources harnessed the Britons to the state apparatus; a radically penetrative road network warped and streamlined Iron Age Britain's sluggish space-time geography. From time to time, rivals of the distant emperors set up shop in *Britannia** but, generally, the province was secure; it paid for itself.

Romanitas, from the colonists' point of view, brought peace and prosperity to the frontiers and security to the empire. For the indigenes, the experience was, at best, mixed. By the middle of the second century, Britain south of Hadrian's Wall was, in some respects, thoroughly Roman. Settlements of army veterans – *coloniae* – were established outside legionary fortresses at *Lindum* (Lincoln), *Camulodunum* (Colchester), *Glevum* (Gloucester) and *Eboracum* (York). The provincial capital at *Londinium*, whose origins lay in its status as a well-connected trading port rather than as a military fortress, must have looked like many other Roman cities with its fora, temples, baths, wharves and stone

---

* Carausius, fleet commander of the *Classis Britannica*, declared himself emperor and severed formal ties with the empire in the 280s; *Britannia*'s independence lasted barely a decade.

houses. *Civitas* capitals like that at Winchester seem to have been enthusiastically patronized by a regional nobility buying into the *Pax Romana*, with its opportunities for social and political advancement. New technologies, direct cash taxation and farming innovations matching eager and sustained demand – chiefly the military – encouraged an intensification of rural production. Roads connected industrial production sites churning out pottery, salt, iron, lead and other precious metals with markets in towns, at forts and abroad, supplied through Britain's ample natural harbours. Meat, grain, timber, minerals and wool made Britain wealthy and its population expanded accordingly. By the beginning of the third century, its inhabitants enjoyed the status of imperial citizenship. Many of the *civitates* were encouraged to govern themselves, more or less, so long as the taxes kept coming.

Under Roman rule Britons were better off. That is to say, those Britons able to enjoy heated baths, the latest design in mosaic floors, good wine, slaves and the gossip of the forum were better off. The fine furnishings, architecture and décor of the wealthiest houses tell us that their owners ate well with silver cutlery off beautifully crafted dishes, embracing a hybrid northern version of Mediterranean life – even if the pressure to compete for professional and social advancement caused the sorts of tensions reflected in pretentious display and the bourgeois moanings of the *Aquae Sulis* tablets.

For the vast majority of the native population, access to such exclusive benefits and mores was at best vicarious. Rome may have been content to franchise out provincial administration and tax collection to native ruling families; but the provinces had to pay their way. As a result, Britain's entrepreneurs made themselves rich at the expense of a large majority of the population who were excluded from most of the benefits. As was the case with the disenfranchised classes of eighteenth-century British colonies, bitter resentment at heavy taxation and the conspicuous wealth and consumption of their betters may have encouraged many Britons to ask if they might not be better off without the dubious benefits of the empire. The further one lived from the ostentatious centres of Roman power and consumption, the greater the alienation or envy likely to be felt.

The empire was in a state of anarchy and economic decline when the town councils, the *curiae*, of Roman Britain began to build enclosing stone walls in the third century. In so doing, they were very probably embarking on a competition with each other to express their sense of civic identity, their enjoyment of privacy and wealth; but it is hard not to see in that particular choice of display a tension between urban and rural, wealthy and poor, security and insecurity; between inclusivity and exclusivity. During the so-called Third-Century Crisis *Britannia* suffered revolts and episodic coastal raids (in St Patrick's *Confessio*, written two centuries later, we have a survivor's personal account of the consequences). No doubt urban and rural riots broke out sporadically too, even if such manifestations of social discontent festered beneath the radar of Continental historians. Despite such instability, *Britannia* remained as solidly a part of the empire as any of Rome's conquests.

Where, then, to place a marker for the beginning of the end? Not, surely, before the elevation of Constantine the Great to the imperial purple at York in 306; nor, probably, in the 340s when an allusive text hints that his son, Constans, came to Britain with a small force to investigate reports of trouble in the province.[6] Something more significant may be indicated in the chronicle of the last great Roman historian, Ammianus Marcellinus,* who recounted the aftermath of a usurpation of the Western empire by Magnentius between 350 and 353. This would-be emperor's sympathizers or supporters included a significant number of British

---

* A non-Christian Syrian-born military officer, whose career was largely spent in the East but also included a spell in Gaul. He was writing in Rome in the late 380s, able to draw on both near contemporary accounts of the provinces and on the personal knowledge of some of those involved in distant events, as well as imperial records, in his *Res Gestae*. Hamilton, 1986.

officers or governors. From Rome, Emperor Constantius II sent a member of his securitat, a sort of notary-cum-inquisitor known ominously as Paulus 'Catena' ('the Chain') to Britain to bring back for trial those suspected of having collaborated with Magnentius. According to Ammianus, Paul was overzealous, denouncing innocent and guilty alike, fabricating charges and having suspects manacled. When Flavius Martinus, the *vicarius* or viceroy of *Britannia*, intervened he was himself accused of treason. A desperate fight ensued and Martinus committed suicide.[7] The Latin theologian and historian Jerome, looking back from the first decade of the following century, could cite a litany of British usurpers following Magnentius's precedent.[8]

Was this a storm in a teacup, or evidence of a deeper malaise that mirrored the general sense of dynastic instability suffusing the Western empire in the fourth century? Did Britain's unique island geography encourage a recalcitrant sense of independence? Whatever the case, political volatility did not prevent a sort of economic heyday in Britain during that century, a time when new villas were built and others were splendidly refurbished. Within a decade of Paulus's heavy-handed intervention, the Emperor Julian (361–363) could send hundreds of ships to Britain to be loaded with grain for a Continental campaign.[9] *Britannia* was wealthy still; and yet, could the province sustain such rapacious demands from its god-like leaders and attendant resentment against their absentee politicking? And, if the countryside was productive, its great towns and cities had long since passed their flowering. Public investment in civic infrastructure, evidenced by inscriptions that speak of pride and of expenditure on baths, fora, temples and statuary, had been superseded by the privatization of town life. Archaeologists detect fewer buildings, less obvious material consumption; less town-like behaviour. The curial classes of the *civitates* seem to have become wearily anti-civic, investing their wealth in villas – rural mirrors of urban grandeur – and, perhaps, spending their social capital on land, family and local clientèle rather than state-centred careerism. Taxation in the late empire was increasingly localized, levied in kind rather than directly in cash.[10] The economic life of the province was, by the middle of the fourth century, sustained by many dozens of small towns and trading settlements and by the shrunken garrisons of the frontier; not, it seems, by an active, enthusiastic metropolitan class. Was regional power flowing away from the *civitates* – in any case more of a Roman construct than a native institution – towards their more local *pagi*? Was Britain reverting to its inherently localist character?

One thinks of the classic Romano-British villa as a sumptuously appointed and spacious single-storey stone house with tiled roof, porticoes, dining suites, corridors giving onto formal courtyard gardens and family shrines; as a display case of social and economic opulence, of discreet showiness and carefully managed privacy. As a one-dimensional, one-size-fits-all model of rural life, the villa tells a dead-straight narrative of economic and social rise and fall.[11] Its ultimate disappearance from the British landscape looks, from the imperial heights of the second century, like failure; and dramatic failure at that.

Signs of more subtle relations between town and country, owner and estate, corporation and farm hint at a more responsive and interesting patchwork of community and economy. What of the large timber roundhouses, such a strong echo of indigenous Iron Age tradition and architectural conservatism, that accompany many comfortably successful rural settlements? What of the substantial complexes that were something less than a villa but more than a native farmstead?

Close inspection of the excavated record shows that buildings and settlements in the late Romano-British landscape lie along a very broad spectrum. Villas have often been compared to the great country estates of the eighteenth and nineteenth centuries, but there is nothing, in the opulent villa dining suite, of those great social gatherings centred on the ballroom. Villas themselves were not, by and large, central places or assembly sites.

Some of the most impressive buildings in the countryside, often found close to more conventional villa complexes, must have been the timber- or stone-built aisled barns or halls, of which an increasing number are being excavated across southern Britain.

Meonstoke: the miraculously preserved first floor arcade of its aisled barn, preserved in the British Museum.

Like the tithe barns of the medieval shires, these are monumental structures displaying engineering skill and architectural sophistication. Some are plain, open-plan halls with columns, high ceilings and hearths (seeming to anticipate the Anglo-Saxon mead hall or the Christian basilica), perhaps of more than one storey; others bear internal partitions. Their simple rectangular ground plans, from which most have been identified by excavators, give little idea of their outward appearance or the possible range of social and economic functions that they fulfilled. But, occasionally, archaeologists get lucky. At Meonstoke, in Hampshire's Meon valley, a small accident of structural failure has preserved part of the upper gable end of such a building. Collapsing outwards from its lower storey as an intact section of façade, it landed more or less complete on the ground outside and was buried for over

1,500 years before being excavated and then, with admirable forethought and technical skill, lifted as a whole.*

The early fourth-century Meonstoke façade, along with other evidence from the 1989 excavation, shows that this aisled building was no mere hay barn: it looks for all the world like a basilica, with clerestory windows set directly over the aisles, false arcades above, decorative flint courses and tile-and-mortar detailing.[12] While the traditional wing-corridor villa proclaims exclusivity and wealth this building, and others like it across the countryside, speak of the communal, of a need to display grandeur not just to the intimates of an élite clientèle at an ostentatious dinner party but to an extended kin group or to dependants. One can imagine great social occasions taking place here – assemblies of dependent households and their servants, where the wheels of patronage were oiled by wine and song, dance and gossip: a more familiar social environment for Jane Austen's sociable characters than any villa bath suite.

Something, then, is missing from the standard model of late Romano-British society; something that seems to presage the Early Medieval. The aisled barns and great roundhouses may also be just the most visible manifestation of a change in the way the empire taxed its provinces, from the direct extraction of cash tribute towards more local renders of goods and services in kind that fostered and cemented local and regional social networks: the keystone of Early Medieval territorial lordship.

If Britain had largely been insulated from the tremors shaking the bloated fourth-century empire, its wake-up call came in 360. In this year, Ammianus Marcellinus tells us, the *Scotti* (from across the Irish Sea or from Argyll) and *Picti* (from *Caledonia*) broke their treaty obligations with Rome and attacked the northern frontier – in response to what provocation or opportunity is not known;

* The Meonstoke façade is now on display in the Roman galleries of the British Museum, the gift of Mr and Mrs Bruce Horn.

some perceived military weakness, perhaps, or a growing sense of indigenous self-confidence. Emperor Julian sent a senior commander named Lupicinus across the Channel with a force of auxiliary troops to intervene; but nothing is known of the expedition's outcome.* The attack of 360 heralded a decade in which 'the Picts, Saxons, Scots and Attacotti were bringing continuing misery upon Britain'.[13] Seven years later, according to Ammianus, reports reached a new emperor, Valentinian, that 'a concerted attack by the barbarians had reduced the provinces of Britain† to the verge of ruin. Nectaridus, the count of the coastal region,‡ had been killed; General Fullofaudes§ surprised and cut off.'[14] Much has been made of this passage in the *Res Gestae*, as a presage of disasters to come and because the two commanders both bore names suggestive of a Germanic background. The loss of *Britannia*'s two most senior military commanders implies overwhelming force or a strong element of surprise and a concerted campaign on several fronts by tribal warbands co-ordinating their attacks. Such a scenario itself implies perceived weakness in the provincial command structure and probably in troop numbers. Those signs of weakness are reinforced by what is known of subsequent events.

---

* Lupicinus is sometimes proposed as the owner of a large stash of fine silverware (now in the British Museum), buried some time in the late fourth century at Mildenhall in Suffolk, close to the edge of what would have been fenland in the Roman period.

† *Britannia* had been divided into two provinces at the end of the second century, *Britannia Superior* and *Inferior*. A century later, under Diocletian's wide-ranging reforms, Britain became a diocese of four provinces: *Britannia Prima*, *Britannia Secunda*, *Flavia Caesariensis* and *Maxima Caesariensis*. A fifth province, not securely located but called *Valentia*, was added during the fourth century.

‡ *Comes litoris Saxonici.* His command included the so-called forts of the Saxon shore: *Othona* (Bradwell), *Dubrae* (Dover), *Lemanis* (Lympne), *Branodunum* (Brancaster), *Gariannonum* (Burgh Castle), *Regulbium* (Reculver), *Rutupiae* (Richborough), *Anderitum* (Pevensey) and *Portus Adurni* (Portchester). Ireland 2008, 139.

§ He was *Dux Britanniarum*, Duke of the Britains [*sic*] whose command included Hadrian's Wall, with headquarters at *Eboracum* (York).

Valentinian's initial response to despatches reaching him while en route from Amiens to Trier (*Augusta Treverorum*) was to send an investigative force across the Channel. A first commander was recalled; a second begged for reinforcements. In 368 a proven military commander named Theodosius was sent with four units of auxiliaries – about 2,000 troops in total. Crossing from *Bononia* (Boulogne) to *Rutupiae* (the coastal fortress at Richborough in Kent) Theodosius advanced on London, encountering what Ammianus describes as roaming bands – coastal raiders from the Rhine delta and beyond, perhaps – weighed down with prisoners and booty. He dealt with them swiftly and entered London, where he received detailed intelligence confirming widespread, effective tribal attacks and army defections. Some of the deserters were induced to rejoin him and he now took an enlarged force north, 'seizing positions suitable for guerrilla warfare'[15] – possibly hilltop sites in Wales, the Pennines and southern Scotland. That he was able to see off the enemy with a relatively small force, and at speed, implies that they were raiders rather than invaders, bent on acquiring booty rather than on a land grab; that in turn implies that the frontier garrisons had been reduced to dangerously low levels.

Theodosius now uncovered evidence of a coup, planned by a political exile named Valentinus. Worse still, he exposed the wholesale institutional betrayal of a force whose role was precisely to gain advance intelligence of enemy movements beyond the frontier. The *milites areani** had been bribed or coerced by tribes north of the Wall to report to them on imperial troop movements inside the frontier; in espionage parlance, they had been 'turned'. Their reports of garrison weakness behind the supposedly impenetrable Wall defences had encouraged the attacks of 367.† Theodosius promptly disbanded them.

The crisis, then, had been both opportunistic and structural.

---

* Frontier scouts; but an alternative name, *Arcani* – a secret service – may also be intended by Ammianus.

† Historians have suggested that the raids were, in any case, undertaken by sea, in which case the land-based defences were irrelevant.

That warbands from either side of the Irish Sea and across the North Sea had co-ordinated their assaults tells of a coherent political and military opposition to the empire in the late fourth century. But there is no record of military victories in the field during the Theodosian campaign; the raiders may have departed hotfoot with their loot rather than risk an open engagement with professional imperial troops. For now, the imperial army could still intervene decisively. Four generations later, the culture and politics of the warband was the dominant force in a fragmented former colony.

Theodosius, accompanied on the British campaign by his son (the future Emperor Theodosius I) and by his nephew Magnus Maximus (a future usurper), returned to the emperor's service with a stellar reputation. But one might be sceptical of Ammianus, a Theodosian loyalist, when he tells his readers that the commander 'restored cities and garrison towns… and protected the borders with guard posts and defence works' so that the province was completely recovered.[16] There is little archaeological evidence of either widespread destruction or rebuilding in Romano-British towns or villas or at the forts of the Wall garrisons in the 360s, although renovations and structural alterations at three Wall forts are recorded around this time. A series of signal stations was constructed along the east coast between Filey and Huntcliffe in the late fourth century; but to date them to Theodosius's time in Britain is to play a dangerous game in which archaeology chases history around the block.

With the single exception of *Cunetio* (Mildenhall in the Kennet valley of eastern Wiltshire), the walls of Romano-British towns make for poor defences;[17] and *Cunetio* seems an odd choice of town to defend against an assortment of attackers from across the Channel or the Irish Sea. Town walls, gates and bastions are better seen as displays of local power and spare cash; and, besides, there is no evidence for any Roman town being attacked or comprehensively razed in the fourth century. On the other hand, it is possible that the late Roman state in *Britannia* feared the theft by its rural poor of strategic food stores. A number of very large stone buildings, urban equivalents of the aisled hall at Meonstoke, were constructed within the walls of fourth-century towns. After Emperor Julian's raid on Britain's grain harvest in 360, hunger may have been the most pressing threat to internal security, but a few packs of vicious-looking dogs and half a dozen well-armed guards might do just as well as a wall for keeping looters at bay. In any case, the majority of monumental civic works were completed long before the Theodosian crisis which seems, on the face of it, to have bequeathed little to the archaeological record.

For a decade and more after 367 Britain's fortunes were peripheral to great events on the Continent and in Africa. No news is good news, perhaps. But Ammianus notes that in 372 Valentinian sent a force of *Bucinobantes*, an Alamannic tribe from the upper Rhine, to Britain under their king, Fraomarius.[18] This is the first British notice of a policy of resettling tribes, more specifically tribal warbands, in other provinces as allied military forces called *foederati*. The potential cultural, linguistic and genetic implications of this move are not lost on historians and archaeologists looking for the seeds of an 'Anglo-Saxon' warrior culture in Britain *before* the end of the empire. Even so, much more ink has been spilt on the figure of Magnus Maximus, Theodosius's Spanish-born nephew, who had seen service in Britain in 368. In 380, now in his mid-forties, he was assigned to *Britannia* by a new emperor, Gratian (died 383) – perhaps as commander of the field army, the *Comes Britanniarum*, or as the senior provincial commander, the *Dux Britanniarum*. Magnus Maximus is significant as an imperial usurper. After defeating a force of *Picti* and *Scotti* in 382, he was acclaimed emperor by his troops in 383, crossed the Channel with a substantial contingent of British field forces the following year and won over much of the Rhine army to his cause. Retreating south and west in the face of this seemingly irresistible military threat, Gratian was caught by a pursuing force and cut down.[19] In victory, Maximus negotiated terms with his cousin and former comrade Theodosius I, emperor of the Eastern empire. Maximus set up his capital court at Trier on the banks of the Moselle and from there administered the Western provinces for the next four years.

Almost nothing direct is known of Maximus's policy towards *Britannia* during this time. A less-than-perfect later source suggests that he withdrew more troops from Britain and elsewhere to support an ultimately fatal campaign against Theodosius in 388.[20] But, thanks to his appearance in the *Historia Brittonum*, in Gildas's *De Excidio*, in medieval Welsh poetry and in a number of supposedly early genealogies, Magnus Maximus has fostered a thriving industry of speculative ideas in which he might be cast as the 'real Arthur', even as the first Early Medieval king. He is occasionally credited with setting up client kings among the *civitates*.

In 395 Theodosius died, leaving two sons to divide the empire between them. In the West, the rule of Honorius (until 423) is indissolubly associated with the loss of control over Gaul, the sacking of Rome by Alaric's Visigoths in 410, a damaging theological controversy and with the final detachment or secession of the British provinces. The last coins from an imperial mint to reach Britain in meaningful quantities belong to his issue of 402. After that, no army pay wagons ever made it across the Channel again.

In about 396 the twelve-year-old Honorius's senior general and regent, Flavius Stilicho, is credited in a Claudian oration – the equivalent of a tabloid front page – with either a military reorganization or a reinforcement of the British garrison, among a number of other pressing military concerns. But these troops seem to have been withdrawn within a very few years and nothing much can be said about the campaign or its legacy. The immediate effect on a formerly cash-based military economy may not have been dramatic: plenty of coin and bullion must still have been circulating and the army was not so significant a driver of commercial demand as it had once been. As a retrospective marker for the end of *Britannia*, its exclusion from the flow of Continental currency is highly significant; but it is doubtful if any Briton or Roman seriously believed that more than three hundred years of colonial rule was about to end.

On the last day of the year 406, dated by the joint consulship of Arcadius and Probus, a force of Vandals, Suevi and Alans crossed the River Rhine.* Edward Gibbon, writing his masterwork, *The History of the Decline and Fall of the Roman Empire*, during the War of American Independence, saw in that epic event a parallel to the empire west of the Alps. He offered his readers the lurid image of a frozen river affording unlimited passage, across the once impenetrable barrier of the northern frontier, to an unstoppable wave of barbarians.[21] There is, in fact, no evidence that the Rhine was frozen; nor of the size of the force that crossed into northern Gaul and penetrated as far as the Seine.

According to Zosimus, writing at the end of the fifth century in far-off Constantinople, but drawing on reliable sources, 'such was the slaughter they inflicted that they inspired terror even among the forces in Britain, who were then forced, through fear the barbarians might advance against them, into electing usurpers'.[22] In short succession Marcus and Gratian, either army officers or provincial administrators, were promoted as candidates for emperor in *Britannia*. Within a year they had both been deposed and killed – whether as a result of counter-coups, or because they enacted unpopular policies, is not known. Britain's senior military commanders may by now have been withdrawn for service on the Continent; nominal authorities – provincial governors and the *vicarius* of the diocese – seem to have been entirely sidelined. In their place, a common soldier bearing the portentous name of Constantine was promoted to wear the purple. He was the last emperor, legitimate or otherwise, to see Britain. By the end of 407, like Maximus before him, he had crossed the Channel into Gaul where he set about campaigning against the Rhine invaders. His progress towards conquest of the whole Gaulish province can be traced most easily by his minting of coins – first at *Lugdunum*

---

* As recorded by Prosper in his *Chronicon* and by Zosimus quoting from the lost history of Olympiodorus (Ireland 2008, 157). Some commentators have argued that the correct date should be the last day of 405, which would resolve some problematic issues with its timing relative to events in both Britain and Italy. Kulikowski (2000, 326–7) argues for the earlier of the two possible readings.

(Lyon), then at *Augusta Treverorum* (Trier) and at *Arelate* (Arles), where he established his headquarters.[23]

If *Britannia*, its armies or whatever administration still held legitimacy there believed that raising its own candidate as Western emperor would strengthen it against prevailing insecurities, Constantine's preoccupation with Gaul must have been a grave disappointment. Honorius formally recognized the usurper Constantine 'III' as co-emperor at Arles in 409. A year later, according to the *Chronica Gallica of 452*, came the following: *Britanniae Saxonum incursionae devastatae* – a terse entry whose Latin needs no translation.[24] An immense hoard containing nearly 15,000 gold and silver coins, given a *terminus post quem* by a coin bearing the name of Constantine III, seems to have been deposited in the village of Hoxne, Suffolk, around this time.* The following year Honorius sent an army to besiege the usurper in Arles and had him killed. The words of Zosimus seem to inscribe an epitaph for *Britannia*:

> The barbarians beyond the Rhine made such unbounded incursions over every province, as to reduce not only the Britons, but some of the Celtic nations also to the necessity of revolting from the empire, and living no longer under the Roman laws but as they themselves pleased. The Britons therefore took up arms, and incurred many dangerous enterprises for their own protection, until they had freed their cities from the barbarians who besieged[†] them.[25]

A more controversial entry in Zosimus's *Historia Nova*, known as the 'Honorian rescript', appears to record an official response from the imperial government in Ravenna to Britain's ultimate political crisis: 'Honorius, having sent letters to the cities of Britain,

---

* Discovered by a metal detectorist in 1992.

† This phrase has also been read as 'billeted, or stationed on them' – a critical difference. Oosthuizen 2017, 27, quoting Bartholomew, P. 1982, 'Fifth-Century Facts'. *Britannia* 13, 261–70.

counselling them to be watchful of their own security...'[26] Much has been made of the context in which this tantalizing phrase occurs – a description of Honorius's tribulations in Italy – and some commentators have argued that Zosimus's *Brettania* is a mistake for *Brettia* or *Bruttium* in southern Italy.[27] But, in any case, Honorius had already made legal provision for the provinces to undertake their own defence* and the reality on the ground was that the bulk of the frontier forces, the *limitanei*, were already composed of locally recruited soldiers. The rescript, if actually referring to Britain, is no acknowledgement that the province had been given up; only that the emperor had more pressing business on his plate.

Whatever the complexities of *Britannia*'s terminal political history, the fragmentary remains that survive from these few manuscripts, remote in time and distance from events on the ground, are unsatisfactory grounds for telling the whole story. In themselves they paint a crude picture of conflict, insecurity, imperial impotence and internal dissension; of military coup and secular abdication. Whether an Insular[†] military or civic élite, self-identifying as 'British' or 'Roman', had formally seceded from the empire or had merely found themselves left in charge, is an enduring question. Gildas, picking up on the theme of catastrophe in his *De Excidio*, describes the aftermath of Roman withdrawal: 'Foul hordes of Scots and Picts, like dark throngs of worms', carried across the sea by their coracles, greedy for bloodshed, seized the whole of the north of the island as far as the Wall, whose lazy garrison troops were torn from their high towers and dashed to the ground. Then, the Britons 'abandoned the towns and the high wall... the pitiable citizens were torn apart by their foe like lambs to the slaughter'.[28]

Archaeologists have enthusiastically taken up the challenge of detecting tell-tale signs of violence and abandonment along Hadrian's Wall and in towns and rural settlements across *Britannia*.

---

* In a compilation of late Roman law, the *Codex Theodosianus*, section Vii.xiii, 16–17. Wood 1987.
† Insular: pertaining to the British Isles.

Hadrian's Wall, Northumberland: A symbol of Rome's
military might... and ultimate weakness.

What sorts of evidence might corroborate Gildas and those
Continental whispers of raids and disharmony? Bodies with blade-
weapon injuries would help, especially if they were left rotting in
the open or slung into pits. These ought to be readily detectable.
The fact that none have been found in locations suggestive of
violent, malevolent irruption – fort towers, town squares, villa
dining suites – may yet prove to be an accident of fate, but most
archaeologists now accept that proofs of anarchy are probably
not there to be found; not, at least, in any significant quantity.
What of destructive fire, then: houses and forts burned to the
ground and never rebuilt are reliable signs of destruction. But a

house may burn accidentally – indeed, it was one of the profound disadvantages of town living in an age when most structures were highly combustible, when lighting sources were unprotected and *vigiles*,* if they operated at all, were poorly equipped. No British town or fort of the late fourth or early fifth century has yielded any proof of having been comprehensively razed, as *Londinium* and *Verulamium* demonstrably were during the Boudiccan rebellion of 60 CE.

So far, there is little evidence to judge the speed at which the population declined. Gildas believed that many Britons had fled their homes and there is a strong case, certainly, for numbers of refugees fleeing domestic crises travelling to and settling in Armorica – what later became Brittany – although the scale of those movements is still debated.[29] But in order to convince archaeologists that homes, forts and towns across *Britannia* were abandoned wholesale, at speed and in the face of imminent danger, a special sort of evidence is required.

Humans are messy: they dig holes, generate rubbish, leave buildings to fall down, manure their fields and garden plots with all sorts of detritus, and are generally unsuccessful at covering their traces. Many of their manufacturing processes – butchery, ironworking, pottery firing – leave admirable and distinctive waste for excavators to find. Archaeologists call this 'primary' refuse – stuff that's left where it falls. Most people do not live comfortably with filth in their living rooms, and workshops have to be kept in good order; so, generally, householders in all ages have been assiduous in sweeping, tidying, mending breakages, collecting rubbish in discrete places and habitually adding to such heaps or pits in a set of maintenance processes that most of us call housekeeping and take for granted. Excavators find plenty of this 'secondary' refuse, too; but not on the floors of living rooms. They find it in rubbish pits, latrines or backyard heaps, so-called midden deposits: the stock-in-trade of archaeologists trying to

* Town watchmen who responded to reported crime and fires. They were also known as *spartoli*, 'little bucket fellows'.

understand past lives through material remains. When such refuse material is found within domestic spaces, it very often relates to activities that took place *after* abandonment.

When people moved to a new home in prehistoric, Roman and medieval societies, just as in our own, they cleared their old dwellings more or less comprehensively, taking portable and precious items – clothes, furniture, tools, lamps and cooking vessels – with them. It might have taken a few cartloads between old and new homes. Immovable, broken, low-value, heavy or awkward items were often left behind – locks on doors; chipped storage jars; pots sunk into the ground as basins; ovens, for example. This material, along with deliberate deposits like hoards, ritual offerings or burials, is called *de facto* refuse.

When people flee danger or oppression – and today's news reports bear eloquent, shocking witness to whole peoples on the move – they do so in a hurry and take what little they can carry, no more: a few clothes and tools; some bedding, perhaps; any saleable portable assets like jewellery or cash. They may hope to return to their homes one day. History tells us that valuable items such as furniture, machinery, fixtures and fittings, left behind by refugees, may be rapidly looted by the soldiers of conquering armies or parties of raiders. Even so, less valuable or portable objects are often discarded, and this is the stuff that excavators are looking for, lying directly on the floors of rooms where people were living immediately before their precipitate departure. Think Pompeii after the eruption of Vesuvius; think Pripyat* after Chernobyl, or any earthquake zone. Pripyat, and Varosha, the abandoned quarter of the Cypriot city of Famagusta, whose inhabitants fled Turkish soldiers in 1974, are fascinating archaeological laboratories in which to observe such processes.

In the now silent streets of Roman Silchester, Wroxeter or Caistor, had they been abandoned by fleeing citizens in fear of their lives, we ought to find the sherds from whole pottery vessels lying where

---

* The evacuated Belarussian town closest to the Chernobyl nuclear plant that exploded disastrously on 25–26 April 1986.

they were dropped; the nails and upholstery pins from beds and dining furniture; ovens with half-baked loaves in them, carbonized by engulfing flames. But we do not. No Roman town in Britain was comprehensively abandoned in a hurry. Building materials, metalwork, furniture, pottery and domestic fittings continued to be recycled by inhabitants, if on a smaller scale than before. Town houses were occasionally refurbished; new structures were erected; cemeteries and mausolea lining the roads outside towns used for burials. Britons did not, so far as one can tell, run away en masse.

Violence, then, will not do as the primary explanation for the profound changes visible in Romano-British towns in the late fourth century and beyond. Those changes include the introduction of burial within walled areas, a practice specifically forbidden in Roman law; the construction of large, apparently public buildings that encroached on existing streets or public spaces; the repurposing of civic structures like basilicas for industrial craft production and recycling; the accumulation of what appears to be garden soil (so-called 'dark earth') above the remains of former houses; and an apparent shift of markets and trading centres from larger towns – especially the *civitas* capitals – to smaller, roadside settlements.

The challenge for archaeologists trying to make sense of these changes is the lack of a broad and persuasive body of evidence: no single town has been excavated in its entirety using modern methods sensitive to the sorts of environmental and stratigraphic subtleties that might furnish the story of their fortunes either side of 400 CE. The necessarily very small scale of most excavations means that signs of town-wide change, of broad social and economic evolution or revolution, are frustratingly difficult to detect and describe. The temptation is to compensate, by gathering the results from lots of small excavation trenches across many towns to create a plausible, if incomplete, mosaic of urban fortunes. But the result is a tendency to homogenize the townscapes of later Roman Britain into a few conveniently straightforward narratives, at just the time when local responses to dynamic political change are at their most strikingly heterogeneous. To aggregate similarities in the fortunes of late fourth-century towns is to obscure diversity; to over-generalize.

Much is made, for example, of the fortunes of *Britannia's* diocesan capital, *Londinium*, and its four *coloniae*: *Glevum* (Gloucester), *Camulodunum* (Colchester), *Eboracum* (York) and *Lindum* (Lincoln).* The latter were originally military garrisons with attached settlements founded by and for army veterans. Three of them became provincial capitals, with London as the fourth† and, in due course, they emerged as medieval cities, the centres of ecclesiastical dioceses with powerful burghal privileges. Each offers tantalizing glimpses of occupation into the fifth or even sixth centuries; but none is able to tell us what town life was really like in the almost two centuries between the Honorian rescript (410) and the arrival of Augustine's Christianizing mission in 597.

To take just one of the *coloniae*, Lincoln offers fragmentary hints of continuing urban occupation. In 314 it sent a bishop to a church council at Arles; it may have supplied one of the bishops for another council at *Ariminum* (Rimini) in 359. An excavation at the church of St Paul-in-the-Bail, in the heart of the Roman forum precinct, produced circumstantial evidence for a very early timber church, with a seventh-century successor probably to be identified with that founded in the city by Paulinus (in about 630) and described by Bede.[30] The Christian history and archaeology are important, both in their own right and in the central political narrative, for even if the emperor in Ravenna had given up on Britain, the pope in Rome had not. There are traces, too, of late fourth-century industrial activity in Lincoln and for the accumulation of dark earth; also of large 'public' buildings and a number of large private houses being built at a similar period. Lincoln's defences were refurbished in the first half of the fourth century. So far, these are features characteristic of other major towns. After about 425, according to a recent survey of the evidence, occupation of the city ceased – or at least becomes invisible to archaeologists; no early 'Anglo-Saxon'-style structures, such as the characteristic

* See Map 2, p. xv.
† *Glevum* may have been supplanted as capital of the Western province by *Corinium Dobunnorum* (Cirencester).

sunken-featured buildings called *grubenhäuser*, have been found here.[31] The total number of sherds of early 'Anglo-Saxon'-style pottery from excavations in Lincoln wouldn't fill a wheelbarrow.

So Roman Lincoln must have 'failed', in Roman urban terms, early in the fifth century at the latest. And yet, the total excavated area of Roman Lincoln is less than 1 per cent of its ground plan. This is a reflection of the modest scale of commercial development, of the sort widespread in Roman towns that became modern cities. So Lincoln's apparent inactivity may be reflective of an absence of evidence, rather than evidence of absence. Archaeologists are right to ask: if Lincoln failed, why did it become the focus, in the seventh century, for the Early Medieval kingdom of Lindsey and for the mission of Paulinus? Something is missing.

At the other extreme, it is worth looking at a more unfashionable town – unfashionable among archaeologists, that is – like the *civitas* capital *Ratae Corieltauvorum* (Leicester), which has been more comprehensively excavated than any other Romano-British town, including the two greenfield sites of Wroxeter and Silchester. A recent survey shows that Leicester has produced more evidence for fourth-, fifth- and sixth-century occupation than any other town in Roman Britain.[32] Perhaps one should not be surprised.

Leicester was superbly well connected in the Roman period: to the *civitas* capital of the *Dobunni* at Cirencester, to Lincoln and points north by the Fosse Way. It lay within a day's travel of Watling Street and was directly linked to the Fens and to East Anglia by a third major cross-country road, while the River Soar, connecting it directly to the major economic artery of the River Trent, may have been navigable during the Roman period. Within 30 miles no fewer than sixteen other substantial settlements or walled towns flourished in the Roman period: *Ratae Corieltauvorum* stood at the heart of the province.

Leicester was constructed as a *civitas* capital, close to a pre-existing major Iron Age settlement. It gained earthen ramparts in the second century and a fronting wall in the later third century. A substantial chunk of a second-century wall, possibly part of a public bath complex, still stands an impressive 26 ft high at Jewry in the west of the old town close to the river.* Internal towers may have been added during the following century and it seems that the wall circuit survived more or less intact into the medieval period.[33] Sanvey Gate in the north-west, Friar Lane to the south-east and Church Gate along the north-east side of the modern city preserve three sides of its perimeter.

At the beginning of the fourth century Leicester's forum was remodelled, with signs of industrial activity encountered in excavations. After a mid-century fire, which might have spelled the end of a declining forum, floors were relaid. A shop floor accumulated silt from the adjacent road; a wall was knocked through and a new floor laid on top. Lying above these, wall plaster fragments and pottery sherds tell of final disuse. To the immediate north of the forum, the *macellum* or marketplace was still being used for the industrial production of glass and metalwork at the end of the fourth century and it is believed to have survived in use into the fifth century and beyond. The baths complex has produced fifth-century material.

One possible temple site and a building tentatively identified as a shrine, along with cemeteries lining the principal roads from the town, seem a poor spiritual inventory for all the excavation that has taken place; but no archaeologist would be so brave as to say that Leicester was uniquely uninterested in cult, memorial or worship. And the fact that it has so far produced no firm evidence for late Roman Christianity should not count as evidence that there was no Christian community here.† Leicester hosted its first bishop relatively early, in 680. The lack of *de facto* refuse lying on shop floors and open spaces tells its own story, if circumstantially.

More than twenty buildings regarded as 'private' have shown

---

* Jewry and the baths area were excavated by the archaeologist Kathleen Kenyon – best known for her work at *Verulamium* and Jericho – in the 1930s.
† Leicester gained its first bishop in the aftermath of the Battle of the River Trent in 679, when the Mercian see of Lichfield was divided (Kirby 1966, 1–2).

evidence of construction or modification during the fourth century; at least three are believed to have been used into the fifth century. A Roman street uncovered by excavations at Freeschool Lane had been encroached on by a series of hearths dated to the late fourth century, after which a timber structure was built into the street's edge and dark earth deposits began to accumulate, containing both late Roman and 'Anglo-Saxon'-style material.* Elsewhere in Leicester a similar picture is emerging: in the north-east corner of the town, where excavation has been most heavily concentrated, the remains of five further timber buildings of mid- to late fourth-century date have been recovered – one of them associated with early 'Anglo-Saxon'-style pottery sherds.

The most intriguing structure in this quarter is a large court-yard townhouse, built in the early fourth century, complemented by a very substantial rectangular masonry edifice with foundations measuring some 75 ft by 40 ft. At some time after the middle of the century several stashes of coins and a lead ingot were deposited within its walls. Hoards are traditionally seen as an extreme form of *de facto* refuse – hurriedly buried for safekeeping in a time of danger, the proof of the danger lying in the failure, by their owners, to recover them. Recent thinking allows that there are many possible reasons for burying precious items in special places – not least as an expedient means of tax avoidance or as a propitiatory offering – a voluntary tax – rendered to the gods. Much of the main structure of this large complex was subsequently demolished, while the rooms fronting onto the street were converted into commercial premises: a bone pin workshop and a smithy. This large rectangular building is recognized as having intriguing counterparts in London, Colchester and Lincoln; one might also include in the same category the large timber halls at Wroxeter and the repurposed basilica building at Silchester, and draw parallels with the aisled barns or halls of rural complexes like that at Meonstoke.

* Interpreted by Speed (2014, 76) as evidence of 'open ground', showing that waste – construction debris, human faeces and other secondary refuse – was being left in 'convenient places'.

This paradoxical interplay of private and public, of spatial negotiation and purposeful reorganization, of domestic, industrial and possibly horticultural innovation, ought to warn us that employing the late Roman town in Britain as a paradigm of urban failure may be as much an error as calling barbarian art 'primitive'. It ought, also, to act as a reminder of the potential complexities of social and economic transitions in those towns with much less solid evidence than Leicester on which to build a model of 'typical' late Roman towns. It is doubtful that there was such a thing as a typical late Roman town; and to ascribe Leicester's dynamic fourth- and fifth-century fortunes to the activities of Picts, Scots, Germanic *foederati* or immigrants, when the available evidence points to indigenous tensions and opportunities being played out here, seems like special pleading.

Even the most enthusiastic proponents of Gildas's narrative of fire, sword and famine would be hard pressed to allow Germanic or, for that matter, Irish raiders a direct role, some 50 miles due west of Leicester, in Wroxeter's remarkable transition from *civitas* capital of the *Cornovii* to small Shropshire village, whose most substantial contemporary structure is an English Heritage visitors' centre. Pioneering large-scale excavation of parts of the Roman town was directed by Philip Barker in the 1970s and 1980s. His identification of the subtly vestigial remains of very large timber buildings, which would almost certainly have been missed in earlier decades, in smaller trenches or in towns more disturbed by later cellars and foundations, radically overturned previous ideas about the end of urban life in Roman Britain.

Viroconium Cornoviorum was a town planted on the east bank of the River Severn after about 57 CE in the shadow of a great Iron Age hilltop settlement – the Wrekin – whose chieftains were dispossessed of their independence and their weapons and, in compensation, connected to the rest of *Britannia* and thence to the wider world by the navigable waters of the River Severn and by the terminal paving stones of Watling Street. At its peak Wroxeter may have supported a population of 15,000 citizens – *Britannia*'s fourth largest settlement. Its eventual successor as a central place was the fortified *burh* constructed at Shrewsbury by the Mercian queen Æðelflæd* in the early tenth century; but the native Brythonic name for the Wrekin, *Uiroconion*, seems to have survived through the centuries as *Viroconium*, then as *Wrocensætna* in the seventh-century list of peoples known as Tribal Hidage.

Like Leicester, Wroxeter boasts a large chunk of upstanding Roman masonry and, similarly, it formed part of an impressive public baths complex without which no self-respecting Cornovian chieftain or local magistrate could feel his life complete. An enormous 192 acres was enclosed by bank, ditch and palisade during the second century. Inside, houses, gardens, a forum, temples and industrial workshops revealed by geophysical survey and excavation speak of a busy, successful urban experiment; and Wroxeter's possible upgrading to a *municipium*, or chartered city, in the fourth century reflects its importance as a centre for provincial administration and the collection of *annonae* – taxes in kind: grain, cattle, woollens and so on – from the regional population.[34]

The concentration of modern, technically accomplished excavation in the area of the forum and baths (as at Lincoln, just 1 per cent of the total internal area of the town has so far been opened) means that the more complex, nuanced geography known from Leicester is missing here; but the compensations are great. The baths were certainly still in use in the late fourth century; but it is during the fifth and sixth centuries and into the seventh that Wroxeter punches above its weight in the sheer scale and dynamics of its post-Roman life. Barker's meticulous recording showed that early in the fifth century the huge baths basilica – an aisled hall some 200 ft long by 66 ft wide – was completely remodelled, in timber, as the core of a complex of more than thirty timber buildings, all aligned on existing structures or streets. The largest of these, directly superimposed on the rubble from the dismantled basilica, probably boasted two storeys. Surrounding buildings showed

* Pronounced Athelflad, the ð or eth character sounding like the 'th' in 'then'.

traces of hearths and ovens, while several structures are interpreted as 'booths or shacks' in a marketplace. The bath's *frigidarium* was reused, perhaps as a church or granary, and in its hypocaust twelve bodies were interred in later centuries.[35] An inscription of the late fifth century, carved into a reused Roman tombstone, commemorates CVNORIX MACVS MAQVI COLINE, an Irish, presumably Christian, chief.* The medieval parish church, perhaps originally a seventh-century foundation, lies within the south-west corner of the Roman town close by the river.

Some of town's principal structures survived into the 600s, providing a unique glimpse of either a very special exception to the standard late Roman model of town 'failure' or an insight into what may have been a more common phenomenon. Archaeologists continue to argue, from the same evidence, whether Wroxeter retained some of its urban functions or had evolved into a mere village supporting a local chief in style. Leicester's evidence should suffice to warn us that Wroxeter may yet reveal unanticipated complexities in its fascinating history.

It is tempting to equate the Roman imperial collapse with the end of urban life. An equally reasonable temptation sees change and novelty as evidence of Anglo-Saxon immigration or invasion. Heavily loaded terms like failure, loss, shrinkage, abandonment, depopulation and the collapse of civic authority are used to describe these changes; and such imagery is amply evoked in melancholy Anglo-Saxon poems like *The Ruin*. A story of political, social and economic discontinuity and dysfunction dominates: an absence of evidence for solidly civic urban functions is read as negative evidence. The resulting model is monolithic – Roman urbanism failed or was comprehensively rejected across Britain; state authority imploded; civil war, anarchy and opportunistic takeover by groups of hostile foreigners forever altered the trajectory of British history. The reality was surely less uniform, more regionally diverse, more adaptive.

If the fates of the large towns, and brief Continental notices of

---

* 'Cunorix son of Maqui Coline'.

events in Britain, tell us anything concrete it is that state control in Britain was weak during the second half of the fourth century. Towns increasingly took the initiative in managing their own affairs. On the Hadrianic frontier, where military forces were concentrated, dissatisfaction – with lousy pay and conditions, with poor leadership – and a sense of isolation and indifference prompted the search for more effective command. Beyond the frontiers, and where state control was in any case tenuous or non-existent, it seems as though a sense of group identity was born out of, or reinforced by,* antipathy towards the empire. Anticipating Rome's inability to mount offensive operations, opportunities arose to cash in on some of the wealth so conspicuously displayed by its lucky citizens. Some chieftains took substantial diplomatic gifts – or bribes – to stay neutral or act as buffers. Raiding parties of *Scotti* and *Attacotti* from Ireland or Argyll, and *Picti* from *Caledonia* increased in scale and sophistication to the point where, in 367, frontier scouts – the *areani* – were comprehensively bribed into complicity. Channel pirates, careless of ethnic distinctions, evaded coastal defences and patrolling fleets to prey with impunity on coastal and river settlements for slaves and bullion.

In the provincial capitals, the corporate solidarity of the second and third centuries morphed into a privatized oligarchy. Fewer but larger structures were built. Civic sensibility and the economics of the marketplace gave way to industrial recycling, market gardening, the large-scale storage and consumption of agricultural surplus and expressions of communal assembly. In place of cash taxes, local impositions in kind (*annonae*) were made on the hinterlands of the towns. But, so far as one can tell, senior officials – for the most part career diplomats of high political and social rank† supported by the forces of law and the *Dux Britanniarum*

---

* Anthropologists use the term 'ethnogenesis' for the process by which disparate groups coalesce around a novel group identity, often retrospectively given divine or mythic origins.
† One of the last named *vicarii* of Britannia, Chrysanthus, later became bishop of Constantinople.

– had either left, lost credibility, been deposed or murdered or – worse – were just ignored. Who, then, was in charge; and of what? Had *Britannia* seceded from the empire or been abandoned by it? Were the emerging lords of the fifth century descendants of ancient tribal families, now styled as magistrates or provincial officials? Were they arriviste entrepreneurs and industrialists; retired army officers, perhaps? Some, possibly, were Christian bishops and priests acting as conduits for a sense of imperial authority and spiritual security. Others may have been the mercenary *foederati* of Continental tribes, or local self-made heavies.

Deep in the countryside, communities like the Salisbury Plain downlanders and the villagers of the Fens probably noticed little difference except, perhaps, that while public tax officials visited less frequently, when they did so they came with spear-wielding mates in tow to ensure compliance. But if and when imperial demand for their produce – their wool and textiles, salt, meat and pottery – went into terminal decline they must adapt or go hungry. They kept smaller flocks of sheep and cattle – and these for their own consumption or to pay renders rather than for a no-longer hungry commercial market.

The stewards, housekeepers and farmers who managed and belonged to the villas may, by the last decades of the fourth century, have given up wondering when their absentee owners would ever visit again and begun to transform and adapt on their own initiative, building grain driers or malting kilns and smithing furnaces within the once plastered walls of grand country houses while they entertained and patronized dependants in their aisled halls.

Archaeologists are increasingly sensitive to sometimes very subtle traces of communities going about their business in the absence of the easily identified and dated material trappings of Roman culture, especially commercially produced pottery and coins. Some of these may have remained in use: repaired, re-circulated, treasured as keepsakes or heirlooms for many decades. Where late fourth-century structures were maintained or refurbished, perhaps over several generations, we have permission to suggest that they survived into a new age. Novel techniques allow archaeologists to see change in a broader landscape context than ever before, so that when a settlement is seen to have been abandoned, its immediate successor can be described not as revolutionary, but as evolutionary.

Across the British Isles local adaptations to new realities allow archaeologists to follow the fortunes of its people into this new age. Occasionally, a candle is held up by a Continental scholar interested in the fortunes of the British church. Against the darkly obscure background of the early fifth century, there are signs of life.

3

Signs of life

Christian communities in the fifth century –
the visit of Germanus – Uley Hill pagan shrine – a village
cult – the military zone – Birdoswald – St Patrick

(I)AMCILLA VOTUM QVOD / PROMISIT CONPLEVIT

*'Iamcilla [servant of the lord?] has fulfilled the vow that
she promised'*. Fragment of a silver plaque showing part
of a *chi-rho* (the Greek initials for *Christos*) monogram
and an offertory inscription from a female Christian.

The names of three fourth-century Christian women, belonging to a community of worshippers living in the East Midlands, have come down to us, engraved on what appears to be a collection of expensive church plate. It was dug up by a metal detectorist in Cambridgeshire, close to the banks of the River Nene, in 1975. The Water Newton treasure, as it has become known, is a stunning cache of silver jugs, bowls, cups (including what may be the oldest chalice known), a dish and strainer and no fewer than eighteen small plaques – many of them damaged – bearing motifs and inscriptions impressed into thin silver sheets.[1] Several of the objects bear *chi-rho* monograms, some flanked by A and W for *Alpha* and *Omega*, the beginning and the end.* One bowl bears the name Publianus, and an inscription dedicating it to a church. Two of the women, whose baptismal names were Innocentia and Viventia, seem to have donated the inscribed cup that bears their names and the monogram. A third woman, probably (I)amcilla – perhaps from *ancilla*, a female servant (of Christ) – dedicated a small, fragmentary plaque, again with *chi-rho* monogram and inverted WA, recording the fulfilment of a promise. The plaques are reminiscent of the sort of votive tokens known to have been placed in 'pagan' contexts at shrines elsewhere in Britain, such as Uley.† But this was a thriving and generous congregation of committed Christians, and the fortunes of such communities are the tell-tale pulse of *Britannia*'s life after Rome.

Christianity made women visible as never before. From the life and work of Jerome (347–420), the Latin translator of the Vulgate bible, from the *Confessio* of St Patrick and from the remarkable diary of an intrepid Gallic pilgrim called Egeria, who toured the Holy Land at the end of the fourth century, we know that women were active in the early church: as patrons and deaconesses, probably as full deacons, certainly as participating members of congregations.[2] The so-called Walesby cistern, one of several late Romano-British lead ceremonial tanks found particularly across

---

* Revelations 1:8, 'I am Alpha and Omega, the first and last'.
† See p. 84ff.

the East Midlands and East Anglia, appears to depict the induction into such a congregation of a female catechumen or baptismal candidate, flanked by two other officiating women.[3] One of the striking painted figures on a frieze in a private basement villa church at Lullingstone in Kent may be that of a wealthy woman like Viventia or Innocentia. The misogynist third-century diatribes of the theologian Tertullian against fashionably made-up and coiffured Christian women are clues that, even before Constantine the Great's edict of imperial tolerance towards the faith in 313, and its official adoption as Rome's state religion in 380, fashionable women might adopt Christianity; and that Christian women might be overtly fashionable. But the chatty, waspish diary written by the pilgrim Egeria from Sinai, Jerusalem and Antioch to her faraway sisters on the Western Ocean should give the lie to any idea that fourth-century Christianity was mere display or modish observance.[4] Christians, especially pilgrims and desert hermits, immersed themselves in a deeply involving set of lengthy, physically arduous and emotionally charged ceremonies, especially during extended Easter festivities. Christian worship was demanding and psychologically intense; baptism more than just a ceremony. Congregations became, in a sense, fictive families or households, strongly bound by ceremonial and by common emotional and material investment in their church. No worshipper could have been unaware of the oppression formerly suffered by Christians under the persecuting regimes of the third century.

A dozen or so credible locations of late Roman churches in Britain include the towns of Silchester, Colchester, Lincoln, Canterbury* and London; coastal forts at Richborough in Kent and at South Shields on the River Tyne; three of the Wall forts

---

* The probable foundations of a Roman-period church lie in a field immediately north of the London road (the A2) at Stone, just west of Faversham, while the church that lays claim to be the house of worship in longest continual use in Britain, St Martin's, lies a little way east of the walls of Canterbury. It may have been built on the site of an extramural mausoleum. An alternative candidate for the Roman church mentioned by Bede (*HE* I.26) is nearby St Pancras. Morris 1989, 20ff.

between the River Tyne and Solway Firth; villas like Hinton St Mary, with its famous *chi-rho* mosaic; and Lullingstone. Possible baptismal fonts have been identified at several sites and a very rare vessel decorated with repoussé copper alloy plaques depicting overtly Christian scenes has been found at Long Wittenham in Oxfordshire.[5] Other communities are indicated by the surviving place-name element 'Eccles' – from Latin *ecclesia*, meaning 'assembly' or 'church' – scattered thinly across the north and west of the former province.[6] But church buildings themselves are difficult to identify from excavation alone. Late Roman Christian church architecture was not necessarily distinct from other religious or secular buildings, so each candidate must be weighed on its own, often circumstantial merits; but the inventory of probables is now substantial.[7] Private and estate church congregations – possibly celebrating their faith in basilica-like aisled halls or in the private drawing rooms of villas – have long been suspected; the Water Newton treasure, and an increasing number of lead cisterns like the Walesby tank, show just how active they were.

It is even more difficult to identify specifically Christian cemeteries, or Christian burial plots within cemeteries – the search hampered by an empire-wide trend for simple east–west oriented graves unaccompanied by diagnostic artefacts of the kind so conveniently buried at Water Newton.[8] Across the Atlantic west of Britain, from Cornwall in the south to Argyll in the north, memorial stones with inscriptions in Latin and, sometimes, in the Irish Ogham script, identify Christian communities alive and active through the fifth and sixth centuries. Such stones, or their wooden equivalents, may also have been erected in the heartlands of the former province; if so, they do not survive.*

The geographical context for the Water Newton treasure is intriguing. Close to, perhaps even incorporating the rather vague find spot, nestled against a bend in the River Nene and once

---

* Aside from the cluster of extreme geographical and chronological outliers at the church of Lady St Mary, Wareham, in Dorset, where five seventh- to ninth-century memorial stones bear inscriptions of British Latin form.

MELI MEDICI FILI MARTINI IACIT.
Fifth- or sixth-century memorial stone to Melus the doctor, son of
Martin. From the churchyard at Llangian, Caernarfonshire.

commanding a major river crossing, lay the Roman town called *Durobrivae*.* This was one of *Britannia*'s 'roadside' towns, quite unlike those planned *coloniae* or *civitas* capitals characterized by grid-square layouts and orthodox civic buildings. Motorists driving south past Peterborough along the A1 look across the faint crop marks and raised banks of its buried walls and streets in a large field just after the sign to the small, now bypassed, village of Water Newton, squeezed between river and dual carriageway. *Durobrivae* was well connected to the rest of eastern England by Ermine Street (running between London, Lincoln and the Humber, right through the centre of *Durobrivae*), to East Anglia via the Fen Causeway and, via the River Nene, to the North Sea. The town was well sited to take advantage of marshland salterns and pasturage, of ample iron ore deposits in the hills to the west and local sources of fine clay. It has not yet been systematically excavated using modern techniques but aerial photography reveals dense, organic-looking, occupation inside its walls, overspilling into suburbs. More than a dozen villas flank the river immediately to the west while across the river to the north substantial pottery kilns – the centre of a thriving industry between the second and fourth centuries – produced high-quality Nene Valley 'colour-coated' wares: beakers, flagons and bowls, often decorated in relief and sometimes in imitation of fine moulded Samian ware.† The colour-coated pottery is found across Roman Britain as far north as the Clyde–Forth isthmus – evidence of widespread internal trade independent of military demand.

Beyond the potteries, on a rise a mile or so north of the river, a magnificent, stately mansion once stood at Castor – the Blenheim Palace of its day, perhaps. Subjected to many programmes of piecemeal excavation over the last two centuries – a sort of death by a thousand cuts – Castor has nevertheless produced evidence of a huge complex, far grander than a mere villa. Its status as a

---

* From Brythonic *Durobriwas*, 'the fort by the bridges'.

† Often highly decorated and coated in a glossy reddish-brown slip, Samian ware, or *terra sigillata*, was the fine tableware of the empire.

possible administrative centre for imperial estates in the Fens, perhaps as a successor to the imposing establishment at Stonea Grange some 20 miles to the east, shows how wealthy and productive the area was.[9] That a successful Christian community was established nearby during the fourth century complements a sense of prosperity, influence and social dynamism in the region. One wonders if those wealthy Christians had made their money in the pottery or salt industries, or from the agricultural bounty of the East Midlands. The latest occupation at Castor runs into the fifth century at least. Suggestively, Castor's estate buildings enclose the site of a medieval church, whose masonry includes recycled Roman quoins, columns and tiles. Three centuries after its Roman heyday it seems to have been home to a monastic community founded and patronized by Cyneburh, a Mercian queen.[10] The lacuna in tangible evidence between the two is the dark matter of the Dark Ages.

Narrative sources record three British bishops attending a church council at Arles in 314, so we know that episcopal administration was established in *Britannia* before or shortly after Constantine's Christian-inspired victory over his enemies at the Battle of the Milvian Bridge in 312 and the official imperial tolerance of Christianity under the Edict of Milan in 313.[11] Three British martyrs, probably of the third century, are mentioned by Gildas. An unknown number of bishops from Britain attended a council held in 343.[12] Records of a synod held at *Ariminum* (Rimini) in 359 tell how three British bishops who were present requested financial support from public funds.[13] We do not know how many others attended at their own or their see's expense, and we can take the report, by the Gallo-Roman Christian historian Sulpicius Severus, in two ways: either the three who claimed expenses belonged to ascetic communities rejecting material wealth; or, British bishops were poor and few in number because of the economic poverty of the province – but this was a time when Emperor Julian could send to *Britannia* for several hundred shiploads of grain. Gaul sent thirty-four bishops to *Ariminum*; did Britain send representatives from each of its *civitates* – perhaps a score and more?

By the 370s a new sort of Christian movement was under way on the Continent. St Martin, a former cavalry guardsman and later bishop of Tours, was much celebrated for his monastic foundations at Ligugé and Marmoutier, for his exemplary life and many miracles; for inspiring followers of the ascetic ideal.[14] At least two British churches, one at the monastery of Whithorn on the Kirkcudbright coast and another, named by Bede, just outside Canterbury, were dedicated in his name. Martin involved himself directly in the fiercely contested ecclesiastical and theological debates of his day, whose antagonists frame a parallel history to that of clashing imperial dynasts and usurpers. The part played by British actors in these dramas is known to us through allusion and the occasional vignette, which make it clear that the island province was not immune to the factions, divisions and religious fashions driving church politics while the empire fell to its knees. By 400 it is possible that at least one monastery already existed in Britain: that at Whithorn, Bede's *Candida Casa*, said to have been founded by the semi-legendary Ninian.*

In 396, the year before St Martin's death at Tours and at about the time when Stilicho, the young Honorius's military regent in the West, was sending a fleet to suppress raids across the Channel and Irish Sea, a bishop of Rouen, Victricius, sailed to Britain (from Le Havre, perhaps) to intervene in a dispute. 'Holy bishops called me there to make peace,' he later recalled.[15] We do not know the precise nature of the fracture in the British church but hindsight suggests that it may have had something to do with an unorthodox British† theologian called Pelagius.[16]

The church's extreme discomfort with this talented, highly educated and articulate thinker and teacher was inflamed by his radical belief that God's grace, a life of asceticism and good works were sufficient qualifications for the salvation of the soul. He argued that Christians might hope for a direct relationship

---

* See Chapter 10, p. 335.

† According to Augustine. Jerome believed him to have been Irish. Pelagius means 'sea-born' in Greek.

with God, without the intervention of a priest or the sacrament. Pelagius's ideas, like those of St Martin and of the Desert Fathers, gave inspiration to followers of the monastic calling. In one sense they anticipated free-will Protestant ideas of the Renaissance; but to many of the established Church Fathers of the day – especially Augustine of Hippo and Jerome in Palestine – Pelagius was a dangerous propagator of schism and heresy.[17] After moving to Rome in about 380 he was first lauded as a brilliant thinker, then came into increasingly bitter conflict with the authorities, particularly since his ideas attracted widespread popular support. He was the archetype of the dangerous liberal intellectual – a fifth-century Peter Abelard, perhaps.

In 416 Pelagius was openly condemned by Pope Innocent I, shortly before that pontiff's death. Two years later he was excommunicated by a new pope, Zosimus (who died the same year), condemned at a synod in Carthage and sent into exile in Egypt. The suspicion that Pelagian ideas had taken root in his native Britannia is reinforced by two of the very few narrative accounts that allude to its fortunes in the fifth century. First, a contemporary chronicler, the enthusiastically orthodox Prosper of Aquitaine (c.390–455), whose Epitoma Chronicon* provides something like an official version of events. During nearly two decades after 410, when Britannia was effectively an independent state, the Gaulish province also lay more or less outside imperial control. Prosper records that in 425 or 426 a new general, Flavius Aëtius (391–454), began to roll back the tide, winning a military victory against the Visigothic king, Theodoric, at Arles. In the following years Aëtius fought and won back territory from the Franks holding the Lower Rhine. In 429 he became magister militum, the most senior military officer in the Western empire.

These successes, alongside fears for continued adherence to Pelagian doctrines in the now-peripheral provinces of the empire (though by no means peripheral to the interests of the Holy See),

* First compiled in about 433 and therefore close to the events it describes in time, if not in place.

encouraged a parallel campaign to recover ecclesiastical control. Prosper tells us that in the year of Aëtius's elevation, 429,

> Agricola, a Pelagian, the son of the Pelagian Bishop Severianus, corrupted the British churches by the insinuation of his doctrine. But at the persuasion of the deacon Palladius, Pope Celestine sent Germanus, Bishop of Auxerre, as his representative and, having ejected the heretics, directed the Britons to the Catholic faith.[18]

As it happens, a longer and more detailed, if contradictory, account of the same event was recorded by Germanus's hagiographer, Constantius of Lyon, writing some fifty years later. His *Vita Germani* was written to establish the sanctity, miracles and achievements of Bishop Germanus, formerly a *dux* or governor of one of the Gallic provinces. Constantius, himself remote from these events, says that 'a deputation came from Britain... to tell the bishops of Gaul that the heresy of Pelagius had taken hold of the people over a great part of the country'.[19] He says that, in response, a synod determined to send Germanus and Lupus, then Bishop of Troyes, to reimpose orthodoxy. Gaul's bishops, it seems, regarded their British counterparts as dependants, while for their own part Pelagians from across the empire might have seen independent *Britannia* as a haven, safe from the stifling hand of orthodoxy.

No matter whose original idea the mission was, Germanus, Lupus and their retinue crossed the Channel, probably from the harbour at *Bononia* (Boulogne). After a stormy passage, during which Germanus poured holy oil on the turbulent waters of the Channel (a conscious metaphor, surely, for theological and disciplinary turmoil and for *Britannia*'s edgy remoteness), they reached the shore safely, where they were greeted by great crowds. There is not the faintest hint in the text to help locate the landing site or the party's subsequent progress through town and country. Logic suggests the fort and harbour at *Rutupiae* (Richborough), where the presence of a fourth-century church is likely.

We are immediately suspicious of the conventionality of the

hagiographer's story: exaggerating the saint's virtues but light on circumstantial detail, such as the rather important (to us) matter of the landing site, the names of bishops met and the locations of meetings. When Constantius does provide detail, it requires sceptical evaluation; even so, the essential bones of the story are striking and invaluable. Constantius says that the Gaulish mission was everywhere surrounded by crowds in churches, at crossroads, in fields and lanes. There is no sense that this is a strictly urban or metropolitan itinerary. At some point a meeting was organized at which the Pelagian faction was brought to debate; there must, then, still have been a functioning assembly site – a theatre or large hall of the type now recognized by excavators on grand villa estates and in towns. Canterbury, London and *Verulamium* had theatres. According to Constantius the Pelagians, far from hiding, 'came forth flaunting their wealth, in dazzling robes'.[20] A vast crowd assembled, both spectators and jury-men. One of those present was a man of high military rank, of 'tribunician authority', who challenged the bishop to cure his blind ten-year-old daughter – which he did, by means of prayer and by holding against her eyes a reliquary that he wore on a chain around his neck. We are to understand that the daughter is a metaphor for the blind willingness of the Britons to follow the heresy; the girl's age is, perhaps, a reference to the duration of the Pelagian crisis.[21] It is tempting to think of the well-dressed, even flashy Pelagians as members of wealthy liberal Christian communities, owners of the sort of showy church plate recovered at Water Newton; but Constantius is deliberately pejorative; he is no disinterested eye-witness.

The *Vita* continues the story. The damnable heresy having been 'stamped out', Germanus was now free to visit the holy shrine of Alban. If we do not know the locations of any other parts of the story, we can at least identify Alban's shrine; or at least its general location in the Hertfordshire city, beneath the cathedral and abbey church that bears his name. The name Alban (literally 'Briton') may, in fact, be Germanus's invention: the personification of Britain's fall and revival as an orthodox Roman Christian

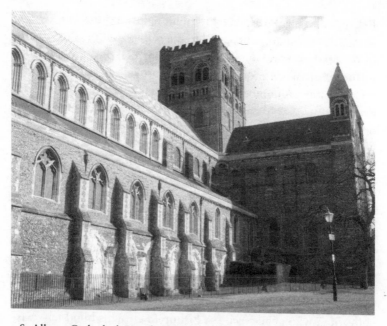

St Albans Cathedral, Hertfordshire, stands on a hill above the Roman town of *Verulamium*. Germanus visited the martyr's shrine here in 430.

state. The apparently very early *Passio* of St Alban* records that Germanus deposited relics of the apostles in the saint's tomb after seeing a vision of the (probably third-century) martyr.[22] By Gildas's day it was supposedly impossible for Britons to undertake pilgrimages to this holy site because of 'the unhappy partition of the barbarians'.[23]

The grand Romanesque church of St Alban carries weighty contextual baggage, overlooking as it does the Roman town of *Verulamium* where excavations have revealed key evidence for urban continuity in the fifth century.[24] *Verulamium*, like *Durobrivae*, lay athwart a major road: Watling Street (later *Waéxlingga Strate*),[25] which joined London to Wroxeter along the line of

---

* A fifth- or sixth-century hagiographic account of the martyrdom of St Alban.

England's internal watershed.* It had been established as one of *Britannia*'s earliest towns, razed to the ground by Boudicca's army in 60 CE. It was rebuilt and, despite an apparent decline in its fortunes, sustained public buildings until at least the end of the fourth century. A number of timber-built structures take the town's history comfortably beyond the end of the empire. A large barn or hall of the fifth century, its foundations later cut by a wooden water pipe overlying an earlier town house complex, allow us to envision Germanus and his entourage at a functioning settlement. Its public theatre would have provided the perfect stage for Germanus and Lupus to preach orthodoxy to the town's gentry and to local Christian followers.† Like other Roman towns, only a very small percentage area of *Verulamium* has been excavated – and much of that before modern recording techniques or the recognition of subtler structures among Roman masonry, spolia and dark earth deposits. *Verulamium* has also suffered much at the hands of the plough. Nevertheless Bede, writing of Alban's martyrdom in the early eighth century, tells us that 'a church of wonderful workmanship', enclosing Alban's shrine, was a place of pilgrimage down to his own day.[26]

On his return from the shrine Germanus was injured in a fall. If the house to which he was taken lay in *Verulamium*, and if Constantius's account preserves authentic detail, we have some idea of its appearance. The wooden house, roofed with reeds, caught fire and several others nearby were consumed. A timely miracle extinguished the flames and preserved a 'tabernacle' (a portable altar?) in the house where Germanus was recuperating.

The Gaulish party may have spent the winter here. The least credible and most controversial episode in the story occurred

---

* To the north and east of this route, rationalized by the line of Watling Street, rivers drain into the Irish Sea or North Sea; to the south and west they drain into the Thames and thence the North Sea, or into the River Severn and Bristol Channel.

† The only known Roman theatre in *Britannia* to be furnished with what we would recognize as a stage.

at Lent, probably in the spring of 430. A force of Saxons and Picts, we are told, was threatening the Britons, whose army was besieged in a camp. Germanus and his party were called upon for help. They responded, baptizing the British troops en masse; the enemy approached and Germanus undertook to lead the Britons' army, deploying their forces 'on a new model' in a valley 'enclosed by steep mountains' (which doesn't sound much like the Home Counties, it has to be said). At a signal, the Britons gave out a terrible battle cry of 'Alleluia' which, reverberating about the confined space between the mountains, panicked the enemy into fleeing. Many of them drowned in a river. This great victory sealed the defeat of Britain's dual enemies: barbarian invaders and theological evils.[27]

Whatever truth lies behind the tale – and much ink has been spilt speculating on its geographic and military possibilities – the story cannot be taken at anything like face value. One can do no more than accept that such miraculous events, the stock-in-trade of providential history, may contain a kernel of historical truth, and move on. The historian Ian Wood has made the highly credible suggestion, based on a knowledge of how the *Passio* of St Alban was constructed, that the story of Germanus's British expedition was originally recorded in *tituli* – explanatory captions for wall or panel paintings displayed in the crypt at the Abbey of Saint-Germain d'Auxerre; that, in effect, the source for Constantius's *Vita* was a series of cartoon images, like a pre-Norman Bayeux tapestry.[28] The idea makes considerable sense given the vagueness of detail and the strong visual imagery of the story's set-piece events.

The chronographer Prosper does not record the second visit to Britain made by Germanus and described by Constantius, so we cannot date it. But credible analysis suggests a time in the late 430s – perhaps 437.[29] On this occasion, we are told, news came from Britain that a few Pelagians were, once more, spreading their vile heresy. This time Germanus was accompanied on his voyage by Severus, bishop of Trier. They were met by a man named Elafius, one of the few fifth-century British individuals whose name has come down to us.* According to Constantius, he was 'one of the leading men in the country'. It is an infuriatingly vague description, although one can easily visualize a painted panel in the crypt at Saint-Germain depicting the scene with its caption: 'Here Germanus is met by Elafius, the leading man in the country.' He, like the man of 'tribunician authority' who had presented Germanus with his blind daughter, asked the bishop to bless a child: his crippled son, whose tendons were withered. This is metaphor again: the crippled son personifies the former province's institutional weakness; neither could stand on their own two feet unless supported – or healed – by the Gaulish mission. A suitable miracle ensured the boy's return to vital health; the heresy was countered and this time its preachers were expelled from the island. If there is a subtext here, it may be the hint that a Pelagian faction was dominated by secular powers – those whose dependants or adherents needed 'curing' – while the Insular bishops, on whom Constantius is consistently silent, were invisibly cast as champions of orthodoxy and loyalty to the empire. Circumstantial as it is, the Germanus story offers the first evidence of political factionalism driving events in post-Roman Britain.

Christianity, its adherents and politics deliver some of the most convincing signs of life after the end of imperial rule. But its places of worship are still elusive and, in any case, Jesus the Messiah of Judea was a latecomer onto the British stage. Older, more mysterious and enduring religious practices have left tangible marks on the countryside of *Britannia*. Excavations at West Hill, near Uley, in the Gloucestershire Cotswolds, have revealed the history of a major shrine complex that thrived and evolved right

---

* A hand list culled from the main sources gives us Gildas, Patrick and his father and grandfather, Agricola the Pelagian, Ambrosius, Gwyrangon, Elafius, Vitalinus, Vortigern and his probably fictitious sons Cateyrn, Pascent, Faustus and Vortimer (*Historia Brittonum* 48); Riothamus, a warlord active in Armorica; Mansuetus the bishop; Belli (a legendary tyrant in *Historia Brittonum* 32); and Germanus's host Cadell Ddyrnllug (also probably fictitious). The names of a few more Britons, such as Barrovadus, Latinus and Senacus, are known from memorial inscriptions.

through the prehistoric and Romano-British periods and beyond.[30] First identified as a special place in the third millennium BCE, the wooded hill top here, once cleared of trees, became a focus for feasting – perhaps at the four quarter days of the solar year. Sacred trees or totemic posts and standing stones, possibly the figurative representations of ancestors, stood within a ditched enclosure. Successive generations remodelled this space and its monuments to their own satisfaction and needs: this was a busily sacred site where placed or discarded objects recovered from pits and ditches suggest interactions with local and perhaps regional communities, as well as with the spirits of other worlds.

The cumulative thinking from ethnography, near-contemporary literature and later tradition suggests the prevalence in native societies of an animistic world view: spirits, often capricious, sometimes malign, inhabited animate and inanimate objects – birds and animals, springs, rivers and dark pools. They were to be found in trees, rocks and caves, places with some sense of attachment or connection to another world; hill tops; crossroads; wet or liminal places; ancient monuments like henges and burial mounds. They infused the physical and psychological landscape with life and meaning, with potential and risk. The fates that governed love, childbirth and health, the harvest, weather, disease and luck could be implored, or invited, to side with mortal humans through offerings, incantations and dedications. Intermediaries – call them shamans, druids or cunning-women as you will – entered altered states of consciousness to communicate with otherworldly spirits or ancestors on their behalf. Natural cycles provided by night and day, lunar month and solar year naturally fostered festivals and ceremonies marking farming cycles, new life, bounty, hunger, marriage and politics, coalescing around the equinox and solstice quarter days.

By the time of the Roman invasions, formal timber structures stood within the ditched enclosure at Uley and a number of contemporary infant burials have been found. Pits were carefully filled with votive paraphernalia: food, weapons, horse and vehicle equipment, querns, coins and tools, in ceremonies whose narratives are hidden from us and whose motives are obscure, but suggestive of both psychological and material investment on a tribal scale. Layer after layer of maintained, disused and partially remembered natural and engineered features, created and modified over many centuries, must have enriched a collective sense of the hill as a very special place – a focus, perhaps, for the ceremonial identity of the *Dobunni*. Although Iron Age mortuary practices and burials are notoriously hard to identify, the shrine on West Hill may have been furnished with the scaffolding structures associated with excarnation or sky burial, suspected elsewhere in Britain.

During the first and second centuries CE the sacred enclosure at Uley acquired a solid timber shrine at its centre – square in form, like so many other contemporary ceremonial monuments identified in Britain and on the Continent. Subsequently a square stone temple, of considerable grandeur, directly replaced its predecessor on the hill top, eventually forming the core of a complex of buildings: shops, baths, industrial workshops and stalls. Imagining Uley Hill in its heyday brings to mind the busy association of medieval mosques or cathedrals, constructed over the shrines of saints, with marketplaces, inns, shops and services clustering around them, designed to relieve enthusiastic pilgrims or desperate supplicants of their wealth,* a set of tensions held in balance by devotional solemnity and gifts to the cult figure; by throngs of people at quarter-day festivals; by feasting, trading, dancing and the machinery of patronage. Inscribed lead tablets, figurines, jewellery and trinkets, a razor, shoe fittings and toilet articles lost or donated across the centuries at Uley Hill carry the distant echoes of their owners' hopes and dreams, like the Bath tablets, the pilgrim flasks of the Holy Land or the special lace made for devotees of St Audrey at Ely, later cheaply copied and known as tawdry.

---

* One thinks of Southwark, Ely and Darlington – of Canterbury and Lincoln, perhaps. That late Roman churches should so often appear to have been constructed in *fora* may be expressions of such mutually attractive crowds.

By the end of the fourth century the temple at Uley Hill had partially collapsed and been demolished. It was now rebuilt on a more modest scale, as an L-shaped structure.* Within another generation or two, at some time during the fifth century, it was replaced by a timber building that looks for all the world like a basilica, with accompanying baptistery – evidence, perhaps, of its conversion from the Roman cult of Mercury to a more fashionable imperial hero of sacrifice and divinity – the crucified Christ. As an expression of psycho-social continuity, the inclusion of much spolia in the new structure – fragments of statues, defaced altars from the old temple, for example – rather than an absolute rejection of unclean pagan practices, suggests incorporation of the inherited power and sensibilities of the place.[31] This looks like the evolution of an indigenous, adaptive culture – not a religious revolution.

Some 200 miles north and east of the Cotswold heartland of the ultra-Roman Britons, a more modest shrine dedicated, it seems, to Ceres, the Roman goddess of agriculture and fertility, was constructed over a spring miraculously flowing from the base of the almost streamless Yorkshire Wolds. Here, in a long-inhabited and very busy landscape overlooking the Vale of Pickering,† rural communities wore the *Pax Romana* lightly. *Derventio,* an auxiliary fort with attendant civilian settlement supporting a cavalry unit, stood at Malton, half a day's walk to the west. A mere handful of villas pockmarked its hinterland; these and a fourth-century signal station on the coast at Scarborough are Rome's modest structural legacies here. The *colonia* and legionary headquarters of the *Dux Britanniarum* at York, two days distant, must have seemed no more than a cloud beyond the horizon.

The inhabitants of the indigenous settlement, guardians of the shrine at West Heslerton, thrived on ample hill pastures and access

---

* Emperor Theodosius closed all pagan temples across the empire by decree in 391.

† Once a huge glacial lake fringed by Mesolithic communities like those at Star Carr and Seamer Carr, and later the focus of elaborate Neolithic and Bronze Age monuments and settlements.

to the River Derwent, with easily tilled farmland and meadow in between. They seem also to have profited from their magical spring because, in the middle of the fourth century, a building was erected across the valley to control access to it. Bread ovens and the copious detritus of street food (oyster shells; thousands of sherds of pottery) betray the commercial management of a religious site. Dominic Powlesland, West Heslerton's excavator, believes that the shrine must have been inundated with visitors in spring, but that for much of the year it was a quiet adjunct to the everyday concerns of subsistence farming: of cattle and sheep rearing, ploughing, sowing, weeding, harvesting and threshing corn.[32] It may be that Heslerton's spring was special because here water seemed providentially to flow from beneath the chalk Wolds where it was always in short supply. Ironically, by the end of the fourth century a period of wetter, cooler summers and rising sea levels threatened to inundate the Vale of Pickering, as it would the Fens, the Vale of York and the Thames Estuary.

West Heslerton, and many other rural settlements, were peripheral to the Roman project. Unlike those towns and forts reliant on the military economy, which saw their fortunes rise and fall dramatically over those four centuries, such communities were largely insulated from the waves of fate that overwhelmed the towns and villas. Heslerton's shrine may eventually have lost its magic, but the settlement survived for several hundred years more. If archaeologists prefer to call its later inhabitants Anglo-Saxons, who can say how they thought of themselves?*

Where should one look for signs of life in the more militarized frontier zone, the 100 miles between York and Hadrian's Wall? The Vale of York is low lying and drains much of the North Pennines. The River Ouse, which gave invaluable navigable access to the Humber, Trent and North Sea, was both York's beating heart and its weak spot. By the end of the fourth century *Eboracum* was

* See Chapter 4.

prone to serious flooding. Two Roman roads, allowing the rapid movement of trade and troops between the provincial Midland heartlands, the northern military headquarters at York and the garrisoned frontier, ran north from Lincoln, one either side of the Trent and the Vale, converging on York from east and west by virtue of (to the west) a terminal glacial moraine and (to the east) a spur of higher ground that linked it to the Wolds and thence to a strategically important ferry crossing of the Humber at *Petuaria* (Brough). To the north, the two flanking roads ran directly on towards another of eastern Britain's major rivers, the Tyne.

At York the imposing Roman legionary fortress lay on the north-east side of the River Ouse in a natural fork provided by its protective tributary, the Foss. The *colonia* lay directly across the Ouse to the southwest. Excavations beneath the medieval minster in the 1960s and 1970s showed that the headquarters, or *principia*, which it overlies directly, was still standing when the last legions withdrew; but by then the *Dux Britanniarum*, the military governor of the north, was barely viable as a command. In the early seventh century King Edwin of Northumbria built his first church in its ruins and rode through his lands preceded by a standard bearer, like a latter-day emperor.* He probably knew of Constantine's acclamation there 300 or so years previously and was consciously tapping into the mythology of Rome's power to enhance his own new-found imperial and Christian credentials. But it is unlikely that he found a functioning settlement. His re-occupation of the ruined city was for show. By Bede's day, a century later, an enterprising group of Frisian traders had set up shop in a small settlement in the fork between the two rivers, anticipating York's Viking heyday by two centuries; but they seem to have been its most active inhabitants.

Around 100 miles north-west of York the Pennine hills are split by a pass at Greenhead, where the headwaters of the Northumbrian River Tyne and its Cumbrian counterpart, the Irthing, provide a natural east–west line of communication between the North Sea

* See Chapter 12, p. 379.

and Solway Firth. Military-grade bridges spanned the Tyne 12 miles or so inland from the sea at *Pons Aelius* (Newcastle) and 20 miles further upstream at *Coria* (Corbridge), while innumerable fords, ferries and smaller bridges provided for local traffic. The military crossings connected Rome's principal northern frontier with the military headquarters at York, while two major supply forts either side of the Tyne's mouth* allowed the shipment inwards and outwards of troops and their supplies, hard imperial cash and the wealth of the north: corn, cattle, wool and lead.

Emperor Hadrian's grand design for a wall was conceived in the third decade of the second century. That a line of military control should be envisioned here, at central Britain's narrow waist, is no surprise. It established a base for direct military intervention among the unruly hill tribes of the *Brigantes* and for the support of forts and patrols to the north. It afforded the state absolute control over valuable lead and silver deposits immediately to the south. A road, the Stanegate, was built from Corbridge westwards to the navigable River Eden at *Luguvalium* (Carlisle), later the *civitas* capital of the *Carvetii*. The Wall made military and political sense. Its more ambitious younger sibling, the turf-built Antonine Wall of about 142 CE, connected an even narrower isthmus between the rivers Forth and Clyde; but it was abandoned less than a decade after construction, repaired and re-garrisoned at the beginning of the third century, then abandoned once again.

That Hadrian's Wall was still relevant at the end of the fourth century is, in some ways, counterintuitive. The frontier, with its forts, garrisons, milecastles, interval turrets, vallum and ditch, regulated traffic into and out of the empire. It was a substantial, ongoing cost to the province. It is true that the cost was offset by the economic benefits of security in the south and by, in effect, a series of customs points strung out along its length, relieving natives of cash and goods in kind – furs, livestock, grain, fleeces, textiles, slaves – whenever they crossed the frontier. But the Wall

---

* *Segedunum* on the north side at Wallsend (whose name speaks for itself) and *Arbeia* at South Shields.

had long since lost its role as an offensive launch pad – as a base for conquering the recalcitrant tribes of *Caledonia* and extending *Britannia* to its natural limits on the wild North Atlantic.

In 367 the Wall's continued relevance must have been in serious doubt when the combined raiding forces of *Scotti* and *Picti* simply bypassed it. A generation ago few archaeologists would have argued that the Wall functioned at all beyond the end of the empire. But excavations at several forts, complemented by geographical analysis, are beginning to tell a different story.

Guarding the pass at Greenhead that links the headwaters of Tyne and Irthing on the modern Northumbrian–Cumbrian border, the remains of a Wall fort at *Banna* (Birdoswald) still stand, nearly 500 ft above sea level. Rain-laden clouds barging in from the west are like a low ceiling; winters can be long; summers short but light until late. Immediately to the south the Irthing rushes through a deep gorge cloaked in dense woodland. From the fort's gatehouse the view to the north is of rough pasture and tussocky peat hags, for the most part blanketed by recent conifer plantations. To the south the lead-rich Pennines rise to over 1,500 ft. The north gate of the playing-card-shaped fort abuts and incorporates the fabric of the Wall: frontier, defence and access were welded into the indivisible fabric of the empire's edge.

Banna's immediate hinterland could never have produced all the grain required to run a fully staffed garrison. Supplies were brought in along the Stanegate, either from Tynemouth via Corbridge or through more local arrangements with the farmers of the fertile coastal plains and hills of eastern Northumberland. Like many military garrisons, and by some unvoiced social and economic chemistry, *Banna* acquired a civilian settlement or *vicus*, attached limpet-like immediately to its east.* Soldiers spent their time on patrol to north and south, collected exit and entry tariffs, administered imperial justice to the locals; married or otherwise consorted with the local women and, eventually, became wholly

---

* At least some of the Wall fort *vici* did not survive the end of the third century, for reasons as yet unknown. Wilmott 2010, 10.

integrated, like their wall, with the landscape and its people. After the second century the *limitanei* or frontier troops would have been recruited largely from local youth under the command of professional officers from the Middle East or from beyond the Rhine frontier. Son followed father into service.

By the late third or early fourth century a striking remodelling and architectural upgrading of the *praetorium* – the fort commanders' quarters – at Birdoswald is a hint that his role was expanding into new social, judicial and administrative spheres – as a local or regional governor, perhaps. A large proportion of *Britannia*'s field armies was withdrawn in various usurpers' campaigns during the late fourth century, culminating in Constantine's Gallic adventure of 407. *Banna*'s garrison shrunk; was rationalized. After 410 no imperial administration functioned in the province. Now, finally, the Wall was useless – at least so far as distant emperors were concerned. But those dependent on it for their livelihoods and security probably felt rather differently.

Civilian authorities might have wrung their hands in a state of impotent shock, retired to their country piles or given up on *Britannia*, leaving the keys under the doormats of their villas and sailing home. Alternatively, and more plausibly, they may have sought to retain control over smaller, more manageable territories – the old tribal lands of the *civitates* or the hinterlands of large towns. Bishops, still invested with Rome's papal authority, if not that of the emperor in Ravenna,* may have maintained their power through the compliance, patronage and protective clout of wealthy landowners and intellectuals, their fictive extended families. Some communities probably noticed little change in the distant workings of the régime. But what was a fort commander on the Wall to do when the last army pay wagon failed to turn up?

It is a conspicuous fact that, with few exceptions, the boundaries of the many historic townships† that lie along the line of Hadrian's

---

* Capital of the Western empire from 402 to 476.
† A northern equivalent of the local civil parishes of the south of Britain; confusingly, northern parishes consist of groups of townships.

Wall do not butt up against it, as one might expect of such a great physical barrier, but straddle it.[33] Historical geographers have established that the origins of many historic townships and parishes lie in their Early Medieval role as productive territories: clusters of farms obliged to render goods and services to a central place – a *vill* – whose lord lived off their surplus and who, in turn, protected them and gave them access to the benefits of patronage: feasting, marriage alliance, identity and legal status. It looks as though the central places that emerged along the now-defunct frontier to form the core *vills* of a novel set of post-Roman administrative and economic realities, were the forts.*

It makes sense. A fort commander suddenly or periodically unable to pay his men lays himself open to a loss of authority; to mutiny and unrest. He must retain that authority by taking upon himself exactly the sort of role that a lord fulfilled in an Early Medieval *vill*. He must feed them, give them something to do – they are, after all, professional soldiers whose chief enemy is boredom – and ensure that they still believe he is the best man for the job. Otherwise, like a shipwrecked crew, it is every man for himself and the devil take the hindmost. The temptation to mutiny and go feral, a very small-scale usurpation compared with that of the would-be British emperors, may have been strong. But the soldiers and commanders of the forts were, by the end of the fourth century, highly integrated into their local communities; socially invested in their fortunes. Each mattered to the other, bonded by mutual interests, obligations and, very likely, by family ties. The solution, for the more pragmatic and capable commanders, was to exact render from the surrounding lands with which to support the personnel of the fort, provide for their families and offer, in return, protection and an even greater measure of social

---

* I have grossly simplified the complex arguments assembled and laid out by Brian Roberts (2010). He rightly points out that simply to map immediately post-Roman territories onto boundaries that were first accurately mapped in the nineteenth century is a fool's errand. Forts may have required very large territories to support themselves.

integration: a model of Early Medieval territorial lordship. It is most unlikely that such evolutions were sudden, carefully planned or contemporaneous: *Britannia*'s increasingly local and privatized post-Roman realities expressed themselves in many ways.

At *Banna* the physical evidence of such an arrangement was written in sufficiently bold form to be recovered by excavation.[34] Like most of the Wall forts its regular, axial layout, familiar to any newly arriving soldier or visiting dignitary, included granaries – *horrea* – where consumable supplies were stored. The *horrea* were substantial, stone-built structures with hypocaust heating, built to take up to a year's supply of dry goods. The two *horrea* at *Banna* stood inside, and just to the south of, its west gate.

The starting point of a suggestive sequence can be closely dated to the mid-fourth century, when the hypocaust beneath the south granary was filled in and refloored. Some time during that period the roof of the north granary fell in and the structure was used as a quarry for building materials or as a dumping ground – classic signs of controlled recycling. The fort, it seems, no longer needed, or received, supplies in such bulk; but as a whole it was not abandoned. The south granary subsequently acquired a stone hearth, a marker for habitation and something of a contra-indication in a grain store, where a year's supply of wheat or barley might be lost to accidental fire. Close to this hearth a worn coin of Theodosius I (*c*.395), a black glass ring and a gold earring were accidentally dropped and lay unrecovered for 1,500 years.

The subsequent history of the north granary is even more suggestive. The site was cleared and a new building constructed above the foundations of the old – on the same pattern but now in timber, with a new stone floor sealing the deposits below. The sequence is reminiscent of that at Wroxeter. How long this building lasted is uncertain, but it was subsequently dismantled and then rebuilt some 16 ft to the north, on the same alignment but a little shorter (about 75 ft in length) and, significantly, partially over the *via principalis*, the fort's main thoroughfare, running east from the gate. This move realigned what was now the largest structure in the fort with the west gate that had been modified to create an

Birdoswald: the foundations of the north granary and the timber hall that replaced it: is this where the 'Dark Ages' begin…?

offset entrance in the third century. One imagines that the new timber building was an imposing sight on arrival.

Birdoswald's excavator, Tony Wilmott, suggests that the whole sequence takes the fort's life into the sixth century and he explicitly makes the connection between the remodelled south granary and the architecture of the 'Anglo-Saxon' mead hall. Was the prototype of *Heorot*, that poetic stage for feasting, patronage, celebration and warrior-bonding, neither more nor less than a barn conversion, the place where the fort commander took up residence, feasted his comrades-in-arms and collected around him the renders of his territorial dependants?

Banna's former *principia* (the official heart of the fort), no longer appropriate in its exclusivity for a novel set of relations between commander, troops and dependants, might by now have been converted to other uses. At *Vindolanda*, some eight miles east along the Stanegate road, the late fourth-century *praetorium* seems to have contained a church; another has been suggested for the forecourt of the *principia* at *Arbeia* (not far from the future site of Bede's monastery at Jarrow). The Wall may seem a far cry from the busy industrial and civilian heartlands of the *Corieltauvi*, where Innocentia, Viventia and Iamcilla flaunted their faith and cash on silver bowls and plaques and where theological crises were played out in public assembly. But the Wall garrisons had always been sensitive to changing fashions in religious belief and Constantine, *Britannia*'s own emperor, had championed Christianity as a soldier's faith in the early fourth century. In these strange new times fort commanders must adapt psychologically as well as practically.

It is tempting, in this context, to follow a line of argument that places in this landscape the young St Patrick, son and grandson of British Christian priests (one of them also a town official), before his fateful abduction by Irish slave raiders at the age of about sixteen. Patrick's is the sole unambiguously British narrative voice from the whole of the fifth century. Two of his works survive in later copies. His *Confessio* is the autobiographical defence of an elderly man, the self-styled bishop of *Hibernia*, who believes himself to have been unfairly accused of various misdemeanours. The *Letter to Coroticus* is an admonition to a British king who has taken Irish Christians prisoner. Neither can be dated in more than very broad terms to the middle or second half of the fifth century. The timing of Patrick's birth and death are unknown (despite much scholarly debate and speculation). Nor can his background be told in any detail, because he is so vague about it. But he recorded the fact that his father was Calpornius, a decurion and a deacon; that his grandfather was a priest called Potitus, who 'belonged to the town [*vico*] of *Bannavem Taburniae*; he had a small estate [*villula*] nearby, and it was there that I was taken'.[35] The name

Bannavem Taburniae has exercised generations of philologists. No such name is known in Roman Britain and its form seems inherently implausible to them.

Charles Thomas, a pioneering student of early British Christianity, suggested conflating the name elements and redividing them, on the assumption of some scribal error in the transmission of the Patrician manuscript over the centuries – perfectly reasonable in itself.[36] He offers a more easily explained *Banna venta B(e)rniae.* * *Venta*, a central place or market, is already well known as a name element from Winchester, Caerwent and elsewhere. *Banna* is a credible Brythonic word for a horn or spur of land – like that on which the fort at Birdoswald was sited; and *Berniae* or *Burniae* appears to be a genitive, a regional identifier, telling us where to look for the assembly place of *Banna*. As it happens, there is a known *Bannaventa*: Whilton Lodge in Northamptonshire, close to Watling Street and the modern town of Daventry. Thomas is uncomfortable with a *villula* so far inland and seemingly immune to the predations of Irish raiders. He prefers the *Banna* of Birdoswald, in the region that later formed part of the Northumbrian kingdom of Bernicia – whose 'bern' element describes a pass or gap such as that at nearby Greenhead. Some 15 miles west of *Banna* lay the *civitas* capital at Carlisle, whose fountains were still a marvel in the seventh century, where Calpornius might have served as a decurion, a civic functionary of the late Roman state. It is only too easy to see Irish raiders predating there and along the Stanegate. Where the *villula* belonging to Patrick's family was situated is another matter.

Signs of life in the towns, villas and forts of late Roman Britain are increasingly visible to archaeologists, despite a paucity of convincingly dated material. But describing the lives of the bulk of fifth-century Britons is by no means straightforward; and the

---

* It must be said that amending the 'm' to 'n' and the 'u' to 'e' makes philologists uneasy.

picture is complicated by the arrival, in the second quarter of that most obscure century, of novel buildings, burials, artefacts and settlements in the south and east of the old province. Are these the smoking guns of Gildas's and Bede's impious Germanic pirates, the supposed enemies of Arthurian heroes?

4

Of grub huts, urns and isotopes

Siþæbæd's urn – Spong Man – Wasperton – a spanner
in the works – *Grubenhäuser* – three key sites –
migrants, invaders, indigenes

Siþæbæd / þicþ / hlaf

Fifth-century cremation urn from Loveden, Lincolnshire –
one of 1,790 cremation burials. The runic inscription, perhaps
the earliest in England, seems to contain the name of a woman,
Siþæbæd. The þ character, Old English 'thorn', has the 'th' of 'think'.
Several variants of its meaning are possible, including one that reads
'Siþæbæd, female servant, her grave'. Findell and Kopár 2017.

The British élites of the towns, villas and forts, of civil service, church, army and trade, needed to adapt quickly to a new political and social environment in the former province. Along with its attendant web of patronage and allegiances, the apparatus of the Roman state had retreated to the Continent where generals, bishops, intellectuals and merchants lay besieged by overwhelming agents of change. After the first quarter of the fifth century, economic realities, the force of arms and local and regional dynamics would determine how state and private powers were devolved in *Britannia*.

The entrails of this devolutionary carcass cannot be read until the later sixth century, when its profound impacts become visible in a radically new political and social landscape. How far such epoch-making events affected the bulk of the population is another matter, and recorded history is largely blind to their fate. But their experience is imprinted in a subtle, often opaque archaeological script, encoded in dwellings, burials, arts and crafts: a message in a bottle. As yet only partly comprehensible, it nevertheless tells us that the peoples of *Britannia* were not mere passive victims of imperial collapse, but that they collectively engineered a cultural and social revolution.

To piece together the life of a man or woman or the community to which they belonged is to reconstruct a face from a thousand faded mosaic tiles. Who was the woman called Sïþæbæd (pronounced 'Seethabad') whose name was inscribed in runes on a 6-inch tall cremation urn from a cemetery at Loveden Hill, Lincolnshire, sometime in the fifth century? Did she make the pot? Were her remains buried in it; or both?

These are among the earliest Germanic runes known from Britain. They were incised by a right-handed person, gently rotating the vessel clockwise as they made each letter, while the clay was still leather-soft. Two bands of horizontal incised lines bordered the shoulder of the urn, where a number of stamped cross-in-circle motifs provided extra decoration. The urn was coil-built, using materials not local to the burial site but obtained from further afield. It was fired in a bonfire at a relatively low temperature. Its wide mouth is a well-recognized marker for the burial of a female; and its biconical shape was deliberately contrived such that both runes and decoration could be seen from above.

Over the centuries many thousands of such vessels have been turned up by the plough and the curious antiquarian, or excavated by archaeologists in advance of commercial development. Often they have been found during topsoil stripping in advance of gravel extraction – the lighter, freer draining soils of East Anglia and the Thames valley seem to have been favoured for both settlement and burial during the fifth century. With few exceptions the cremation urns are found, sometimes in very large cemeteries like that at Loveden Hill, in eastern and central southern England: as far north as the River Tees and as far south as the Thames estuary – that is, across much of the heartlands of the former Roman province. They first appear some time in the early decades of the fifth century,* reflecting new – or revived – ideas and practices about disposing of and commemorating the dead. The cremation rite was a radical departure from the empire-wide practice of inhumation – burial in an earth-cut grave – seen in both pagan and Christian cemeteries of the late empire, although it had often been practised in Britain in earlier centuries.†

Cremations are incomparably rich sources of evidence for ideas about life and death, if only their message can be unravelled. The journey of an urn from potter's shed to burial tells of an elemental transformation from life to death, from earth to fire, from domestic to heavenly. It has traditionally been thought that the cremation urns of the fifth and sixth centuries were purpose-made for burial; such vessels occur only very rarely on settlement sites, where their presence is far outweighed by simple undecorated cooking pots, jars and bowls. But much can be said about how and why pots are made – meat and drink for archaeologists, especially in periods

---

* The exact dating is a vexed question.

† Although, as Hills and Lucy (2013, 300) point out, late Roman burial practice was more diverse, and is less well documented, than is often supposed.

lacking coins – and the work of modern ceramic analysts suggests that many, if not most, of these urns had useful lives before they contained cremated bones. These new insights draw us more intimately into the lives of people like Sïþæbæd.

Take the materials used in making a pot. Clay is found widely across Britain, the legacy of a glacial past. It varies in quality, texture, colour and firing properties. After the decline of industrial pottery production, some time in the first half of the fifth century, pottery was locally made, without a fast wheel, and fired in what are called clamp kilns – in effect, bonfires. To ensure that the clay withstood the thermal shock of firing, it was tempered – hardened by the addition of grit, wheat chaff, dung, flint or some other fine crushed mineral. These, also, are available across Britain, with distinct local and regional characteristics that allow archaeologists to build maps of their distribution. A pot with alien clay and minerals must have moved from its place of manufacture; and pots don't move on their own. If the pots were moving, so were people.

Oddly enough, the potters of the fifth century and beyond did not always use the best materials available to them. The distinctly localized oeuvres within which they mixed their clay and shaped their pottery, reinforced by many ethnographic studies of potters from around the world, suggest that the determinants of form, fabric and decoration were a combination of utilitarian need, aesthetics and the idea of *habitus*: we do it this way because this is the way we do it – an expression of social conservatism and a modest display of regional, community, perhaps even household identity.[1] Sometimes, quite distinct and exclusive patterns of pottery manufacture are found in the same settlements, but in separate zones. People made positive as well as passive choices about what they liked and what they did not like. The same goes for local and regional traditions in weaving and spinning. People were concerned to express their identity and affiliations in functional, visible, material arts and crafts.

Pottery is by no means essential to settled life, as the apparently aceramic farms and hamlets of other parts of Early Medieval Britain show; but this plastic, artificial stone is marvellously useful and adaptable, and the lowlanders of the fourth century had been accustomed to buying cheap vessels available in a wide choice of designs. The provincials of Roman Britain had a full array of crockery to choose from: fine dinnerware; mortaria for grinding and mixing; amphorae for storing and transporting liquids; cups, beakers and jugs for wine and ale; cooking pots in all shapes and sizes.

The pottery of their successors was both utilitarian and diverse, if less showy, and totally divorced from industrial mass production. Fifth- and sixth-century householders suspended large, lugged cooking vessels over their fires; used bowls to prepare and mix ingredients; stored grain, dough, dried goods and liquids in jars. A pot's capacity, the design of the rim and base, the width of its mouth, all offer clues to both a new aesthetic and to its particular function in the household. Large, wide-mouthed pots were useful for ladling potage or scooping out dried goods like flour or peas. Pots with narrow mouths and everted (out-turned) rims slowed evaporation and allowed perishable contents, especially liquids, to be covered by a cloth secured with cord to prevent insects, pets and stray hands from getting at the contents. They may also suggest some use in packing precious commodities like salt for regional trade. Flat bases allowed pots to stand on solid floors or tables, while a rounded base worked well for heating over a fire or for resting in cool earth. Some pots – and this goes for cremation vessels as well as those more commonly found on settlement sites – had small holes pierced in them, low on their sides, and these seem to indicate that the vessel was used for straining – whey from curds, perhaps.

The life history of a pot leaves scars: sooting on the base shows that it was used at some time in its life for cooking, for example; and many pots must have been reused for multiple purposes before they broke irretrievably, the sherds recycled as gaming counters, trivets or wedges or thrown on the dung heap. But more subtle traces of use wear are now being recognized. Pitting and exfoliation of the internal surface of many cremation urns – something that until recently was not even routinely recorded – suggests that, by and large, they were not made bespoke for the collection of funeral remains but had already been used for brewing ale – not once, as for a funeral feast, but often, over a long period.[2] Others seem to have been used for food storage or processing; and some were probably used to prove dough.

Long years of scholarly study, backed by statistical analysis, have shown that vessels used in cremations were chosen carefully, even if they had not been manufactured solely for the purpose of burial. They and their decorative motifs played a key symbolic and functional role in a consciously constructed set of rituals, whose elements can only be recovered at second hand from what remains after the fiery destruction of the funeral pyre. The archaeologist of the cremation cemetery is an artist of forensic imagination.

To cremate the dead of a community was to invest emotional, material and social capital in a ritual display that transmuted a person and their corpse into elemental, then intangible, then back into material existence. Whether in a household plot, a small burial ground close by a hamlet or in a large communal cemetery serving several settlements, the cremation rite was organized, structured and ordered. After death a body was laid out, dressed in appropriate clothes. Knife hung from girdle or belt; tunic was pinned with small objects of personal adornment: toilet and grooming implements; brooches, perhaps. Items had to be appropriate for the age and sex of the deceased, perhaps also for their social standing within a household and in accord with family tradition. Bodies must be transported, on a bier or in a cart or wain, to the place where the pyre would be constructed. Pyres were built with care, and a suitably large supply of brushwood and larger logs was required to ensure the very high temperatures and structural stability needed for a complete and seemly burning. The scene is painted vividly by the *Beowulf* poet, who describes the communal gathering of materials, the thick black smoke of the fire, the weeping and songs of grief that mingled with the roaring of the flames.[3] How many people, and who, attended the lighting of the pyre we cannot say; but the investment of time and materials and the fact that a funeral bonfire must have been visible – and

Spong Man: the stopper of a cremation urn from the cemetery at Spong Hill, Norfolk, an enigmatic clay figurine.

reminiscent of a full-size alder-wood chair or throne – carved from a whole trunk in the round – excavated at Fallward near Cuxhaven in Lower Saxony. It was found in a boat grave, that of a Roman military officer, and its carved decoration would not be out of place on a cremation urn.[7] Other images are brought to mind: the seat belonging to King Hrothgar, lord of Heorot, in the *Beowulf* poem; and the so-called Frith stool, carved in stone, from Hexham Abbey in Northumberland.[8] If Spong Man's seat is a throne, what does it say about the man depicted as a lone, contemplative figure whose ashes were contained in an accompanying urn? Was his temporal kingdom a mere hamlet; or had he been a great warrior, forced into humble exile? Because the two were separated in antiquity, tying Spong Man to a real human life is impossible, except in the imagination; the chain of detection is broken.

Sentiment aside, why do people deliberately place valuables in the graves of their loved ones? It seems, if nothing else, a waste of precious resources: metalwork that cannot be recycled, kept as memento or passed down as heirloom; perfectly good knives, weapons and pots chucked away by people who can, ostensibly, ill afford to lose them. The archaeologist Martin Carver has suggested that such public disposal of valuable personal items in graves and cremations, and the consumption of surplus foods in the feasting that went along with funerals, may be explained as a sort of voluntary personal and communal tax or render.* After the invisible and God-like emperors ceased to hold sway in *Britannia* and lost the power to tax their provincials centrally, a sense of propriety and the need to feel invested in the fates who governed fertility, health and wealth encouraged people, Carver argues, to invest part of their surplus in the next world. The great communal cemeteries like Spong Hill may, then, be expressions of investment in their shared fortunes: a spiritual spread bet. In such displays they were echoing the practices of their Bronze Age predecessors, who buried some of their dead with similar goods under mounds still visible in the Early Medieval landscape and present in the collective consciousness. When accompanied burials died out again, as they did in the late sixth century, the change of funerary practice was paralleled by the reimposition, in those areas, of the formal mechanisms of the render by an emerging state apparatus.

Much of lowland Britain did not experience, or was not interested in copying, these new, or reinvented, means of disposing of their dead. The most westerly cremations so far found come from a community as solidly Roman, and 'middle England', as it is possible to conceive. The small village of Wasperton (Old English: 'pear orchard by the land that floods') sits in a bend of the Warwickshire Avon a few miles north-east of Stratford. Its Roman predecessor, situated close to the Fosse Way, was excavated in the 1980s in advance of gravel quarrying.[9] Its inhabitants, buried in an inhumation cemetery of the late fourth century conveniently

* See Chapter 11.

sited in a disused rectangular field nearby, belonged to a very long-lived community with roots deep in the prehistoric past. Twenty-three individuals lay spread out across the enclosure, apparently in small family or household groups and carrying a variety of markers of pagan sensibilities, including ritual decapitations and the provision of hobnail boots. Orientations of the bodies were diverse, but predominantly north to south.

Towards the end of the fourth century two urned cremations joined them – apparently unsegregated from the rest. In the fifth century another thirty-seven bodies were interred in dug graves, but with no accompanying goods, lying predominantly in the south-east corner of the enclosure and oriented east–west, with some evidence of stone and plank linings. These are considered to be strong, if not conclusive, markers of Christian affiliation. In the late fifth century further cremation burials took place, inside a small fenced enclosure within the larger cemetery. A few more individuals were interred in dug graves during the same period. The cemetery continued in use into the sixth century, when interments were once again dominated by north–south grave alignments, but now furnished with what are conventionally regarded as 'Anglo-Saxon'-style possessions – eighteen of them with weapons. Some new burials were, at this time, also inserted into very ancient but presumably still visible prehistoric barrows nearby.

Isotope analysis* was successfully carried out on twenty of the individuals from the cemetery.[10] Just over half of these appear to have been raised locally; four were tentatively identified as originating from western Britain and another four – slaves, perhaps – as having grown up around the Mediterranean. None showed signs of having been nurtured in nearby Continental Europe. Despite the temptation to see the adoption of new rites and new styles of possessions as evidence for settlers moving into the Avon valley over the course of the sixth century, there is every reason to

---

* Tooth enamel contains a record of mineral intake during childhood. One trace mineral, strontium, is associated with localized geology, offering the chance to compare populations from areas with distinct soils.

think that the dead of Wasperton belonged to a community that had remained substantially stable for generations. Wasperton's villagers survived the dawning of a new age, adapted to the winds of change enveloping fifth-century Britain with their local and regional identity intact. They went with the flow.

The earliest cremation urns seen in eastern Britain have long been recognized as having direct Continental counterparts in the lands of north Germany and southern Scandinavia, rather neatly tying the fifth-century inhabitants of eastern England to the poetry of *Beowulf* and to Gildas's apocalyptic history. On the face of it, the Early 'Anglo-Saxon' cremation rite is incontrovertible evidence for a Germanic cultural invasion of Britain, its warriors displacing many of the indigenes and subjecting the rest to slavery and oppression. Ostensibly, that story is reinforced by a range of Germanic- and Scandinavian-inspired artefacts; by the evident fact that English is a Germanic language; by distinctly un-Roman Anglo-Saxon law codes, and by the testimony of Bede: that, in his day, Briton and Anglo-Saxon were broadly separate, often antagonistic competitors for territory and power. Terms for 'Briton' and 'slave' were interchangeable: to be *wealas*, or 'Welsh' meant both those things.

That simple, convenient and appealing narrative, which underpins all inherited ideas of Englishness, has begun to look rather shaky in recent decades. Objects and cultural values are transmitted by migrants, it is true. But they are also moved by more subtle, often intangible processes; by trade and gift exchange and through the socially advantageous mimicry of powerful patrons – people who, these days, would be called 'influencers'. Sometimes ideas about and expressions of identity seem to change because of some unfathomable zeitgeist. No foreign invasion or power influenced the late nineteenth-century readoption of cremation in Britain, which seems to have been primarily a response to changing ideas about hygiene and the overcrowding of urban churchyards. Fifth-century artefacts and their decorations are, to be sure, strongly suggestive of affinities between communities on either side of the North Sea; but the nature of those affinities is not nearly so easily characterized as cause and effect. What can now be said with some confidence is that apparently dramatic social changes seen in burial and settlement sites began *before* the traditional dates for migration suggested by Gildas, the Nennian texts and contemporary Continental sources.[11] Archaeology has thrown a spanner in the works.

If cremation was a new or revived rite in Britain from the early fifth century onwards, its adoption seems to be matched by a novel style of building with a similar distribution in eastern and central southern England and, again, counterparts in the traditional Continental homelands of the Anglo-Saxons. No new villas were built in the fifth century; no new towns were founded; few forts were constructed on virgin soil. Evidence for continuity in late Roman settlements is hampered by problems with dating, so archaeologists have quite naturally seen, in novel structures appearing in the same landscapes as the cremation rite, the imprint of migration. More than 130 years after antiquarians first associated cremation cemeteries with ancestral Germans,[12] the much more subtle signs of their supposed dwellings and settlements began to be detected in excavations. In 1921 E. T. Leeds, excavating at Sutton Courtenay in Oxfordshire, identified the now diagnostic sub-rectangular voids – often about 13 ft by 10 ft and perhaps 3 ft deep, sometimes larger, and frequently showing signs of load-bearing posts at either end – that became known as *grubenhäuser*: pit dwellings. The assumption that these apparently squalid hovels had housed immigrant German peasants prompted the search for more sophisticated and permanent structures in which the lords of early Anglo-Saxon England, like their counterparts in *Beowulf*, might have feasted and caroused with their warriors.

Such halls, if disappointingly modest in size and in engineering sophistication, were also eventually recognized, along with the need to develop excavation techniques sufficiently sensitive to recover their ephemeral, organic remains: shadows of former post holes; traces of hearths; thin scatters of refuse. A surprising amount of information can now be gleaned from such traces. Entrances in fifth-century buildings almost always occur at the

Reconstructed Early Medieval house at West Stow, Suffolk.
Fifth- and sixth-century houses recovered from excavation are
remarkably alike in size and ground plan.

centres of the long sides. These are hardly conducive to thermal
efficiency and seem more likely to reflect ideas about social space.
In some buildings, posts seem to match those on opposite long
walls, suggesting the use of tie-beams; in others, extra sets of
external post holes point to the use of raking supports, designed
to prevent the roof loading (heavy turves or thatch) from forcing
the walls out. Hearths, when they are found, seem to have been
the central focus of the building from where, in the words of one
ethnographer, women could 'see all, manage all'[13] during the day
and around which, at night, families must have spent long hours
singing or telling stories of lost times and wonders; perhaps even
of distant homelands. These buildings make a dramatic contrast

with both the native roundhouse and with the spatial organization and overt pretension of the villa, where chosen guests were
ushered through and past carefully engineered, exclusive displays
of private power. Fifth-century domestic architecture looks as
though it belonged to farming households living in dwellings
much like every other farming household. It is an architecture
of very limited privacy and of external social equality, entirely
compatible with the undifferentiated social ranking apparent in
cremation cemeteries.

No archaeologist now believes that the sunken-featured *grubenhäuser* were dwellings, or that simple rectangular patterns of
earth-fast timbers might not have borne impressive and cleverly-
wrought superstructures with carved and painted lintels and doors.
Modern understanding of how these new structures appeared in
the British landscape, and what they tell us about fifth-century
communities, has been informed by the excavation of hundreds
of sites discovered by chance or strategy since the 1950s. Three
key excavations dominate discussion: Mucking, on the Thames
estuary in Essex; West Stow, in Suffolk; and West Heslerton on the
north edge of the Yorkshire Wolds, where *grubenhäuser* are found
in abundance close to the former Romano-British spring shrine. *

Mucking was excavated with very little funding, in extremely
difficult conditions during the 1970s, in advance of gravel extraction. A complete record of the settlement and its accompanying
cemeteries is impossible to reconstruct now, and much that may
have remained was already removed or truncated by mechanical
excavators. Nevertheless, it was, for many years, the only substantially excavated settlement of the period from the fifth to the
seventh centuries in England, and its dozens of *grubenhäuser* and
Germanic-looking finds seemed to offer confirmation of at least
part of Gildas's story, of Saxon warriors settling as mercenaries to
protect London and the lower Thames from pirates and raiders.
Mucking† lies on a gravel terrace overlooking the Thames estuary

---

* See Chapter 3.
† Either 'Mucca's people' or *Mucing*, 'muddy place'. Watts 2004, 425.

downstream from Tilbury. It commands an uninterrupted view of the marshy Hoo peninsula and of the estuary as it opens out to the sea, towards the Continental 'homeland'. Just upstream at East Tilbury is one of the narrowest crossing points on the lower Thames.

The site yielded a staggering 1 million artefacts from 203 *grubenhäuser*, 53 timber post buildings, 468 cremations and nearly 400 inhumations.[14] Here, for the first time, one might offer a narrative account of the founding and development of a new, fifth-century settlement with very evident Germanic cultural affiliations. The Mucking excavation plan (Figure 1) – which gives archaeologists the all-important hard evidence of layout, chronology and structural complexity – has become a classic.

The most striking feature of the Mucking layout is that it sprawls over several hundred yards, with no evident centre or spatial focus; there is no village-like core of manor house and church with surrounding houses and fields. To all intents and purposes it looks like a long-lived campsite or shanty town. The earliest fifth-century buildings, constructed perhaps two centuries after the heyday of its Romano-British predecessor, cluster in the south, where a scatter of *grubenhäuser* look, on the plan, like tumbled dice. The original ground surface has been lost, so how many structures may be missing, particularly rectangular framed houses like those present in the central and north part of the site where recovery was better, is not clear.[15] Chronologically, the settlement seems to have spread slowly and inexorably north over the two centuries following the construction of Mucking's first distinctive buildings in about 420–450. The earliest structures were erected when the ditches of Romano-British fields must still have been visible, and recent analysis of late Roman pottery from the site by Sam Lucy suggests that Mucking's new (or relocated) inhabitants were conscious of their antecedents.[16]

When the site was first excavated, military-style belt fittings, the location of the site on the Thames estuary and the novelty of the buildings suggested to many scholars that Mucking must have been a settlement of *foederati*, engaged by British authorities to

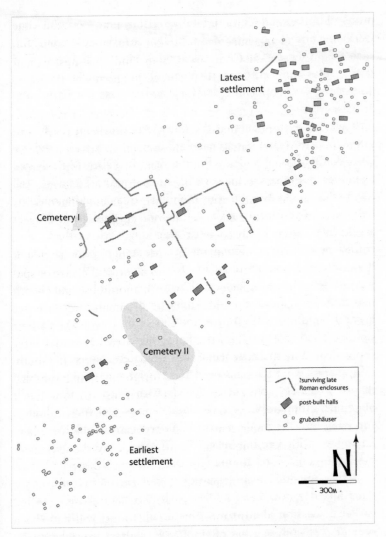

Fig. 1. Plan of excavated structures at the Early Medieval settlement at Mucking, Essex. Shaded areas are cemeteries. After Lucy 2016.

protect London and its hinterland against raiders from the same Germanic homeland. That idea is no longer fashionable; but still, such a fluid sense of space seems at odds with the highly focused farms, villas and roadside settlements of the provincial centuries. Something was happening at Mucking that was not happening at Wasperton.

It was once thought that the finds retrieved from the fills of *grubenhäuser* would tell archaeologists what they were used for, while constructional evidence from increased numbers of excavated examples would reveal the sorts of superstructure that might tell them what made these curious buildings so fashionable over the best part of two centuries. Two-, four- and six-post *grubenhäuser* are known. Some seem to have been dug with vertical sides, consistent with a plank lining; many more seem to have had plank floors suspended above the void – for aeration, perhaps, or just to stay dry when working indoors in winter. No scholar now doubts that the sunken areas stand for larger, perhaps much larger, above ground buildings, with ample floor space and a variety of possible wall and roof designs. Essentially, they must have looked like sophisticated, permanent tents: well-insulated against wind and rain, if somewhat dark inside. Their chief virtue may have been that they could be constructed quickly, with as it were off the shelf materials. Ethnographers have found examples of such buildings surviving into the modern world and reconstructions have been attempted with varying success.* To say that they must have looked 'organic' is to do no disservice to their builders.

A fundamental misunderstanding over the nature of *gruben-haus* fills has now been addressed by archaeologists.[17] As the earlier discussion about town abandonment has made obvious, only *de facto* refuse – material directly related to contemporary use, which has been abandoned and left *in situ* – is likely to offer direct clues about a building's function. A number of *grubenhäuser* destroyed by fire have been excavated; and some of these

---

* Easily accessible examples can be found at Jarrow Hall on Tyneside and at the West Stow Anglo-Saxon Village in Suffolk.

have yielded what seem to be tell-tale rows or heaps of clay loom weights – the warp-tensioners from a vertical frame loom. Many *grubenhäuser* may well have been weaving sheds. In his *Natural History* the Roman writer Pliny the Elder associated the German women of the first century CE with weaving carried out in pits dug underground.[18] That women wove and spun yarn as they went about their daily business at Mucking, where loom weights and spindle whorls are found across the site, shows, if nothing else, that the settlement was no mere military camp but a fully functioning community, reflected in the mixed population of its two cemeteries.

But not all *grubenhäuser* – perhaps even a minority – were weaving sheds. Some archaeologists have argued that suspended plank floors would have been ideal for grain storage, and cereal grains have indeed been recovered from their voids and post holes. This is *primary* refuse, consisting of debris too small or insignificant to tidy away and very likely to reflect contemporary use. Other sunken-featured buildings must have had diverse or multiple functions, sometimes being used as workshops, sometimes as stores for agricultural surplus, or as temporary animal shelters or calving pens. Planks might be removed temporarily to give extra working height. Several of the Mucking examples yielded hearth-bases, cut into the fills after initial abandonment, and slag from iron working; others bore signs of use in working bone and antler, even lead.[19] *Grubenhäuser*, like cremation urns, had complex life histories.

Careful analysis of their fills reveals something more. Several of those at Mucking – and this is broadly true of sites across the zone where they are found – have three fills: a dark base layer, sometimes described as sticky, which excavators recognize as decomposed turf from roof collapse or from the pushing in of turf walls; then less organic, gravelly material that may represent erosion or backfilling, and which contains domestic and industrial debris; then a silting or topsoil layer that had slumped into the void as it compacted.[20] Some sunken-featured structures have one, two or several more complex fills – indicating diverse histories of use. Many *grubenhäuser* fills contain large, unabraded pottery fragments and other refuse such as bone (including animal carcasses and meat joints), even coprolites.* These might imply a general secondary use of the voids as convenient rubbish pits. But the most complete analysis so far of these structures shows that their contents, rather like those of cremation urns, were by no means random; that the voids were filled deliberately after the superstructure was dismantled.[21] There is a suspicion that, in some cases, these are what are known as closure deposits, where the life of a building is deliberately ended in some form of ritual filling, possibly involving feasting. If, indeed, such buildings were ritually closed after the death of the owner, the voids might be seen as analogous to graves. A number of *grubenhäuser* have even yielded human bone, generally of very young infants. The idea that such deposits were not casual is reinforced by another look at the Mucking plan: almost no *grubenhäuser* are seen to cut or disturb existing or former structures. This was no random spread of haphazard temporary shelters, but a self-consciously coherent settlement with a life spanning two centuries, which itself replaced earlier, dense occupation on the same site in the Roman period. Helena Hamerow, who has studied the Mucking evidence in detail, estimates a functioning population in the region of 110 people.

Those curious to know what the settlements of this period might have looked like can make the journey to West Stow in Suffolk. Here, on a sandy knoll overlooking the River Lark on the edge of the Brecklands, a much more compact and well-preserved settlement, excavated in the 1960s and 1970s, has been partly reconstructed in an experiment to test various theories about its buildings and the lifestyles of its inhabitants.[22] Anglo-Saxon West Stow, sitting in a landscape densely occupied since the Middle Bronze Age (*c*.1600–1000 BCE), was protected by medieval wind-blown sands from the depredations of modern ploughing and mineral extraction, so archaeologists have been able to record its stratified layers intact. The Lark flows out onto the Fens some

---

* Fossilized human or animal faeces.

8 miles to the west at Mildenhall, where a fabulous fourth-century treasure of Romano-British silver was found in 1942. A little nearer along the valley lies Icklingham, where a probable fourth-century church and cemetery are associated with a lead baptismal tank depicting a *chi-rho* monogram flanked by a reversed *alpha* and *omega*. Closer still, a Roman road runs east, just to the north of the site, while one of Britain's most ancient trails, the prehistoric Icknield Way linking Norfolk with Wiltshire, passes to the immediate west. A large sixth-century cremation cemetery has been excavated at nearby Lackford.

The settlement at West Stow was established at the beginning of the fifth century in an already busy landscape. From the site plan (Figure 2) it looks much more like a compact, small village or hamlet than the sprawl of Mucking, with several rectangular earth-fast post-framed buildings surrounded by a scatter of *grubenhäuser*, establishing a key relationship between the family house or hall and its outbuildings. These seem like rectangular counterparts of the indigenous tradition of the large family roundhouse surrounded by smaller, sibling stores and workshops, presaging a familiar medieval pattern. However apparently novel the buildings, the lives of its inhabitants are unlikely to have been very much different from those of Iron Age or Romano-British inhabitants of the area.

The large range and quantity of artefacts recovered from West Stow allow archaeologists to compile an inventory of everyday life from the fifth to the seventh centuries, while the reconstructed halls and *grubenhäuser* paint a picture of domestic activities that allowed this comfortable community to thrive. They herded sheep and cattle on the sandy heaths of the Breckland, ploughed the well-drained gravel soils of the valley and fenced their stock in sturdy pens. They made pottery in a variety of forms and styles for a range of craft and culinary uses. They spun yarn and wove textiles; fashioned pins and needles from bone; made buckets to carry water and milk; forged their own tools, harnesses and weapons and enjoyed access, through exchange and trade networks, to glass beads and copper alloy jewellery. They combed

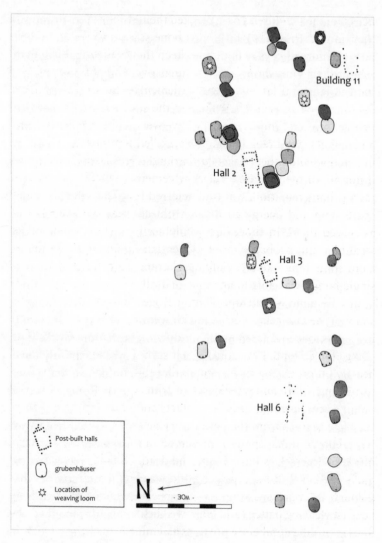

Building 11

Hall 2

Hall 3

Hall 6

Post-built halls

grubenhäuser

Location of
weaving loom

N

- 30M -

Fig. 2. Plan of selected excavated structures, West Stow village,
Suffolk c.440–600. Early halls and their associated outbuildings.
Dots are individual post-holes. Successively darker shading
indicates later phases. After West 1985.

lice from their children's hair, plucked their eyebrows and trimmed their moustaches. They fashioned bone stamps to decorate their pots and forged keys and locks to keep their valuables safe. They rebuilt their workshops and dwellings over the generations; but the fundamental layout of the settlement, representing perhaps five or six or households, remained the same. They were crafts-people, farmers, smiths, potters,* weavers, cobblers, woodsmen and hunters: a self-reliant, adaptable, skilled community of families interacting with other settlements around them. They buried most, if not all, of their dead in a nearby cemetery where inhumation, rather than cremation, was the preferred rite. They had sufficient spare time and energy to fashion objects that pleased as well as served them. In time, one family seems to have emerged as wealthier and probably more influential: an apparent evolution from something like a socially level community to one where a single family was able to aggrandize itself.

Textile analyst Penelope Walton Rogers has made a detailed study of the artefacts associated with weaving at West Stow, open-ing a precious and fascinating window on its female inhabitants going about their daily routines.[23] Self-sufficient communities relied heavily on producing their own textiles for clothing, bedding and furnishing. Cloth and woollens, like pottery, bear coded messages about status, fashion, cultural contacts and utility. Unlike pottery, very few textiles from the period survive – in some cases only as fragments of thread pattern preserved in the corrosion products of metal accessories buried with the dead. But the technology of Early Medieval dyeing, spinning and weaving is well understood through its more enduring tools, especially spindle whorls, pin beaters, weaving battens and loom weights. These have come down to us in prolific numbers: a precious assemblage of objects that link manufacture directly with display and function. All calculations of clothing requirements indicate that prodigious quantities of yarn

---

* A heap of unused clay was found on the site, and among the artefacts were antler-motif pottery stamps.

Reconstruction of a warp-weighted loom at West Stow, Suffolk:
the presence of the doughnut-shaped weights in many excavated
settlements opens a window on domestic life.

were spun and, indeed, spindle whorls* are found scattered across
settlements and buried with females. Along with later medieval
illustrations they confirm the idea that women of all ages and
social strata spun as they went about their daily chores.

* Spindles were slender shafts of wood, bone or shale, a hand span in
length, rotated by the deft fingers of the spinner while drawing wool, hemp
or flax fibres from a distaff or skein. The whorl, a disc of pottery, bone or
stone perforated with a central hole, was wedged onto the spindle and acted
as a flywheel. Different weights and sizes allowed the spinster to adjust the
fineness and amount of twist in her yarn to suit the cloth being prepared
on a loom.

Yarn came from three principal sources: wool, flax and hemp. Cotton was virtually unknown and silk was an exclusive preserve of the wealthiest. Sheep were fleeced in early summer, probably more by plucking than shearing. Fleeces were taken to the farmstead and processed: washed, carded, sorted for quality and fineness, all under the supervision of the female head of the household.[24] Flax was harvested in summer; hemp a little later. Flax had to be pounded, scutched and heckled – involving some physically unpleasant, heavy manual work – to release fibres that could be spun. Each yarn, designed for a particular cloth and weaving technique and chosen for strength, appropriate thread count, weatherproofing or softness, was spun by hand on a drop spindle.

At West Stow, spindle whorls were not found on the floors of houses, but in most of the *grubenhäuser*. Had they been lost or discarded in the domestic living space, they would be recovered or swept up in regular maintenance, while *grubenhäuser* voids and the outdoor areas immediately around them naturally accumulated such easily lost items. Doughnut-shaped clay loom weights, by contrast, were found clustered in a much more restricted range of locations, showing that one of the larger *grubenhäuser* associated with each household was probably the designated weaving shed, where a vertical loom was set up and where spare sets of loom-weights – chosen and balanced to achieve even tensioning on the vertical warps – were stored close by on wooden rods. Like spindle whorls, pin beaters – thin, cigar-shaped rods made of bone or antler – were found in or near *grubenhäuser*, indicating that women carried them around – and lost them – during their daily routine. They may have acted as multi-function tools, tucked into a belt or holding hair in place. Each household at West Stow, then, produced its own clothing and accessories: from rugs, hangings, coarse blankets and rough working tunics to the attractively patterned hems, cuffs and braids woven on smaller tablet looms, perhaps by the evening light of the household fire.

In stark contrast to the wealth of information from the settlement, very little is known of the last resting places of West Stow's inhabitants. Two small cemeteries were discovered during gravel

extraction in the middle of the nineteenth century and only anecdotal accounts survive to tell of the 100 or so skeletons recovered.
They were, we know, oriented with their heads towards the south-
west. Many artefacts were recovered without their provenance
being recorded; we cannot say how grave goods were disposed
about the bodies except by analogy from other sites of the period;
but they included a handful of Roman coins (four of them perforated for use as pendants); more than fifty brooches, various
bracelets and finger rings; two swords; combs; nearly 200 beads;
toilet items and a variety of spinning and weaving implements. The
context is 'pagan', for Christian burial eschewed grave goods.

At both Mucking and West Stow our view of people's burial
customs and individual pathologies is hampered by the limitations
of the original excavation or the physical state of the site. Only
one largely complete settlement of the fifth to seventh centuries
has been excavated with its cemetery intact and, such was the
abundance and complexity of the data from West Heslerton,
excavated during the 1980s and 1990s, that the full report has
yet to be published. Nevertheless, evidence from its *grubenhäuser*,
houses, stock pens, rubbish pits and associated burials has already
overturned many long-held preconceptions about the centuries
immediately after Roman withdrawal. For the first time, it has
been possible to address one of the sixty-four-thousand-dollar
questions of British archaeology: where did the inhabitants of
these new-style settlements come from?

West Heslerton had been the site of a Roman-period shrine
focused on the spring that rises from the foot of the Yorkshire
Wolds and flows north into the River Derwent across the clays,
peats and sandy glacial gravels of the Vale of Pickering.* By the
end of the fourth century Britain was experiencing cooler, wetter
decades that would lead to the flooding of the Fens and the Vale
of York. By the middle of the fifth century much of the lower-
lying land between wold edge and river had become untenable.
A string of Roman-period settlements along the south side of the

* See Chapter 3.

vale was abandoned in favour of drier, more elevated locations close to the spring line and the shrine. This area now saw the establishment of a densely occupied settlement, which has been excavated to the highest modern standards in open-area fashion in advance of gravel quarrying.

The 'Anglian' settlement at West Heslerton was a close-set but organized affair, with discrete areas devoted to animal husbandry and crafts, housing and burial (Figure 3). On either side of the stream that emanated from the spring, dozens of *grubenhäuser* used for grain storage were enclosed by clearly defined rectangular fenced or ditched pens. A mill tapped the stream's flow to grind corn that had been threshed and stored nearby. Downstream on the west bank lay an area devoted to metal crafts, bone working and other small-scale industries. A large cluster of rectangular post-framed houses with attendant *grubenhäuser* stood opposite, on the east side of the stream. Between the domestic living space and the animal pens a small patch of woodland might have included orchard trees. The whole settlement, with its discrete activity areas and careful layout, was sustained from the early fifth century for at least 200 years.[25] This was no transient campsite; nor yet a small hamlet like West Stow, but a busy, populous and prosperous village whose inhabitants acted co-operatively to get the most from their land and their own talents. It has something of the downland villages of Salisbury Plain about it. The final excavation report should offer unprecedented detail about the lives of its inhabitants: their diet and daily routines, their choice of animals, crops, building styles and pottery. It will tell us much about the evolution of a community in its contemporary land-scape – a community that spans the most obscure centuries of the last two millennia. Archaeologists excavating Knook Down on Salisbury Plain might one day find similar riches there. The fact that West Heslerton seems never to have been enclosed by any sort of defensive earthwork or palisade, nor to have suffered the depredations of raiding or razing to the ground, ought to bury the myth, once and for all, of a dangerous, violent countrywide aftermath to the end of Roman rule.

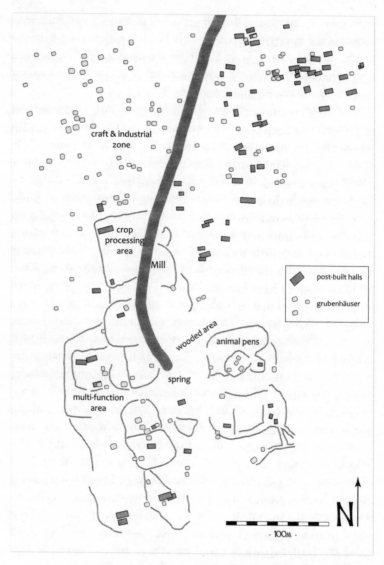

Fig. 3. Plan of excavated features at the Anglian settlement, West Heslerton, North Yorkshire. After Powlesland 2020.

Legend within figure:
- post-built halls
- grubenhäuser

Labels within figure: craft & industrial zone, crop processing area, Mill, wooded area, animal pens, spring, multi-function area, N, - 100M -

The dead of West Heslerton's post-Roman community were taken to a similarly well-organized cemetery, lying some 440 yards to the north-east (now bisected by the modern A64 trunk road between York and Scarborough). The cemetery site seems to have been chosen because of some folk memory, possibly even the upstanding remains of a set of prehistoric funerary monuments, tapping into a deep sense of belonging to the land and an already powerful idea of ancestry that pervades the archaeology of the vale. The 'Anglian' burials were placed in dug graves, many of them accompanied by personal adornments such as brooches with distinct artistic and technical similarities to material found in Scandinavia and northern Germany. Unusually, a significant number of infants and juveniles was buried alongside adults of both sexes, with little indication of any great disparity in wealth or status but, like the cemetery at Wasperton, in evident groupings of what seem to have been household members.

It was natural that, with such a wealth of information at their disposal, the excavators took advantage of newly developing isotope tracing techniques to test theories about where the population had come from.[26] Forty individuals of both sexes were tested, including infants and young adults and several from demonstrably prehistoric graves whose origins might be expected to offer a reliably local baseline. The excavators were keen to compare these with individuals accompanied by 'Continental'-style grave goods, such as Scandinavian wrist clasps and northern German bucket pendants.

Results of the tooth-enamel tests confirmed that the prehistoric burials bore predominantly local strontium markers, as did the majority of the so-called 'Anglian' dwellers of the vale. But several bore isotope signatures incompatible with a local childhood – including both males and females and two juveniles. Their specific origins cannot, in the present state of the science, be pinned to any one part of Continental Europe or of the British Isles; but they had not been nurtured in north-east England. Even those individuals with isotope traces most likely to have come from Scandinavia or the traditional Anglian homeland must have migrated over several generations, rather than in a single wave.[27] The 'Anglian' settlement at West Heslerton was not founded by European immigrants, but by local people whose ancestors had lived nearby for many generations. What archaeologists have long suspected can be tentatively confirmed: 'foreign' grave goods do not tell us about the ethnicity of the people they were buried with. Nor is there any sense of social 'apartheid' operating at West Heslerton: non-locals do not seem to have had pride of place in the cemetery; nor were they buried close to one other; and nor does the architecture of the village suggest the establishment of a single élite family. Naturally, isotope analysis cannot help with the identification of the children of migrants, who could only be identified by detailed DNA analysis of family groups within cemeteries. But there are, perhaps, more important problems to address.

West Heslerton's legacy will be to challenge many long-held assumptions about the decades and centuries after the end of Roman provincial rule – and, indeed, about how to excavate their remains. But it is, so far, exceptional. What we cannot yet say is whether its outstanding evidence for organized Early Medieval settlement, with deep roots in the prehistoric and Roman landscape and the apparently small number of individuals who joined the community from elsewhere, will turn out to be typical or atypical of the lands that became England. West Heslerton had never been at the heart of *Britannia*.

If its inhabitants were, by and large, direct descendants of the local population and yet adopted a radically novel set of cultural behaviours, it begs the question of how we should read or re-read the traditional narrative of Anglo-Saxon invasion or mass migration indicated by historical sources and also, apparently, by waves of new buildings, burials, pottery and metalwork. That evidence, solidly bolstered by decades of scholarly research on the linguistic triumph of Old English and by the apparent hiatus in occupation of Romano-British towns, villas and other settlements, is now shown to rely heavily both on assumptions about identity, race and material culture, and on the perhaps too-persuasive testimony of the few available, highly partisan narrative sources. A resolution to this paradox requires some fancy footwork. Either the evidence is lying, which would undermine some very well-established disciplines, or we have been looking at it the wrong way.

Leaving aside, for the moment, the testimonies of Gildas, the Nennian texts, Bede, the *Anglo-Saxon Chronicle*, the *Gallic Chronicles*, the earliest English laws and a host of other Continental notices, and postponing thoughts about linguistics, it is worth going back to basics and looking at the foundations of the archaeological case for migration and invasion. Architectural, funerary and material fashions change, influenced by such social phenomena as early adopters, influencers, élites and by the diktats of a state apparatus. No one has ever argued that an Italian élite migrated en masse into Britain after the middle of the first century CE, to account for millions of 'Roman' artefacts and cultural fashions. In fact, it seems that there is only one known burial from the Roman period in Britain of an individual who was actually born in Rome.[28] Nor is the global dominance of American fast food and drink brands or the spread of Japanese automotive technology to many countries across the world attributable to overwhelming numbers of immigrants or to actual military conquest. In some parts of the world, the history of colonialism offers a more nuanced picture of the impact of incomers on indigenous societies. In South America, India and Africa, for example, a small military, mercantile and civil service élite generated the momentum for legal, linguistic and technological change, alongside its more invidious effects. At the other end of the spectrum, the immigration of waves of Europeans to the New World from the seventeenth century onwards swamped and largely marginalized the indigenous cultures of farmers, hunter-gatherers, plains tribes and pueblo dwellers, by a combination of aggression, assimilation and legal oppression. Even so, these enormous events wrought their changes over centuries, not in a few short decades.

Against these historical, and by no means directly comparable, examples, a number of models has been developed to explain the adoption by parts of Britain's population of new, or revived, burial rites and novel buildings alongside the apparent rejection of villa and town life and of the heavier agricultural lands where Romano-British settlements abounded.

The dominant model, compatible with and inspired by the narratives of Gildas and the Nennian compiler, proposes the arrival from Germanic lands of a male warrior élite, identified by the weapons with which they were buried, who married into locally dominant indigenous families.[29] They enacted a political and social coup whose results included the subjugation of the native British élite and the linguistic dominance of Germanic place names: Rodings, Basings, Barkings, and so on.* Some archaeologists, notably J. N. L. Myres, argued that new types of pottery and of military-style belt buckles were decisive evidence for the implanting of Germanic *foederati* in Roman towns and key coastal settlements as early as the late fourth century.[30] The early settlement overlooking the Thames estuary at Mucking might fit such a model, presaging the better-attested arrival of a male warrior élite into northern Britain during the first Viking Age (*c.*796–950).

A broader model, following Bede's account of a folk movement involving three distinct peoples – Angles, Saxons and Jutes – has sought to identify evidence for migration on a much larger scale.† It emphasizes indications of an apparent emptying of the ancestral homelands of these historically attested peoples on the Continent and the contemporary arrival of their cultural paraphernalia in eastern Britain during the early and middle decades of the fifth century. Distinct regional variations in pottery, metalwork, textile manufacture and burial rites have tended to support this model, even if the precise dating needed to confirm it is lacking.

A twentieth-century interest in migration theory and an examination of trends in historical emigration (from Europe to America

---

* See Chapter 8, p. 242. Roding, for example, derives from OE (Old English) *Hroðingas*, 'Hrotha's folk'. The asterisk indicates a linguistically reconstructed form.

† Bede names those three peoples in his *Historia Ecclesiastica* (I.15) but later, in the same work (V.9), he adds Frisians, Rugians, Danes, Huns, Old Saxons and *Bructeri*.

or from Asia to Europe, for example), has given rise to ideas about so-called chain migration: small numbers of pioneering migrants followed by periodic, long-drawn-out arrivals of relatives and dependants over several generations: less a revolution than an evolution. Such migrants tend to cling to cultural norms from their homelands as a means of reinforcing their sense of identity, only slowly adopting indigenous cultural behaviours, if at all; taking their time to integrate. In such scenarios second- and third-generation children of such migrants can find themselves speaking a language barely understood by their grandparents. This model allows a more inflected reading of the highly complex and apparently contradictory evidence from settlements and cemeteries. It does not address the reaction of the indigenes to their new neighbours.

The most radical model suggests that there was no, or a negligible, immigration from the Continent; that social and cultural innovations in the fifth century were driven by internal forces in response to imperial collapse and wider environmental and social dynamics.[31] Recently, ideas about a sort of North Sea mercantile zone of fluid population movement and a Germanic lingua franca have shown that some imagination is required to address the many apparent paradoxes that confront archaeologists and historians.[32] One might, lastly, consider the idea that a substantial number of warriors and their dependents came, perhaps repeatedly, impacted dramatically on their hosts' cultural lives, and departed again, as an often-overlooked passage in Gildas suggests.[33]

A striking feature of these contrasting models, each of which must bear the weight of an increasing body of apparently conflicting evidence, is not that they might all be wrong; but that they might all be right. No single model or combination of scenarios seems to accommodate all the evidence. What characterizes much of the debate within the archaeological community is a strong tendency to argue from the particular to the general: to offer one model exclusively at the expense of others. The diversity of Britain's climate, soils, cultural histories and sense of local identity suggests a mosaic of challenges, opportunities and accommodations faced or embraced by the communities of the former Roman province.

Unless forcibly coerced, people adopt new cultural values and material expressions of identity because they see them as socially advantageous. Warriors, pirates, refugees, economic migrants and family followings all have their place in any picture of the emerging native societies of Early Medieval Britain. A seemingly inescapable concentration on, if not obsession with, ethnicity (either native or Germanic) is intellectually unhealthy and redolent of a late Victorian mindset, fixated on the origins of formative 'nations' and races. Even the almost universal employment of the terms 'Early Anglo-Saxon' or 'British' or 'Migration period', to describe the archaeology of eastern Britain in the fifth and sixth centuries, is a straitjacket.

It might reasonably be argued that, in those areas where archaeologists find both *grubenhäuser* and large communal cremation cemeteries – that is, in East Anglia, the East Midlands, Lincolnshire and Essex – some permanent settlements of migrants from across the North Sea were established over the century from 400 onwards. It is not much; but to say more is, perhaps, to stretch current evidence beyond breaking point.

Communities in what is now eastern, central and southern England found much that was attractive – and familiar – about the warrior values, ideologies and material culture of societies across the North Sea, societies whose histories had been wrought in tension with the Roman empire but who were less subject to its cloying colonial dominance and rapacious taxes. Those peoples had traded and mixed with Britons since before the Roman invasion of the first century CE, and they continued to do so during and after its heyday. The cultural historian Michael J. Enright has argued persuasively that so-called 'Celtic' and Germanic societies shared many social and material attributes; that they borrowed imagery, mythology and their material expressions from one another.[34] Northern Europeans and peoples of the maritime north-west share cultural bonds as distinctive, and as ancient, as those of the lands that flank the Mediterranean.

The absolutely decisive shift in the history of eastern Britain in the fifth century may not be so much the willing or unwilling embrace of Scandinavian and Germanic cultures, but the rejection of much that was Roman: town life, villas, privatized wealth and display, conspicuous consumption, crushing centralized taxation, martial rule, corruption and absentee landlords. Disgust with imperial politicking at the expense of local needs reflects, perhaps, the sorts of recurring motivations that drive relations between an island people and their Continental neighbours. The complex expressions of that shift are hardly explicable in the current state of knowledge about that most interesting and opaque century after Rome's fall, but tantalizing glimpses of such processes at work in the villas, towns and forts may yet hold some of the answers.

Political and cultural rejection of Rome did not solve the profound economic or infrastructural problems facing *Britannia* after the disappearance of a cash economy, state taxation, a professional military and the imperial administration. If, in eastern England, a sort of collectivized, smaller world was the crucible in which Early Medieval politics was forged, a late and ironic adoption of Latinate Mediterranean culture found new life in those parts of the west and north that had been the most antipathetic to Rome. Diverging trajectories were acted out over the course of the fifth and sixth centuries, subtly recorded in some of the most intractable archaeological evidence in Britain's history and, more crudely, in a narrative whose ill-wrought offspring comes down to us in the words of Patrick, Gildas and the traditions later recorded by Bede and the Nennian compiler. This is the story of civil war, perfidy, mystery and mythology that fuels enduring interest in the search for the origins of medieval Britain.

5

Of famine, sword and fire

Gildas – a Faustian deal – false witnesses – Patrick –
the *Historia Brittonum* – landscapes of conflict –
good fences; good neighbours?

ᚷᚫᚷᚩᚷᚫ ᛗᚫᚷᚫ ᛗᛖᛞᚢ

GÆGOGÆ MÆGÆ MEDU

The Undley bracteate, a fifth-century gold pendant modelled on a
coin of Constantine the Great, found near Lakenheath in Suffolk. It
is regarded as the earliest runic inscription from the British Isles. The
untranslatable inscription begins with what may be a battle cry or
imprecation, followed by something like 'reward for kinsmen'.

Picture the British landscape, sometime towards the end of the fifth century. Wide plains and rolling hills are productive of the fruits of the soil and abundant in good pasture; wild flowers delight with their colours; clear springs feed rivers that glide in gentle murmur. These natural blessings are bejewelled with more than a score of cities, defended by towers and solid gates and filled with sturdy houses. This is a Britain largely free from the strife of war or the menace of plague and famine, a fatherland where those who lie on the banks of rivers and lakes refreshed by the cold rush of living waters enjoy sweet sleep.

If this description sounds like the promised land, that is no coincidence, for the author who speaks thus of his native country is steeped in the imagery of the Old Testament. Such an idealized portrait is not, perhaps, too hard to reconcile with the snapshots that archaeology offers of the lives of farming families at West Heslerton, Mucking, and West Stow – modest and industrious as those inhabitants appear to have been. But it strikes a resounding discord with the litany of tragedy and destruction offered by the same author in the same brutal lecture addressed to his contemporaries.

De Excidio et Conquestu Britanniae, 'The Ruin and Conquest of Britain', written in Latin by a British monk known only as Gildas, is the founding text of post-Roman history.[1] It is part finger-wagging sermon, part allegorical biography of a nation, part providential history. *De Excidio* tells how the obstinate Britons, having thrown off the civilizing might of Rome, were subjected to conquest; how they rebelled and were forced into servitude. It tells how they became prey to heresy, tyranny, plunder, famine and plague; how flames of devastation tore across the land from coast to coast.

Like the putative murals from which Constantius drew vivid inspiration, if not strict historical truth, for his hagiography of St Germanus, the chaff of Gildas's extravagant imagery must be winnowed from the grain of credible fifth-century history with care. A grand drama has been constructed by generations of historians on the basis of just seven short chapters (out of 110) in *De Excidio* that purport to account for the fortunes of the Britons after the end of the empire; and its rhetoric is pervasive. A bare précis of Gildas's account, stripped of biblical allusion and oratorical flourish, runs as follows.

On the departure of the Roman administration, 'foul hordes' of Scots (from Argyll, or from across the Irish Sea in *Hibernia*) and Picts (from *Caledonia*) began to prey on the northern part of Britain, landing in their curraghs (*curuci*) with bloodshed in mind.[2] They took control of the north of the island, 'right up to the Wall'. Britain's defenders, too lazy to fight them, were overthrown. In the aftermath, towns were looted and abandoned, citizens fled, hunger was rife. The 'miserable remnants' then wrote to the Roman commander in Gaul, begging for help. Gildas purports to quote from the letter:

'To Agitius, thrice consul: the groans of the British'. Further on came this complaint: 'The barbarians push us back to the sea, the sea pushes us back to the barbarians; between these two kinds of death, we are either drowned or slaughtered.' But they got no help in return.[3]

Famine followed; then, after years of plundering by their foes, the British won a victory that stemmed the tide of their enemies' audacity. The Irish raiders returned to their homeland and the Picts were, for the most part, quietened. Now the island was flooded with abundant goods and luxury; but the licentious British were purged of their sins – fornication, murder, falsehood, drunkenness – by a virulent plague, so that 'the living could not bury all the dead'.[4]

'*Tum omnes consiliarii una cum superbo tyranno*', 'Then all the members of the council, together with the proud tyrant' resolved to invite three shiploads of Saxons 'like wolves into the fold' to beat back the peoples of the North.[5] They came in 'keels' (*cyuli*) followed by a second, larger contingent, 'fixing their claws' first on the east side of the island. For a long time these mercenaries were granted regular, monthly supplies (Gildas uses three specific Latin terms: *epimenia*, *annonae* and *munificentia*). Soon, they found that these were insufficient and, exaggerating tensions over individual 'incidents', threatened to mutiny. Mutiny turned to plunder; towns were laid low; fires licked across the land as far as its western shores. 'There was no burial to be had except in the ruins of houses or the bellies of beasts or birds.'[6]

In the aftermath of this onslaught, some were enslaved; others fled to the mountains or emigrated. Then, when the 'cruel plunderers had gone home', the survivors gathered together under the leadership of a man named Ambrosius Aurelianus whose parents, who had 'worn the purple', had been slain in the conflict. The people regained their strength, challenged the enemy to battle, and won. For some years, it seems, a conflict raged in which both sides won victories and suffered defeats, up until a year marked by the siege of Badon Hill – 'pretty well the last defeat of the villains, and certainly not the least'.[7] Gildas tells us that at the present time (forty-four years after his own birth during the year of the siege) all is 'calm' but that, even so, cities are deserted and lie in ruins – an image set in striking counterpoint to the bucolic description of Britain in his introduction to the historical section of *De Excidio*.

Gildas presents enough problems of interpretation to keep scholars busy for generations. Who exactly was Agitius – handily dated, it would seem, by his third consulship? If the famous battle at Badon Hill took place forty-four years before the *present*, when was the present? And who were the *superbus tyrannus* and his ill-advised councillors? Was Ambrosius the commander at Badon? Where did these battles take place, and whose were the armies who fought them? How big were they? How far can Gildas's testament be trusted when it is so vague in detail and so laden with melodrama? And why no mention of Arthur, regarded by later historians of the Britons as an epitome of indigenous military leadership?

To begin at the beginning: Gildas is a suspect witness because his account of Roman Britain betrays significant ignorance and confusion. He was no trained historian and, if he had access to chronicles or annalistic material, he played fast and loose with them. He knew of Magnus Maximus and he alludes to what might be Honorius's admonition of 410 to the Britons to look to their own defences – but he dates the early second century construction of Hadrian's Wall to the same period. On the other hand, the link he makes between the Romans' departure and the arrival of Irish and Pictish raiders may be based on a stock of oral memory. And there is every reason to suppose that the well-attested raids of the late fourth century continued into the fifth: St Patrick's early experience of abduction across the Irish Sea, assuming it occurred in the first half of the fifth century, vividly confirms the reality of transmarine piracy. It is surely significant that Gildas associates the letter of appeal to Roman authorities with these northern raids, rather than with any predations from across the English Channel. The geography of conflict is, at this point of his historical narrative, wholly northern.

Much has been made of the letter to Agitius.[8] The only Agitius known from this period was a *magister militum per Gallas* and possible ruler of the kingdom of Soissons, a rump state of the Western empire in what is now northern France: properly Aegidius, who died in about 465. But he never held the consulship. Most historians accept that Gildas, or a scribe in the succession of those whose latest manuscript we possess,* misheard or miscopied; that he must have meant Aëtius, the famed Roman commander who recovered much of Gaul for the emperor from the late 420s onwards. Aëtius was indeed consul on three occasions: in 432, 437 and 446. If a real letter had been sent, from which Gildas was able to quote directly, it must have been composed during or after 446, the date of his third consulship. This has set the accepted date for what is now conventionally known as the 'Letter to Aëtius', providing a convenient *terminus post quem* for the Saxon episodes that follow. But Gildas's knowledge of any letter seems no more

---

* The earliest surviving but severely fire-damaged manuscript is *Cotton MS Vitellius A VI*, copied in the late ninth or early tenth century from earlier manuscripts. It was transcribed before the damage occurred.

than anecdotal – its authors were 'the miserable remnants', rather than any named officials. All that can be said with reasonable confidence is that any appeal was sent after Aëtius's appearance as the dominant Roman force in control of the Western provinces in 430, because Gildas's 'thrice consul' may be his interpolation, rather than an original quote.

As it happens, and given the context of Germanus's visits in the late 420s and the 430s, the first consulship of Aëtius is a perfectly credible window for an appeal, at just the point when it seemed as though Rome would recover Gaul. For the first time in more than a decade Britain might look for imperial military help, as it had so often in the past, against raiders from the north and east.[9] Diplomats were still crossing the Channel during this decade, as the appeal from British to Gallic bishops proves. But hope was, in the event, illusory. If Ravenna's civil and military authorities, like their ecclesiastical counterparts in Rome, had ambitions to recover *Britannia*, they did not succeed.

Precedents for an alternative solution to the problems facing the former province – to settle *foederati* in the island for security – had been set during the previous century. The Saxons had a reputation as tough, fearless sailors and raiders whose services might be bought. But it seems doubtful that Saxon federates were hired to protect *Britannia* from Picts and Irish operating in the north. The garrison forces still in place on or behind the Wall were best placed and most experienced in that field of operations; and the evidence from Birdoswald suggests that at least some of the forts retained fighting strength. Besides, Gildas says that the northern threat was subdued by the time the council, to which he refers so vaguely, invited Saxon forces across in their three keels. A more plausible threat was posed by other seaborne raiders, including Saxons themselves, operating in the Channel and North Sea from Jutland down to Brittany. The enemies against whom Germanus supposedly defended the Britons were both Picts and Saxons. Official policy was, one imagines, to keep the Channel open for trade and communications. Sidonius Apollinaris, a Gallic diplomat, poet and inveterate correspondent in the mid-to-late fifth century, wrote to his friend, a naval commander called Admiral Namatius:

> I whiled away some time talking with [the courier] about you; and he was very positive that you had weighed anchor, and in fulfilment of those half military, half naval duties of yours were coasting the western shores on the look-out for curved ships; the ships of the Saxons, in whose every oarsman you think to detect an arch-pirate. Captains and crews alike, to a man they teach or learn the art of brigandage; therefore let me urgently caution you to be ever on the alert. For the Saxon is the most ferocious of all foes. He comes on you without warning; when you expect his attack he makes away. Resistance only moves him to contempt; a rash opponent is soon down. If he pursues he overtakes; if he flies himself, he is never caught. Shipwrecks to him are no terror, but only so much training. [10]

That a deal was brokered to protect *Britannia*'s southern and eastern shores from sea-born raids, and that it failed because of greed or mistrust or misunderstandings on both sides, is in itself credible. The history of the Viking Age is littered with accounts of precisely such arrangements and their almost invariable failure. Setting a thief to catch a thief is a high-risk strategy – the strategy of a desperate, undefended élite. But the practice was a well-tried policy of late Roman armies. Companies of Saxon marines might well have been recruited as standard military units of the late Roman state, under an established set of protocols and with set rates for remuneration and billeting. [11]

Gildas was a religious conservative; a partisan sermonizer. Doubts about his sources are amplified by his distance in time and space from events in whose retelling he recast Insular history in the apocalyptic rhetoric of the Old Testament. His chronology floats ethereally in Brownian motion; circumstantial detail is virtually non-existent. Even so, and in anticipation of some corroboration in the archaeological record, it is possible to suggest the following as the political essence of his history. In the years after the failed appeal to the *magister militum* of Gaul (which, if true, I tentatively date to the 430s), a council of provincial leaders agreed to acquire the services of a small fleet of patrolling marines to protect key sites in the south and east, the backbone of British naval policy ever since. These were reinforced by others – perhaps many others. Families, associates and refugees from the conflicts and environmental stresses troubling the lands north of the Rhine joined them. In due course, the mercenaries decided that they might dictate the terms of their contract more agreeably – perhaps demanding an extra monthly allowance, *epimenia*, for their followers but, just as likely, claiming land on which to settle their dependants and rights to collect their own taxes in kind – *annonae* – from the locals. Friction led to trouble. The south of the British province had not possessed its own military force in centuries and so, eventually, the federate warbands took lands of their own, dispossessed the native ruling élite and ruled in their stead. This was how Gildas's generation remembered those far-off days.

The emergence of a resistance leader, the son of aristocratic parents who had held high office in the former province, is confirmed by Gildas's ability to name him, alone among the Britons of the period. Gildas allows him no geography or milieu, and his floruit is uncertain; but Ambrosius Aurelianus must have enjoyed a sufficiently memorable career that his name survived to be credited with great victories – even if he cannot be securely placed at Badon Hill. In later centuries he featured in nationalist legends recording his miraculous emergence as a champion of the British against their Saxon foes.[12]

Gildas's silence on Arthur says one of three things: that he was unknown to Gildas (perhaps his orbit was local; perhaps he was not yet famous when Gildas wrote); that his story came with inconvenient baggage (a reputation for extreme brutality or licentiousness, perhaps, like Gildas's *tyranni*); or that he is a poetic figment of later imagination.

If *De Excidio* could be dated it would help enormously to elucidate this bare framework for fifth-century political history. Gildas says he is writing at the age of forty-three, and that the siege of Badon Hill – as famous a victory as Ambrosius was a commander – took place in the year of his birth.* Traditionally Gildas's death was accepted, by virtue of an obituary notice in the *Annales Cambriae* (a ninth-century compilation), as 570. The same annals offer 516 as a date for a battle at Badon Hill, giving Gildas a perfectly reasonable life span of fifty-four years. These dates seem to be corroborated by another entry in the *Annales*: the death, in a great plague in 547, of Maelgwyn, king of Gwynedd – one of five contemporary '*tyranni*' cited by Gildas for their unspeakable sins.† It is all rather neat. But in recent decades serious doubts have been cast on the credibility of the *Annales Cambriae*, as they have on the whole Nennian compilation. The *Annales* were set down several hundred years after the events that they purport to record; they were compiled in a more or less overtly nationalistic political climate; and they are not, by and large, corroborated by other independent sources.

And then, Gildas's educational background has been shown to be classically Latinate, as formally taught in schools of rhetoric. His overwrought prose is littered with the sort of precise, technical vocabulary – the *epimenia*, *munificentia* and *annonae* of the Saxon federates, for example – that many historians find hard to square with an adult of the middle of the sixth century. Lastly – and to précis very detailed arguments and counter-arguments by those who have devoted years to studying *De Excidio* – what little sense of time can be gleaned from Gildas's account of the northern raids, the letter of appeal, famines, plagues and the Saxon revolt, hardly seems to fill a century, let alone a century and a half; especially if one accepts a date in the 430s for a letter of appeal to Roman authorities. Even allowing for a decade or two of war followed by forty-three years of peace leaves one struggling to place Gildas later than about 500.[13]

* That is the accepted reading; but there are doubts about Gildas's some-times opaque Latin and some scholars have argued that Badon Hill and Ambrosius's victory are the events separated by forty-three years, and that the siege occurred in the year in which Gildas was writing. Wood 1984, 23.
† See Chapter 6, p. 197ff.

Continental sources offer some hope for shoring up Gildas's shaky foundations. The *Chronica Gallica of 452* recorded under the year 441–442 that 'the Britons, having hitherto been overrun by various calamities and events, are subject to Saxon authority'. A second annal, the so-called *Chronicle of 511*, offers 440 for the same event.[14] For what it is worth, there is nothing improbable about an unanswered appeal to Roman authorities in the early 430s followed by the arrival of mercenaries on the Channel coast, their rebellion and a takeover – however limited – of political control in parts of the south-east during the following decade.

Such a simplistic account of the founding of the English nation may be satisfactory for primary-school picture-book learning and for the grossest politics of nationalism; but it hardly does justice to the nuanced and localized picture emerging from the archaeological record or, indeed, to hints provided by the Germanus narrative and by entries in the *Historia Brittonum* that evoke a parallel picture of political and religious factionalism within the British establishment. Unless one is to picture the takeover of *Britannia* as a distant mirror of the mercurial conquest of the Aztec empire by Hernán Cortés in 1520, the historian must attempt to tell a subtler tale.

Two Insular sources purport to furnish Gildas's account with credible people, places and dates. The *Anglo-Saxon Chronicle* compiled at, and on behalf of, King Ælfred's West Saxon court in the 890s, gives the dates of a number of battles supposedly fought by key protagonists half a millennium before, in the second half of the fifth century: at *Ægelesthred* in 455 and at *Creganford* in 456; at *Wippedesfleot* a decade later; at an unnamed location in 473; then at *Cymenesora* in 477; on the banks of the *Mearcredesburna* in 485; at *Andredesceaster* in 491 and *Certicesora* in 495.[15] Each was said to have been fought by a 'Saxon' warlord against a 'British' or 'Welsh' army. The locations range from Aylesford (*Ægelesthred*) on the River Medway in north Kent to the Roman shore fort at Pevensey (*Andredesceaster*) in East Sussex, with several unidentified. The named combatants are Hengest, Horsa, Æsc, Ælle and Cissa (for the 'Saxons') and Vortigern (for the British). Ambrosius does not appear.

The *Chronicle* is both propagandist and, for these early centuries, unsupported by independent sources. Like the other ninth-century annal compilations, it is framed by nationalist conflict (West Saxons against 'foreigners'). Serious flaws in its chronology and the overtly political motives behind its construction have driven scholars towards a hyper-cautious, almost dismissive use of its early material.* It goes almost without saying that no pagan Germanic warlord employed, in his retinue, a Latin cleric jotting down on wax tablets *Anno Domini* dates (not, in any case, invented until the sixth century) for his famous deeds so that they could later be set down in a great chronicle. The records of such battles might, at best, have been remembered by attaching them to a sequence of regnal years[†] passed down, in Bede's phrase, 'by those who compute the dates of kings'.[16] Such calculations, without knowing where or when they were first written down, need to be treated with due scepticism. In any case, several of the protagonists are regarded by modern historians as semi-fictional: eponyms invented or co-opted to explain distinctive place names. Nevertheless, and with all due caveats, these entries tell a story of a long-running, if periodic, conflict between warlords whose martial deeds on behalf of the 'Saxons' against the native British were remembered and celebrated by later generations.

For a British view of the fifth century, historians have one absolutely authentic contemporary voice in St Patrick.[17] Here is no grand narrative but a very affecting, personal story of human tribulation, a small, bright gem from a turbulent century. Taken from his home at the age of sixteen 'with so many thousands', Patrick endured the life of a slave in Ireland for six years, herding his master's sheep. In his early twenties, inspired by a vision, he ran away and found passage on a ship, which sailed for three days

---

* Simms-Williams 1983; see also Chapter 10.
† Regnal lists, like those found in the Nennian compilation, comprise formulae such as 'Freodwald [son of Ida] reigned six years and in his time the kingdom of the Kentishmen received baptism, from the mission of Gregory. Hussa reigned seven years.' *Historia Brittonum* 63. Morris 1980, 37.

before making landfall. It seems that Patrick travelled with a large number of companions, but he is silent on the ship's destination and on the purpose of the voyage. Were the captains of such ships, like modern-day people traffickers, carrying escaped slaves across the Irish Sea in return for what money they could raise, then landing them on a deserted shore – no questions asked? One way or another, Patrick and his companions were landed in a wilderness through which they wandered for a month without finding human habitation, surviving only because they came across a hive full of honey and a herd of wild pigs, which they slaughtered. At some later period in his life Patrick was taken prisoner for a second time, but was 'delivered' from captivity after two months.

There is no way of knowing where he landed after his first sea voyage. Three days' sailing from, shall we say, Strangford Lough,* might take one as far north as Argyll or as far south as Wexford on the Irish coast or Pembrokeshire on the Welsh coast. Much has been made of internal textual hints that Patrick spent some years in Gaul, perhaps visiting and being trained for the priesthood at Tours; but that is to stretch his own testimony beyond what it will credibly bear.

After 'a few years' Patrick was able to return to his family. This is remarkable: how on Earth was a young man, stolen from his home at sixteen, able to navigate his way back in a country with no maps or road signs and not much more than local knowledge of place names? In the end, another vision drew him back to Ireland and precipitated his long, sometimes troubled career as a bishop there. Patrick's heart-on-sleeve defence of his time among the Irish might easily be placed during the generation of relative calm described by Gildas after the Irish Pictish raiding died down. But Patrick's writings and career cannot be dated to other than

---

* The geography of Patrick's enslavement is totally obscure; later tradition associates him with Armagh and Downpatrick in the south-east of what is now Northern Ireland. Such a geography would be consistent with a birthplace for Patrick close to the northern Roman frontier; and with direct raiding across the Irish Sea.

very broad decades across the fifth century. Like Gildas, he was concerned to admonish kings and fellow clerics for their failings. Unlike Gildas, he was not classically educated – his Latin was, by his own testimony, uncultured. The backdrop to his life is a landscape in which arbitrary violence, extreme wealth and poverty, kindness and cruelty are shadowed by a functioning, literate institutional church capable of conducting business with daughter churches across the Irish Sea. If Patrick has nothing to say about grand events further south and east, one can at least say that embracing these apparent paradoxes may be the key to unlocking the mysteries of the fifth century.

There is no more challenging, intractable or tantalizing source for this period than the ninth-century text often known by the name Nennius.* The standard manuscript text,† which survives in copies no earlier than the twelfth century, contains the *Historia Brittonum*; a set of useful genealogies; a very brief but possibly significant Chronography; a list of twenty-eight 'cities'; the 'Wonders of Britain, Mona and Ireland' and the *Annales Cambriae*, or Welsh Annals.[18] None of these is either straightforward or trustworthy. The earliest time at which the author might have collected these disparate and contradictory fragments together is the first half of the ninth century, perhaps fifty years before the *Anglo-Saxon Chronicle* and in a similar, if opposed, climate of nationalist wish fulfilment.

In fleshing out Gildas's vague political narrative of the fifth century the *Historia Brittonum* looks, on the face of it, like a gold mine. Gildas's 'proud tyrant' is given a name: Vortigern (*Guorthigirnus*).‡ The three keels in which the Saxon federates arrived have two named commanders: Hengest and Horsa. They land on the shores of eastern Kent as exiles and are given the island 'that

---

* From the autographed preface to later editions.
† British Library Harleian MS 3859.
‡ The association had already been made by Bede in 731 (*HE* I.14). 'Vortigern' might be a direct translation of an office: high king, or indeed *superbus tyrannus*.

in their language is called Thanet, in British *Ruoihm*'.[19] Up until the medieval period Thanet was an island, separated from the Kentish mainland by the Wantsum Channel – now no more than a modest burn over whose bridges cars pass without a thought.*
At either end of this navigable channel stood a major Roman fort: *Rutupiae* (Richborough) at the south-east end and *Regulbium* (Reculver) on the north coast, overlooking and guarding the mouth of the Thames Estuary. If one accepts the broad historicity of the account in the *Historia Brittonum*, it points to a force of seaborne Continentals guarding the entrance to the Thames and protecting cross-Channel trade destined for Canterbury and the other Kentish ports. That they were stationed in semi-isolation on their own, circumscribed, plot of land strikes a credible note.

The *Historia Brittonum* is explicit that the deal promised by Vortigern was to provide food and clothing (equivalents of Gildas's *epimenia*) in return for protection against his enemies. Then, the compiler says, another sixteen ships arrived as reinforcements. The rider to this extended contract, cast in the light of a tale of intoxication, extortion and trickery, was that Vortigern should be given Hengest's daughter and that, in return, Hengest should be given the whole of the country called *Canturguoralen* – that is, the lands of the *Cantiaci* (Kent), tacitly deposing its king, Gwyrangon. A third deal was also struck between the two men: Hengest's son and his cousin, Octha and Ebissa, were to bring a force of forty ships to Britain to be stationed 'in the north about the Wall' to fight against the Irish.[20]

After a legendary interlude set in Snowdonia, the *Historia Brittonum* reports a war between Vortigern's son, Vortimer, and the Saxon federates. The Saxons were expelled to Thanet and besieged there, whence they sent to their homelands for further reinforcements, precipitating the wars that followed. The *Historia Brittonum* lists three battles: on the River Darent (which flows

---

* Today's Wantsum flows north; the southern part of the channel is now the outflow of the River Stour, which executes a smart U-turn at Sandwich and enters the sea at Pegwell Bay.

north into the Thames at Dartford); at Rhyd yr afael (called Episford in 'their' – i.e. the English – language), a conflict in which Horsa and Vortigern's son Cateyrn both died; and a third in open country, by an inscribed stone on the shore of the Gallic Sea (the Channel), in which Vortimer defeated the Saxons. A fourth battle said to have taken place is not described.[21]

After Vortimer died, the two sides negotiated a peace in which Vortigern was said to have been coerced into ceding several districts (*regiones plurimae*), namely *Est Saxum* and *Sut Saxum* (Essex and Sussex).[22] A brief but important entry, detached from the main body of this narrative and known as the Chronography,[23] counts twelve years from the beginning of Vortigern's reign to a quarrel between Vitalinus and Ambrosius – 'that is, Wallop, the Battle of Wallop (*Catguoloph*)'. The Chronography also gives the year of the Saxon arrival as the fourth of Vortigern's rule, which began in the year of the consulship of Theodosius and Valentinian – 425 – so dating their arrival to a year before Germanus's first visit and the Battle of Wallop to 437, roughly the date of his second visit. The battle at Wallop would, on that reckoning, have taken place eighteen years before the first battle recorded by *the Anglo-Saxon Chronicle*, in 455. Again, the chronological framework for conflict is the 430s – a decade before the traditional *adventus Saxonum* of Bede and the Continental chroniclers and at a time when Roman imperial forces were enjoying success in northern Gaul. Those successes might be seen as prompting warband leaders to look overseas for new opportunities.

It is obvious that the shape of the Nennian narrative parallels, perhaps copies, that of Gildas: a deal struck between a British council and a federate force; its failure through perfidy or accident; the resulting war. The Nennian compiler had access to Gildas's account and so his apparent corroboration of the role of Ambrosius in a civil war, echoed in the legendary Snowdonian tale of Emrys (the Brythonic form of Ambrosius), cannot itself be read as an independent corroboration.[24] The Chronography, which seems to frame the initial phase of the conflict in the 420s and 430s, looks to have been derived from an annal recorded using consular

years so it may have independent value.* To some extent, the
incongruity between the Nennian battles and those of the *Anglo-
Saxon Chronicle* is suggestive of independent strands of tradition
– victories for either side being remembered at different times and
with different names. But, as historians have often pointed out,
names like Vortigern (perhaps a direct Brythonic translation of
Gildas's *superbus tyrannus*), Hengest (Old English 'stallion') and
Horsa ('horse') do not inspire confidence that these are much more
than legendary figures.

Section 56 of the *Historia* has been flogged to death over the
years. It tells how 'at that time' the English grew in number; Octha
came south from the Wall after the death of his father, Hengest,
and sired future generations of Kentish kings. And then, enter
Arthur who, alongside the kings of the British, fought against
them as leader in battle (*dux bellorum*). There follows a list of
twelve engagements:

> The first battle was at the mouth of the river called Glein. The
> second, the third, the fourth and the fifth were on another river,
> called the Douglas, which is in the country of ?Lindsey [in
> *regione linnuis*]. The sixth battle was on the river called Bassas.
> The seventh battle was in Celyddon Forest, that is, the Battle
> of Celyddon Coed. The eighth battle was in Guinnion fort, and
> in it Arthur carried the image of the holy Mary, the everlasting
> Virgin, on his ?shield/shoulder and the heathen were put to
> flight on that day, and there was a great slaughter upon them,
> through the power of Our Lord Jesus Christ and the power of
> the Holy Virgin Mary, his mother. The ninth battle was fought
> in the City of the Legion. The tenth battle was fought on the
> bank of the river called Tryfrwyd. The eleventh battle was on
> the hill called Agned. The twelfth battle was on Badon Hill and
> in it nine hundred and sixty men fell in one day, from a single
> charge of Arthur's, and no one laid them low save he alone;
> and he was victorious in all his campaigns.[25]

* See Chapter 6, p. 200.

Most of these battles are located on rivers with Brythonic names that cannot now be securely identified; nor can the hill called Agned. One was fought in a forest that should be located in Scotland (*Celidon*, as in Caledonia); one in a former Roman town (perhaps Caerleon; possibly Chester) and another in an unidentified fortress. The last battle is located on Badon Hill (dated to 516 in the *Annales Cambriae*), providing an apparently neat cross reference with Gildas. Another entry in the *Annales Cambriae,* under 537, records Arthur's death in a battle at Camlann (possibly *Camboglanna*, a fort west of Birdoswald on Hadrian's Wall). Suddenly, 100 years have elapsed since the conflict between Ambrosius and Vitalinus; something is seriously amiss. Like the traditional dating of Gildas's letter – which frames both his life and the chronology of the wars – the Nennian events are stretched over an uncomfortably long period. Nothing adds up.

It would be superfluous to add to the mountain of literature that picks over the very thin fare served up by the *Nennian* texts and traces the origin and development of the Arthurian mythology that it has attracted ever since.[26] However garbled the truth, two parallel sets of myths were perpetuated by communities who identified themselves with a 'British' or 'Saxon' heritage and for whom, by the eighth and ninth centuries, national identity was a potent political touchstone.

Despite the efforts of many historians and archaeologists and an army of speculators, the careers of a tangible Arthur, Ambrosius, Vortigern and the rest of this cast of fifth-century antagonists still lie out of reach. The most that can be said is that if there was no Arthur, there were probably Arthurs: those who, assuming or being appointed to Roman-style commands of infantry or mounted warriors, were deployed to protect towns and trade and the interests of the contemporary ruling élite. The same loose interpretation must suffice for the leaders of perhaps dozens of bands of federate troops or pirates crossing from the Continent in that century, and for the politicians whose judgements and policies towards them were vilified by later generations. That is not to say that no more useful information can be mined from

Gildas, Patrick or the Nennian texts – they contain other precious nuggets.

An obsession with identifying the sites of putative Early Medieval battle sites – a mug's game if ever there was one – has diverted attention from the solidly real landscapes in which fifth-century communities lived and sometimes fought. Gildas's wistful portrait of the countryside of his day is slowly coming into sharper focus. Seen, in the mind's eye, from the basket of a hot-air balloon, fields, woods and hamlets are busy with people. Most are going about their daily business, largely oblivious to the great games played by their leaders and acting out parts ordained long ago by the necessities of the farming year and the ever-turning cycles of birth and death. Many are still ploughing fields first laid out during the Iron Age and in the Roman period. Others are turning the soil in new furrows, but perhaps in sight of their grandparents' homesteads. Settlements are smaller and more mobile than those of the Roman period, less tied to central markets and the impositions of imperial tax gatherers. Land is less intensively managed. Lordship is weak. And there are signs of conflict. Competition and opportunity bring mixed fortunes to those enslaved by poverty, crime or kidnap, and to those made wealthy by that ancient trade. Other precious commodities – salt, bullion, cattle, exotic imports of oil and wine – are worth fighting for. Those who would rule their neighbours find means to enforce their demands.

Thousands of fifth- and sixth-century men were buried with weapons – spears, shields and short swords or battle knives. No citizen of Roman Britain would have been buried with equipment; few, outside the professional military, would have owned such things. Many of these new weapon bearers were buried alongside women and children – their families – in new cemeteries close to settlements like Mucking and West Stow, where novel forms of building and village layout were once thought to tell of incomers. Others were interred beneath ancient burial mounds seeming, in some sense, to tap into older martial and ancestral traditions. The thought that identities were under threat from real or perceived conflict is echoed in the apparent re-occupation of Iron Age hillforts – reminiscent of Gildas's image of citizens fleeing into the mountains – particularly in the south-western counties of England and in Wales. Inside the massive Iron Age ramparts of South Cadbury in Somerset, the focus of celebrated excavations by Leslie Alcock in the 1960s, a great timber hall was built inside refurbished defences during the fifth or sixth century.[27] At Dinas Emrys, a rocky knoll on the southern slopes of the Snowdon massif, structures that might tell of Vortigern's legendary conflict with Emrys (Ambrosius) have been excavated.[28] Further south, overlooking the Severn estuary from the north, Dinas Powys is a very modestly sized hilltop enclosure, occupied for the first time in this period, where signs of lordly feasting and acquisition have been found in excavation. At Congresbury, close to the opposite shore in Somerset, archaeology has revealed a re-occupation of the Iron Age hillfort by people who were able, like their counterparts at Dinas Powys, to import fine luxury goods from the eastern

Tintagel: rocky promontory on the north Cornish coast: a site of importation for Mediterranean goods and probable centre of Early Medieval kingship.

Mediterranean at a time when *Britannia* had fallen off Rome's own radar.[29] Tintagel, the magnificent, naturally defended rocky promontory on the north Cornish coast, is heaving with the debris of such trade and with buildings that tell of wealth and power enduring on that site across the centuries. Beyond the edge of empire, fortress sites on the Kirkcudbright coast, in East Lothian, Strathclyde, Moray and Argyll, evoke ideas of Iron Age tribalism, much debated in the scholarly literature.

These naturally defended hilltop sites, whose dramatic physical presence and mythological trappings are manna for any passing airborne archaeologist, hint at political and social tensions that are even more dramatically chiselled onto the landscape by the great, enigmatic earthen dykes that belong to the centuries after Rome's province cut itself adrift. From Wansdyke, striding across Wiltshire's downs, to the Fleam Dyke of Cambridgeshire, apparently built to block the lines of prehistoric trackways and a Roman road between East Anglia and the south-east Midlands; to Wat's Dyke in the Northern marches, which prefigures the monumental eighth-century frontier of King Offa, and others scattered across the former province, it is hard to avoid a sense of co-operative, or coercive, military effort expressed in new or revived ideas about martial display. It is, or will be, possible to date some of these earthworks, especially with new thermoluminescence techniques becoming available that allow archaeologists to tell how long soil horizons have been buried.

Beneath the imposing ramparts of the medieval castle at Richmond, in North Yorkshire, the wild waters of the River Swale have carved a gorge through solid bedrock, and here they cascade down a spectacular natural staircase. In winter spate the river's roar is deafening: a positive cataract. The Swale flows east, then south to join another Pennine river, the Ure, at Boroughbridge. But downstream of Richmond, as it breaks out into the Vale of Mowbray, it is a tamer affair. Close to the village of Brompton-on-Swale it passes benignly beneath the streamlined dual carriageway of the A1 and flows past the village of Catterick.

Catterick was *Cataractonium*, a walled Roman town on Dere

Street, the road that ran north from York via the *civitas* capital of the Brigantes at *Isurium* (Aldborough) towards Corbridge in the north and Carlisle in the northwest. The town that guarded this important crossing, lying between road and river, seems to have been named after the waterfalls at Richmond, for there is no white water here. Like many other Roman towns positioned at key crossings of strategic routes, Catterick has yielded evidence of significant activity during the fifth and sixth centuries – including *grubenhäuser* and what appear to be 'warrior' burials.[30] Some time towards the end of the sixth century a great battle was fought here, celebrated in Aneirin's British poem *Y Gododdin*, which tells of a last, heroic but tragically fateful campaign by the *Gwyr y Gogledd*, the Men of the North, to oust the Anglian kings of Northumbria.[31] In the seventh century the Roman missionary and bishop Paulinus is said, by Bede, to have baptized many Christians in the purifying waters of the Swale.[32] In later decades it became a kingly residence and, later still, the location for royal marriages.[33] Catterick seems to look north and east towards the fertile valley of the Tees and the North Sea more than it does to the hinterland of York and the Brigantian heartlands further south and west. Higher up the valley from Richmond, in Swaledale proper, a series of enigmatic earthworks seems designed to block access from Catterick to a route across the Pennines. This is a landscape of conflict and ambiguity.

Large-scale earthworks are often described as defensive – that is, they are perceived as having been built to keep out hostile groups of armed people. Realistically, not many earthworks function like that. Invaders tend to go around them or over them if they want to. Most linear earthworks function in complex ways that have little to do with fortification. They are predominantly displays of prestige and power, like the grandiose walls and gates of country parks. Even the massive ramparts of the great Iron Age hillforts say much more about display than they do about direct military threat. In an unmistakeable code they signal exclusivity, separation and the power to control labour. An earthwork might also function as an expression of a bilateral treaty: the mutual recognition of a frontier (although rivers take the lead role in boundary forming). Prehistoric Britain was full of boundaries: many of them modest streams, some formed by lines of burial mounds marking watersheds, others by rows of pits or modest stone and earth banks. In most cases their purpose was probably to mark and reinforce rights to pasturage, accompanied by injunctions to herders like St Patrick and St Cuthbert not to cross them or else. Some dykes were evidently unilateral statements – an unequivocal message to keep out – but more effective psychologically and, perhaps, legally than physically.

As material barriers, many of the larger linear earthworks of the Early Medieval landscape functioned most effectively to control the movement of livestock. Small armies might ignore a ditch and bank or climb over or around it; cattle and sheep are much less inclined to scale something as massive as the Wansdyke, especially if they are being herded at speed by a raiding party; and cattle were the currency of tribute, of portable wealth and theft in these centuries. Pictish raiders may have sailed around Hadrian's Wall; but to take any four-legged booty home with them they needed to find a gate, and an open gate at that.

In several parts of Britain what look like coherent systems of Early Medieval earthworks have survived into the modern landscape. Andrew Fleming, the archaeologist who has made a special study of Swaledale's dykes, has shown that the linear earthworks strung out across the dale near the villages of Reeth and Muker are sealed, as it were, beneath a more familiar and much more recent rectangular pattern of drystone walls, barns and green sheep pasture that characterizes this country. He believes that they reflect territorial tensions between rival groups in the post-Roman centuries.[34] This landscape had already been cleared of rough stones and laid out in rectangular parcels, perpendicular to the line of the river, as long ago as the middle Iron Age, perhaps in the third century BCE.[35] It was a land in which, like the pastures of Salisbury Plain, the Yorkshire Wolds and the Cheviot Hills, farming revolved around livestock management: wintering cattle and sheep close to valley farms; manuring their small fields; driving herds and flocks up into improved pastures in spring and onto higher, rough moorland pastures in summer. In this integrated system, whose now fragmentary low walls form a distinctive co-axial plan from above, Romano-British farmsteads maintained the traditional economy and a high density of population through the centuries of provincial rule.

In Swaledale, three sets of substantial dykes stand out from both the prehistoric/Romano-British field systems and those of medieval and later date. One blocks the narrow flood plain of the Swale and its tributary, the Arkle Beck, above Reeth. A second blocks the valley at the point where these two rivers meet, just below Reeth, close to the villages of Grinton and Fremington. A third survives only on the south side of the Swale at Marrick, some 2.5 miles downstream. Each was constructed at right angles to the river and with a ditch on the east – downstream – side of the bank. In other words, the message is addressed by people in upper Swaledale to those who would advance from the east – from Richmond and Catterick.

Fleming has demonstrated the likelihood that these dykes are later than recognizably Romano-British settlements (at Dykehouse Close) and earlier than the establishment of the Anglo-Saxon place names of Grinton and Fremington. He believes that the early name of the valley, *Swar* – from *Swalwe*: Old English for 'rushing water, whirlpool' – is an equivalent of the Latin *Cataractona* which stood for both river and Roman town. *Swar* was, he suggests, the Anglian name given to a small polity – a petty kingdom – of upper Swaledale, whose extent he has mapped by back-calculating from medieval documents and boundaries.* An earlier, Brythonic identity for this territory seems to be indicated by *yr Erechwydd*, a name that survives in poetry attributed to a celebrated Welsh bard, Taliesin, and which carries the same meaning again: of

---

* It has been pointed out to me that more recent study has cast serious doubt on Fleming's interpretation of 'Swar', and on the date of some of the Swaledale earthworks. See http://www.swaledalemuseum.org/swaledale-reviews-the-first-kingdom-max-adams.html

waterfalls or rushing waters. The distinguished Taliesin scholar Sir Ifor Williams believed that the legendary warlord Urien, described in an elegy as *Udd yr Erechwydd*, Lord of Erechwydd or Rheged, is a precise counterpart to the *Llyw Catraeth* of the battle poem *Y Gododdin*.[36] If it has any historical credibility, this poem tells of conflicts in the late sixth century; nevertheless, it shows how careful archaeological fieldwork might combine with historical analysis to identify landscapes where post-Roman conflict – the wars remembered by Gildas's generation – left its mark; and that some of these might be hiding in plain view. Whether or not they can be used to construct a kingly narrative of ethnic rivalry and blood feud is quite another matter.

Such evidence is not confined to the less intensively developed landscapes of the north and west. Between the Fenland edge at Cambridge and the scarp that forms the north-west edge of Essex a series of dykes survives that seems designed to control, or prevent, access between East Anglia and the Chiltern heartlands, some time between the late fourth and sixth centuries.[37] This narrow strip, perhaps formerly the northern border of the *Trinovantes*, was successively interrupted at right angles by the Bran Ditch, the Brent Ditch (which blocks the Roman road running north-east from the small Roman town at Great Chesterford), the Fleam Dyke and the highly impressive, dead-straight Grim's Dyke. They appear, also, to have blocked passage along a series of prehistoric trackways, including the Icknield Way. Like the linear earthworks of Swaledale, they proclaim bold political and strategic statements whose immediate historical context can only be guessed at, but which must express regional political tensions.*

The scale of these earthworks offers some indication of political control and capability. Wat's Dyke runs south from the Dee estuary to Shropshire for some 25 miles, even if it is much less physically impressive than its famous neighbour. The Wansdykes of the south-west, two discrete (but by no means discreet) earthworks that may belong to a single grandiose scheme, are massive in all respects.

* See Chapter 6.

Wansdyke, looking west along the crest of Tan Hill
near Avebury, Wiltshire.

The east section runs for 13 miles along a high chalk ridge looking south across the Vale of Pewsey. The great prehistoric monuments of the Kennet valley – Avebury and Silbury Hill – lie in prominent view to the north from the breast of the earthwork. At its most impressive the bank and ditch together create a formidable 100 ft-wide, 23 ft-high barrier. West Wansdyke runs for some 9 miles, shadowing the Somerset Avon south and west of Bath before crossing – blocking or controlling – the Fosse Way at right angles. The dykes, then, speak to both local and regional landscapes and politics; to peoples whose sense of identity and security may, as in so many other periods, have been defined as much by who they were not as who they thought themselves to be.

Any study of the great and small linear earthworks of the British landscape must reach beyond ideas of conflict and chronology to consider the labour and organization involved in their construction. Such joint enterprises must have grown out of a sense of place, of belonging and ownership. They involved coercion – slaves or defeated enemies – or payment as well as codes of obligation and shared purpose. Above all, the land must have yielded sufficient surplus produce that the workforce could be spared from the everyday toil of farm and field. Unless they were constructed entirely by captives from war (and that is not impossible), one has to imagine the inhabitants of settlements like West Stow, Mucking and West Heslerton leaving their homes for weeks at a time, spade or hoe in hand, either willingly or unwillingly. Later testimony, from the trials and toils faced by Ælfred in the ninth century when confronted with a sustained and determined Viking threat, shows how reluctantly people embraced public obligations; how dishonoured they were by the imposition. The institutional mechanisms that allowed and fostered the refurbishment of hillfort defences and crumbling town walls, the construction of the dyke systems and the patching of Roman roads and bridges, evolved or re-emerged during the fifth century. To understand and reconstruct those mechanisms is to explore the anthropology of lordship: of hall and hearth, of kinship and obligation; of weaving loom, mead cup, spear and shield.

Chronography I: 350–500

AC	*Annales Cambriae.* Morris 1980.
Adomnán *VC*	*Vita Sancti Colombae.* Sharpe 1995.
Ammianus *RG*	*Res Gestae.* Hamilton 1996.
ASC	*Anglo-Saxon Chronicle.* Garmonsway 1972.
AT	*Annals of Tigernach.* Online edition.
AU	*Annals of Ulster.* Online edition.
Bede *HE*	*Historia Ecclesiastica Gentis Anglorum.* Colgrave and Mynors 1994.
CG 452	*Chronica Gallica of 452.* Online edition.
Constantius *VG*	*Vita Germani.* Hoare 1954.
Eddius *VW*	*Vita Wilfridi.* Colgrave 1985.
ELGG	*The Earliest Life of Gregory the Great,* by an anonymous monk of Whitby. Colgrave 1968.
Felix *VG*	*Vita Guthlaci.* Colgrave 1985.
Gildas	*De Excidio.* Winterbottom 1978.
Gregory *HF*	*Historia Francorum* or *Decem Libri Historiarum.* Thorpe 1974.
HSC	*Historia De Sancto Cuthberto.* South 2002.
LGG	*Letters of Gregory the Great.* Schaff and Wace 1895.
Nennius *HB*	*Historia Brittonum.* Morris 1980.
Orosius	*Seven Books of History Against the Pagans.* Fear 2010.
Patrick	*Confessio.* Hood 1978.
Procopius *BG*	*Bellum Gothicum.* Dewing 1914–40.

Prosper *EC*	*Epitoma Chronicon*. Mommsen 1892.
VS	*Vita I Sancti Samsonis*. Taylor 1925.
Zosimus *HN*	*Historia Nova*. Buchanan and Davis 1967.

350	Magnentius usurps imperial crown (to 353); provinces that support him include Britain. Emperor Constans killed by cavalry unit near the Pyrenees; his brother Constantius II succeeds as sole emperor (to 361).
351	Magnentius engages Constantius II in battle at *Mursa Major* (Croatia); he is defeated in one of the bloodiest battles in Roman history.
353–354	Under Constantius II, Paulus 'The Chain', an imperial agent/notary/inquisitor, is reputed to have carried out savage reprisals against the propertied class in Britain, after the fall of Magnentius (Ammianus *RG*); Flavius Martinus, *vicarius* of *Britannia*, commits suicide; more accountants sent to investigate widespread abuses in the province.
359	Julian 'the Apostate' opens Lower Rhine to imports of British corn (Zosimus *HN*) and builds fleet of 600 ships to carry it across. British bishops attend Council of Ariminum (Rimini) convened by Constantius II, but three of them need subsidizing from public funds.
360	Picts and Scotti attack northern frontier. Julian sends reinforcements to Britain. Christianity is now widespread across Britain, but there is a two-year official apostasy under Julian (361–363).
367	The so-called Barbarian Conspiracy, in which tribes north of the Wall overrun it with connivance of garrisons. Army deserters and runaway slaves maraud through countryside (Ammianus *RG*).
368	Count Theodosius sent to Britain: recaptures London; restores order and re-establishes forts. Meets marauding bands between London and Richborough.

369	Theodosius routs invaders (possibly from the Rhine delta), and begins refortifying northern frontier. No Roman troops now stationed north of the Wall. Watch and signal towers between Filey and Huntcliffe on Yorkshire coast probably built at this time.
371	Martin made Bishop of Tours. Founds abbey and monastery a year later.
372	Valentinian I sends contingent of Alamanni to Britain under Alamannic king Macrianus (Ammianus *RG*).
375	Valentinian I dies and is succeeded by Valens, Gratian and Valentinian II as joint emperors.
*c.*375(–80)	British cleric Pelagius departs for Rome.
379	Theodosius I (the Great) succeeds Valens in the East (from 379) and Honorius (from 392) in the West. Last emperor to rule both halves of the empire (to 395).
380	Magnus Maximus, Spanish former officer under Count Theodosius, assigned to Britain. — Edict of Thessalonica: Theodosius I (son of Count Theodosius) orders Christianity to be the imperial state religion.
381–384	Pilgrimage of Gallic woman Egeria to the Holy Places; her journal survives partially as the *Itinerarium Egeriae*.
382/3	Magnus Maximus defeats armies of Picts and Scots (*CG 452*).
383	Magnus Maximus, commander in Britain, usurps throne from Emperor Gratian (375–383); crosses to Gaul with elements of British army. Gratian killed at Lyon or Belgrade. Magnus Maximus crosses into Italy and is confronted with army sent by Theodosius I.
384	By agreement with Theodosius I, Magnus Maximus is made emperor in Britain and Gaul. Rules from Trier in Gaul. — St Jerome has by now probably completed the textual revision of the Bible known as the Vulgate.
388	Theodosius marches on Italy with Valentinian II; defeats Magnus Maximus at Save (in what is now

Croatia). Maximus retreats to Aquileia where he is captured and executed.

389–390   Emperor Theodosius I enters Rome: the first emperor to do so since Constantius in 357; sends expedition against the Picts. 'First Pictish war'.

c.391   Theodosius closes all temples in the empire and bans pagan cults, by decree.

395   Emperor Theodosius dies. His sons Honorius (in the West, to 423) and Arcadius (in the East, to 408) succeed. The Vandal General Stilicho is effective military regent in West.

c.396   Victricius, Bishop of Rouen, visits Britain to intervene in episcopal dispute, possibly against Pelagianism.

397   Death of St Martin of Tours, according to Sulpicius Severus.

396–398   Stilicho ordered by Emperor Honorius to send expeditionary fleet against Picts and Scots; defeats seaborne forces of Saxons and Scots. Picts defeated (on land?) in the Second Pictish War (from Stilicho's court poet Claudian).

c.400   Marine inundation of Thames estuary; other similar floods occur later in Fens and elsewhere.

401   Stilicho withdraws a legion from Britain to fight against Alaric's Goths in Italy. Yorkshire coastal watchtowers abandoned.

402   Last issue of Roman coins to be found in Britain in substantial quantities, probably reflecting a breakdown in imperial payment mechanisms. This is a possible trigger for the disbanding of regular armies.

403   Rome mint strikes *VRBS ROMA FELIX* coin. Does not reach Britain in meaningful quantities.

405   Irish warlord Niall of the Nine Hostages raids southern coast of Britain.

— Vandals, Suevi and Alans invade Gaul, crossing the frozen Rhine on the last day of the year (or 406) (Prosper *EC*).

406 or after   Army in Britain revolts and proclaims Marcus emperor; then murders him and elevates Gratian (who may be British, acc. Mattingly); four months later the army murders Gratian in turn and raises Constantine 'III'.

— Rebellion of Constantine 'III' in Britain.

407   Constantine 'III' crosses to Gaul with British forces (Zosimus *HN*). Takes Gallic prefecture; takes Spain.

408–409   Constantine 'III' recognized as co-emperor by Honorius.

— Army in Britain rebels against Constantine 'III'; ?Britons expel Roman administration (Zosimus *HN*).

410   Emperor Honorius warns British *civitates* to look to their own defences.

— Britain is devastated by Saxon incursions (*Chronica Gallica* of 452). British take up arms against barbarians and defend themselves (Zosimus *HN*).

— Rome sacked by the Gothic king Alaric.

411   Death of Constantine 'III' in the Siege of Arles; Rome regains control over Gaul but is unable to recover Britain (Procopius *BG*).

— At a conference in Carthage Honorius condemns Pelagianism as heresy.

413   'At this time, Pelagius, a Briton, asserted with his supporters Caelestius and Julian [of Eclanum] the dogma named after him, which attacked the grace of Christ. He won many people over to this heretical opinion' (Prosper *EC*).

415   Possible approximate date for birth of St Patrick.

418   Council of Carthage condemns Pelagianism.

423   Death of Emperor Honorius: he is succeeded by his nephew Valentinian III, son of Constantius 'III' and Gallia Placidia, daughter of Theodosius I (to 455).

425   Vortigern comes to power in Britain (Nennius *Chronography*).

428 Invitation to Saxons under legendary commander Hengest in their three 'keels' (Nennius *HB*).

— The Roman general Aëtius regains parts of the Rhineland from Franks (Prosper *EC*).

429 Germanus of Auxerre visits Britain to help put down Pelagian heresy propagated by Agricola (Prosper *EC*). He becomes ad hoc commander in field against sudden combined Saxon/Pictish attack in so-called Alleluia victory (Constantius *VG*).

— Aëtius becomes *magister militum*.

430 Aëtius gains overwhelming control of Western provinces.

431 Date of Bishop Palladius's ministry to existing Christian communities in Ireland, sent by Pope Celestine I.

— Possible date for Patrick's abduction by pirates, who send him into slavery in Ireland.

430s Privateer operations of Octha and Ebissa against Picts and Scots in Northern waters (Nennius *HB*).

432 Patrick: supposed date of return to Ireland and the beginning of his ministry there (*AU*).

— Aëtius holds consulship for the first time.

433–4 Prosper records the expulsion of Pelagians from Britain.

— First record of assault by Saxons in Ireland (*AU*).

437 Battle of Wallop, as dated by Nennius's Chronographer (Nennius *HB*): British Civil War? The quarrel between Vitalinus and Ambrosius.

— Possible date of second visit to Britain by Germanus.

441/2 An entry in the *Chronica Gallica of 452* records that Britain is now ruled by Saxons.

446 Aëtius's third consulship. Supposed date (Bede *HE* and *ASC*) of the British authorities' letter to Aëtius/Agitius begging for help (but perhaps more credibly 432).

449	'Traditional' (i.e. calculated by Bede *HE* and the *ASC*) date of arrival of Hengest and Horsa in Kent; wars against Vortigern (but see 428–429).
450	Earliest possible date for siege of Badon Hill (*Mons Badonicus*) based on internal evidence from Gildas.
	— Large-scale emigration from Britain to Armorica cited by contemporary Gaulish chroniclers begins in this decade.
454	Possible birth date of St Brigit.
455	Hengest and Horsa fight 'Vortigern' at Ægelesthred (?Aylesford in Kent) (*ASC*) – possibly equivalent to second battle cited in Nennius *HB* at 'Episford'.
456	Hengest and Aesc fight Vortigern at *Creganford* (Crayford, Kent) (*ASC*), where they slay four companies; Britons flee to London: possibly equivalent to first battle cited in the *Historia Brittonum* (44) on River Darent (*Derguentid*).
458	Childeric, son of (semi-legendary) Merovech, becomes leader of Franks (rules to 481).
459	Possible date of Patrick's death; noted in the *AC* sub anno 458 as his 'passing', or 'going to the Lord'.
461	Mention of Mansuetus, 'Bishop of the Britons', in Continental church sources.
	—Aegidius proclaims creation of kingdom of Soissons
465	Hengest and Æsc fight against the Welsh at *Wippedesfleot* and slay twelve Welsh nobles; Thane Wipped is slain there (*ASC*): possibly equivalent to the third battle by Gallic Sea recorded in Nennius *HB*.
	— Death of Aegidius, Roman general in Gaul; ruler ('king') of Soissons from 461; formerly *magister militum per Gallias* under Aëtius. Succeeded by his son Syagrius, second and last king of Soissons.
470 or after	Floruit of Riothamus in Brittany, who receives a letter from Sidonius Apollinaris.
473	Hengest and Æsc fight the Welsh and capture innumerable spoils; the Welsh flee (*ASC*).

475 or after	Rough date for the beginning of post-Roman imports to south-west Britain and the Irish Sea from the Mediterranean via the Atlantic.
477	Traditional date of arrival in Sussex of Ælle and his three sons – Cymen, Wlencing ('Lancing') and Cissa ('Chichester'): they land in three ships at *Cymenesora* (near Selsey Bill) and fight the Britons (*ASC*), slaying many Welsh; others flee to *Andredesleg*.
*c.*480	Letter of Sidonius Apollinaris to his friend Admiral Namatius warning of the dangers of Saxon piracy.
480	Earliest plausible date for Gildas writing the *De Excidio*; possible date for composition of Patrick's *Confessio*.
481	Childeric, king of the Franks, dies; his son Clovis succeeds him as king (to 511).
485	Ælle fights the Welsh near the bank of the *Mearcredesburna* (*ASC*).
486	Battle of Soissons. Clovis defeats Syagrius, last Roman 'prefect' of northern Gaul and second king of Soissons.
488	Æsc succeeds to the kingdom (?of Kent) for thirty-four years.
491	*Andredesceaster* (Pevensey Saxon shore fort) besieged by Ælle and Cissa; all of its British inhabitants are slaughtered (*ASC*).
493	Possible date for death of St Patrick (*AU*).
495	Traditional date of Cerdic's and his son Cynric's arrival in Wessex in five ships at *Certicesora* (*ASC*; but 494 in the genealogical preface); they fight a battle against British forces.
?496	Battle of Tolbiac: Franks fight against the Alamanni; Clovis subsequently converts to the Catholic faith.

PART II

AFTER HISTORY

449. Marcianus and Valentinianus ruled as co-emperors for seven years. In their time the English came to Britain on the invitation of the Britons.

538. There was an eclipse of the sun on 16 February from six to eight in the morning.

547. Ida began to reign, from whom the Northumbrian royal family trace their origins. He reigned for twelve years.

BEDE, *Chronica Maiora*[1]

6

Private enterprise

Governors – households – the render – local power –
bucellari – big men, small ponds – women and lordship –
Sidonius Apollinaris – Gildas's tyrants – Rendlesham

MEMORIA VOTEPORIGIS PROTICTORIS
The memorial of Voteporigis, the Protector

Fifth- or sixth-century memorial stone from Castell Dwyran,
Carmarthenshire, Wales; with Latin and Ogham inscriptions.
Ogham is an Irish rendering of the Latin alphabet, scored in
vertical and diagonal strokes, generally onto the edges of stone
Christian memorials, with a distribution largely in Wales and
Ireland. Thomas 1971, 103 and 110.

Archaeologists excavating rural settlements of the fifth and sixth centuries are sensitive to signs of what one might call 'big men': the equivalents of later squires or lords of the manor, of Gildas's judges and watchmen, of Patrick's *decuriones*, and of the sort of people whom Bede would call *reges* and *principes* – kings and earls or dukes. At West Heslerton, Mucking, West Stow, Wasperton and their like, excavators have so far drawn a blank. These settlements were inhabited by people who lived in similar-sized houses to each other and were buried in household groups, with no signs of grand mausolea or princely burial chambers. Projecting the aisled halls and villas of the late Roman province, which tell of thriving rural lordship, into the century after, say, 450 is a tough ask. Archaeology has little to say of individuals like Vortigern, Hengest, Arthur or Ambrosius, although one might ascribe to them, as a governing class, the planning and execution of the linear earthworks. The re-occupied hillforts, with their displays of material wealth and specialized craft skills, hint at such figures in Wales, Scotland and the south-west, but there is nothing comparable in the central and eastern heartlands of the former province; no headquarters for these elusive lords in the lands of socially equal cemeteries and off-the-shelf houses. If they are hiding in plain view, then perhaps they are to be found in the refurbished town houses and 'public' buildings of *Britannia*'s 'failed' towns.

The immense social and economic gulf between emperor and slave narrowed after the end of the empire. The people of the fifth-century British countryside, especially in the east, seem to have got along without kings or the stupendously wealthy landlords of the third century. To be sure, there is a material disparity between richly and poorly furnished graves, but how far that reflects the spectrum of power and status enjoyed by people in life is not all that clear. People got by with little access to the material trappings of a major market economy. The sorts of private exclusivity displayed in villa and townhouse, preserves of the curial classes during the imperial centuries, are not seen in either settlements or cemeteries. The household, consisting of an extended family and probably a number of unfree dependants, was the fundamental, and seemingly universal, unit of social life. Inhumation burials, difficult as they are to read as social history, appear to reflect hierarchies within households, not between them: a world of masters, mistresses and servants rather than competing dynasties.[1] The largest cremation cemeteries hint more at a regional sense of community than at élitism.

On the other hand, there are signs that some sort of state governance functioned well into the middle decades of the fifth century – possibly longer. In the 430s, if not later, a governor of sorts – Gildas's *superbus tyrannus*, the *Historia Brittonum*'s Vortigern – was able to make significant policy decisions supported by councillors, likely representing each of the *civitates*. Germanus, in the same decade, identified and dealt with 'leading men' and officials of tribunician authority. In the West, perhaps at the very end of that century, Gildas wrote of Britain's governors, if not in flattering terms. He named five contemporary 'tyrants' whose writ ran in territories – generally identifiable as former *civitates* – that had not been overwhelmed by the disaster of the supposed Saxon takeover. The state that he knew supported an institutional, if dysfunctional, church. Both his and Patrick's careers testify to a Christian Latin education system. In Gildas's day, western Britain still had its judges (*rectores*); its watchmen (*speculatores*).[2] Here, competition for precious resources – cattle, sheep, slaves, salt, wood pasture – and a tradition of tribal leadership ensured the survival of petty kings and their rival dynasties.

Warfare, which Gildas believed to have been endemic in the province immediately before his own lifetime and periodically since, and which is attested in semi-legendary form in the annals, is predicated on the existence of a fighting élite, or militias, under the control of leaders – the Arthurs of the *Historia Brittonum* or the Ambrosiuses of Gildas and the Chronography. Where, then, is the material evidence for the sort of lordship promised by the historical sources? One might argue that a tiny, self-serving élite was an irrelevance in the lives of ordinary people; that such tyrants were peripheral. But each level of hierarchy and state apparatus had to be supported by some form of taxation; and taxation is relevant, sometimes overridingly so, to people. Who was obliged to cough up for the sort of centralized spending that enabled the recruitment of federate troops from overseas; that supplied workers' needs as they constructed mammoth earthwork frontiers; that kept leading men and bishops in style as they counselled and ruled? How, during the first half of the fifth century, with no functioning imperial machinery in *Britannia*, were these taxes and renders collected, and from whom? How and when did such a system evolve? If 'big men' were able to live off the surplus of farming communities in the fifth century, archaeologists ought to be able to find them. If the mechanism that drove the imposition and collection of renders can be reconstructed, we may be able to track the evolving social and political institutions of the Early Medieval kingdoms.

Even during the economic heyday of the second century, farms produced food and materials primarily for domestic consumption and taxation rather than for the market. After the collapse of the empire-driven coin-based economy, with its industrial output focused on supporting a military and patrician superstate underpinned by huge social and material inequalities, communities carried on subsistence farming: they got by. They may even have felt material relief from the end of swingeing state taxes. But if the world had shrunk, it was still connected. Regional trade in pottery, in specialized goods such as salt[3] and highly crafted art, particularly fine metalwork, continued while a rump state was maintained for a generation and more.

In the two decades leading up to Germanus's visit of about 429, and the supposed recruitment by the ruling council of federate troops, the internal supply of bullion – coin, family silver, stores of ingots – was probably sufficient to underpin state expenditure. Lower echelons of the social and political hierarchy fell back on an age-old system of food and labour dues drawn from tenants and dependants, sufficient to indulge themselves in politicking. To envisage such a system for the fifth century, in the absence of other evidence, is only to extend a trajectory already established under the later emperors. Underlying that system is a basic principle, called the *feorm* in Old English, *iugum** in Latin and the *treth* in Brythonic. Unlike coin, paid out from the imperial treasury in wages and taxed directly at markets, tax raised in kind and consisting primarily of consumable, perishable foods – ale, honey, meat and cheese – along with grain, wool, linen, underwood, timber and crafted items, could not be moved over great distances. Their production and consumption were, essentially, locally closed loops. The provision of direct services – carrying wood, hay and grain; fixing roofs; offering hospitality – was also organized locally. Two mechanisms functioned to link renders with lords: food renders must either be delivered personally – effectively within a day's, perhaps even half a day's, travel – or an itinerant landlord must consume or collect them where they were produced. Labour dues must be delivered directly, probably seasonally. The reforms of Diocletian (emperor from 284 to 305) had given legal force to the collection of taxes in kind from the provinces, rendered under local and regional administration, so there was no need to reinvent the rules in the fifth century.[4] All the evidence that alludes to such arrangements suggests that these renders were levied directly from the principal social unit: the household, with its workshops, compounds, fields, meadows and wood pastures.

The fort at *Banna* (Birdoswald) on Hadrian's Wall is, perhaps, the best place to catch sight of localized lordship in its early development.† The last army pay wagons cannot have arrived here much later than the 390s; the last visit by a *Dux Britanniarum* probably occurred in the same decade. *Banna*'s fifth-century commanders responded by expediently remodelling one of its former grain stores, turning it into a large residence where locally rendered supplies might also be stored, distributed, displayed and consumed.[5] The fort's second grain store, rebuilt in timber during the same period and maintained, perhaps, into the sixth century, looks for all the world like an incipient Early Medieval mead hall: the expression

---

* A term derived from the Latin word for 'yoke'.
† See Chapter 3.

of a re-forged relationship between a commander-cum-squire and his dependants. It seems as though, in the militarized zone along the Wall, new arrangements for protecting locals, maintaining discipline in the garrison and feeding the commander and his troops (along with their wives, children and collateral family members) were being established at a local level.

In some respect these relationships must have been adapted from the practices of tribes beyond the Wall where no centralized state held sway, and from existing customs maintained alongside more artificial imperial arrangements imposed along the military frontier. It is not possible to be certain over what period such changes occurred – whether they were dramatically sudden or generational. But adaptations to new realities probably began well before the end of the fourth century, as an increasingly debased coinage was worth less and less and army wages effectively declined in value. They continued well into the sixth century, when metal was worth its scrap or bullion value only and when livestock on the hoof became a principal unit of currency and long-distance tribute.

Even at the height of imperial expansion, Europe's economy had still been based on subsistence farming. As the economic historian Keith Hopkins has pointed out, peasants produced most of what they themselves consumed, and consumed most of what they produced.[6] The end of the money economy looks to archaeologists, probing the faded ruins of its heyday, much more disruptive and catastrophic than it probably was. The apparatus of the state, even of the *civitas*, seems to have survived fundamentally intact across the province into the 430s. But, by the end of that century, the political institutions of *civitas* and state in Britain may only have been patchily maintained, if at all; rather, power had devolved to the level of the fort, the town, the *pagus* or the estate. Over those four generations cumulative changes had dramatic effects; but their workings are like the darkly obscure contents of the black box of physics.

First principles apply here. Birdoswald's soldiers and their officers must eat; so must their wives and children. Farms had to remain productive; sheep must still be herded and fleeced, cows milked, ale brewed, yarn spun, clothes woven and stitched; grain sown, reaped, threshed, stored and milled into flour for bread and oats for porridge. Buildings, roads and bridges needed to be repaired, insofar as they were required to keep the fort functioning. Wood had to be regularly cut, from well-established and managed coppices, for fuel and construction. Tools, wheels, carts and wagons, weapons, harnesses and horseshoes must be kept in working order by smiths and farriers. Soldiers must continue to act as soldiers, going out on patrol; showing the flag, so to speak. Occasionally, when the harvest was poor or when the commander's table lacked meat, his soldiers probably went a-raiding, as their reiving successors would a millennium later.*

Local farmers and families enjoyed the garrison's protection from other, competing Wall garrisons and from tribal warbands to the north and across the Irish Sea (the sort that stole young men like Patrick from their homes). In return, those households maintained the Roman system of giving up a tenth of their annual surplus, and this was stored in the former granary.† Part of that render, especially in years blighted by a poor harvest or by cattle disease, might be supplemented or replaced by their labour – serving the commander's meals and working in his quarters; tilling his private fields, looking after his own small herd or flock; mending his fences or the roofs of the fort's buildings; perhaps fostering his children. His responsibilities, in turn, extended to judging local disputes – enforcing military law when necessary – and preventing small-scale conflicts from getting out of hand. Social bonds developed and were maintained between the garrison and the dependent farmers of its hinterland. Friendships and enmities between families were

---

* The Border reivers, acting very like tribal warbands with strong family affiliations (the so-called 'surnames'), dominated life on both sides of the Anglo-Scottish border for two centuries up to the beginning of the seventeenth century.

† See Chapter 10, p. 320, O'Brien (2002, 66), for seventh-century evidence of a 10 per cent tax in kind.

inherited by their children; favours were reciprocated; gifts and insults remembered; traditions, stories, songs and famous episodes in their lives pooled as a communal cultural legacy.

It is impossible to know how large *Banna*'s hinterland was; but the extent of the historic township in which Birdoswald lies may be instructive. Now called Waterhead, it consists of a parcel of land, bounded on the south side by the River Irthing, as far north as the stream called King Water and west as far as the Wall turret marked 52A on modern maps.* This gives an area of about 10 square miles, a large chunk of land that reflects the mixture of rough and improved pasture, woodland and a small amount of arable suitable for growing barley and oats. Only a dozen or so families farm the township at the present time. It is a country for hardy people and animals. By the middle of the fifth century the grapes, figs, apricots and almonds enjoyed by earlier generations in the garrison canteen must have been hard to come by.[7] Birdoswald's tax régime and its hinterland were, one suspects, flexible: they reached as far as they had to, to sustain the fort community in good and bad years.

At harvest time and in winter, when animals were slaughtered to save on feed, there must have been an abundance of meat and grain in good years, and a wise commander would invite his dependants into the hall inside the fort to share his hearth, tell stories of the farming year and of the old days, and feast on the fruits of the land: meat, ale and bread. The soldiers would bring their families in; three generations of a socially and economically interdependent community would consume and celebrate the fruits of their labour. And, if the soldiers cast aside their now idiosyncratic uniforms to relax and join in the family fun, their shields and weapons, hung on the walls of the hall and shining brilliantly in the firelight of autumn and winter, were a reminder

---

* Ordnance Survey maps at 1:25,000, the Explorer range, give admirable detail including existing township boundaries. The First Edition 6-inch series of the mid-nineteenth century provides the earliest comprehensive record of all local administrative boundaries.

that they sat as an élite under the leadership and patronage of the most powerful man in the district.

A smart commander might think to build up a surplus of grain in his hall, to distribute in lean years. A poor commander might find himself displaced. The archaeologist David Petts suggests that late Roman military commanders might have played twin roles: as both officers and gentlemen.[8] But these forms of male display – feasting, hospitality, grand wooden buildings, weaponry – are much less tangible than the imposing stone walls of the great towns or the showy private spaces afforded by villas. Women expressing a new sense of self-confident identity in their dress and hairstyles, perhaps also in their language and social vocabulary, are much less visible than those inscribing their names on church plate. Archaeologists must find their burials to read anything of their changed aspirations and inspirations; and the Wall forts have not so far yielded the bodies of commanders and their wives.*

If Birdoswald provides an outstanding example of the evolution of forts as centres of locally sustained power in the fifth century, there are other candidates for similar developments across the so-called militarized zone. Next to the major Roman fort of *Vinovia* (Binchester) in County Durham, close to a crossing of the River Wear along Dere Street,† a large extramural civilian settlement continued in use after 400.[9] The dominant activity in the areas excavated in recent seasons was large-scale processing of animal bones – strong evidence that the economy of the fort and settlement depended on goods acquired by render; that it had become the *vill* for its district. The periodic ceremonial consumption of harvest surplus in feasts – betrayed by characteristic finds of animals bones and fragments of drinking paraphernalia – is a vital

---

* None of the Wall fort cemeteries has been comprehensively excavated. Recent work at Birdoswald (*Current Archaeology* 353) has revealed a number of cremations, yet to be fully analysed; but none are likely to belong to the fifth century.

† 30 miles north of another Dere Street river crossing: the Swale at Catterick.

Dere Street, the Roman road heading dead straight and due south from the fort at Binchester towards Piercebridge, County Durham.

key to identifying the archaeology of lordship during the post-Roman centuries.

Small, self-sustaining territories based on military installations across the north may now be suggested at *Arbeia* (South Shields, close to the mouth of the River Tyne); at *Vindolanda* (along the Roman Stanegate road in the Tyne valley); at Catterick; and at *Magis* (Piercebridge in County Durham), where Dere Street crosses the River Tees.[10] Several of these, in addition to their potential for gathering surplus from a productive hinterland, enjoyed key strategic positions where the Roman road network coincided with the crossing of a major river. Such locations may have been advantageous for controlling, and therefore taxing, regional trade in valuable goods like salt and woollen cloth. In East Yorkshire, the Roman fort and settlement at *Derventio* (Malton) on the River Derwent is a good candidate for the development of a territorial centre into the caput or chief place of what later became the kingdom of Deira. It can now be argued that these military garrisons, although much diminished from their imperial heyday, were still relevant in the fifth century.

The bulk of *Britannia* south of the River Trent and east of the Severn possessed few working forts at the end of the fourth century. Several of those coastal fortresses that survive to such impressive heights along the Channel coast (so far, Portchester, Pevensey, Bradwell, Brancaster, Dover and Richborough)* have begun to yield signs of occupation after 400; but there is not yet enough evidence to characterize that occupation, let alone to people it with lords.[11]

Where else might archaeologists look for local centres of control and power? The towns of *Britannia* are widely held to have failed before or during the crisis of the 400s; but that is to measure their fortunes by the yardstick of Mediterranean urbanism – or by modern ideas of how towns should look and function. Buildings constructed and modified, the privatization of urban space and distinct traces of industrial activity in many of those towns indicate their continued, if modified, value in strange new times. The survival of an institutional church based in *civitas* capitals and smaller towns is suggested by the material wealth and confidence of Christian communities, by the direct evidence of Germanus's visit and by Patrick's testimony. The name of a British bishop, Mansuetus, is known from a document dating to 461.[12] Might such evidence also be read as an indication that some towns functioned as territorial centres of power in the fifth century, as lowland counterparts to the garrisons and hillforts of the west and north?

At the close of the previous century towns might have been civic shadows of their former selves; that does not mean that they had no functioning administration. Patrick's father held civic office. The councillors who advised Gildas's *superbus tyrannus* were recruited, surely, from the *civitas* élites of the province. From *Coria* (Corbridge) in the north to *Noviomagus reginorum* (Chichester) in the south we can identify about fifteen of these cantonal or *civitas*

---

* *Portus Adurni, Anderida, Othona, Branodunum, Dubris* and *Rutupiae*.

capitals. Adding to that number those *coloniae* that were not also centres of tribal authority – Colchester, Lincoln, Gloucester and York plus *Londinium*, the provincial capital – gives about twenty major centres of provincial, or tribal, power reaching as far east as *Venta Icenorum* (Norwich); as far west as *Moridunum* (Carmarthen) and as far south-west as *Isca Dumnoniorum* (Exeter). In the ninth-century Nennian compilation, twenty-eight 'cities' (*civitates*) are listed, perhaps indicating some fragmentation of the old regional cantons. It would be unsurprising if some of the leading families in each *civitas* sought to ally themselves with, or promote family candidates as Christian bishops, figures of secular and spiritual authority who maintained links with Rome, if not Ravenna, well into the fifth century. One might even suggest that some of the councillors who met to advise the *superbus tyrannus* were both bishops *and* senior figures among élite urban families – a twin role enjoyed by Germanus in Auxerre.

Any speculative portrait of the powerful families who held high office in the last decades of the empire sees them controlling the assets – both land and people – of valuable rural and urban estates. Their rights and responsibilities included tax gathering (from which they creamed a comfortable profit); rights in markets and the trade in minerals; judicial powers in criminal and civic law; representation at provincial councils; and perhaps, also, the authority to appoint or nominate bishops and to raise militias or recruit auxiliary units for defence. They are likely to have been responsible for the upkeep of roads, bridges and town defences, the labour for which was part of the *iugum*, the render.

Despite the political crisis threatening the province and the end of the cash economy in the first decades of the fifth century, it is hard to imagine that these families, the apex of a highly developed web of patronage and exploitation, gave up their status easily. They were forced to adapt. The conspicuous consumption so blatantly on show in the great villas was no longer sustainable, either materially or politically; likewise the construction of new town walls and grandiose mausolea, the importation of luxury goods in bulk from the Continent and the lavish patronage of elaborate Romano-Celtic temples and civic statuary. Like the fort commanders on the Wall they must collect dues from the general population, protect their assets – by force if necessary – and create, or re-create, social and political bonds with large numbers of dependants. They had also to compete for precious resources with other regional urban élites. In the larger towns this might have been a tougher trick to pull off than in the forts, where a system of military command and codes of martial behaviour were long ingrained. Archaeologists might, nevertheless, look for key signs of such behaviour.

The widespread occurrence of industrial activity in once-public town spaces has been read as evidence of 'squatter' activity; but it might make more sense as indicating the concentration of taxation in kind, as bullion in the form of lead piping, tools, cullet (scrap glass), coins and valuable family plate was delivered to a central place for conversion into new products. These newly crafted high-value items of display – brooches, weaponry, hanging bowls, beads and other adornments – became the currency and lubricant of Early Medieval patronage and political influence. The repurposing of town centres might also be seen as an expression of lordly control over the specialized craft skills of the smith; and the same might apply to regional pottery industries.* So, instead of reading civic failure into such activities, archaeologists are increasingly open to reading them, along with the debris of feasting, as signs of incipient urban lordship.

Very large timber and masonry buildings appearing in several towns at the end of the fourth century and beyond hint, like the converted granaries of *Banna*, at storage facilities for rendered agricultural surplus, and/or assembly sites on a scale suitable for a large urban hinterland. Wroxeter, Colchester, Leicester and London have already produced evidence for such large, non-domestic buildings, constructed late in their provincial histories.

---

* Black Burnished Ware from the Poole area of Dorset; Huntcliffe ware from East Yorkshire; Verulamium ware from St Albans and Lincoln's Local Coarse Pebbly Ware, are strong candidates for fifth-century survivals. Fitzpatrick-Matthews and Fleming 2016.

Wroxeter, with its long post-Roman history of impressive timber construction, later gave its name to a small kingdom, *Wrocansæte*. Leicester, the most extensively excavated Romano-British town,* shows vigorous signs of activity into the fifth century and beyond, including the continued use of a large 'warehouse' and the presence of *grubenhäuser*.[13] And, rather than reading 'abandonment' and 'waste ground' into the presence of widespread dark earth deposits, one might see those as evidence that cattle were being stalled within town walls – as rendered goods themselves, or as a landlordly perquisite – producing not just meat but also manure, so that private townhouses might fertilize their own kitchen gardens secure behind town defences.† An extensive late Roman cemetery at Poundbury, close to *Durnovaria* (Dorchester in Dorset) is thought to have served that town well into the fifth century.[14]

There are several ways of looking at the *grubenhäuser* and 'Anglo-Saxon'-style burials that appear in and around many towns in the fifth century. Traditional interpretations favour the idea of either large-scale migration across the North Sea leading to the expulsion of the native citizens, or bands of Germanic mercenaries being recruited to defend towns, then taking control in military coups. Few archaeologists are still arguing for mass Germanic migration, although there is little doubt that people moved across the Channel in both directions during every century of the First Millennium.

Evidence for private military arrangements is accumulating slowly but persuasively. The earliest so-called barbarian law code from the Continent, the *Codex Euricianus* of about 480, provides for a caste of freemen beneath the noble class, called *bucellari*, who acted as military escorts and who could transfer their allegiance between lords.[15] Some of the paramilitary trappings – so-called quoit brooch style and zoomorphic-style military buckles

---

* See Chapter 2, p. 59.

† The historian of the Franks, Gregory of Tours, describes a siege of Chastel-Marlhac, in the Auvergne, whose inhabitants farmed land and reaped a generous harvest within its walls. *HF* III.13.

– found in late fourth- and fifth-century burials close to towns like London, Winchester and Dorchester-on-Thames, as well as in cemeteries like that at Mucking, look as though they may have belonged to retinues of *bucellari* recruited by town councils or dominant families.[16] Even a small retinue, supported by the render of a town's immediate hinterland, might provide security for élite urban families whose dependants, like hungry pets, eyed their masters' stores jealously. Such a retinue would ensure the efficiency of their tax gathering and look very pretty on parade. In some cases, the right to collect local renders was very likely devolved to the retinue, or *comitatus*. In due course the *comites* must have been allotted, or otherwise acquired, land on which to settle and raise families – like the Roman *coloniae* – in a similar process to that recorded by Gildas and in the *Historia Brittonum*, if on a smaller scale. Several scholars have pointed out that the first material signs of such free enterprise seem to date *before* any historical evidence of migration or invasion.[17]

Close to the boundary between Essex and Cambridgeshire, on a Roman road apparently blocked by a series of major fifth- or sixth-century linear earthworks,* lies the town of Great Chesterford. This is a landscape of crossroads and frontiers – between the boulder clay plateau of north-west Essex and the Fenlands of Cambridgeshire – where the old tribal lands of *Trinovantes*, *Iceni* and *Catuvellauni* met. Great Chesterford sits on the east bank of the River Cam just below its highest navigable point, giving it access, across the Fens, to the Wash beyond. In the Roman period the town seems to have guarded this narrowest gap between plateau and marsh, through which all traffic must pass between East Anglia and the centre of the province. Through the late Iron Age, the Roman period and the Early Medieval centuries a confluence here of distinct regional identities is reflected in material culture, building tradition and governance.[18] Lying on the cusp of these distinct traditions, Great Chesterford was typical of those towns, originally planned as forts and later remodelled as urban centres,

* See Chapter 5.

that outlasted some of their larger regional counterparts by virtue of vigorous fourth-century trade and industry. Geographers might classify it as a 'break of bulk' location, where goods were transferred between river and road at a point where those networks met. Goods landed here from along the River Cam would pass close to the grand Fenland tower house at Stonea; thence south, west and east into the province's heartland. By the time it gained stone walls, Great Chesterford was the second largest settlement in the region, after the *colonia* at Colchester. It was flanked by two substantial walled *vici* or civilian settlements that might boast a large central *macellum* or market (identified by geophysical survey). The presence of a *grubenhaus* and scatters of early 'Anglo-Saxon'-style pottery in the small number of excavations that have taken place here, and the uncovering, in the 1950s, of two Roman and post-Roman cemeteries,[19] have prompted questions about the town's fortunes after 400. One of the cemeteries, in the walled settlement that lay just outside the south-east corner of the town, was later the site of its medieval parish church, inviting the idea of a possible late Roman predecessor. In the later fourth century a substantial masonry building was constructed nearby.

The most recent review of Great Chesterford's archaeology interprets the post-Roman evidence within a traditional ethnic framework of Germanic immigration. Its author suggests that it may have become either a 'border town' within a surviving Romano-British power base centred on the Chilterns, or the focus of inter-tribal conflict.[20] But several authors have also noticed a very striking feature of the surrounding townships, whose historic boundaries, as recorded in the nineteenth century, seem to form a radial pattern around it. Stephen Bassett, reviewing the origins of Anglo-Saxon kingdoms, proposed that this radial pattern preserves the extent of a large *territorium* (some 30 square miles) that provided the town with its food and service renders; that the fifth- and sixth-century evidence from the town indicates peaceful co-existence between its population and 'newcomers'.[21] Whatever the merits of the migration argument and its ethnic overtones, the presence of a possible territorial demarcation around a late

Roman walled town hints at the emergence of a form of lordship here and of the survival of a 'minor' town as an independent caput. In such towns excavators might hope to identify the missing 'big men' of fifth-century lowland Britain.

In the south-west, the situation of Ilchester in Somerset is highly suggestive. The Roman town, which sits at a key crossing of the River Yeo by the Fosse Way and a second major road linking Dorchester with the Severn estuary, was elevated to the status of a cantonal capital during the late empire and became *Civitas Durotrigum Lendiniensis*.[22] The town has barely had its surface scratched by excavation, but a sherd of imported Mediterranean pottery is said to have been found here.[23] The River Yeo links Ilchester with the Bristol Channel by way of the River Parrett, an important regional boundary and navigable waterway; it also lies at the centre of a well-defined and productive landscape of wetlands, cultivated fields and hill pasture, rich in the remains of Roman-period villas. Ilchester apparently lost its official status and its regional importance during the fifth century, but its role as a lordship centre may have been inherited by the massive hillfort at South Cadbury, 7 or 8 miles to the east.

Cadbury's immensely impressive prehistoric ramparts were rebuilt some time after about 475: laced with a timber frame and revetted with stone. The gateway was reconstructed and at least two large timber buildings were erected.[24] One of these was a rectangular hall some 66 ft long with opposed central doors, an internal partition and slightly bowed sides, constructed on a double square formula: a super-sized version of the domestic halls at West Stow, West Heslerton and Mucking. It had been built partly over the remains of a circular structure, which may have stood and been in use when the defences were being refurbished. Sherds of imported pottery and glass found here are indicative of both access to exotica and of feasting – essential components of lordly display and consumption. Whoever controlled sufficient resources to invest in Cadbury's revival as a centre of power was a mighty lord. But if Cadbury represents the peak of indigenous power in the fifth century – and there are few more impressive sites of the

South Cadbury hillfort: perhaps the hillfort successor of the
Romano-British town at Ilchester, and the site of an Early
Medieval feasting hall and lordship site.

period – it shows that *Britannia*'s horizons were shrinking. The late
Roman state had been privatized.

Maintaining social cohesion in the hinterland of a large town, let
alone across the former tribal lands of the *civitates*, may have been
a much greater challenge than managing the immediate environs
of a fort from an experienced, functioning garrison. Ultimately, the
provincial leaders, if they survived or re-emerged as an institution
after 410, would be divorced from their urban powerbases. By the
beginning of the sixth century there is very little, if any, evidence
that major towns still functioned as central places. Canterbury
and Wroxeter are the possible exceptions.

If the scale at which political and economic authority was exercised in the former province was shrinking; if classical towns,
with their markets and social functions, had become something
of an irrelevance, archaeologists and geographers must try to
identify suitably smaller territories in which localized power
was exercised among the vast bulk of rural communities. Great
Chesterford provides a tentative model. Boundaries demarcating

the hinterlands of the thriving settlements excavated at West Stow and Mucking cannot, yet, be drawn. But East Yorkshire's Vale of Pickering, in which West Heslerton lies, offers compelling evidence for such landholding units. The vale runs more or less east to west between the North Sea coast at Filey and the Hambledon hills, bounded to the north by the North York Moors and on the south side by the chalk wolds. From the flood plain of the River Derwent, up through successively higher ground to the south – including the spring line along which the settlements lie – to the wold scarp and the high pastures of the chalk plateau, the land's resources are stretched across river, water meadow, arable, pasture, woodland and, finally, on the plateau, extensive summer grasslands. As early as the Bronze Age, burial mounds demarcated neighbouring parcels of land on the high plateau – the limits of a community's pastoral rights. At intervals of roughly a mile along the south side of the vale, prehistoric linear earthworks and pit alignments bounded strips running across the grain of the land, ensuring that each settlement had access to a cross-section of these resources. Small Iron Age forts, built on knolls at intervals along the scarp, reinforce the pattern, as do the later sites of manor houses and parish churches. Parish boundaries still follow many of these ancient lines. Clusters of *grubenhäuser* occurring at the same intervals along the south edge of the vale dramatically confirm the persistence of that pattern into the Early Medieval period.[25]

Territories like that proposed for Great Chesterford reflect a more centripetal version of the need to demarcate lands from which a suitable range of resources might legitimately be drawn by render. In Kent and Sussex the formidable geography of the densely wooded Weald led to a fan-shaped pattern of land units (called rapes in Sussex and lathes in Kent), each ensuring access to its rich timber stands, wood pastures and iron deposits for communities whose core settlements lay some distance away.

Several authors have tried to identify similar territorial patterns around the sites of known Roman villas, seeing in them the sort of broad-based estate capable of functioning successfully in the subsistence economy that emerged, or re-emerged, during the fifth century. Roman estate boundaries are notoriously difficult to identify on the ground, but those villas where there is strong evidence of survival beyond the end of the empire are candidates for central places. Once again, the sorts of markers that might help identify villas as emerging central places include large buildings like the aisled barns of Meonstoke, Rivenhall in Essex and elsewhere; the repurposing of domestic spaces for industrial processing – smithing hearths punched through mosaic floors at villas like Lufton in Somerset, for example – and a rising incidence of corn-drying or barley-malting kilns. In these processes archaeologists detect an obvious association between modest surplus, recycling, renders, feasts and beer. Such features are an indication of produce being drawn towards a villa whose dependent tenants looked to its owners for protection and patronage. The patron – or steward – supported by the render was able to keep managing it as a coherent unit with the aid, possibly, of a small retinue of *bucellari*. Roman villa estates and buildings apparently functioning into the fifth century are convincingly attested at Orton Hall, near Water Newton in the East Midlands; at Barton Court Farm in Oxfordshire and at Frocester in Gloucestershire; many more must lie as yet unrecognized.[26] Latin terms surviving as place-name elements, such as *wicham*, *camp*, *funta* and *port* also hint at such continuities.[27]

One of the most convincing candidates for a villa-based *territorium* lies in the ultra-Roman Cotswold hills 6 miles north-east of the *civitas* capital of the *Dobunni* at Cirencester, in a fork between the Fosse Way (heading north-east to Lincoln) and Akemann Street (the principal Roman route between London and Bath), straddling the River Colne. A prehistoric rampart overlooking the river from the south at Ablington encloses a site of more than 10 acres. At Bibury Mill, a little over a mile downstream, the site of a large and 'opulent', but as yet unexcavated villa is known from accidental discoveries in the nineteenth century. Bibury parish, which spans the river and covers 10 square miles, was the site of a minster church by the eighth century and became a hundredal centre.* The historian Christopher Dyer has argued that the Early Medieval estate centre was a direct successor to the villa and its possible predecessor, the hillfort at Ablington.[28] Although the villa at Bibury Mill has not been excavated, another, at nearby Barnsley Park (2 miles to the south-west), was investigated in the 1950s and 1960s. Questions have been raised about its excavators' methods and interpretations;[29] even so, its development from a farmstead in the second and third centuries into a modest villa in the late fourth century and its continued use as a working farm over succeeding generations establishes the continuity of the landscape. Barnsley Park is one of the few excavated settlements of this period to have preserved the fields and boundary system that surrounded it and there have been suggestions that it became an assembly site in post-Roman centuries.[30]

If the Bibury estate, with dependent farms like that at Barnsley Park, developed from a Roman predecessor, one might speculate about its relations with the *civitas* capital at Cirencester. Were these the lands of a tenacious élite native family maintaining their position by returning to their rural property and successfully managing it as a small *territorium*?

Not all landowners and lords were men; women could and did control substantial holdings in late Roman Britain, sometimes inheriting estates from their fathers or husbands.† At least two female landowners are known from *Britannia*. Melania, a celebrated Christian patron and the immensely wealthy wife and cousin of Valerius Publianus, owned estates across the empire, including land in *Britannia*, at the beginning of the fifth century. Her portfolio is known to historians only because she and her husband were induced, by no less a figure than Augustine of Hippo, to

---

* Hundreds (in the south) and wapentakes (in the north) were administrative divisions of the late Anglo-Saxon shires, many preserving early territorial groupings of vills. The Welsh equivalent is the *cantref*: literally, a hundred farmsteads.

† Boudicca went to war in the first century to establish her right to her dead husband's lands.

donate much of their fortune and estates to the church. Melania's subsequent career as a Desert Mother in Palestine assured that a *vita* was written celebrating her career. It is most unlikely that she ever visited the province. Another very wealthy woman, a citizen of *Dumnonia* in the south-west, possessed large estates in what is now Devon.[31] There has always been a suspicion that semi-legendary early Christian martyrs like St Juthware (who may have inherited a villa at Halstock, in Dorset) – and St Winnifred (from the Welsh marches) may have been owners of substantial villa-based estates. Wealthy Christian women who devoted all or part of their fortunes to founding Christian communities might attract the unwanted attentions of jealous men. Juthware and Winnifred both lost their heads.[32] It is not until the seventh century that such women come into sharper focus as royal and ecclesiastical entrepreneurs – visible in extravagant bed burials, in the verses of the *Beowulf* poem and in Bede's political narratives as 'peace weavers' and political and religious activists.

Some villas – Lullingstone in Kent, with its house, church and sumptuous accommodation, is a notable example – have been touted as the residences of provincial governors and it would be surprising if some members of those élites did not attempt to maintain their country estates as private fiefdoms after the expulsion or withdrawal of the imperial administration. Other villas are thought to have been the houses of retired army officers and, in these cases, one might speculate on the sort of local arrangements that Birdoswald typifies. Estates whose absentee owners lost control over their assets in the turmoil of the fifth century might have been appropriated by neighbouring lords. In some cases it is tempting to imagine opportunistic land grabs by the 'squatters' whose presence is often touted by archaeologists; or the elevation of bailiffs to *de facto* lords by virtue of their social seniority on an estate. The career path from steward to Stuart is well-trodden in Scotland while, in Gaul, the Carolingian dynasty emerged from former mayors of the palace.

Nothing concrete is known of the lives of those who exercised lordship in *Britannia*; but from fifth-century Gaul not just names and partial histories, but a wealth of private observation and opinion survives. Sidonius Apollinaris (c.430–489), whose father had been a prefect of Gaul, was an indefatigable correspondent. A poet, diplomat and bishop, he politicked with the great men of his day, travelled widely, took an interest in everything and generally enjoyed life.* His was still a connected world, recognizably Roman despite the fluctuating fortunes of the Gaulish province. From his villa estate at *Avitacum* (perhaps modern-day Lac d'Aydat in the Puy-de-Dôme), which he acquired as his wife's dowry, he wrote of enervating summer heat; of his spacious baths, luxurious but unpretentiously decorated with plain white stucco; of the 'place where the maids do our weaving'; of the winter dining room where a roaring fire burned; of watching fishermen row their boats on his lake.[33] He says disappointingly little about the extent of this estate: it has 'spreading woods and flowery meadows, pastures rich in cattle and a wealth of hardy shepherds'; but it was evidently sufficiently large to support an opulent lifestyle. Sidonius's hankering for the good old days of empire may have been wildly out of touch with the trajectory of his times, as we see them from a distance but, in the late flowering ultra-Roman *Britannia* of the fifth-century Cotswolds and Severn valley such men – counterparts to conservative ecclesiastics like Gildas – may still have enjoyed congenial lives. Did the owner of the Bibury estate, like a British Sidonius, correspond decadently with potentates and merchants across the province and beyond?

Any idea of a bucolic Golden Age of fifth-century rural governance, of a province liberated from its oppressors and overseen by genial squires, should be tempered by the knowledge that fifth-century politics was generally a pretty filthy business. Gildas may have over-coloured his satanic portraits of contemporary leaders, but he cannot have invented them. Britain's tyrants and judges plundered and terrorized, waged war, kept political prisoners and swore false oaths.[34] In Gaul, competition for political power

* See Chapter 5, p. 140, for Sidonius's warnings about Saxon raiders, of whom he had heard by repute.

The West Stow Anglo-Saxon village reconstructed on the original site of the excavations: most people existed below the radar of kings and great lords.

and landed estates could be bloody and unforgiving. Smaller and more liminal communities like West Stow and the downland villagers of Salisbury Plain, perhaps also people in the Fens, may have thrived below the radar of those politicking on a grander stage; but even comparatively modest landowners and garrison commanders may have been drawn into disputes by virtue of their allegiance to more powerful contingents, or to defend the interests of their dependants.

Once again, the letters of Sidonius Apollinaris offer instruction. He is to be found intervening on behalf of a friend, Donidius, who had lost and wished to recover lands abandoned in the face of barbarian invasion.[35] He also praised his brother-in-law Ecdicius, *magister militum* in Gaul like Aëtius before him, in a much-cited letter that described how Ecdicius had taken charge of the defence of Clermont against a Visigothic invasion. He had protected those lining the half-ruined walls from disaster with 'no more soldiers to back you than you often have guests at your table'.[36] Such heroics underlie the legendary careers of fifth-century commanders like Ambrosius and, perhaps, Arthur. Indeed, Sidonius Apollinaris corresponded with one of the very few known British commanders to enjoy demonstrable success in the late fifth century. *Rigotamos*, to use his Brythonic name, or Riothamus, as Sidonius knew him, was a British *dux* active in Armorica – or Brittany as it would become – in the 470s, capable of bringing substantial forces into the field to side with Roman commanders against their Gothic enemies. His existence is independently attested by Jordanes in the *History of the Goths*.[37] Sidonius refers only allusively to Riothamus's military exploits; his concern is for a supplicant who complains that Bretons are enticing his slaves away; might Riothamus intervene and judge the matter on its merits?[38] Riothamus is periodically offered up as a model for either the historical Ambrosius or the legendary Arthur; but there is no need to entertain either connection.[39]

Where, then, should one look for the *duces* of *Britannia*? There is no particular reason why commanders of British forces fighting political opponents – domestic or external – should not have been based in walled towns or the garrison forts of the northern frontier, although there is no positive evidence, from any of the towns or forts so far investigated, for armed conflict. A number of extramural cemeteries have yielded burials whose artefacts and even skeletons have been claimed to prove the presence of Germanic mercenaries; but the evidence is capable of supporting more than one interpretation.[40] The search for tangible signs of the warfare recorded by Gildas, the Nennian compiler and the *Anglo-Saxon Chronicle* has traditionally been directed towards the hillforts of Wales and south-west England, partly because of a tiresome preoccupation with the location of Badon Hill and the archaeology of Arthur; partly because excavation of several of the hillforts has produced strong evidence for occupation and refortification during the two centuries after Rome's fall. Excavations at South Cadbury (Somerset) and Dinas Powys (Glamorgan) by Leslie Alcock; at Cadbury Congresbury (Somerset) by Philip Rahtz and others and at Dinas Emrys (Gwynedd) by H. N. Savory have all revealed significant lordly activity: the presence of goods imported from outside the British Isles, substantial halls and the refurbishment of defences.[41] But despite much wishful thinking and wrangling with spurious place-name evidence, only one Early Medieval battle site before the Viking Age has ever been identified in Britain by the only evidence that counts: multiple bodies with bladed weapon trauma;* and that tentatively. The undeniable and bloody massacre very obviously identified by Alcock at South Cadbury took place early in the Roman period.

The role of hillforts in Iron Age society has been much debated over the decades. Many of the larger forts were regarded by the Roman state as *oppida* – in effect small, elevated towns with large numbers of dwellings, religious structures and trading facilities. They must have enjoyed administrative and ceremonial status, controlling territories the size of *civitates*. Hundreds of smaller forts, spread all over the highland zones of Scotland and Wales, the Pennines, the south-west and the Cheviots, where settlements were generally small, dispersed and materially conservative, look like little more than farmsteads in prominent, defensible locations. In between, many seem to have been occupied only periodically or seasonally, as summer assembly sites for tribal gatherings and fairs, the collection of tribute and the fostering of kinship ties. For the fifth-century revival in their fortunes, questions have focused on the status and length of their occupation and on identifying

---

* Graves excavated at Heronbridge, just south of Chester, have been claimed to be casualties from the battle fought in 616 between the forces of King Æðelfrið of Northumbria and the armies of King Selyf ap Cynan of Powys and his allies. See Chapter 12. See also www.webcitation.org/67hhMeYza?url=http://www.chesterarchaeolsoc.org.uk/heronbridge.html.

whether such sites once again became central places or were no more than strongholds used by local or regional warbands during times of conflict. A resurrection of tributary tribal assemblies – a sort of post-Roman Iron Age flowering – has been touted by several authors, along with the possibility that some of the hillforts became kingly residences for the likes of Gildas's *tyranni*.* The jury is still out.

Those five *tyranni* excoriated by Gildas in *De Excidio* cannot be located in more than a very tentative geography of western Britain.[42] His long address of complaint against them begins immediately after the historical section of *De Excidio* and so their behaviour is drawn in direct contrast to that of Ambrosius Aurelianus. Had Gildas been more of a poet he might have cast their deeds in a sonnet, as the poet Shelley would the early nineteenth-century Hanoverians, as those of 'Old, mad, blind, despised and dying king[s]; princes, the dregs of their dull race...'[43] Constantine, whom Gildas accused of adultery and of murdering two young princes, was the 'tyrant whelp of the filthy lioness of *Dumnonia*', and can therefore be securely placed on the peninsula between Exeter and Land's End. The Early Medieval settlements of Devon and Cornwall have barely begun to be identified, let alone excavated† and only one defended site has yet produced the sort of evidence, present at Cadbury Congresbury and South Cadbury, for a princely residence. The rugged, romantic promontory of Tintagel, whose exploitation as a self-serving Arthurian trope is quite unnecessary, has produced abundant evidence of British contact with the Continent after the end of the Roman period and may tentatively be identified as a stronghold of *Dumnonia*'s secular rulers. If the majority of its rectangular stone buildings belong to the fifth and sixth centuries, as the material finds indicate, it was a busy place – more *oppidum* than palace and probably unique in the British Isles. The presence of luxury items like fine pottery,

---

* See Chapter 9, p. 281, for the role of hillforts in trade with the Continent in the fifth and sixth centuries.

† But see Chapter 9 for the élite settlement excavated at Trethurgy.

glass and metalwork may be taken as evidence for the highest levels of lordship; but in general, if fifth-century warlords were as itinerant as their successors in the seventh century, one should probably look for campsites rather than palaces.

The second of Gildas's tyrants, Aurelius Caninus – a good candidate for one of the degenerate grandsons of Ambrosius who were disappointing contemporaries of Gildas – was guilty of fomenting civil war; of parricide and of adultery, his crimes 'a slime like sea-waves'.[44] He is not located in De Excidio but Nick Higham, who has made a detailed study of the text, suggests that Caninus might be associated with the Cunignos whose name is found on a memorial inscription to his daughter Avittoriga: AVITORIA/FILIA CUNIGNI.[45] The inscription, in both Latin and Ogham, is carved on a pillar found in St Margaret's churchyard, Eglwyscummin, in Carmarthenshire. If this is correct, Caninus's territory bordered very tightly on that of Gildas's third tyrant, the ageing Vortipor of the Demetae, a white-haired 'bad son of a good king' whom he accuses of having committed many murders and adulteries.[46] The Demetae, like the Dumnonii, were a civitas of the Roman province, located in what is now Pembrokeshire. Their remoteness from the centre of state power and military authority suggests that they enjoyed a greater degree of autonomy and independence than tribes elsewhere in Britannia. Far from reinventing an idea of kingship in the fifth century, they may never have lost it. As it happens, another memorial inscription, with an incised cross inside a circle, whose Latin reads MEMORIA/VOTEPORIGIS/PROTICTORIS, might seem to locate Vortipor in neighbouring Carmarthenshire.* Protictoris is, literally, 'protector'. The term is redolent of Gildas's own words, that 'Britain has her governors; she has her watchmen'.[47] Doubt has been cast on this idea by linguists who suggest that the missing 'R' in the name in the inscription tells definitively against the identification.[48] But Vortipor, in any case, surely belongs in south-west Wales.

Cuneglasus, the fourth of the tyrants who attracted Gildas's

---

* See the illustration of his memorial at the head of this chapter, p. 171.

opprobrium, may be identified with *Cynlas Goch*, the Brythonic equivalent of the Latin name, known from the genealogies of the kingdom of Rhos which lay immediately east of the River Conwy on the north coast of Wales.[49] Cuneglasus was the 'driver of the chariot of the Bear's Stronghold, despiser of God... in Latin "red butcher"', wager of war against 'our' countrymen.[50] Suggestions have been made that Bryn Euryn, a hillfort overlooking Colwyn Bay recently excavated to reveal massive – if undated – fortifications, might have been Cuneglasus's stronghold, on the grounds that it lies in the medieval township of Dineirth – 'Bear's Fort'.[51] It seems like wishful thinking. Intriguingly, though, Bryn Euryn lies just 3 miles east of another hillfort, Castle Deganwy, whose twin rocky promontories directly overlook the mouth of the Conwy and seem to guard access to both the river and the huge copper mines of the Great Orme. Deganwy has been touted as a possible residence of Maelgwyn Gwynedd: Maglocunus, 'Dragon of the Isle'. Last in Gildas's list of tyrants, he was nevertheless 'first in evil'.[52] Deganwy hillfort was excavated by none other than Leslie Alcock, between 1960 and 1961, and produced finds of the right sort of date. But, as he himself pointed out, it can hardly have been the principal court of the early kings of Gwynedd, which is securely located at Aberffraw on *Inis Môn* or Anglesey, just across the Menai Strait.[53] Gildas produced a very long charge sheet against the man who was 'higher than almost all the generals (*duces*) of Britain'. As a youth Maglocunus had killed his uncle. After seizing the kingdom he publicly vowed to become a monk, but the vow came to nothing. He married, then took his nephew's wife as lover, and proceeded to kill them both. We are to understand that Maglocunus had had, as his worthy teacher and mentor, 'the refined master of almost all Britain', and one suspects that here Gildas is referring to himself.

The same king appears in several genealogies, and his death during a great plague is recorded in the annal entry for 547 in the *Annales Cambriae*. If this date is sound, and if he was a direct contemporary of Gildas, then Gildas himself can be dated – and many another duck, including Badon Hill, is lined up. Unfortunately, few scholars are now confident that it is.[54] The most recent and detailed calculations, woolly as they necessarily are, have offered dates for the composition of *De Excidio* between about 485 and 545. If nothing else, the very large possible timespan warns those wishing to pin down a chronology for Gildas (and Badon Hill... and Arthur) to be exceedingly cautious.

On the other hand, there is little point in going to the races without placing a bet. My money is on a date for *De Excidio* close to the end of the fifth century, on the following grounds. Gildas says unequivocally that he was a contemporary of the grandsons of Ambrosius Aurelianus, whose parents had 'worn the purple' and had, therefore, held high rank in the province before about 410. One of the very few passages in the Nennian compilation that may have been drawn from a genuine written annal is the Chronography tacked onto the end of the *Historia Brittonum* in Section 66. It places Ambrosius in a conflict with the otherwise unknown Vitalinus* at Wallop (in Hampshire) in about 437, twelve years after the beginning of the reign of Vortigern in the year of the consulship of Theodosius and Valentinian (dated to 425).† This could be a Nennian invention; but consular dates are inherently more likely to come from a contemporary source than retrospectively calculated *Anno Domini* dates, because that is how they would have been recorded, if at all, in contemporary annals. Very well: suppose that Ambrosius was active in the 430s, like Germanus, Vortigern, Vitalinus and Aëtius. His parents had been prominent a generation earlier, in the first decade of the fifth century when Britain had been 'fertile in tyrants'. Calculating generations on the basis of arbitrary averages – twenty-five or thirty years – is not much more than a guessing game; but the grandchildren of Ambrosius, Gildas's contemporaries, must on this supposition have been active adults close to the end of the century. I offer a date around 500 for Gildas writing *De Excidio*, which suits his educational background and does not unduly

---

* Section 49 of the *Historia Brittonum* gives what looks like a spurious genealogy for Vortigern, in which Vitalinus appears as his grandfather.
† See Chapter 5, p. 149.

stretch his thin historical narrative beyond breaking point. It is an each-way bet; no more.

The geography of Gildas's kings is very clearly western and confined to areas where no *grubenhaus* was ever constructed. Wales and the south-west, peripheral to the heart of the Roman province, seem to have retained ancient institutions, including kingship and those governing the customs of the render. But there are peculiarities: if the current consensus is sound, Gildas's Britain consists of one 'king' of the *Dumnonii* in the south-west peninsula; two in south-west Wales and two in north Wales. There are large gaps in between; and two pairs of geographically adjacent kings make an odd imbalance. Either some nuance in Gildas's choice of targets is being missed, or his list is not as comprehensive as historians would like to believe.

Gildas's own location is not revealed and the geography of his *tyranni* is imprecise. On the other hand, the scale of territories that these rulers controlled is consistent with that of the *civitates* and, indeed, with the known Early Medieval kingdoms of the west. It is, in that case, tempting to associate them with the sort of power structure that produced the councillors and the *superbus tyrannus* of Gildas's historical account. But there is danger in projecting an idea of the size of a *civitas* onto its name; the tyrant-led territories might, by Gildas's day, have been small, circumscribed by their rulers' limited ability to extend their reach over former tribal lands. The lords of the *Demetae* and *Dumnonii* might, by the end of the fifth century, have been ruling territories the size of Birdoswald's township or the immediate hinterland of Great Chesterford. Certainly their residences, if they are the complexes excavated at contemporary hillforts like Dinas Powys, are hardly more pretentious than the two-by-four houses at West Stow or Mucking.

Back in the east of the island, where Rome's legacy was ultimately much more comprehensively rejected, scholars have barely even begun to ask where the *superbus tyrannus* might have been based. In London – supposedly derelict or empty by the middle of the fifth century? Surely not at Canterbury in Kent, which he is supposed to have handed over *in toto* to a couple of small-time pirates, deposing its rightful king, Gwyrangon. Where, then? Several towns bear evidence of large, late houses that might do very nicely as governor's residences, together with locations that would give them the strategic advantages of a central place. The headquarters of the *Dux Britanniarum* at York is an obvious site for a militarized state to concentrate its political resources, especially in the face of threats from Picts and Scots; but York may have been more or less uninhabitable by the second quarter of the century, being so prone to flooding. One might do worse than suggest *Verulamium*, *Britannia*'s third largest city. It was the Iron Age tribal caput of the *Catuvellauni* before Rome's arrival. Burned by Boudicca's Icenian forces in the first century, it was rebuilt, and thrived. Later chartered as one of Britain's two *municipia* – a sort of civic promotion* – it sustained very late, probably fifth-century buildings and has notable historical associations with Germanus. Its unique theatre offered a possible assembly site.† It was well connected to the major transport routes of the former province and the presence of the shrine of a celebrated martyr – a focus for pilgrimage – bolsters its credentials. Major linear earthworks to the east and south, blocking (or controlling access along) roads to London and East Anglia, emphasize its importance in the emerging structures of fifth-century power. It may have become the *Caer Mincip* listed as one of the twenty-eight cities of Britain in the Nennian compilation.

Onto this tentative picture of emerging fifth-century lordship, based in towns, forts and the surviving *civitates* of the west, an analysis of recent fieldwork in East Anglia has daubed a colour from another palette. Rendlesham, a small village on the navigable River Deben in Suffolk, is associated with the archaeology of a Golden Age of Anglo-Saxon glamour. It was named by Bede as the site of a royal marriage in the seventh century;[55] more obviously, it lies less than 4 miles upstream of the ship burials at Sutton Hoo. In the face of threats from illegal metal detection, a detailed survey

---

* Wroxeter is the other possible example.
† See Chapter 3, p. 79.

of the village and its environs was conducted in the mid-2010s, revealing widespread concentrations of high-status artefacts of fifth- to eighth-century date and probable contemporary buildings scattered over an area that the surveyors liken to the expanses of West Heslerton and Mucking.[56] From the late Roman period, coins of Honorius, military belt fittings and clipped silver coins seem to indicate what the surveyors call 'the exercise of authority' here. If such a presence was followed by *grubenhäuser*, then halls, then the township of a *villa regia* – the caput of King Rædwald's early seventh-century court – an otherwise unrecognized sequence of continuous lordship can be suggested for Rendlesham. Its riverine and Continent-facing location and its early emergence as a high-status power base, may be hints that Rendlesham started life as the fifth-century equivalent of a Viking *longphort*, or pirate base. Significantly, by the sixth century, its lords – if that is what they were – were importing the bulk of their material trappings from Merovingian France and from further afield in Byzantium. Were they outstandingly entrepreneurial in their own right; or the subject lords of bigger fish across the Channel?

It seems, then, that the elusive 'big men' of the fifth century might be found in a number of characteristic places: at Roman forts with evidence for continued life; in some, perhaps many of the smaller towns with coherent hinterlands; on some villa estates; in the hillfort country of the west and north and along Continent-facing navigable rivers. As archaeologists and geographers get better at spotting and interpreting the vital signs, the map will come into focus. Most of these scenarios have an overtly indigenous origin. The logical conclusion to draw is that, by and large, fifth-century *Britannia* was controlled by an evolving, native élite – not as a unified whole but as a mosaic of adaptations, each with distinct social, economic and political consequences that come into focus for historians only at the point when much of that diversity was being lost, towards the beginning of the seventh century. Is there room in this mosaic portrait of *Britannia* for a great migration of Germanic warriors and their followers?

7

Belongings

The mythical past – Bede's *gens Anglorum* –
the Lakenheath warrior – the silence of the
graves – the language enigma – apartheid –
altered states – art – lordship

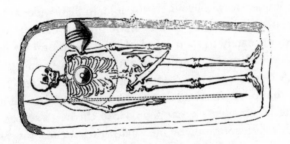

Drawing of an Anglo-Saxon warrior
grave from Ozengell, Kent.

Sometime in the sixth century, in a cemetery on the Isle of Thanet, a man was buried with spear, fighting dagger, shield and a jug that might have contained beer. One would like to know who placed these possessions with him and why. He must have been a member of an affluent family; perhaps the head of a household. His funeral may have been attended by large numbers of his kin group; perhaps also by tribal elders. He spoke a language shared by his *gens*, a group later known as the Men of Kent (or perhaps Kentishmen); his clothes and the manner of his burial were accepted and understood to be appropriate for a man of his age, rank and ancestry. As his weapons belonged to him, so he belonged to family and clan. He also belonged to the land that he farmed, may have fought for and in which he was buried. Just as he had probably inherited his weapons and the right to bear them, so he inherited his language and a cultural outlook.

In largely non-literate societies, people's sense of belonging – to their immediate family and household, to their wider kin and to the clan or tribe with whom they share broader cultural affinities – is tied intimately to their sense of past; to an oral tradition of landscape and memory, to ideas about ancestors and the spirit world. Archaeologists looking for insight into such intangibles have to read the coded messages that survive in those other belongings: the material possessions that people lose, throw away, pass down through the generations or bury with their dead. But, as every undergraduate archaeology student knows, pots are not people. Something of the life of the villa owner can be described because the testimony of people like Sidonius Apollinaris has come down to us. The inhabitants of West Stow, West Heslerton and Mucking are mute, save for the structures, memorials, arts and crafts that they left behind. A psychological void remains between pot sherd and living inhabitant. Ethnography, art history and linguistics help to fill that void and tell a story of what it was like to belong, and to possess, in the centuries after Rome's fall.

Looking back from the seventh century and beyond, the poets and historians of Britain mythologized their past, brilliantly embroidering dimly remembered heroic tales onto a canvas of social

Aberlemno II: a magnificent battle or hunting scene relief carved on a stone slab in the kirkyard at Aberlemno, Angus. The enigmatic Z-rod, mirror and comb symbols are expressions of rank and/or kinship.

and ethnic tropes. Kings rewarded followers with rings and feasts, with honour in their household and lands on which to raise future generations of warriors. Those followers swore oaths of loyalty unto death to follow their lord into battle or on cattle raids for glory, honour and booty. Hunting, song, poetry and hospitality were honourable pursuits, whose depictions on Pictish memorial stones and high crosses endure more than a millennium later.

Noble men rode horses and wielded swords; lower ranks carried an ash spear and a fighting knife; a shield if they were lucky. Receiving one's lord in hospitality was honourable; surrender, and the payment of tribute, were dishonourable. Both gift and theft demanded reciprocity: gift with gift; praise with praise; theft with pursuit; blow with counter-blow; insult with revenge; murder with blood feud, in an unending cycle. Noble women also appear in dynastic histories and in poetry as warriors; but more often as cup bearers, prophetesses and peace weavers: valuable diplomatic assets to be deployed by marriage and alliance. They graced the mead hall and honoured the brave; they incited the timid to action.

The evidence from excavated settlements shows that lower ranks – the ceorls and their wifmen, heads of small households – engaged in agriculture and homespun crafts. Monastic records and charters surviving from the seventh century onwards show that communities rendered services and surplus from their ploughland and pasture to a lord at his *vill*. Men were duty bound to follow and supply their lords in battle. Age-old rules of patronage suggest that on their part they enjoyed a sense of belonging, of vicarious honour as his dependants. In turn, they exercised a form of miniature lordship over the members of their own household: children, unmarried women, the elderly, the unfree.

Smiths fashioned cunning blades and exquisite jewellery, some of which survives to dazzle the museum visitor; potters moulded bowls and jugs. Bards sang; cunning-women and wise men healed, prophesied, cursed and presided over ceremony and burial, if later sagas are to be believed. Boys became men when they could carry a spear; girls became women when they were married. The earliest written laws suggest that the unfree toiled on land on which they would be born and would die, belonging as much to their physical landscape and to the earth as to their caste and their lord or lady. Men ploughed and sowed; women spun and wove; families drove their beasts into the woods in autumn to feast on acorns and beech mast. They coppiced trees for fencing, tools and charcoal; cut timber for their houses; collected bundles of faggots for firewood by hook or by crook; loaded their carts and wains with provisions for their lords. If Thomas Hardy, transported in time, would find life in fifth-century Britain strange – without the marketplaces, churches, gentleman farmers, manors or towns so familiar in his day – Leo Tolstoy, a serf-owning estate owner in the pre-industrial Russia of counts, peasant farmers and artisans, would probably have felt quite at home there.

Men and women belonged to families; families to their kin, sept or *pagus*; kin and sept to their tribes, each with its totem – boar, goat, stag, bear. They looked to their legendary progenitor, a warrior or god or combination thereof, for aid and inspiration. Their mythological origins lay obscurely among generations buried under dark mounds in the days when ruined walls and cities, built by a lost race of giants, had stood proud and tall.

Surviving epic tales and poetry from Irish, Anglo-Saxon, Welsh and northern bards bear witness to the deeds of kings, warriors and queens and the fortunes of their tribes; to daring raids and fabulous wealth; to the intercession of more or less exotic beasts and capricious spirits in peoples' lives. The Irish epic *Táin Bó Cúailnge*, 'the Cattle Raid of Cooley', tells of a war between the impulsive, bellicose Queen Medb of Connaght and her consort Aillil, and their enemies in Ulster; of their attempt to steal a magnificent and famously fertile stud bull; of heroic resistance by the young and very bloodthirsty Cú Chulainn; and of supernatural interference by a cast of exotic, shape-shifting beings.[1] Medieval collections of Welsh legends seem to preserve tales of earlier centuries, celebrations of heroic warriors like Geraint riding to bloody battle on swift horses with spears glinting in their shafts; even of Roman usurpers like Magnus Maximus, recast poetically in the *Dream of Maxen Wledig*.[2] From the same tradition, the battle poem *Y Gododdin* recounts a disastrous campaign, late in the sixth century, by a confederacy of the Men of the North – the *Gwyr y Gogledd* – against the Anglians of *Catraeth*: Catterick, the Roman town lying at the mouth of Swaledale.[3] The greatest epic of Anglo-Saxon mythology is *Beowulf*, whose eponymous hero gains glory by defeating the dreaded monster Grendel and whose final, noble death in battle with a dragon is followed by an iconic description of his funeral pyre and obsequies.[4] Other poetry tells of exile and melancholy, of blood feud and of cunning smiths. The earliest folk narratives of what is now Scotland do not survive. Pictish was never a written language, but its evocative and enigmatic stone-carved art portrays many of the characters and themes common to all the peoples of the Atlantic islands: huntsmen, warriors, fertile bulls and fantastical water beasts; a sense of self-conscious nobility infused with expressions of rank and honour, feasting, kinship and alliance.

Such myths are wrappings for cultural packages that include language; a sense of shared and far-from-passive attachment to landscape; customs and customary laws, the cult of leadership and museums-full of material trappings. Looking at the whole, their outstanding feature is a shared expression of ideology and values that seem, if anything, to cut across the cultural boundaries conventionally used to separate them: British or Anglo-Saxon, Middle or East Saxon, dwellers of the Marches or Fens. Despite their strongly diverse sense of local and regional identity, the peoples of the British Isles were much more like each other than they were alien. That should be no surprise: their languages and cultural histories came out of the shared experience of Indo-European civilization.[5] They were preoccupied with rights over land and animals; with the passage of time; with compensation for injury or accident; with trespass (including the technically complex question of trespassing bees);* with marriage and divorce; with class, or rather caste; with fertility and with the value of everything, down to the amount of compensation due for a pig that died before it had been fattened on the autumn acorn crop.[6] Time, and people's passage across life's wide arc, was marked in festivals and ceremonies by the motions of moon, Earth, sun and tide. The poetry that survives is full of wit and riddle, of ironic philosophy:

---

* The Irish solution was to accept the principle of mutual trespass, so-called 'flying trespass'. Kelly 2000, 145.

Mæst sceal on ceole... sweord sceal on bearme
The mast belongs on the ship... the sword belongs in the lap.[7]

One suspects, with no possibility of proof, that families and communities enjoyed rich traditions of dance and song. The wise archaeologist wields a sharp trowel, while dreaming of Brueghel's peasant dances or carnivals.

Bede, writing in the first half of the eighth century, listed five languages spoken on the island of Britain: Irish, British, Pictish and English, plus Latin; he probably had functional knowledge of at least three of those himself.[8] So far as he was concerned, the first four were spoken by distinct peoples, or *gentes*. His *gens Anglorum*, the English, had arrived during a great wave of immigration – the *adventus Saxonum* – in the middle of the fifth century, from the homelands of three powerful Germanic tribes: Angles, Saxons and Jutes. Ethnicity – the sense of belonging to a *gens* – was implicit in his world view, recognized and endorsed by God, in which moral failings were ascribed to whole peoples. The Britons, for example, were all tainted with the crime that they had failed to preach Christianity to the English after the *adventus* – more than two centuries before his own day.

Opposite ends of the social scale were also, Bede believed, separated by an unbridgeable gulf.[9] His ideas about rank are expressed in the language he used to describe the hierarchical secular society of distinct castes that he knew: kings (*reges*), their immediate subordinates (*principes*), the *gesiths* of their warbands, free ceorls and the *paupere vulgo* or *rustici* of the countryside: the unfree. Early Medieval Irish laws testify to clerics' preoccupations with even finer grades of rank, although one may doubt how far their minute concerns reflected social realities. In the ecclesiastical world, the pope was equivalent to an emperor or *imperium*-wielding overlord; archbishops to kings; bishops to *gesiths* and clergy to ceorls, with lay brothers and sisters as their equivalent unfree subordinates.

Nowhere is Bede's sense of social rank and propriety more carefully sculpted than in the story of a man named Imma, injured in a battle on the River Trent in 679.[10] Imma came to his senses after the end of the fight, in which the Northumbrian King Ecgfrið's own brother had been killed, to find himself bloodied but alive among the unmoving corpses that lay strewn about the battlefield. Looking for friends to help him, instead he was taken up by an enemy patrol and brought to their lord, a *gesith* or thegn belonging to a *comitatus*, the warband of the Mercian King Æðelred. Under interrogation, he declared himself a poor man, and married – a mere camp follower, bound to bring food to his lord's soldiers.

By his own testimony, then, Imma's position lay below the social radar of the *gesith* and so he was unworthy of ransom or the executive revenge of the blood feud. His captors tended his wounds and chained him to prevent his escape; but the chains would not bind him. Bede does not explain why the unfettered Imma did not run away; but the miraculous element to the story explains its inclusion in his history. Eventually, Imma's captors realized 'by his appearance, his bearing and his speech' that, far from being a *rusticus*, he was, in fact, of noble family (*de nobilibus*). They had every right, therefore, to execute him by the rules of the feud, as Bede recognized. In the event the *gesith*, his moral right to revenge compromised by having kept the man for so long in his household under his protection, eventually sold him to a Frisian merchant in London. If social inferiority was rigidly clear, moral dilemmas might still be troubling.

Bede also recognized society's need to accommodate those who, in some way, did not belong – at least, not to the system defined by familiar secular rules. When Augustine, Pope Gregory's missionary, arrived in Kent in 597 the pagan King Æðelberht did not know quite what to make of him, despite the fact that his own queen, Bertha, was a Frankish Christian. Æðelberht kept the cross-wielding party at arm's length on the Isle of Thanet while he took counsel (one imagines quite a bit of pillow talk in the royal household, as well as formal debates in the hall).[11] Hostile magic was suspected; auguries (entrails of sacrificed animals, perhaps) are likely to have been read with great interest. But Augustine's status as the leader of a large party of followers, the fact that he bore an embassy from a great lord (the pope) and, perhaps, the pseudo-bellicose symbolism of their Christian paraphernalia, eventually persuaded the king that Augustine could safely be regarded as belonging to the rank of land-owning warriors – and so Æðelberht gave him 'suitable' lands on which to settle his followers.[12] Æðelberht became his *de facto* lord, protecting the party with his authority, or *mund*, against aggressors and thieves. At the other end of the social spectrum, laws written during the reign of King Wihtred of Kent (*c*.690–725) made provision for dealing with those persons discovered abroad in the land outwith the protection of a lord.* They were to be taken up as thieves.[13] Lords needed to know who owed them loyalty; the non-noble free and unfree needed to know and name their lord.

Bede's sometimes unstated cultural rules, underpinned by mythological literature (much of it romantically retrospective) and by nineteenth-century ideas about race, rank and genetic superiority, have heavily informed historical views of the inhabitants of early Anglo-Saxon England. From the first antiquarian discovery and recognition of Early Medieval burials in the eighteenth century, to the aftermath of the sensational discovery of the Sutton Hoo ship burial on the eve of the Second World War, archaeologists have looked for, and found, confirmation of these supposed cultural rules. A male, Germanic warrior élite dominated, even defined, the culture of early Anglo-Saxon England. For archaeologists and historians wishing to reinforce or test received ideas about identity, belonging and social status, the accompanied graves of the east and south offer rich possibilities. Here, the presence in abundance of buried possessions with strong stylistic similarities to artefacts from across the North Sea basin seems to reinforce historic accounts of migration and conquest from north-west Europe to Britain during the fifth century.

From the third quarter of the fifth century onwards, for more

* See p. 278.

than 100 years, the dead of the *gens Anglorum* were, by and large, interred in dug graves, often accompanied by various belongings, sometimes with weapons. The fashion for cremation, especially in large cemeteries, was in decline. The classic warrior grave, typified by a carefully elaborate late fifth- or early sixth-century chambered burial at Lakenheath, Suffolk,[14] is that of a male (in this case in his early thirties), interred with a spear, a fighting knife or *seax*, a shield and a heavy iron pattern-welded sword. Lakenheath lies on the western edge of Norfolk's Breckland, a few miles across the Fens from Ely and a long day's walk from West Stow to the south-east. It is a landscape rich in settlements and burial sites of the prehistoric, Roman and Early Medieval periods.

In addition to sword, spear and shield, the Lakenheath man was buried with the remains of a horse and its harness, a metal-bound bucket (containing ale for the funeral feast, perhaps, or for his journey beyond) and animal bones representing faithful hunting companions, or joints of meat. The burial plot was circumscribed by a ring ditch, perhaps betraying the presence of a mound or barrow sealing and marking his last resting place. The horse had suffered a stunning, if not fatal, blow to the side of the head, fracturing its skull and dinting part of its harness, preparatory to sacrifice in honour of its master. The dead man was about 5 ft 10 in tall and well built, with no obviously fatal weapon injuries or crippling pathology. He was, it would seem, a real-life Beowulf. But compared with the vast majority of contemporary inhumations his grave is exceptional; all the more so because, surrounding him, lay the ephemeral remains of a number of children's graves. Some of these, too, were accompanied by weapons, and skeletal analysis shows that the children may have been his.

The evidence of thousands of burials in southern and eastern Britain belonging to the late fifth and sixth centuries shows that most people were buried with few grave goods, and that these were modest in character: grown men took their knives with them; women were buried with their spindles and perhaps keys or miniature toilet articles and the odd bead necklace. Containers – small drinking or cooking vessels especially – are common finds in graves. A much smaller number contain a broad suite of more desirable objects: wrist clasps and fine jewellery for women;* swords, spears and shields for men. In contrast to the apparent social equalities of earlier inhumation and cremation cemeteries, the special nature of a few individuals, from this period onwards, is emphasized by their deliberate interment within the mounds or surrounding ditches of prehistoric tumuli.

On the face of it, there is a clear hierarchy: the more exclusive the burial space and the more diverse the set of objects, the fewer the number of individuals wealthy enough or superior enough to be buried with them. Warriors and noble women of the sixth century onwards belonged on an élite plateau – a supposedly Germanic plateau at that – supported by swathes of free but not noble ceorls and unfree – often, by implication, 'native' – *rustici* of the sort impersonated by Imma. Between them, the furnished inhumations and cremations have become an irresistible focus for computational analysis and for the study of Early Medieval social anthropology. All sorts of claims have been made for reconstructing Early Medieval ideas about the afterlife and the nature of their households.[15]

The geographical distribution of these accompanied burials is similar to that of the *grubenhäuser* and cremation urn cemeteries and an understandable, almost pervasive belief has grown up that these are the descendants of Bede's Anglian, Saxon and Jutish *gesiths*: warriors marked in death as in life by their appearance and customs and doubtless by the speech and bearing of those who mourned them. The skeletal evidence, that weapon-bearing bodies are on average an inch or so taller than their unarmed counterparts, has led to the belief that warriors came from a distinct genetic pool – that is to say, from the Germanic homelands. Despite 'pots are not people' warnings, the evidence has historically been read as confirmation of Bede's *adventus* narrative: of a Germanic-speaking warrior élite dominating a subordinate native culture.

---

* Perhaps as part of a self-consciously 'traditional' costume, or *tracht*. But see Harland 2019 for a critique.

The evidence presented in the previous chapter suggests that there are other possible interpretations.

Was the man buried with such ceremony at Lakenheath a German warrior? Part of that question is easy to answer: isotope analysis of his teeth places him locally.[16] That is not to say that he was not the child of immigrants; but he was brought up in East Anglia, drinking its water and eating the produce of its soils. As for his martial prowess and career, that is by no means so straightforward. Analysis by Heinrich Härke of forty-seven cemeteries containing nearly 4,000 individuals dating from between the fifth and eighth centuries showed that nearly half of all male inhumations were accompanied by weapons of some sort.[17] Weapon burials increased in frequency during the late fifth century (when the Lakenheath warrior was buried), reached a peak in the second quarter of the sixth century and declined slowly thereafter. It seems very unlikely that half of all men in that period were professional warriors; if so, they would hardly constitute an élite. Such a 'normal' distribution in the statistics suggests the growth and decline of a fashion, rather than responses to changing levels of endemic violence or formal warfare.

Given the evidence for widespread violence between warbands in the dynastic inter-tribal wars of the late sixth and seventh centuries, when weapon burials were declining or absent, the direct association of weapons with professional careers as warriors begins to look a little shaky. Härke also points out that the sets of weapons found in most graves are incomplete – often just one or two components are found. By and large, these are not full sets of military kit. And then, there is the very strong evidence of the graves of children, also buried with weapons, who can hardly have been battle-hardened warriors. The incidence of weapon-blade injury in Early Medieval graves is very low, less than 2 per cent.[18] The bodies accompanied by weapons turn out to have had a wide range of physical attributes, including severe arthritis; and, conversely, some of those individuals showing the pathologies of actual violence – cut marks on the skull, for instance – did not merit a weapon burial.

Most archaeologists now believe that weapons and other display items are markers for more complex social identities, rather than simple badges of professional merit. In other words, like the making and use of distinctive pottery styles, weapon burials were a function of *habitus* – of appropriateness, tradition and a sense of cultural affinity, rather than mere biographies; a manifestation of privilege, probably of family prestige and wealth and, perhaps, only an honour accorded to the head of a household. Burial may also have been aspirational, so that those interred with a spear or fighting knife were able to enjoy in death a privilege they may not have merited in life. One wonders if their relicts were despatching them as, in some sense, a gift (or render) to the spirits of another world or to the earth whence they had sprung. If some of those buried with weapons were, or had been, professional fighters, such a career was not a prerequisite for being buried with weapons.

One further thought occurs. Membership of a warband or *comitatus* was restricted to a tiny élite; but it was not the only manly pursuit requiring prowess and shiny equipment. In a more localized landscape of less intensive meat production and more extensive wood pasture, with large areas of woodland, rough grazing, heath and moorland surrounding many settlements, hunting with spear and shield – for boar, deer, wolves and wild cattle – might have begun to preoccupy the male householders in many settlements, especially those wishing to enjoy, vicariously, the glory of the professional warrior. As a rite of passage, a marker of belonging, as a badge of protective valour and in the provision of meat, many weapon burials might be concealing a more subtle story than that of the mythologized and romantic noble warrior. Somewhere between the huntsman, the reiver, the squire and the soldier, ideas of manhood were being expressed as they had not for generations. The man buried so splendidly on the edge of the Fens at Lakenheath may or may not have tasted battle. He may be one of the elusive 'big men' who inherited some of the privatized powers of the late Roman state, controlling local territories and enjoying the fruits of a suitably large render. Those who arranged his obsequies thought him battle-worthy.

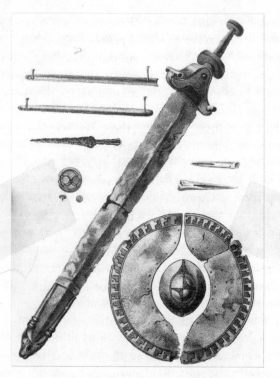

Weapon burial assemblage from Grimthorpe on the Yorkshire Wolds, excavated by John Mortimer in the 19th century and drawn by his sister, Agnes.

Much less has been made, for obvious reasons, of those communities who buried their dead with few or no grave goods. So-called unfurnished graves have been notoriously difficult to date before recent refinements in radiocarbon* dating techniques. To the west

* Carbon¹⁴ is a radioactive isotope of the element. It decays at a rate that can be measured and calibrated against dendrochronological (tree ring) sequences to give approximate dates for organic materials, which absorb atmospheric carbon. For the Early Medieval period the accuracy of C¹⁴ dating may be limited to the nearest half century because of widely fluctuating levels of atmospheric carbon during those centuries.

and north of the core lands of *Britannia*, it is often difficult to distinguish between the graves of people buried during and after the Roman centuries. Warrior and camp follower, slave girl and noblewoman were buried with few, if any, grave goods; only the existence of an above-ground memorial might offer a clue to their language or caste. Sometimes, as in the case of the memorial stone raised to *Voteporigis Protictoris*, there is an explicit statement of the deceased's authority in life. Rarely, such inscriptions reveal an individual's own sense of belonging, as in the case of a Christian man named Aliortus, buried in a graveyard in the Welsh village of Llanaelhearn, Gwynedd, who was 'Elmetiacos' – that is, a British-speaking native of Elmet, in what is now West Yorkshire.[19] Another remarkable memorial, from Ceredigion, records the last resting place of Corbalengus (an Irish name), who belonged to the *civitas* of the *Ordovices*, further north in central west Wales.[20] In one case, we are told of a professional vocation: *Meli Medici fili Martini iacit* – 'Meli the doctor, son of Martin, lies here'.[21] These are fascinating glimpses into dynamic communities. Even so, they are thin materials from which to sketch a whole society in action, especially since it has almost never been possible to match a body – with its tell-tale genetics, scars and diseases – to a memorial inscription. Many cemeteries, especially those close to Roman towns or villas, have understandably been classified as 'late Roman'. But there have always been suspicions that some of these cemeteries lasted well into the fifth century, and probably beyond.[22]

The Somerset village of Cannington overlooks the flood plain of the navigable River Parrett a few miles before it empties into the Bristol Channel. A small hillfort perches above the river. An as yet unexcavated Romano-British settlement lay on the slope between the hillfort and the later village. In the early 1960s quarrying destroyed a large part of a nearby cemetery before archaeologists were able to intervene and excavate the remainder. Several thousand people may have been buried here during its long period of use; more than 500 of them were recovered by careful excavation.[23] Most of the graves are typical of those found close to late Roman towns and in areas beyond the core lands of the former province. They are generally arranged in rows, with a broad east–west orientation, consistent with Christian practice but by no means exclusively Christian. Some are lined with stone, seeming to echo an ancient tradition of cist burial.* Radiocarbon dates, and some of the more diagnostic of the few grave goods recovered, show that the community here buried their dead in much the same way across a period spanning the fourth to eighth centuries – half a millennium. What do these taciturn interments have to say about people's sense of belonging; about their own material possessions and preoccupations; about the supposedly martial culture portrayed by later historians of the British and monumentalized in hillfort and battle poem?

Cannington's large cemetery looks as though it may have been the communal burial site for a territory centred on the adjacent hillfort: the caput of a small tribe or sept, perhaps, to which the dwellers of those parts looked for lordship and a sense of affinity. The hillfort has not been meaningfully investigated; nor have the contemporary settlement or settlements of the people who were buried here been located. But elsewhere in Somerset contemporary hillforts have been excavated – at South Cadbury, most famously; and at Congresbury, situated in a comparable location to Cannington further north along the Bristol Channel. If warrior élites are to be found anywhere it is surely here, in hillfort country where prominent defensive locations, seemingly abandoned in the early Roman period, were busily being refortified during the fifth and sixth centuries.

These are the sites where Ambrosiuses and Arthurs, if they existed, belong. But, if archaeologists have uncovered the graves of great warriors and the lords of these lands, they cannot tell them apart from the householders whose food renders supported their bellicose activities. In death they seem to have been undifferentiated. What does that say about social ranking, or a shared sense of identity? Newly refurbished hillfort defences may, like the ostentatious weapon burials of the east, be kidding us into

* Interment in a stone-lined grave or stone coffin.

believing the all-too-credible narratives of epic conflict that make the Heroic Age so beguiling. Palisades, ramparts and sturdy gates may be expressions of lordly pretensions, like Roman town walls and weapon burials, rather than the infrastructure of warfare.

Ordinary settlement sites of the fifth and sixth centuries almost never offer up evidence of defensive works; and those few burials of this period that exhibit pathologies of violence – weapon-blade injuries, depressed skull fractures and the like – are likely to reflect hunting injuries or the result of drunken bust-ups as much as warfare. None of which is to argue that fifth-century Britain was not run by thugs.

If the search for an archaeology and anthropology of Hengest, Horsa and Arthur has proved to be something of a chimera, those looking for evidence of élite migration, even of a wholesale replacement of the indigenous British population by hordes of pagan Germanic pirates and peasants, have the comfort of knowing that language and place-name evidence is firmly on their side. At least, it used to be.

By the year 500 many – perhaps a substantial minority – of the inhabitants of much of the former Roman province of *Britannia* spoke a language evolved from Old Frisian or Old Saxon, alongside or in place of Late Spoken Latin and/or Brythonic. They buried their dead in graves with personal adornments and weapons like those found across the North Sea in Frisia, Scandinavia, Francia and north Germany. Most archaeologists now dismiss the idea of an overwhelming invasion of warrior-led peoples from across the North Sea and instead talk of small numbers of immigrants: a warrior élite, able to quickly dominate an ultimately subservient native population who had forgotten how to fight or were too weak from hunger to resist. Some, trading on ideas about twentieth-century racial ideologies, speak of a sort of social apartheid developing.[24] But others suggest that there was, in effect, negligible population movement.[25] DNA and isotope studies have promised a resolution of the ethnic question, only to be subjected to rigorous scrutiny in turn, and so far Angles, Saxons, Jutes, Danes and Swedes are not turning up in graves in significant numbers; the genetic verdict is still open.

Linguists and place-name scholars have, on the other hand, held out for the wholesale replacement of the bulk of the native population, believing that the complete loss of Brythonic and Latin in favour of what would become Old English, in the east and south of Britain, cannot otherwise be explained.[26] Old English inherited very few words from either the Latin of the late empire or from Brythonic, and especially few words that relate to basic everyday matters like agriculture, domestic tools and implements and the days of the week. There are said to be just ten Brythonic words surviving in modern English.[27] By comparison, medieval French is heavily infused with Latinity, despite Gaul having been subject to well-documented Germanic invasion by Frankish kings and their armies in the fifth century. Medieval Welsh, too, retained hundreds of Latin loanwords and is a direct descendant of Brythonic.[28] Even more decisively for linguists, no obvious Brythonic linguistic structures, such as its phonetic system or syntax, made their way into Old English, as one would expect if there were several generations of bilingual Brythonic/Frisian/Saxon speakers.[29] That is to say that, if Germanic-speaking immigrants taught the natives their language, the natives would learn to speak it with an accent – the sort of tell-tale that instantly marks a native speaker from one who has learned a second language; and that accent would be betrayed in its Insular development. The most respected place-name scholars have, therefore, argued that the overwhelming replacement by English place names of British names for settlements and topographic features in lowland landscapes (river names, like Ouse, Derwent and Avon are notable exceptions) cannot be explained other than by an influx of large numbers of immigrants of relatively low status: peasant farmers displacing the indigenes. They believe that the idea of a takeover by a small warrior élite cannot account for the wholesale replacement of settlement and topographic names; and that any hypothesis arguing for negligible immigration is simply untenable.[30]

A recent analysis threatens to turn this received wisdom on its head, just as the remarkable site at Rendlesham in Suffolk is shaking up ideas about the contemporary emergence of lordship and central places. Peter Schrijver, a specialist in Celtic languages, has shown that although Old English, as it emerges into the written record at the beginning of the seventh century, shows no signs of having been influenced by the so-called Highland Brythonic of the west and north (reconstructed from inscriptions and from the development of Early Welsh), its characteristic sound patterns did borrow heavily from an indigenous, now lost, language. Schrijver reconstructs this lost language as a distinct but defunct Lowland Celtic – whose so-to-speak visible offspring can, oddly, only be traced in Old Irish.[31] Despite the lack of inherited vocabulary from this language, its distinct pronunciation shows that there was extended contact between Germanic speakers and indigenous Britons. In other words, Old English was spoken with a native British accent. Its southern twang comes from the natives, not any incomers. One of the joists supporting the argument that Anglo-Saxon invaders and colonists physically displaced the natives of *Britannia* has been sawn half-through.

It is a common trope in studies of the emergence of the English to argue that native Britons were regarded as socially inferior by their Germanic conquerors.[32] Bede (who was biased) implies as much. The seventh-century laws of King Ine of Wessex appear to discriminate between *Englisc* and *wealh* or *wilisc*. The former apparently enjoyed a higher legal value in cases of compensation and oath taking. The word *wealh*, with its plural *wealas*, has come down to us to mean Welsh; originally it meant 'foreigner', and by extension 'Briton', but it then became a pejorative term implying 'unfree'. A substantial number of English place names – Walcott and Walton, for example – preserve the word in descriptions of minor settlements, and these have often been regarded as small enclaves of surviving British speakers in areas of Germanic dominance.

There are counterweights to the argument that Ine's laws reflect a form of social discrimination against natives. First, they survive only in a set of ninth-century laws compiled at the court of King

Ælfred; there is a substantial possibility that they do not accurately reflect seventh-century practice, let alone fifth-century social and legal reality. Second, the earliest law codes that survive intact, those from Kent where legend says the first shiploads of predatory Anglo-Saxons arrived, contain no such clauses. Thirdly, there is a possibility that the association between native ancestry and social inferiority might originate in a process opposite to that usually inferred. It may be that the British epithet was negatively applied to a group of the socially disadvantaged, rather than the other way round – that is, the lowest caste came to be called Britons, rather than Britons becoming a lower caste. Belonging and not belonging are twin faces of identity.

Simplistic ideas of cultural domination, many of them leaning on historical analogies from colonial history that may or may not be pertinent, tend to simplify processes by which people choose and express their sense of belonging – to a place, a tribe, a social stratum or whatever. Far too little is known about the social upheavals of the fifth and sixth centuries to say how such profound changes in culture and language came about. That applies equally to the monolithic idea of immigration. People have been moving to and from the Continent to the British Isles and Ireland since they were sundered by the inundation of the land bridge that once joined them. People from across the Roman world arrived and settled in Britain over three centuries and more; and it would be surprising if none of them hailed from those coastal areas of Europe closest to *Britannia*. The legions and cohorts that served in Britain were drawn from across the empire. Two named senior commanders who fell in the troubles of the late fourth century bear German names: Fullofaudes and Nectaridus.* The existence of so much material culture crossing the Channel and North Sea – both before and after the departure of the legions – and the later dominance of the Old English language, demands dynamic contact between peoples; but it may never be possible to characterize that contact in detail. Traders may bring back more than just goods when they travel.

* See Chapter 2, p. 46.

Fashions are mutable. In the Netherlands, the Dutch language may conceivably be replaced by English within a few generations: the result of the cultural dominance of English as a language, not of the physical displacement of the Dutch population by invaders from Essex. The social advantages of adopting new languages and customs are, at 1,500 years' remove, obscure.

This chapter is about belongings, both the material possessions of Britain's population and their sense of identity and affinity with place, kin and community. People belonged to the land where they were born. They belonged to their household; to their lord; to their sept or *pagus*; to a broad group who recognized a shared kinship; to a tribe and, perhaps, to an ideology echoed in distinct burial practices, in craft traditions and the layouts of settlements. People also belonged to a caste, which, for the most part, dictated their trajectories and opportunities in life. Early Medieval society was ordered. But it was also dynamic, with all the subtleties and nuances so familiar from modern cultures across the world. Look at a painting depicting the life of a late medieval Flemish village, with its children playing, beggars begging, its flagellants and pilgrims, eccentrics, cripples, traders and artisans; people going about their everyday business but fully human in the complexities and curiosities of their lives: sometimes rational, often not. Could the modern anthropologist infer such richness of social expression from a grave or the pot that lies shattered on the ground? Even if one were able to ask them, the inhabitants of fifth- and sixth-century Britain might not know themselves; or they might not say.

Historians and archaeologists, whose primary materials are the artefacts of a patriarchal élite and the narratives of tonsured male ecclesiastics living in closed communities, have at times been guilty of peddling facile, misogynistic ideas about, or ignoring, women. The simple model of Insular society based on the provision of render, by those tied to the land, upwards to a mobile, sword-waving élite, which provides a tidy image of Angles, Saxons, Picts and Britons, hides much that is complex and conceals a more socially competitive society than is sometimes imagined. It is generally presumed that fifth- and sixth-century lowland society was patrilocal and patrilineal – in other words, married couples lived with the husband's family, and ownership of rights and property were passed down through the male line. The social and cultural implications are profound: married women were dislocated from their parents and siblings and had to adapt to the lives and rules of their in-laws. They worked on their husband's land, on his behalf. But alternative arrangements – particularly of matrilocality, where the husband goes to live with the woman's family and farms her land – should not be discounted; not, at least, in such a dynamic period of social change. Surviving law codes from medieval Wales and Early Medieval Ireland, which hint at such social arrangements, also suggest that women might own property, including land but particularly equipment related to textiles and farmyard production; that divorce was more equitable than in the later medieval period; that widows might inherit their husband's interests.[33] And it is surely significant that the inhumations and cremations of lowland women are more amply furnished with goods of value than their male counterparts. For the most part, the material remains of hair fashion, textile design and other indicators of social solidarity among women do not survive; that is no excuse for imagining that they did not exist as expressions of a new age just as vibrant as the bling of the warrior-hunter.

Linguists talk of parents raising their children to speak one or another socially advantageous language. But many parents of the Early Medieval period did not raise their own children; they were put out to fosterage with other families as a form of two-way patronage, sometimes as an expedient form of political alliance, so that the foster child was part apprentice, part hostage. Edwin Ælling, exiled prince and later king of Northumbria, who died in 632, was an English-speaking pagan of Deira fostered at the Christian Welsh-speaking courts of Gwynedd and possibly Rheged.[34] His daughter Eanflæd was brought up, also in exile, as a Christian in the courts of Kent and then of Dagobert I in Paris.[35] Her experience of sophisticated Frankish politics was to play a key role in the development of the Northumbrian state. Oswald, a Bernician pagan prince, was similarly exiled in youth and educated far from his Northumbrian homeland among the Irish-speaking kings and clerics of Dál Riata in Argyll. His immersion in the teachings of the abbots of Iona had a profound effect on British history. It is not clear how far down the social ladder fosterage was commonplace but its implications for the movement of people and their exposure to new cultures and ideas can well be imagined. And besides, women carrying their own familial and cultural mores into new households were agents for change, just as traders and warriors were. Mothers may decide what language their children learn.

Lordship and patronage dominated ideas of political belonging. The farming household and its lordly counterpart, the *comitatus*, were the fundamental social units. But people's world views were also shaped by their relationships with shamanic figures: cunning-women and -men who intervened with animistic spirits and who may have overseen the ceremonies that marked life, death, marriage and the fortunes of their communities. Occasionally a grave is excavated that looks as though it belonged to such a figure. The best known of these in Early Medieval Britain are a female grave from Bideford-on-Avon and a male grave placed at the entrance to a great hall at the Northumbrian royal township of Yeavering. Each seems to have been buried with the tools of their trade – bucket pendants, curious triangular spangles and a pouch of talismanic odds and sods for the woman; a slender iron staff for the man.[36] During the dramatic social and economic upheavals of the fifth century one can only imagine the importance of their roles in helping communities to understand and cope with a variety of challenges, from population movement to infant mortality, famine, unrest and loss of certainty. With charm and incantation, propitiatory gift and judicious nods to the ancestors they improved, or were thought to improve, the odds of success in harvest and reproduction, and of good fortune with wealth and weather. Modern Western societies value rationality highly; they look askance, in general, at altered states of consciousness as religious fanaticism, wastrel hippiedom or as the preserve of 'difficult' artists. The material culture of Early Medieval societies, with its exuberant zoomorphism and fantastic geometry, its miracles and omens and its shape-shifting other-worldly inhabitants, was more embracing of the mind's visionary potential; much less inclined to compartmentalize magic and reality. Shamans and priests in their trances; epileptics and migraine sufferers; fasting monks, fume-breathing smiths and droning poets are likely to have experienced and shared episodes of heightened reality that enriched the lives of their communities, deeply informing and embellishing their cultural repertoire.

In the elaboration of funerary rites seen so widely across the south and east of Britain one might see these spiritual specialists helping to construct a sense of what was proper or appropriate ceremonial for burying and commemorating their dead. Siþæbæd, the woman whose name was etched in runes on a funerary urn, may have been such an individual. Shamanism dealt in ideas about transformation from one state to another, mediated between the pragmatic, empirical world of everyday life and the more negotiable world of ancestors, magic, gods and fates. Its self-consistent rules allowed for humans to transmogrify into trees, beasts and birds. Funerary rites in the fifth century were at one and the same time structured, formalized and collective but also characterized by the bespoke detailing of each individual event. The cremation cemeteries developed as communal burial facilities and places of commemoration in the early fifth century look as though they were focused on prominent hilltop sites – like Loveden in Lincolnshire and Spong Hill in Norfolk – that may also have been places of assembly and public display.[37] Lordship, shamanism, household and kin groups may, then, have periodically coalesced to express common affinities through burial and, perhaps, also through marriage and alliance, regional trade and law making. Towns like Great Chesterford and Ancaster, with their extramural cemeteries, may also have continued to operate as focal places, forging and reinforcing relationships with both living and dead; and here one might see a parallel with the hillfort-focused revival of communal and regional identity in the west and north. In troubled times, people wanted to know how they belonged, and with whom, more than ever. In the Bronze Age, the burial of certain people had been seen as an investment in the earth itself, part of a sense of both ownership and responsibility. In this new, pre-historic age, such investment may also have seemed worthwhile. Language, art, ceremony and custom were all means of securing those identities, even as they were being renegotiated for a new age.

Cultural changes in language, burial, buildings and possessions were driven both by external agency and by the mechanics of the *feorm* or *treth* – the render of produce and services to a central place. Dues must be acknowledged and collected, and since such mechanisms are held in place by social relations, archaeologists need to understand them. The materials at their disposal are everyday rubbish, deposited as a function of conscious and unconscious behaviours; objects buried with the dead and whatever spirituality can be inferred from such heavily structured remains; building designs and construction. Craft products like pottery and textiles and the rituals surrounding burial were conservative expressions of identity and affinity; of *habitus*. On the other hand, there is no doubt that some of the art produced by the hybrid societies of Britain and the Atlantic west was of a very high imaginative order of beauty, exuberance and skill. That art does not speak of an oppressed, morally vacuous, or anarchic society; but of aspiration and imagination, of wonder and mystery; of empirical knowledge and technical mastery.

Artistry, like lordship and an institutional priesthood, requires that some special people are relieved of the need to spend long days tilling the soil, threshing corn, endlessly spinning yarn, tending fires and herding beasts. Art is, above all, labour intensive; creativity is time consuming. The forges, kilns and weaving paraphernalia that archaeologists find in towns and rural settlements all speak of investment in time – not just for conception and creation but in training craftspeople, developing and maintaining their skills; acquiring specialist raw materials. And, since jewellery, glassware, architectural embellishments, decorated pots and luxury textiles were not, so far as one can tell, being traded for cash profit in urban markets, their production must have been fostered by patronage, through gift and commission. Lords acquired weapons, salt, wine, brooches, poets and well-bred hunting dogs; kept and displayed many and distributed the rest as gifts, tokens of the relationship between patron and client. As readers of the Anglo-Saxon poem *Beowulf* will know, patronage cemented the bonds between lordly household and dependent community. Lords, in return for the gift of food and services, engineered their dependants' access to prestige goods, land, positions of honour and advantageous marriages. Those dependants praised and legitimized their lord's authority, earning protection and honour vicariously through his reputation as a warrior, judge and gift-giver.

Lordship, like shamanism or the equally dark arts of the smith, itself occupied a specialized social niche supported by the render, involving intense training from birth in governance, display, fighting skills, ceremonial behaviour, the exercise of privilege and responsibility to one's dependants. The ties that bound this closely regulated society together were founded on an idea of reciprocity – the exchange of gifts, favours and service in a closed, perpetual loop in which debt and obligation were never fully acquitted.

For the fifth century these rules cannot be reconstructed with certainty, even if they emerge well formed into the histories and poetry that looked back from the seventh century and beyond. But the social codes that governed lordship emerged from smaller, tighter social units such as those of the garrison command at Birdoswald, the town council of Great Chesterford and the villa estates of the Cotswolds. At this level, food and services were brought directly to the centre – and a central building – where they were consumed. The web of exchange and patronage was tight, involving small numbers of carefully calculated family and client connections, acutely sensitive to age and sex and probably partly communal. Archaeologists are able to tap into this system when they look at housing, rubbish disposal and burial; geographers when they are able to reconstruct the size of territories; ethnographers when they study contemporary tribal society.

The display of art and architecture, personal dress and adornment, poetry and song; the embellishment of weapons; parades, feasting, ceremony and martial prowess: each allowed individuals in household and community to express their marital and social status and their affiliations with kin and with authority. Much could be read into the quality, antiquity and design of a brooch and, perhaps, as much more from the way it was attached to clothing, alongside other fashions. A pair of penannular brooches with La Tène swirls attached at the shoulders, or a cruciform brooch pinned across the chest, might be read almost as a *curriculum vitae*. Such jewellery might be acquired through inheritance; more likely, perhaps, as a bride gift reflecting the mutual honour of two families. The items that hung on a woman's girdle marked

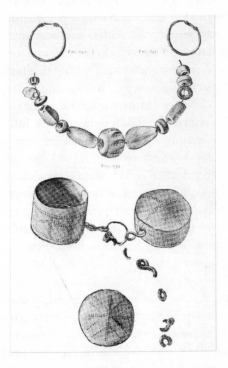

'Anglo-Saxon' women took their portable wealth with them to the grave, marking them out, perhaps, as the head of a household or cunning-woman. Objects from a grave near Garton Slack in East Yorkshire, excavated by John Mortimer in the late 19th century and drawn by his sister, Agnes.

her out as the head of a household or weaving atelier or as a cunning-woman. A man's facial hair, the coarseness of his tunic and language, the poor quality of the knife that hung at his belt, told of his status as a slave or junior member of his household. Dress placed an individual as a relative, friend, potential partner, social superior or inferior just as much as learning, language and accent. Display was reinforced in death by the sacrificial burial – or absence – of high-value goods and the everyday tools of personal grooming, by feasting and lamentation; and these may be read as social investments in the patronage system.

A comparatively modest but exclusive dwelling built on top of an inaccessible hill and encircled by a bank, ditch and fence displayed the credentials of lordship just as surely as the mighty stone walls of a town or the swanky dining room of a villa. Use of a certain sort of pottery for serving ale or the choice of yarn and weave for one's clothes was as sensitive to ideas of identity and fashion as the choice of trainers or home furnishings or holiday destinations is today. The elaborately manifested funeral rites of east and south Britain allow us a rare insight into a world deeply imbued with symbolic forms and constructed identities; with ceremony, ritual and carefully imagined ideas about life and death. The highly regionalized mosaic of British communities in the Iron Age had operated on such principles, and it is doubtful whether the super-centralized Latin Mediterranean culture of the empire had added more than a thin veneer of homogeneity to that reality.

Lordship in the fifth century and later was predicated on extracting food and services from households farming recognizable units of land. Since, as we understand it, the *feorm** rendered on land of varying productivity was uniform in rate, the units themselves must have varied widely in size, as the mosaic of historic townships suggests. As yet, there are only hints of their extent from later

---

* Our word 'farmer' is derived from the office of one who 'farmed' rents and renders – i.e. they were tax collectors.

hundreds, *cantrefi* and shires; and at the level of forts, villas and towns we are still guessing. The largest territories so far identified – by implication from Gildas's five tyrants – were the *civitates*, but they may have been fragmentary even in his day. The cremation cemeteries of East Anglia and inhumation cemeteries like that at Cannington suggest a broader sense of regional belonging, if not necessarily lordship, at the level of the sept, or *pagus*. The villa estate may provide another focus and level at which lordship, and social identity, emerged, or continued, as may the town under authorities as diverse as local magistrates, bishops or arrivistes. There is no reason at all to discount the possibility – indeed the likelihood – of a number of overseas entrepreneurs taking possession, by fair means or foul, of territories of varying size and desirability, from the Thanet of the *Historia Brittonum* and the Bamburgh of Bede to the Rendlesham identified tentatively by archaeology. Those who plump for one model of emerging lordship at the expense of others may be missing the point; the diversity and regionalism that emerges into the historical record suggests that all these variants of control and belonging are plausible – even necessary.

But if lordship evolved predominantly in those places identified in Chapter 6 – towns, forts, villas, hillforts, and coastal or riverine townships like Rendlesham – it was fundamentally an indigenous development. Perceived or real threats of unrest might have provided the impetus for concentrating lordship in discrete locations; but only rarely can it be argued that the manifestations of lordship came directly from overseas. Rights over property, land and people existed and were well understood in the fourth century. There is little reason to believe that those who benefited from such rights vacated their patrimonies en masse. Perhaps, over the space of two or three centuries, hundreds – even thousands – of households or individuals crossed to and from Britain seeking opportunity or fleeing crisis at home. Unless one stands by the idea of actual invasion, most of these scenarios involve lordship at local and regional levels developing as a largely indigenous phenomenon – from old families claiming existing rights over others.

In a socially and economically competitive world there is every reason to believe that local and regional lords acquired the services of what would now be called private security contractors – the *bucellari* of the Continental sources. In some cases these might have been recruited locally; in others, freelance warbands from beyond the old frontiers might have offered their services in return for payment – or for the right to collect renders to support themselves.* Agents and traders may have travelled to and from the lands bordering the North Sea, brokering arrangements that were eventually to underpin parts of the classic narrative – between humbler versions of the *superbus tyrannus* and any number of small-time Hengests and Horsas. The rather stiff and unsatisfactory model of Germanic élite takeover has always presupposed the displacement of the indigenous nobility and curial classes. But it is more likely that in most cases the privileges of lordship remained in native hands. The culture of the lordly household, centred on and in thrall to the supposed romance of the warband or *comitatus* may, over three or four generations, have adopted an overtly Germanic or Scandinavian flavour, a North Sea cultural *lingua franca* – so much so that native families came to think of themselves as belonging more to that world than to the old empire.

For the indigenous élite in eastern Britain, part of the attraction of adopting the new language and half-familiar customs and possessions of Continental traders, brokers and *bucellari*, may have lain in embracing a culture that was both exotic and decidedly *not* Roman. The apparently wholesale rejection of Christian practice in the south and east by the beginning of the sixth century may be a function of the same sentiment. In the old west and north, reactionary forces seem to have inclined many lords to assert a paradoxically stronger sense of Roman identity which, under the empire, they had not felt. In any case, archaeologists are wary of adopting an either/or model of fifth-century *Britannia*. It seems, in reality, to have been characterized by a myriad adaptations and identities.

---

* A Roman concept known as *hospitalitas* and tentatively suggested for some Germanic military settlement in the late Empire. James 1989.

In a milieu in which otherness was expressed with as much enthusiasm as sameness, it is doubtful whether, during three centuries of Roman military and cultural domination, the threat of violence within and between communities had been more than contained. By the beginning of the sixth century social and political relations were predicated on the existence of a fighting élite, on whose success in war and raiding hung communal, kin and regional fortunes. Tensions between communities must sometimes have erupted into group violence, played out by competing lords and their kin, reinforcing a sense of tribal loyalty and affiliation among dependants. For the most part, the social mechanisms of marriage and alliance, customary law and communal inertia held society in balance, waiting for some new force to alter its trajectory forever.

Away from the emerging centres of lordship fixated on the culture of the Continental warband, communities chose varying expressions of both conservative and progressive identity. They revived some anciently remembered customs and invested in the imaginative worlds of their shamans, artists and poets to help navigate their way through uncharted waters towards the future, rejecting much that they saw or heard of worlds beyond their horizon. Some communities may have thrived for generations without either imposing lordship on others or having lordship imposed on them; no one can now say. The chances are that, however modern archaeologists and anthropologists reconstruct such obscure and distant times in their thought experiments, any native of those days transported to the present would assure us that we had got it all wrong.

8

Territories

Tribal Hidage – kingdom, district, *pagus* – cultural
corelands – *Magh Tóchuir* – common rights – evolutions –
Britons and Picts – vills and townships – rivalries
and competition

Myrcna landes is þrittig þusend hyda þær mon ærest Mrycna hæt...

'The area first called Mercia is thirty thousand hides...'.
Eleventh-century copy of Tribal Hidage. British Library
MS *Harley* 3271 folio 6v.

Contained in an Old English manuscript dating from the eleventh century is a schedule, or tariff, of the tributary sums owed by thirty-four kingdoms and peoples to an unidentified overlord. It reads like the little black book of a racketeer, on a grand scale. By common consent the origins of the list lie in the seventh or eighth century, despite its having been edited and amended, perhaps several times, during its passage through the hands of various royal administrators.[1] Some of the names on the list, like Mercia or *Westsexena* (the land of the West Saxons) are familiar. Others, like *Hwicce* around the lower Severn valley, can be located through charters recording donations or sales of land, or from the pages of Bede's *Historia*. More obscure geographies, such as the region called *Wixna,* are suggested by clusters of place names surviving on modern maps. The least easily identifiable items on the list, like *Ohtgaga* and its apparent companion *Noxgaga*, can only be tentatively placed on a map of Early Medieval Britain.

The list of peoples and territories is accompanied by figures, measured in hides,* that appear to indicate the value of tribute owed by each kingdom, province or district to their overlord. The hidage values are neither comprehensive nor consistent as a description of the Early Medieval peoples and regions of *Britannia*. But, in spite of many difficulties with the text known as Tribal Hidage, it contains unique and precious clues to the emergence of England's first kingdoms and, lurking below, it offers an idea of how and where the earliest regional and local territories developed in the fifth and sixth centuries.† It is a fossil of political and administrative evolution. One imagines its inception at a great feast held by an overlord, at which those whom he has defeated, in war or by superior diplomacy, must swear loyalty to him and offer up such tributary spoils as their

---

* The Early Medieval hide was not a measure of area, but of a nominal number of households – Bede's *familiae* – that might render surpluses to a lord at his *vill*.

† See the Appendix, p. 427.

importance and wealth allow. In return he bestows gifts, honours, oaths of alliance and praise on them; agrees concessions and rights of redress. The order of seating at this feast is a matter of delicate diplomacy: slights are remembered and bragging rights cherished. A notary – a literate cleric able to write in Old English script – scribbles with a stylus on wax tablets as the names of kings and subordinate ealdormen are intoned, along with their ancestry and the value of their tribute. The overlord's consort, the 'lady with the mead cup',* presides over formalities; offers each subordinate warlord the cup in strict order, dispensing compliments; oiling the wheels like Queen Wealþeow in the *Beowulf* poem. Later, a formal list is drawn up on vellum to record the proceedings for all time – until domesday. The precursors of such lists must have been maintained orally, by recitation; but in the seventh century, an age of intellectual renaissance and Christian kingship, as wooden churches were being rebuilt in stone and as royal coinage was beginning to replace bullion and cattle as currency, so the infallible written word was to triumph over fallible memory.

Tribal Hidage is separated into two halves, each with a summary figure at the end. The second of these, as we have it, has been added up incorrectly – a clue to some error in transmission. The first half of the list is headed by 'the original lands of the Mercians', rated at 30,000 hides. That is to say, the king of Mercia was required to render as tribute the amount of taxable wealth expected from 30,000 households or farm holdings. But these are not calculations reflecting the physical size of a kingdom or district. This is about the amount of surplus that a subordinate territory was expected to render as tribute by virtue of its wealth and status or, as is probable in the case of Wessex, its perceived crimes.[2] The hidage value is not a fixed sum, in the sense that we would understand it; it would have equated to a material value calculated in heads of cattle and weight of gold or silver.

---

* To use Michael J. Enright's phrase. Enright 1996.

It has long been recognized that there is a rational numerical and geographic scheme behind Tribal Hidage.[3] In a more or less clockwise direction from the west, the first part of the list accounts for the *Wrocansæte* (the dwellers of the Wrekin, based on Wroxeter) at 7,000 hides; *Westerna* (lands seemingly lying west of the Severn and also rated at 7,000 hides); the *Pecsætna* of the Peak District at the south end of the Pennines (a much more modest 1,200 hides); then *Lindes Farona* (Lindsey and Hatfield: 7,000 hides); South and North Gyrwa (both of a diminutive 600 hides, located south of Lindsey on the western edge of the Fens); and so on, down to some very small territories like the *Gifla* of north-east Bedfordshire and the *Hicca* of Hitchin in Hertfordshire, assessed at just 300 hides each. Some of the names identify geographical units and their dwellers; others identify peoples: *gentes*.

The second part of the list contains the names of mostly more southern districts and kingdoms, including East Anglia (assessed, like Mercia, at 30,000 hides), the East and South Saxons (7,000 hides each) and Kent at 15,000 hides. Standing out from the second list is the kingdom of *Westsexena*, assessed at a whopping 100,000 hides. Historians see in this scheme a numeric ranking of tributary kings and kingdoms: larger, more prosperous and politically significant kingdoms, able to muster powerful warbands, at or above 30,000 hides; smaller kingdoms at 7,000 hides; and then progressively less significant territorial units – Bede's *provinciae* and *regiones* and, perhaps, lands at the level of *pagi* below that. The huge assessment for the West Saxons is regarded by some as evidence of a deliberately punitive tribute imposed after a significant military defeat.* There is no suggestion that any of the kingdoms identified in Tribal Hidage existed as such before the middle of the sixth century. The birthplace of Tribal Hidage is variously argued to have been Mercia (because it opens the list) or Northumbria (precisely because it is left off the list).[4]

Many of the smaller territories or regions were later swallowed

---

* See Chapter 12, p. 382.

Barwick-in-Elmet: the name of a Tribal Hidage kingdom, conquered by and absorbed into Northumbria in the 7th century, survives in a West Yorkshire place name.

by the larger kingdoms of the so-called Heptarchy* in the seventh or eighth century. The most precious feature of the list is its inclusion of such minor regions or districts, below the tier at which they might boast kings, which betrays the survival of discrete and formerly independent lordships into a period when they were in the process of being annexed, subjected to permanent overlordship by dominant kings, and swallowed whole. Territorial geography being generally conservative, many of even the smallest districts survived as the names of administrative units into the era of Domesday Book and beyond. In West Yorkshire, Barwick-in-Elmet and Sherburn-in-Elmet preserve the name of a kingdom that was already defunct in Bede's day.

* The seven kingdoms that made up the Heptarchy were Northumbria, Wessex, Mercia, East Anglia, Kent, Essex and Sussex, a tradition popularized by Henry of Huntingdon in the twelfth century.

The clustering of assessments in convenient multiples – 300, 600 and 1,200 hides, for example – offers historians the chance to look at the lower tiers of territorial lordship as they came through into the seventh century, while the basic kingly unit of 7,000 hides, multiplied up to 15,000, then 30,000 hides, recalls the size of the territory given to the legendary Beowulf for his services to King Hygelac. The 300-hide units are so small as to be indivisible, while many of the larger units can be shown from charter evidence to consist of groupings of such districts and peoples, revealing some of the most fundamental structures – the periodic table, as it were – of Anglo-Saxon lordship. Thus, the extensive but not very valuable 600-hide kingdom of Elmet, in what is now West Yorkshire,* contained districts called *Loidis* (around Leeds) and Burghshire (around the old *civitas* capital of the *Brigantes* at Aldborough). *Hwicce*, a 7,000-hide kingdom comprising lands on both sides of the lower Severn valley and roughly coterminous with the medieval diocese of Worcester, consisted of peoples and districts called *Husmerae* (around Kidderminster), the territory that would later become Winchcombeshire, the *Eorlingas* (Arlingham in Gloucestershire), the *Beansæte* and the *Stoppingas*. The equally ranked kingdom of the East Saxons contained many smaller districts too, often named after supposed immigrant Germanic entrepreneurs: *Rodingas, Deningæ, Berecingas, Haningas, Hæferingas* and *Wigingas*. Such names were once regarded as very early formations: the fingerprints of colonizing German migrants.[5] The names as we have them are more likely to date from the seventh or eighth century; but the coherence of the territory, the geographical entity to which the name was given, betrays its greater antiquity.

Further clues allow historians to describe several of these smaller districts with confidence, and in some detail. The *Stoppingas*, a *regio* belonging to the kingdom of the *Hwicce*, can be closely identified, by means of an eighth-century charter entry, with a number of contiguous medieval parishes along the upper Alne

---

* Its last king was expelled by King Edwin in about 630 (*Historia Brittonum* 63).

Valley in Warwickshire, centred on the village of Wootton Wawen.[6] Of the Essex names, *Rodingas* is celebrated in the academic literature because its ancient geography can still be traced on the ground.[7] The River Roding, which falls into the Thames just below the Docklands as Barking Creek, rises just beyond the north-east end of the main runway complex at Stansted Airport in Essex. A modest stream, it winds gently through water meadows, shadowed by a Roman road that ran south-west towards the provincial capital at London. The Rodings, eight contiguous parishes with their medieval churches and manor houses, together form a coherent and natural riverine territorial unit, each enjoying the benefits of strips of land rising up from the river on either side.* Together, they look as though they comprise a small *pagus* or *regio* of the sort encapsulated by the 300-hide entries in Tribal Hidage, with the farms of each *vill* probably rendering their dues to a single central place but, perhaps, collectively supporting a grander lord. The legendary founder of this territory, Hroða (in Anglo-Saxon terms it is a nickname, like 'Ed' or 'Bob'), may or may not have existed; he may or may not have thought of himself as Roman, German, Briton or pure-bred East Saxon boy. Whether he existed or not, apparently early district units like the Rodings suggest a model of local territorial formation that parallels the emergence, or re-emergence, of the 'big men' of the fifth and sixth centuries. Here, the logic of the food render is laid out in three dimensions, with a small river and its tributaries, their meadows, ploughed fields and wood pastures providing the resources from which a lord's surplus and power might be drawn. Their geographical coherence engendered a sense of belonging and loyalty to cement the relationship. From other Insular evidence one might hazard the guess that every household, or every few households, was expected to supply an armed man for his lord's retinue or *comitatus*.[8] The lord, in turn, was obliged to bring his warband to the aid of a grander lord to whom he owed tribute.

---

* Recorded as thirteen manors in Domesday (Bassett 1997).

The River Arrow near Alcester, Warwickshire: a Roman town and river lying at the heart of the Early Medieval territory of the Arosætna.

Delving into the names of the smaller districts* that lie beneath the regional entries in Tribal Hidage, one can identify a number of other territories that also seem to have been focused on river valleys: the *Grantesæte* on the River Granta in what is now Cambridgeshire (perhaps the territorium of Great Chesterford);

---

* Many of these are named in credible Anglo-Saxon charters of the eighth century onwards; others are first recorded in the pages of Domesday and are, therefore, to be treated with some caution.

Bromic along the Breamish valley in upland Northumberland; *Dunutunga* on the River Dent in Cumbria; the *Meanware* on the River Meon in Hampshire; the *Temesæte* of the Teme Valley in the West Midlands; the *Stursæte* on the River Stour in Kent and several more in East Anglia. In Tribal Hidage itself larger valley-based territories can be identified: the *Arosætna* were the dwellers on the River Arrow in Warwickshire, assessed at 600 hides; the East and West *Willa* lay along the Old Well in Cambridgeshire; the *Gifla* on the River Ivel in Bedfordshire. Cases have been made for some of the larger early kingdoms, such as *Bernicia* on the River Tyne and the *Hwicce*, flanking the lower reaches of the Severn, to have formed as substantial and coherent geographical lordships in the post-Roman centuries – emerging from the landscapes of cultural corelands.[9] In the case of the *Arosætna*, one of its districts was, in later centuries, recorded as *Halsæte*, the dwellers at the Roman town of Alcester.[10] If some river basins made natural cultural cores, the Roman towns antecedently sited to exploit their hinterlands made equally convenient centres for the development of lordships during and after the imperial centuries.

In Chapter 1, following the work of the geographer Brian Roberts, the idea of the cultural coreland was introduced to show how very ancient human investment in tractable, fertile and coherent landscapes created natural, governable territorial entities – call them tribal chiefdoms if you will. They were agriculturally productive and socially and economically congruent, fostering an idea of common identity, of belonging. Rivers united communities on both sides, rather than defining boundaries between them. By the early seventh century, and probably for several generations before that, the fortunes of the corelands were indissolubly bound in the person of their lord: his economic, military and procreative success was their success.

In the modern landscape these corelands seem to make only peripheral sense, overridden as they are by the economics of coal and gravel extraction, of conurbation, overseas trade and the huge post-war expansion of industrially drained, ploughed and managed agricultural prairies. But they can still be identified by distributions of early place names – the -*tuns* (centres of population) and -*leahs* (clearings) that differentiate settled from more marginal lands as they come through into Domesday Book and other medieval documents.[11] The archaeological heritage of those landscapes has been scarified, buried, flattened or simply forgotten. Ancient monuments, settlements and boundaries survive mostly as sub-surface shadows, detectable by geophysical survey, by aerial photography during droughts, or when they are exposed by development or agriculture. It is hard, these days, to see cultural cores for what they once were. One must travel to a much less intensively exploited landscape to see an early cultural coreland in the flesh.

In Stephen Bassett's influential 1989 collection of essays, *The Origins of Anglo-Saxon Kingdoms*, the distinguished scholar of early Welsh and Irish literature Thomas Charles-Edwards directed students of early kingship in Britain towards the ample contemporary literary and archaeological evidence from Ireland. Anticipating the work of Brian Roberts, he saw that 'the primary base of the typical Irish king was a territory of small extent, often a single area of well-cleared land, called *magh* or *campus*'.[12] One of these, *Magh Tóchuir*,* was recorded in the seventh century as the site of a church originally founded by St Patrick.[13] Regardless of Patrick's real or imagined involvement in its founding, the church became *Domnach Mor Magh Tóchuir*, 'the mother church of the Plain of the Causeway', identified with the small town of Carndonagh on the Inishowen peninsula in Donegal. Inishowen, a diamond-shaped tract bounded by Lough Swilly to the west and Lough Foyle to the east, protrudes from the boggy outskirts of Derry north towards Ireland's northernmost point at Malin Head. In the middle of the first millennium it was the heartland of a successful tribal dynasty called the Cenél nEogain† whose kings were, at one time or another, also high kings of Tara. The people

---

* The gutturals in 'Magh' and 'Tóchuir' are pronounced like softer versions of Scottish 'Loch'.

† Pronounced Kennel Nogan.

Magh Tóchuir: the 'Plain of the Causeway' on the Inishowen peninsula.
A prehistoric and Early Medieval cultural coreland, its landscape still
bears the monuments of its kings and saints.

who dwelt in *Magh Tóchuir* belonged to one of the myriad tribes
or *tuatha* of Early Medieval Ireland. Enclosed by heather-clad
hills to north and south, the *magh* drains the watersheds of three
rivers flowing north-west into Trawbreaga Bay and thence to the
wild North Atlantic. Four prehistoric hilltop enclosures encircle
the *magh* and look down from peat-rich slopes onto its pastures,
woods and ploughlands and the bay itself. In living memory
the rivers were full of salmon. The *magh* is ringed by standing
stones that tell of ancient emotional and physical investment in
the ancestral landscape and of claims to its resources. Ringforts,

raths* and souterrains† similarly frame this natural amphitheatre of belonging.

Magh Tóchuir was one of four small early territorial units in Inishowen. Each seems to have been defined by its productive coreland, its defensible hilltop enclosures and its mother church. The sites of several early monasteries, marked by a number of grave-yards and outstanding high crosses, reinforce a sense of investment in and of spiritual ties to the land. They stand as eternal markers of productivity and élite patronage.[14] The *Magh Tóchuir* and its neighbours were cleared, settled and farmed long before Patrick's claimed visit in the fifth century. Lordship, and the extraction of the land's surplus as food and service renders, is written into every monument, grassy field, burial ground and high cross. In Ireland, where oral tradition, archaeology and early literature combine as nowhere else to entwine the pragmatic and the metaphysical, continuity in such cultural corelands is deeply felt, tangible even.

In the lands that were once *Britannia*, the standing stones have largely been prised from their sockets and unsentimentally broken up for hard-core or used as gate posts. Churches are divorced from their pre-Reformation traditions, if not from their medieval parishes; hillforts are antique curios rather than living testaments. No one now living sees the *tumuli* dotting the skyline of wold and fell as the burial places of an unbroken line of their own ancestors; such connections were fractured long ago. The names of Early Medieval peoples – the dwellers on the River Arrow; the descendants of Hroða; the Gododdin of battle poetry – are forgotten or culturally meaningless. Even so, and with large gaps and due caution for the inconsistency and fragility of the sources, an archaeology and geography of emerging lordship and identity in the fifth and sixth centuries is beginning to crystallize.

In Chapter 6 I suggested that early lordships might be identified in some *civitas* capitals; in late Roman towns and forts; at some villas and perhaps also coastal and riverine pirate enclaves. A

* Small, élite, circular enclosed settlements.
† Underground food stores associated with aristocratic food renders.

number of Tribal Hidage territories provide credible examples to support the idea. Wroxeter, where Philip Barker's sensitive excavations produced such vivid confirmation of life after the end of the empire, and whose name is derived from the Iron Age fortress on the dramatic summit of the Wrekin, gives us *Wrocansæte*. The *Westerna* of the Hidage are elsewhere associated with a small kingdom called *Magonsæte*, whose lands seem to have centred on the Roman town of *Magnis*, modern Kenchester near Hereford. Immediately to the south, the Early Medieval Welsh kingdom of *Ercyng*, although not cited in Tribal Hidage, was apparently based on the Roman town of *Ariconium*.[15] A minor people of the Middle Saxons called *Brahingas*, first mentioned in a charter of the early ninth century, were centred on the Roman town whose modern name is Braughing, north-west of Bishop's Stortford. The small South Saxon district called *Ondred*, referred to in the early eighth-century Life of St Wilfrid, may have been the *territorium* of the shore fort at Pevensey, called *Anderida* by the Romans.[16] The *Wæclingas* of Watling Street, people belonging to a district that formed part of Tribal Hidage's *Cilternsætna*,* looked to *Verulamium*, that focus of fifth-century power politics. *Caesterware*, one of the six lathes or *regiones* of Kent, directly references a fortified Roman town, *Durobrivae*: Rochester, on the River Medway.[17] Kent was itself a *civitas* with tribal origins in the Iron Age. The relationship between the eponymous kingdom of Deira, the River Derwent and the Roman fortress at *Derventio* (Malton in East Yorkshire) suggests a neat link between the siting of Roman forts at strategic locations and the natural affiliation of central places with both their *territoria* and the headwaters of significantly fertile river valleys.

Much less easily located are those smaller districts that might equate to the *pagi* of the Roman countryside. The *Dibussi*, whose name only survives on a Roman woodland sale document, lay somewhere in Kent. Elsewhere, *Hæmele* – modern Hemel Hempstead in

---

* Assessed at 4,000 hides and based on the Chiltern massif that separates the Thames Valley from the Midlands counties.

Hertfordshire – is cited in a charter of about 704 as a *pagus*, perhaps belonging to *Cilternsæte*.[18] How many more of the minor districts whose names survive, like the Rodings, to suggest landholdings belonging to a named and apparently Germanic lord are, in essence, the ghosts of *pagi*, supporting small lordships with their renders through the Roman period and into the Early Medieval centuries?

Not all early peoples and districts were necessarily subject to direct territorial lordship. West Heslerton shows no sign of having been dominated by an élite dwelling and there are no princely burials here. But, like its neighbours, it enjoyed an apparently entrenched set of rights to a strip of resources, including valuable summer pasturage on the high Wolds. Eventually, if not originally, its lords were the kings of Deira. The downlanders of Salisbury Plain, encountered in Chapter 1, seem to have rubbed along very well with no sign of the estate centre that would betray the presence of local lordship. The dozen or so villages that flanked the western plains during the Roman period may, then and later, have enjoyed and managed common rights over the high pastures of the central plateau without a protecting and extorting chieftain looking over their shoulders and greedily counting their herds.

Where critical resources – wood pastures, water meadows, summer grazing – were shared between multiple communities, it seems likely that intercommunal rights must have been negotiated between groups with a mutual interest in protecting, defending and exploiting them. Commoners might always have managed their extensive resources co-operatively, as the verderers of the New Forest do, administering justice from courts at which each community was represented and militantly upholding their privileges. An outstanding Early Medieval example is preserved in the Domesday entries for the six Kentish lathes, at least three of which – *Weowara*, *Limenweara*, and *Burghware* (the *territorium* of the Roman town at Canterbury) – enjoyed rights to wood pasture in the dense woodlands of the High Weald even if, as in the case of *Burghware*, they must travel across a neighbouring territory to access them. Such rights may even have originated in the Roman period or Iron Age. Ancient routeways through these lands, still etched on maps, betray the physicality of those rights.

Even so, lands free of direct local lordship may have owed tribute to some external, overarching power. A recent, detailed analysis of early 'Anglo-Saxon' material from Kent and Sussex concludes that the very productive coastal lands and iron-rich wood pastures of the Weald were subject to tributary overlordship, perhaps even political control, by Frankish kings from across the Channel.[19]

It has long been recognized that there is a significant clustering of small territories in the Tribal Hidage entries for the East Midlands and the Fenlands that surround the Wash. These *regiones* or provinces, none of which survived in later centuries as independent kingdoms, offer vital clues to the evolution of England's early political geography. The first of these, south of the kingdom of *Lindes Farona* or Lindsey, are a pair whose names are absent from modern maps: *Suð Gyrwa* and *Norþ Gyrwa*: South and North *Gyrwa*, assessed at 600 hides each. Bede knew that the monastic church founded at *Medehamstede* (Peterborough) lay in the lands of the *Gyrwe*. Indeed, the immense estates with which it was generously endowed in the seventh century may, essentially, have consisted of that territory.[20] Bede could even name one of its ealdormen: Tondberht, whose widow Æðelðrið, later famous as a monastic entrepreneur, married a Northumbrian king in the late seventh century.[21] By Bede's day, then, lands on the western edge of the Fens, including the area around *Durobrivae* that had once been so rich in grand villas, pottery industries and affluent Christians, were known as *Gywre*. The name, appropriately, has the same root as Bede's own Jarrow, meaning 'fen' or 'marsh'.

Next on the Hidage list are East and West *Wixna*, assessed at 300 and 600 hides respectively. Susan Oosthuizen, who has made a special study of the Early Medieval Fenlands, believes that the *Wixna* may be located along the River Wissey* and as far west as the mouths of the rivers Ouse and Nene at Wisbech. They

---

* A likely derivation for the names *Wisse* and *Wixna*, it rises near Bradenham in Norfolk and joins the Ouse near Downham Market.

probably describe the same region as the *Wisse* recorded in the early eighth-century *Vita* of St Guthlac, the hermit of Crowland.[22] West of *Wixna* and north of *Gyrwa* lay *Spalda* – home of the 'dwellers by the drain' (their name passed down to us in the southern Lincoln-shire town of Spalding) – a 600-hide region of fenland bounded on the north-east by the Wash and consisting of a number of *vills* occupying the silt band that protects the inland fens from the sea.

The *Wigesta*, dwellers in a 900-hide territory somewhere close to the Fenland zone, cannot be securely located, perhaps because their lands lay within the kingdom of the East Angles; but the larger, 1,200-hide region called *Herefinna*, next on the Hidage list, survived into the medieval period as two hundreds called *Hyrst-ingas*. As the 'hirst' name suggests, they enjoyed rights to wood pastures on the relatively high ground north of the River Great Ouse; but they also laid claim to a share of the rich resources of the south-western Fens. Likewise, their neighbour to the north-west, *Sweodora*, was a modest 300-hide territory whose name is pre-served in Sword Point, a spur of elevated land projecting into the southern edge of Whittlesey Mere,* which belonged among the medieval possessions of Sawtry Abbey.

Tribal Hidage, then, describes a ring of districts and larger regions around the Fen edge that owed tribute to its seventh-century overlords in Mercia or Northumbria. It has nothing to say about the central marshes penetrated by the Roman Fen Cause-way, once dominated by the establishment at Stonea Grange and where a number of economically important islands came to promi-nence from the late seventh century. Susan Oosthuizen, allowing Bede to intrude on the otherwise neat but incomplete Tribal Hidage pattern, supplies the missing territory: *Elge*,† forming the

---

* Until the last few centuries it was one of the largest areas of open water in England – some 5 square miles in extent – but only about 3 ft deep.

† *El* + *-ge*. The first element may refer to the island; or to eels (Oosthuizen 2017, 35). The *-ge* element is rare and early. It is found in Surrey (*Suþrige* – the Southern district), in four Kentish districts, Eastry (*Eastorege*), Westry (Brooks 1989, 69), Sturry and Lyminge and also in Vange in Essex. Cox 1976, 64.

core endowment with which the Northumbrian queen, Æðelðrið, later St Audrey, founded her monastic church on the Isle of Ely in 673.[23] Oosthuizen has also identified a number of potentially early territories lying on the periphery of the Fens: *Meahala*, *Ælm* and Gruntifen; and districts identified by groups called *Bilsingge* and *Beorningas*.[24] None of these is recorded in Tribal Hidage; they may indicate smaller districts – *pagi* even – within larger, named *regiones*.

The names of such territories are telling. Some are descriptive of topography: islands, marshes, edges, boundaries or rivers. Some are deeply obscure toponyms first coined in Brythonic, on whose origins it is not worth speculating but which reflect the survival into later centuries of communities still speaking the native language. A few names hint at the logic of the system: the district called Oundle in Northamptonshire, for example, where St Wilfrid founded a monastery at the end of the seventh century, derives from a word – *Inundulum*[25] – meaning 'division or share' or, perhaps, 'undivided'.[26]

A significant number of early districts are either named for territorial centres – Roman forts like *Anderida* on the Sussex shore, for example – or for the people who inhabited them. Names ending *-inga*, of which more than a score can be shown to originate before the eighth century, are, by and large, compounded with a personal name – the Hroða of the Rodings in Essex, for example, or the Dene of the Dengie peninsula in the same county.[27] The *-inga* names look as though they were formed during the emergence of dominant households in small settlements. Some of these households were later able to assert rights of lordship over, first, their neighbours and then over whole districts. The names are unlikely to belong to the fifth century, when the settlements and cemeteries so far excavated show few signs of dominant households or local lordship. They belong more credibly to the middle of the sixth century and after when, as in the later phases at West Stow, a single household came to achieve prominence. By attaching the name of a probably long-dead (if not fictional or semi-legendary) founding individual to both their group and the wider district, households and dynasties claiming lordship and render rights over others were able to assert that such rights had *always* been theirs. Like the lathes of Kent, Fenland districts and groups with strong and enduring identities were defined by the rights that their commoners had claimed, time out of mind, to the precious riches of the lower, uninhabitable Fens: water meadows, salterns, turbaries (peat cuttings), fishing pools and streams; and the hay, reeds and sedge that grew there so abundantly.

Rights held in common elsewhere have survived, improbably, into the modern age because they were fossilized by the Forest Laws of the twelfth century. Royal forests were hunting preserves – more or less wooded, often predominantly open heathland – but the Norman kings who identified, appropriated and protected them came into conflict with those defending ancient claims to their resources. The verderers of the New Forest in Hampshire successfully claimed, and still claim, rights to common pasture, estovers (wood cut for fuel), turbaries, marl (clay diggings), pannage (autumn grazing for swine on acorns and beech mast) and fern (bracken). The foresters of Epping enjoy similar rights under the 'lordship' of the Corporation of London.

The approximate geographies of Fenland districts and minor territories can be reconstructed retrospectively because communal rights in those communities were still being claimed when Domesday Book was compiled in 1086; and even later medieval documents – tax rolls, manorial records and so on – show how those rights were jealously defended against encroaching neighbours and acquisitive overlords across the centuries.[28] The survival of many early place names supports the general case.

In other parts of the former Roman province, such detailed knowledge of groups and their rights of access to resources in common is beyond reconstruction. But the parish boundaries along the edges of Salisbury Plain form characteristic strips cutting across the contours, like those seen along the northern edge of the Yorkshire Wolds and elsewhere. As in the Wolds, Fens and Weald, perhaps also the high ground of Dartmoor, rights of exploitation over high summer pastures on the downs are likely to have been held in common, demarcated as much by long practice and locally curated knowledge as by strictly defined boundaries.[29]

That Ely, and several other identifiable early territories of the Fenlands, are absent from Tribal Hidage reflects some of the problems that royal administrators from the seventh century onwards encountered when attempting to fit the real geography of district, region and province into a theoretical scheme. Wessex, Kent and the lands of the *Gyrwe* patently occupied different tiers of the lordly hierarchy. While the exorbitant tribute demanded from the West Saxons might be delivered in person, in cash, by their king in a ceremony of submission and fealty in which he was both honoured and judiciously humiliated, the ealdorman of South *Gyrwa* might not even be eligible to sit on the same bench at a feast; might by no means have been able to realize the sort of cash asset – bullion and treasure – that West Saxon kings could lay their hands on. Cattle and sheep, prized horses, valuable commodities like salt, fish and locally crafted metalwork were portable alternatives, directly reflecting the bounty of each region. Administrators may also have lacked detailed geographical knowledge, which may explain why parts of the Hidage list seem to follow in a logical scheme while others appear dislocated. They had no maps to go by. In attempting to rationalize, they also categorized: *Gyrwa* was divided for convenience into northern and southern provinces of equal-sized assessments, while both *Willa* and *Wixna* were divided into east and west districts, albeit in unequal hidages.

Put together, the Fenland districts and provinces named in the Hidage* add up to a convenient 6,900 hides – in other words, about the size of a 'standard' unit of the third tier of kingdoms, like that of the South Saxons, Lindsey and *Hwicce*. Seven thousand hides seems to be the assessment threshold for territories whose lords were kings (Bede's *reges*) with generations of royal forbears behind them, rather than mere ealdormen (Bede's *principes*). But

* Counting, as a coherent geographical group, North and South *Gyrwe*, East and West *Wixna*, *Spalda*, *Wigesta*, *Herefinna*, *Sweodora*, *Gifla*, *Hicca* and East and West *Willa*.

it is doubtful if such theoretical conveniences reflected the way that the inhabitants thought of, or named themselves.

It is a frustrating feature of Tribal Hidage that the internal political geographies of the larger seventh-century kingdoms, assessed as single units, are thus obscured. It was convenient for an overlord – King Edwin in Northumbria or, perhaps, Wulfhere or Æðelred in Mercia – to deal with a single tributary king even if, in reality, that king himself ruled, or claimed rule, over a mosaic of disparate provinces and regions. When, in 577, King Ceawlin of the West Saxons went to war with his neighbours, he killed three British kings whose territories were apparently based on former Roman towns at Bath, Gloucester and Cirencester – at least, according to the *Anglo-Saxon Chronicle*. The latter pair belonged within the later Tribal Hidage kingdom of *Hwicce*, while Bath must have sat close to its border with the West Saxons. And when King Penda of Mercia was killed in battle against his bitter rival King Oswiu of Northumbria in 655 at a battle on the River Winwæd, no fewer than thirty *duces* were said to have fallen with him.[30] One of these was his ally, King Æðelhere of East Anglia; many of the others must have ruled provinces within greater Mercia whose names are lost to us.*

It is tempting to see, in this profusion of smaller and larger political units, a snapshot of an apparently smooth evolution from small, local, independent lordships towards the agglomerations of regions and provinces under increasingly powerful kings; and many would see the middle of the sixth century as the time when such overlordships first emerged. It may be an illusion, however. Many polities may have come into temporary being, as political fortunes waxed and waned, only to fall into obscurity or be wiped out by a successful rival. Territories were subject to all sorts of fissile and agglomerative forces, most of which can only be inferred from a distance. It is, nevertheless, a striking feature of Tribal

* Some of these districts can be suggested from clues in later charters or Domesday. See the Appendix.

Hidage that the partial geography it describes coincides with the core area of the Roman province bounded by the Vale of York, the Trent valley, the Severn and Wye valleys and the River Parrett: the province of town and villa. The early kings of these lands were, in many respects, direct inheritors of the Roman state.

Outside the heartlands of *Britannia* listed in Tribal Hidage, even less detail is available to draw political maps of the fifth and sixth centuries. Gildas's lopsided portrait of tyrants in the west* shows that at least four of the former *civitates* survived, albeit in fragmented form, under the rule of nominally Christian men he called *tyranni*: *Dumnonia* under Constantine; the *Demetae* of Dyfed, perhaps split between Aurelius Caninus and Vortipor; the *Deceangli*, later Tegeingle and then Rhos, ruled by the very wicked Cuneglasus; and the *Ordovices* of what later became Gwynedd, fiefdom of the imperious Maglocunus.

A twelfth-century poem describes Dyfed's seven *cantrefi* – a rough Welsh equivalent of *pagi* and the Anglo-Saxon 'hundred'.[31] The names of other districts within the former *civitates* occur sporadically in late material: the *pagus* of the *Gangani* in Gwynedd; Gwŷr, Ystrad Tywi and Cedweli in Dyfed on the Bristol Channel. A number of additional territories, perhaps with origins in the fifth or sixth centuries, are recorded from the eighth century onwards: *Gwrtheyrnion* and *Buellt*, west of the River Wye, whose king was said to be descended from no less a figure than Vortigern; *Brycheiniog*, whose kings built a royal residence on Wales's only crannog in Llangorse lake; and Gwent, the lands of the *Silures* based on their *civitas* capital at *Venta Silurum* (Caerwent). In *Dumnonia*, there have been suggestions that medieval hundreds such as Penwith, Pydar, Trigg and Kerrier may preserve older territorial divisions.[32]

The large central and eastern part of Wales that would become the very powerful Early Medieval kingdom of Powys, territory that had once belonged to the *civitas* of the *Cornovii* centred on Wroxeter, is curiously missing from Gildas's account. The name

* See Chapter 6, p. 197.

Powys derives from Latin *pagenses* – 'country folk', perhaps a western division of the *Cornovii* of which the eastern part would emerge as the relatively more urbane *Wrocansætna* of Tribal Hidage. Confirmation that names current during the Roman period survived into later centuries comes from the memorial stone raised to Corbalengus the Ordovician.* The unaccountably large gap in Gildas's Welsh geography prompts one to wonder if his acquaintance with the political landscape was confined to coastal provinces; whether his intelligence was essentially drawn from seaborne correspondents.

Early Welsh arrangements ought to offer an insight into the ways in which the former province adapted late Roman taxation arrangements to native ideas of lordship, renders and common rights. Unfortunately, the earliest evidence is very late – much of it belonging to the twelfth century. But charters recording gifts of land from kings to found churches, supported by the food rents of designated estates, may yet preserve some of the earliest territorial arrangements – their abbots, in effect, inheriting lordship rights to collect services and food renders from the lands over which they were granted control. Thomas Charles-Edwards has teased out the essence of some very complex material to show that in Welsh tradition there was a strong relationship between the extent (*uncia*) of land whose lords had rights over it and the quantity of food render (*modii*) that it could be expected to yield. Thus, an estate of so many *unciae* might yield to its lord a designated render in *modii* of ale, barley, meat, honey or wheat. These ideas eventually evolved into a more formal equation in which twelve *modii* constituted one *uncia*.[33] Wendy Davies, who has studied both the Welsh arrangements and the peculiarities of Tribal Hidage, sees the *uncia* as a late Roman unit of land heritable by a member of the *curialis* – the local nobility of the *civitates*, among whose number Patrick's father counted himself.[34]

Such a system, if it can be applied to the heartlands of the former province during the fifth century, might have survived longest in

* Referred to in the previous chapter; see p. 219.

territories dominated by towns like Canterbury, Lincoln, Leicester, Great Chesterford, Wroxeter and Alcester. In early Wales, evidence for territories emerging from shared access to resources like pasture, river and woodland are difficult to identify. But it seems that when large estates consisting of several *trefi* (equivalent to townships or *villae*, like the individual parishes of the Essex Rodings) formed to manage a variety of resources under a single lordship, the shape of their lands was dictated by the needs of transhumant economies: low-lying, winter settlements of small enclosures, manured fields and paddocks, meadows and rivers connected physically or by customary right, as in the case of *Burghware* in Kent, to distant summer pastures. Whole communities may have spent their summers in these broad uplands.[35]

Surviving sources for territorial geography in Caledonia are thin. Cultural cores that emerged as powerful kingdoms in the seventh century and later can be identified in Strathclyde, whose kings ruled from the imposing massif of Dumbarton Rock or *Alclut* overlooking the River Clyde; the lands of the *Wæteras* – later Fortriu – around the Moray Firth; and probably Strathearn, a southern Pictish heartland. Other territories, or peoples, can be roughly reconstructed: *Aeron* in what became Ayrshire; *Fib*, or Fife in the east; *Athfotla* in Atholl; *Cat* in Caithness and Sutherland; *Ce* in Aberdeenshire; *Manau* at the head of the Forth valley; and the *Gododdin* of Lothian. By the time that written sources begin to refer to the Gaelic-speaking west, a kingdom called Dál Riata, claiming lordship on both sides of the North Channel, had emerged as a powerful federation of clans or *cenéla*. Their names are recorded in a tenth-century document in Old Irish known as the *Senchus Fer n'Alban*, 'The History of the Men of Scotland', which purports to account for their origins. The *cenéla*, like those in Ireland, are associated with legendary founding dynasts and homelands: the Cenél nGabráin in *Corcu Réti* (Kintyre), Cowal, Bute and Arran; the Cenél nŒngusa on Jura and Islay and the Cenél Loairn in northern Argyll and Mull. The *Senchus* records that households in Dál Riata rendered military services, providing armed oarsmen for the amphibious assault forces of their kings.[36]

Smaller territorial units – equivalents of the *villae* or townships that give such a detailed picture in England – are textually invisible for the centuries before literate monks began to incorporate their geographies into the *vitae* of holy men and women. Excavating and dating the settlements of Early Medieval Scotland is also challenging. But Scotland is rich in surviving stone sculpture and in the remains of duns, brochs, souterrains and crannogs – all signs of a vigorous pattern of lordship unlikely to have been interfered with by Rome. Archaeological research in Aberdeenshire around the medieval lordship centre of Rhynie,* on Shetland and, in particular, on Orkney, with its long summer days, fertile soils and fine building stone, has revealed an incomparable degree of agricultural and architectural sophistication in settlements both before and right through the first millennium.[37] Livestock were central to the pastoral life: for subsistence in meat, milk, cheese, leather, wool and bone; for pulling plough and harrow and hauling fuel, grain and wood; for renders and gift giving; as a focus for displaying wealth, status and a sense of pride and honour in household and kin.[38] As in Ireland, where animals figure prominently in the lives of saints and in law tracts, the earliest Scottish saints' *vitae* are full of incidents reflecting the intertwined existence of communities and their beasts. Bulls and stallions and their frequent representation in the art of power speak of the mythical potency of animal fertility and strength evoked so marvellously in the Irish epic *Táin Bó Cúailnge*. The pastoral life was supplemented by foraging, fishing and hunting over extensive tracts of land. A widespread practice of transhumance is probably reflected in the hundreds of crannogs known from across Scotland. The remains of souterrains, underground stores or refuges reflective of élite prestige, are concentrated on the more fertile soils of Angus, Perth and Aberdeenshire. A unit of land defining a territory from which a cross-section of resources might be obtained to sustain a community all the year round, like Welsh *uncia*, survives in the term

* See Chapter 12, p. 393.

dabhach* – a measure, it seems, of land that could support so many oxen.

Between Caledonia and *Britannia* proper, thanks to the survival of archaic remnants of food and service renders in medieval written sources and the relative conservatism of regional landholdings, a more coherent map of political geography can be drawn, at least for the seventh century onwards. In north Northumberland, as elsewhere, territories that had only briefly been subject to direct Roman rule evolved a system of drawing renders from parcels of land containing diverse resources: rivers, water meadows, tractable arable land, woodland and hill pastures. Some territories, like *Bromic* on the upper reaches of the River Breamish, consisted of river valleys whose people were probably closely connected by kin, like the *cenéla* of Ireland and Argyll. Food renders and services – both agricultural and military – were drawn from a number of smaller units (later called *villae* or townships) towards a centre of lordly residence (called, by the seventh century, a *villa regia* or royal township). In the early seventh century, when Bernician kings began to donate extensive land holdings to their Irish monastic clients on Lindisfarne, they were able to portray a detailed hierarchy of territorial lordship – that is, they knew what lands they possessed, what those lands consisted of, and where their boundaries lay.†

Congruent groups of adjoined *villae*, with a single royal township at their centre, were called shires. Thus, Lindisfarne was endowed with estates consisting of its own hinterland (later called Islandshire) and an adjacent territory surrounding a *villa regia* at Norham on Tweed (later Norhamshire). These territories were made up of contiguous, smaller lordship units (the *villae* or townships) which were said to be dependencies (*appendiciis*) of the shire. The shire was thus both a whole political and economic

* Pronounced 'dawvach'.
† Territories and their boundaries must have been dynamic, responding to the vagaries of economic and political fortunes over generations. Geographers and archaeologists are seeing mere snapshots of these dynamics; rarely the processes of change.

unit and a collection of coherent adjoining territories. The case for a similar shire-type system of thanages operating in southern Pictland during these centuries, predicated on the control of the same set of landscape and cultural resources, in which *cain* – the agricultural surplus – and *conveth* – obligations of hospitality – were key reciprocal ingredients, has been made by archaeologist Stephen Driscoll.[39] Colm O'Brien has reconstructed the Early Medieval shire units that comprised northern Bernicia and shown how one of these, Gefrinshire, was the *territorium* of *Ad Gefrin*: Yeavering, the royal Bernician township with roots deep in the pre-Christian tribal past of the *Votadini*.[40] The *villa regia* here, described by Bede in his account of the fortunes of Bernician kings, drew on precisely the range of resources that sustainable lordship required; drew too on very ancient associations with tribal assembly (Yeavering Bell hillfort looks down on it) and cult practice.*

Early Medieval kingship did not emerge from chaos; nor did it invent new rules as it went along. It was a more or less organic development of the fundamental mechanisms by which territorial lordship operated and sustained itself, in a land without direct state administration but underpinned by the impeccable logic of the seasons, the needs of farmer and pastoralist and long investment in cultural corelands inherited from generations of forbears.

From a dazzling kaleidoscope of territories and lordships, communities, rights and local geographies, the tensions driving fifth- and sixth-century society come into focus. Gildas, living on the western periphery of the action, saw ethnic and dynastic rivalries behind a social and moral decline that governors and watchmen were powerless to resist, while 'British' kings and clergy were complicit in the political and religious failures that he witnessed. Geographers and historians are latter-day witnesses to some of the mechanisms driving these tensions across the heartlands of the former Roman province.

* See below, p. 353.

Communities competed for a share of the most precious resources: wood pasture for grazing cattle, sheep and pigs; water meadows, their fertility constantly renewed by silts deposited in annual floods; easily ploughed and well-drained rich soils; brine springs and salterns. In some regions ancient custom fostered a sense of shared rights, maintained and enforced by custom. A sense of communal self-interest was expressed in undifferentiated housing and central burial sites that also served as assembly places. Where such communities resisted internal and external pressures to compete with each other, some very early, often Brythonic topographic district and regional names survived into the written historical record: *Spalda*; *Gyrwa*; *Arosætna*. Over a span of more than a century tensions within and between these communities may have propelled the fashion for warrior burial or the dominance of a single household within a community. The scores of district names that survived as -*ingas* are eloquent testimony to these forces operating at local level.

A quite different sense of territorial control and lordship is expressed in the fortunes of the smaller late Roman towns, where a privatized élite asserted lordship over, and rights to collect renders from, local territories. Some of these rights seem likely to have been franchised out to bands of *laeti* or *bucellari*, recruited to protect both economic interests and, ironically, an idea of *Romanitas*. Commanders of forts isolated from political, civil and military support negotiated with or imposed dependent relations on their communities. Elsewhere, pirate bands from across the North Sea carved out niche territories for themselves and extorted renders from their hinterland while, in the west and north, tribal remnants of the *civitates* of Britannia were the nascent kingdoms whose objectionable rulers so exercised Gildas.

Nothing is inevitable in history; but it is not surprising that, without the controlling forces of an overarching state, these myriad strategies should come into conflict with each other. Disease, climatic deterioration, ethnic rivalry or resentment and social competition, displayed so overtly in language, weaponry and burial custom, tested relations between neighbours, lords and dependants to their limits. Warlords and their *comites* must flex their muscles, expand the lands from which they could draw renders; must, above all, fight to display their credentials against neighbours and rivals. Dynastic claims to territory led to tensions between families and probably the extinction and amalgamation of clan affiliations and group names – not necessarily a linear or irreversible process. Commoners resisted outsiders' claims on their rights; resisted the imposition of tributary taxes from outside. Small, self-sufficient communities were first imposed upon, then absorbed; sometimes they must have broken free from external lordship. The resolution of, or failure to resolve tensions: between lords, attempting to extract render and control the flow of services in local districts, and people defending customary rights with vigour is, in essence, the story of the Middle Ages.

In a socially and politically competitive world, it seems that an outwardly Germanic cultural affiliation – in identity, language and material possessions – offered significant advantages to many communities and would-be lords. And in these evolutions it is also striking that over most of the former province* the hide became the standard unit of land: not equivalent to acreage but to the value of its taxable resources. Bede, using the term *familiae* as a Latin equivalent to the hide, made explicit the link between render and household, the principal social unit in Britain. When the earliest royal endowments were made to the church in the early seventh century, the form of the grant recorded rights to exact render from so many hides or *familiae* – usually in multiples of ten. The geographies, fossilized in ecclesiastical grants, that come into focus from the seventh century onwards are monuments to those tensions and processes at work.

---

* Kent is an exception, with sulungs, a rough equivalent of the hide, as a unit of landed render.

9

Horizons

The view from the hill – naming places – salters – travellers in an antique land – navigators – *Ennor* – feasting – Trethurgy – the North Sea basin

E Ware jar found at Loch Glashan crannog in Argyll, manufactured in the Bordeaux region of France in the late sixth to seventh century and thought to be the domestic pottery of Gaulish traders.

S tand on top of the Wrekin, the 1,300 ft-high tree-clad massif on which the indomitable tribal fortress of the *Cornovii* once stood, and your view encompasses a vast horizon: from the peak of Caeder Idris almost 60 miles away on Cardigan Bay to Lancashire's Forest of Bowland at more than 80 miles; from Birmingham, 30 miles to the south-east, to the Brecon Beacons and Long Mynd in the south-west. Closer by – an hour's walk, no more – one can make out, with the aid of a map, the squat square tower of St Andrew's church, Wroxeter, sitting on the bank of the deep, swift waters of the River Severn in a quiet corner of a once great Roman city. Shrewsbury,* Wroxeter's eventual Anglo-Saxon replacement built by King Ælfred's daughter Æðelflæd early in the tenth century, lies another hour or so's walk beyond, protected by a penannular loop of the river. The Severn linked Wroxeter to other towns downstream and, eventually, to the seas that connected it to the mother city of the Roman world.

The Wrekin sees, and can be seen from, a dozen Welsh and English counties – a reminder that the horizons of *Britannia*'s fifth- and sixth-century inhabitants may not have been limited solely to the daily compass of farmyard and field. For the most part, it is true, farmers living in its shadow inhabited a smaller world. At Wrekin's western foot lies the hamlet of Rushton, 'Rush farm', a score of houses set alongside a lane that forms a small loop. Five minor roads and footpaths radiate out from, or converge on, Rushton. The suffix *-tun* implies a central place or functionally significant settlement. Together with the radial routes the name suggests that, early in its life, Rushton lay at the heart of a small estate whose most notable resource was its harvest of rushes – valued as bedding, hygienic flooring and as a roofing material. The pattern of minor routes at whose centre it lies covers a modest area of perhaps 1.5 square miles. Outlying farms and homesteads, whose people rendered food and services to the more senior household at Rushton, would not have had to walk more than a mile or so to deliver their dues. Some of the inhabitants may have spent their

* OE *Scrobbesbyrig*: 'Scrubby fortress'.

The still-standing masonry of the public bath complex at Wroxeter,
with the Wrekin in the background.

entire lives without ever bothering – or having the time – to climb
Wrekin's steep slopes for the sake of the view. But it is perfectly
possible that the Wrekin saw festive assemblies that marked the
passing seasons; that, a few times every year, local people gazed
out from the hilltop and wondered, or could even say, what lay
over the horizon.

Rushton was long ago incorporated into a larger landholding, the medieval parish of Wroxeter in the Domesday hundred of Wrockwardine.* If farmers rendered their goods to a petty lord at Rushton, Rushton in turn rendered to Wroxeter. As both excavations and the evidence of Tribal Hidage show, the principal settlement and royal estate centre of the *Wrocansætna* must have been a rather grander affair, even in the centuries after 400, than it is now. Rushton's minor lord did not have to travel more than 3 miles to pay his respects to the chief of the *Wrocansætna* and deliver his cartloads of rushes to thatch the great timber hall there.

For the dwellers of West Heslerton, on the north edge of the Yorkshire Wolds, the world must have been experienced along a pair of perpendicular axes. Landholdings here took the form of long strips, about a mile wide, running from the flat, peaty carrs† by the River Derwent south towards higher, drier ground where modern roads run and settlements lie, where West Heslerton's Early Medieval population lived and were buried. From here, tracks and lanes led either directly up the scarp face onto the chalk grasslands of the Wolds or by more tractable, zig-zag ways suited to cattle and wheeled vehicles. From the edge of the Wolds the view to the north takes in a splendid panorama: the wooded slopes and bleak plateaux of the North York Moors and the marshier Vale of Pickering. A little further back from the scarp edge the high, dry wold where flocks grazed in summer offered a paradoxical sense of isolation: the North Sea coast between Scarborough and Filey cannot be seen from up here; nor can Malton, site of the Roman fort of *Derventio*. But although the abundant resources of the Vale of Pickering forced its dwellers to live much of their farming lives traversing this narrow belt, they must also have travelled east and west along the daisy-chain route that linked their village with its neighbours on either side. That route had once brought pilgrims bearing offerings to

* Recorded in 1086: 'Enclosure by the Wrekin'.
† Low-lying, seasonally flooded former wetlands.

celebrate festivals at Heslerton's spring shrine. It also connected a string of settlements with each other, with the fort and probable later royal centre at Malton and with the coast, a day's journey to the east.

Much longer seasonal journeys, the routes taken by transhumant pastoralists with their livestock and sheep, can still be traced in areas like the Waveney Valley in Norfolk and in East Kent, where dozens of parallel roads, lanes and paths have fossilized the rights of dwellers in Kent's lathes to graze their swine, cattle, horses and sheep on the High Weald. The common rights of the Middle Angles – the *Spaldingas*, *Gyrwe*, *Sweodora* and others – to drive their beasts down to summer grazing in the Fens have also left their marks in boundaries and trackways. The downlands of Salisbury Plain, the uplands of the Pennines, Cheviots, Dartmoor and Exmoor, are similarly laced with ancient routes that brought people into contact with more distant horizons and the dwellers of other lands. Visitors and seasonal travellers brought news, stories of the trail, perhaps also craft goods for trade and occasional exotic curios from afar.

The most significant meeting places – hillforts, shrines and temples, cremation cemeteries, burial mounds, ancient boundary markers and royal townships – speak of a regional geography focused on coherent landscapes like the cultural coreland of *Magh Tóchuir* or the hinterland of Cadbury hillfort. Those landscapes affected, even defined, people's horizons from the pragmatic viewpoint of farming, craft, trade, render and assembly. They also inspired loftier ideas, the pains and joys of poets and wanderers. Being exiled from one's homeland, cut off from one's kin and the protection of a lord, was experienced as physical pain,* while the urge to explore and venture beyond the horizon is as old as humankind. Standing stones, great dykes, massive ramparts and town walls, Bronze Age burial mounds and henge monuments: these were active characters on the same stage. In the minds

* In the poem called *The Wanderer*, for example (Crossley-Holland 1999, 50).

of Early Medieval poets they had been built by a lost race of giants,* while rocky outcrops, bottomless lakes, magical springs, remarkable trees and winding rivers were inhabited by spirits of more or less benign temper whose caprices must be indulged to ensure safe passage, fertile beasts and abundant crops. If most people's lives, most of the time, were circumscribed by the small-scale economics and politics of farm, *vill*, lordship and render, their cognitive journeys traversed multiple, interwoven and sometimes otherworldly landscapes.

The inhabitants of Early Medieval Britain were acutely sensitive to the topography, the physical character of their environment. They scrutinized it in minute detail for every nuance of shape, form, meaning and potential, as evidenced by many thousands of words preserved in place names of Brythonic, Latin, Old English, Gaelic and Norse origin. Travellers through the Early Medieval landscape were significant observers and describers of the routes along which they passed, of the land's opportunities, curiosities and quirks.[1] It is, to be sure, useful to know that there is a steep path ahead where ox-carts may founder; that the name of a distinctive hill profile marks a deviation in one's route; or that on the road beyond lies a ford[†] where it crosses a river. Settlements close to rivers crossed by Roman roads often acquired the useful name *Stræt-ford*, or Stratford; but there are many much more nuanced words for such important places, describing the likelihood of encountering difficult crossings, rivers impassable at certain times[‡] or even the nature of

---

* In *The Ruin*, for example (Crossley-Holland 1999, 59); and in the Wonders of Britain, part of the Nennian compilation (Morris 1980, 40).
† The Brythonic word for 'ford', which barely survives in names, was *ritu* – as in *Anderitum*, the Roman fort (and ford) at Pevensey in Sussex; and in Penrith in Cumbria.
‡ Great Somerford, for example. OE *gelād*, found in Lechlade and Crick-lade on the upper reaches of the Thames, implies a liability to flood. Nearby Fairford was a more reliable crossing place after heavy rains. Cole 2013, 34.

the riverbed.* The systematic oral mapping of a far-reaching network of tracks, paths, roads and navigable rivers assures the geographer that the horizons of post-Roman *Britannia* had not shrunk nearly so much as one might suppose. Decoding the treasure trove of information contained in such names has been one of the enduring achievements of Early Medieval scholarship.

Both native Britons and their English-speaking successors used many words to describe the shapes of hills and valleys: flat hills with rounded ends (the suffixes *-ofer* and *-ora*), concave and convex slopes; prominent, rounded hills (*-beorg*) and those cloaked with trees; steep-sided, bowl-shaped combes and denes and narrow defiles; places where otters, wolves, foxes and geese were to be found. Prominent landmarks on well-frequented seaways were named descriptively to help sailors recognize them. Names told of land cleared of trees (*-leah*) and scrubby heathland; of woods where pigs were grazed in autumn (*bær-*) and riverside settlements where assistance might be had with overland portage, or where boats might disgorge their cargoes (*-hyth*). Trees were not merely trees or woods (generally *-wudu*) but might be regarded as distinctively small (*-bearu*, as in Bagbear, Devon – a 'small wood with badgers'), regularly coppiced (*-græfe* as in many 'grove' names), lying on a slope (*-hangr*, as in Moggerhanger, Bedfordshire), in a narrow strip (*-sceaga,* as in Wythenshaw, Cheshire), or consisting of a single species (*-holt,* as in Bircholt, Kent). Large expanses of wooded uplands that acted as barriers to travel or seemed impenetrably hostile were described by the term *wald* or weald.

Settlement names, equally, betray acute sensitivity to both location and facility. They might be described by their relationship with major routeways. Names with the suffix *-stræt* invariably indicated a settlement on a Roman road, while *-peth* or *-weg* applied to those places sited on respectively shorter or longer

---

* The gravelly bed of the Cam at Shalford – shallow ford – downstream of Great Chesterford, for example. Stapleford, on the same river, was marked by posts (OE *stapol*). The many Stanfords told the traveller where to expect a solid crossing underfoot.

distance routes; -*anstig* or Ainsty-type names suggested steep roads that might challenge draught animals pulling carts or wains.* Central places, or the equivalents of service stations where repairs and lodgings might be had, often bore the suffix -*tun*; equally a name might mark a settlement as isolated (such as Stanhope in County Durham: a 'remote, stony place'). Latin -*ecles* – from *ecclesia* – comes through in several Eccles names that betray the presence of a British church with Latin speakers surviving into the Early Medieval period, while -*wicham* names (containing the Latin element *vicus*, such as Wicken Bonhunt, near Great Chesterford in Essex) imply the survival of a recognizable Roman settlement into later centuries.[2]

It is not possible to be sure how many of the thousands of names that come through into the enormous corpus of Domesday Book (compiled in 1086) were in existence during the fifth or sixth centuries. Only 224 place names are recorded from surviving documents up until the time when Bede was writing in the 730s.[3] Many of these are, by the nature of the sources recording grants to ecclesiastics, associated with churches and places visited by churchmen and cannot have existed in their recorded form before the arrival of the first Christian mission at the very end of the sixth century. Notably thin on representation in this collection are the -*tun* settlement names, which look as though they were in the process of being created by administrators only from the middle of the eighth century onwards. Some names, especially those with Brythonic or Latin roots like the -*funta* ('spring') in Chalfont, can be securely placed in the centuries either side of 400; others, like the suffixes -*leah* ('woodland, wood pasture or a clearing in a wood') and -*ham* ('farm') are sufficiently common before Bede's day to be regarded as reliably early. Many words used to describe routeways or facilities along routeways probably belong to a time, after the seventh century, when kings and their entourages and long-distance traders and churchmen were in the process of establishing coherent networks of roads over much of

---

* A cart is a two-wheeled vehicle; a wain has four wheels.

Britain. Historians cannot be sure whether Roman roads used enthusiastically by Anglo-Saxon kings and traders and often given the name *herepath* ('road fit for an army') were continuously in use from 400 onwards or whether they were rediscovered or reconstructed in later centuries. But it would be presumptuous to suggest that contemporaries of Gildas and Patrick (who, after all, found his way home from Ireland or Gaul) did not enjoy the use of Roman and even more ancient routes like the Icknield Way or the Ridgeway.

Place-name scholars have, perhaps understandably, taken it as axiomatic that Old English settlement and topographic names were introduced by Germanic settlers 'exploring new lands', as it were overpainting an existing topographical canvas of British, Latin, Pictish and Irish names. But no one can be sure if the majority of Old English names were translations of equivalent native names or new observations by fresh eyes. The most famous cautionary example of a name evolving over the centuries, and changing its meaning, is York. *Caer Ebrauc* (Brythonic, meaning the 'city of the yew tree'), became Latin *Eboracum*; then *Eoforwic* ('the trading place of the boar', as a result of English-attuned ears hearing 'boar', *eofor*, rather than 'yew', *eburos*); then *Yorvik* in Old Norse. Characteristically peaty blueish-black rivers, often *Dubhglas* in Brythonic, became *Divilis*, then Devil's Water in English. Many thousands of names have been forgotten or are only preserved in the names of fields and copses or individual farmsteads.

The idea of a clean sweep of names brought in by hordes of foreign settlers does not convince the many archaeologists who cannot see ethnic migration on such a large scale as linguistic scholars envision. There may be several reasons for this apparent incompatibility in interpreting the evidence. First, Bede is quite clear that, even in his day, when the narrative of solid, virtuous Anglo-Saxon Christianity had become dominant, many contemporary settlements still bore more than one name in more than one language – often English and Brythonic; sometimes Irish or Latin.[4] And then, any newcomer moving to an unfamiliar part of contemporary Britain or Ireland will have experienced the humiliation of finding that the natives not only pronounce names differently* but often use very local, sometimes inconsistent names for places, handed down orally. Administrators are not always sensitive to such niceties, as the Ordnance Survey name books of the nineteenth century amply testify.† So one must allow for both settlements and landscape features to have enjoyed parallel names, of which only the 'official' version survived into written documents from the eighth century onwards. The passage of more than 300 years between the fall of Rome and Bede's *Historia Ecclesiastica* allowed many generations to discard old names and adopt new ones more suited to a changing political and social climate.

Very many names for places and features in the landscape were coined by travellers as aides-mémoires, descriptive mnemonics and mental maps like songlines;[5] many others must have been brought into existence by people referring to neighbours who might have called themselves something else (something more flattering, for example, than the cold comfort of Caldicot ('cold hut') in Monmouthshire or the ethnic pejorative *Wealas*).‡

Place-name scholars have sometimes been shy to embrace the political and social realities in which the majority of names probably evolved. Those realities are predicated on the geography and anthropology of petty lordship and the renders that supported

* A recent visitor told me that he came from Southwell, in Nottinghamshire. 'You mean Suthall,' I said, 'as in the minster.' 'Oh no, only posh outsiders think we call it that,' he replied. Dwellers on the Yorkshire Wolds are apt to condescend when reminding visitors to Fridaythorpe that the correct pronunciation is 'Frithup'.

† These are often the earliest records of local names, collected by surveyors from 'respectable' local sources during the surveying for British and Irish maps in the 1850s and 1860s. For England, only those covering Cumberland, Durham, Hampshire, Northumberland and Westmoreland survived bombing raids in 1940. Scotland's name books survive intact.

‡ See p. 110.

it. Toponymists regard the so-called 'functional -*tun*s'* as features of eighth-century lordship.[6] But it seems plausible that their entry into the written record merely cemented and codified a more organic naming process evolved during previous centuries. Describing and naming one's horizons is as fundamental to human culture as spotting familiar faces in clouds.

Petty lords gathered the bulk of their consumable goods and services from their immediate hinterlands, and the radiating patterns of footpath and lane around many early *vills* testify to their importance as long-lived central places. The rendering of goods and services was fundamentally a centripetal activity. But lords also enjoyed broader horizons. The abundant resources of the British landscape are not equally distributed. Places where wood, iron, salt, good clay, shale and jet, lead, silver, copper and tin might be found warp the geographer's ideal, concentric world. Rivers, bogs, hills and Roman roads distort the mathematically flat Early Medieval model of settlement and resource distribution into all sorts of marvellous contortions. Artistic endeavour and regional specialisms in textiles, metalwork, pottery and architecture were prized then as now; and sometimes they must be sought from afar. Fifth- and sixth-century lords, attempting to live in a manner they thought appropriate to their rank, must extend their reach to acquire suitable trappings.

Droitwich Spa ('dirty market', or perhaps 'noble market') lies on the River Salwarpe ('waters that throw up salt'), a tributary of the Severn in north Worcestershire. The river, together with a convergence of Roman roads and the Latin name *Salinae*, are clues to Droitwich's importance in earlier centuries as an unusually productive and pure source of cheap salt, from the brine springs

---

* -*tun*s are those important settlements, like Rushton, whose names include descriptions of resources that might be found there, such as water, a night's lodging, timber supplies, a smith or a ferry.

that rise naturally there.* Both before and during the Roman period salt was a highly marketable commodity, otherwise obtained from salterns in the Fens and from several sources around the British coast; used as both a preservative for butter, cheese, meat and fish and for flavouring food. The Latin word *salarium* – giving us modern 'salary' – derives from its use as a currency of payment to soldiers.

Brine from Droitwich was especially prized because it contained sodium chloride in concentrations ten times that of seawater.[7] As with all minerals, the salt concession at Salinae was a Roman state monopoly, probably franchised out to merchants and members of local *curiae*. By the early eighth century the settlement at the springs, then part of the kingdom of *Hwicce*, was known as *Saltwich*, indicating its continued economic importance.[8] In the ninth century the springs were regarded by the Nennian compiler as one of the Wonders of Britain.[9]

Salt was won from the brine by boiling it to evaporate the water – using wood or charcoal as fuel – then graded and strained in baskets.[10] Rights to obtain and trade in the salt were jealously acquired and defended. Forty Domesday estates would later lay claim to a share of the profits accruing from its production or trade and it is likely that royal courts regarded salt as a kingly perquisite, suitable as part of a tributary payment and even worth going to war over.

Evidence for regional trade in fifth- and sixth-century Britain has been hard won. Perishable commodities often defy detection by the archaeologist and the recognition that pottery production continued in Britain after the end of the imperial market economy has been hampered by the difficulty of dating such conservative technologies in the absence of regular coin issues. But there are increasingly persuasive signs that regional potters were still thriving in those centuries, and the wide distribution of sherds from known production sites, like the Black Burnished Ware kilns of southeast Dorset, suggests much more than merely local

---

* As they do further north in the Cheshire 'wiches'.

interaction. The forms of many of the pots suggest that they were being made not as trade items in themselves but to contain and transport goods of high value. Several scholars have suggested that a regional trade in salt may have kept the potters in business.[11] By way of confirmation, the landscape archaeologist Della Hooke has plotted evidence* for the routes along which salt was traded from Droitwich, locally and regionally and, by way of an overland route via the River Thames, to a wider clientèle.[12]

Salt was generally transported by pack mule, a train of which might carry as much as 2–3 tons.[13] Transporting salt in sacks has its obvious downside: one is reminded of Aesop's fable in which a merchant overloads a reluctant ass with sacks containing salt; in response, the ass learns to dunk itself in the waters of a ford, shedding much of its burden. Sealed ceramic vessels containing salt of a suitable and consistent volume to trade with those who could afford it would ensure the security of a high-value salt-based economy across substantial distances. In turn, the salt trade supported and encouraged other commodities to move through the landscape. Salt pans required lead, perhaps obtained from mines in the Mendip hills or recycled from the redundant plumbing of Roman towns and villas, while the incidence of settlements containing the elements _græfe-_ and _-tun_ along the Droitwich salt-ways suggests that brine pans were fuelled by regular supplies of coppiced wood, carried by returning packhorse trains.[14] In future, archaeologists might hope to close the loop on this trail and connect potteries directly with salterns.

Regional travel was not confined to traders in raw materials like salt, dyer's madder, cloth or pottery, or even less tangible commodities like the skills of itinerant craftspeople. Gildas, complaining that in his day pilgrims were unable to reach the sites of celebrated martyrs like Alban, implies that such journeys were not in themselves unrealistic.[15]

Archaeologists pondering the ethnicity of people buried in graves accompanied by weapons or jewellery sometimes fail to appreciate

---

* In the form of place names and road names referring to salt.

some of the mechanisms by which people, fashions, materials and finished goods moved through the landscape. The finest craftsmen – capable of producing swords, helmets, gold and garnet brooches and great bronze cauldrons – were probably itinerant, journeying between lordly patrons. Several important routes seem to have given travellers continuous access to distant parts of the former province: notably the prehistoric Icknield Way that runs from the Channel coast in Dorset to Norfolk, much of it using the heights of the Berkshire Downs and the scarp edge of the Chiltern hills; and the Fosse Way, the Roman road that runs for some 180 miles between Exeter and Lincoln. Many major Roman roads and navigable waterways – especially Watling Street, Ermine Street and Dere Street; the Severn, Trent, Ouse, Thames and Fenland rivers such as the Nene and Welland – remained substantially in use during the Early Medieval centuries, travelled by pilgrims and bishops, traders in salt, pottery and exotica, envoys and messengers, warbands and drovers.[16] In this context, some of the major earthworks of the period might have played a role as tariff barriers, or in keeping out competitors' goods. But the *mund* of a king was sufficient to ensure safe passage for those bearing his authority. About the year 600 Pope Gregory's missionary, Augustine of Canterbury, seems to have had no difficulty in locating suitable British bishops with whom to hold a synod at a site on the border between the West Saxons and *Hwicce* well known to Bede's generation.[17] A clause in the laws of King Wihtred of Kent shows how important it was that travellers established their bona fides:

Gif feorran cumen man oþþe fræmde buton wege gange...
If a man from afar, or a stranger, quits the road, and neither shouts nor blows a horn, he shall be assumed to be a thief, [and as such] may be either slain or put to ransom.[18]

Markets as we understand them – *emporia* where producers, distributors and merchants met in semi-urban locations at key nodes in trading networks – were not established features of the British landscape before the first decades of the seventh century.

By then, seemingly under royal patronage, trading settlements or *wics*, in regular contact with European equivalents like Dorestad on the Rhine, Quentovic near Étaples on the River Canche and Ribe on the Jutland peninsula, had been established at *Hamwic* (near modern Southampton), *Lundenwic* (on the Thames river beach or Strand, by Aldwych), *Gipeswic* (Ipswich) and *Eoforwic* (York). Their emergence coincides with the resumption of coin minting by royal moneyers.

The revival of more or less formalized international trade in the early 600s does not mean that British markets and producers had been isolated from Continental Europe and beyond in the intervening 200 years. Far from it. Many more informal trading sites came into and went out of existence, often at small harbours or on the beaches of accessible coastlines, and generally under the eye of interested lords. The locations of some of these are betrayed by suggestive clusters of -*wic* names found on the Cumbrian coast, on the Northumberland coast between Bamburgh and Berwick, along the lower reaches of the Severn estuary and on the Yorkshire, Essex and Kent coasts.* Other beach market or port sites, such as Bantham in south Devon and Longbury Bank near Tenby in South Wales, have been identified by finds of exotica that cannot have been produced in the British Isles. From an unprepossessing sand bank on Cheshire's Wirral† next to the village of Meols (pronounced Mells), thousands of artefacts have been washed up or excavated over the centuries. Their chronological spread and far-flung origins shows that high-value goods from many parts of the former Roman empire – including such wonders as a pilgrim's holy water flask from the shrine of St Menas in Egypt – were being landed here over hundreds of years.[19]

---

* OE -*wic*, from Latin *vicus*, is a common suffix in the names of small, specialized farming settlements such as Keswick (cheese) and Goswick (geese). Distinguishing such farms from possible beach markets is a circumstantial enterprise, as yet insufficiently researched.

† The tooth-like peninsula formed by the mouths of the rivers Mersey and Dee.

By chance, an Egyptian tale preserves the exploits of an un-lucky, or perhaps serially incompetent, sea captain who sailed to Britain from Alexandria in the early seventh century. St John the Almsgiver was patriarch of Alexandria (c.610–619), a man of great holiness and beneficence deemed worthy of two contem-porary hagiographies by men who knew him.[20] According to the second of these, by Leontius, bishop of Neapolis in the island of Cyprus, a sea captain once came to the patriarch pleading for succour because he had fallen upon evil days. John gave the man five pounds of gold and the captain used the money to buy a cargo; but the ship foundered within sight of the famous Alexandrian lighthouse, Pharos. Returning to the patriarch, the captain was admonished for his sins (there was something dodgy about the cargo, one infers) and given a further ten pounds of gold with the admonition that it must be spent wisely. Again, the captain bought a cargo and again his ship ran into difficulties. This time, both ship and cargo were lost entirely. Early Medieval hagiography is, it must be said, littered with such stories of woe and of persistent supplicants. But St John, possessing the proverbial patience of his calling, gave the ill-starred captain one more chance. This time, seemingly throwing caution to the wind, he offered him command of one of his own ships, laden with 20,000 bushels of corn.

The captain's testimony, on returning, was that he had sailed the ship for twenty days and nights through such violent seas and winds that he could not tell where they were. Then, after the twentieth day, they caught sight of the island of Britain, whose inhabitants were suffering terribly in a great famine. On landing, they told 'the chief man of the town' of their precious cargo. In return for the corn the chief man offered the captain either one *nomisma* – that is to say, hard cash – for each bushel, or a return freight of tin. The miraculous dénouement of the story recounts that on the return journey to Alexandria the captain stopped to trade some of the tin with an old business associate in Pentapolis,* and there found that the tin had turned to silver. As

---

* Cyrenaica, on the coast of eastern Libya.

literal truth it will not do but, even if the story is apocryphal, it gives archaeologists permission both to confirm that knowledge of Britain was current among Alexandrian traders in the sixth and seventh centuries and to suggest a basis for intermittent trade in high-value commodities – to justify such long, perilous and expensive journeys. And if Alexandria knew of Britain and its valuable copper and tin deposits, then Britons knew of Alexandria. One would very much like to know more about the 'chief man of the town' – which town, and where? – and about the date of such a severe famine, otherwise unrecorded.*

The Almsgiver's captain was trading in two commodities more or less invisible to archaeology: the corn was consumed; the tin alloyed with copper to make bronze. The precious metals of the Late Antique world are still being recast into every new generation of jewellery, sculpture and coinage. In theory excavation might one day yield charred grains of wheat from an African variety in a British excavation; otherwise, the concrete evidence that corroborates this anecdotal trade comes from more durable glass vessels and the ceramic containers in which goods such as olive oil and wine were carried to thirsty or pretentious British lords.

Pottery characteristic of eastern Mediterranean and north African production sites first began to turn up in quantity during Ralegh Radford's 1930s excavations at Tintagel in Cornwall.[21] These ceramics were of forms – fine slipware dinner plates, bowls and amphorae used for transporting liquids – superficially similar to material arriving during the late Roman empire. But on close inspection this pottery proved to be quite distinct from such wares in both fabric and source, and it was not turning up during excavations in the latest stratigraphic levels of Roman towns. If the petty lords of London, Birdoswald, Leicester, *Verulamium* and Great Chesterford could no longer drink decent wine and eat off posh plates, how were such luxuries available to the residents of a rocky outcrop on the Cornish coast?

---

* See Chapter 11, p. 360, for an account of sixth-century famine in Britain; no such famine is recorded for the seventh century.

Over the decades since, more material of Mediterranean origin has turned up – never in the large quantities found at Tintagel, where the stuff lies in heaps of discarded worn sherds, but in significant places, nevertheless. Alcock's excavations at South Cadbury produced both Mediterranean and Gaulish wares. At Congresbury on the Bristol Channel the recovery of amphorae, including their stoppers, indicated not just a trade in nostalgic curios but the arrival of whole containers of liquid with their lids intact. Other hillfort sites like Dinas Powys in Wales, Dunadd in Argyll, Mote of Mark in Dumfriesshire and Castle Deganwy in north Wales have also produced imported material. Many Irish sites yield small quantities even far inland, as does the Isle of Man. Monasteries like Iona and Whithorn have yielded ceramic exotica too.

Increasingly, imported pottery turns up at otherwise rather unprepossessing places – mostly overlooking small harbours or close to beaches where vessels might anchor or be drawn up. Several sites along the Atlantic seaboard and Irish Sea basin, like Peel on the Isle of Man and Dalkey Island off Dublin, became intermittent, if not regular, ports of call for ships sailing from the south. Bantham, the site of a small fort at the mouth of the River Avon in South Devon, which flows into Bigbury Bay, has now been shown by excavation to have been an important trading site, where shipments were landed, material processed and contents consumed in copious quantities. Forty-four tin ingots, probably the contents of a sixth-century wreck – perhaps on its way to Alexandria – have been retrieved from the sea here.[22]

Vanishingly few sherds of Mediterranean pottery or glass have been found away from the western seaways, or east of Exeter.* The latest analysis, by Maria Duggan, of all the available evidence shows that between about 470 and 550, wine and other less easily identified commodities were being shipped from the eastern Mediterranean

---

* Cadbury Castle is connected to the Bristol Channel by association with Ilchester, via the rivers Parrett and Yeo. The hamlet of Wick lies near the mouth of the Parrett, close to Cannington and another harbour site, Combwich.

and from north Africa, out through the Straits of Gibraltar and along the Iberian coast as far as Vigo in north-west Spain.[23] From this major international emporium ships sailed a coastal route around the Bay of Biscay, stopping specifically at Bordeaux and then periodically making their way across the English Channel to the British Isles and Ireland. It is by no means impossible that ships originating in Britain sailed the same route in reverse. After about 550 this trade stopped, for reasons that are not yet entirely clear.* Later in the sixth century a new trade network developed, centred on Bordeaux. It shared some of the destinations of the old Mediterranean trade but was subtly different in character: Tintagel, for example, has produced none of the pottery – so-called E Ware – made in or near Bordeaux and apparently used by the traders themselves. It can no longer be argued that the odd lost vessel, like the swift sailing ship full of grain despatched with such trust in providence by St John the Almsgiver, washed up on the rocky shores of Britain by chance.

To stand on the island of Tresco during the hours either side of a low spring tide is to watch a 1,500-year-old veil being drawn back: a full 20 ft tidal range filling, then emptying what was once Scilly's central plain, like a colander. The islands that form this sub-tropical archipelago are modestly hilly, nowhere more than 170 ft above modern sea level. Small fields hedged against the salty Atlantic weather enclose sheltered, inward-looking slopes fringed by golden sands and the oddly luxuriant flowers and trees that attract tourists here from far and wide. Outer-facing slopes and crags are exposed to the elements: wind-ripped, grizzled by crashing surf. The shallow sea that both isolates and connects these islands is a tempting jade. But at low spring tide the flotilla of small boats that ferries tourists, goods and post between the

* A general economic and, perhaps, climatic downturn associated with both volcanic activity and great plague, are implicated. See Chapter 11, p. 360ff.

Low spring tide in the Isles of Scilly reveals the inundated plains of what was once a single land mass in the Roman and Early Medieval periods: Ennor.

dozen or so main islands of Scilly vanishes as, one by one, skippers draw alongside a pier or buoy and tie their craft up. Cruise ships pausing overnight on their way to and from the Mediterranean and all points north lie far offshore in deeper waters. As if under the spell of some Old Testament prophet, the turning tide drains Scilly of its turquoise sea and from nowhere, it seems, citizen and tourist alike begin to pick their way, more or less dry-shod, across low sandy causeways to what had recently been a neighbouring island – to visit friends, to take advantage of the free passage or, more likely, just for the hell of it.* On several days during

---

* The channel known as The Road, between St Mary's and the northern islands, stays open to shallow draughted vessels even at low tide. The last causeway that linked St Mary's to Tresco and St Martin's seems to have finally been inundated in the medieval period, around 1200; but the now submerged sandbank of Crow Bar along which the causeway ran can still be seen from the air.

the year the seaweed-clad remains of ancient roundhouses and drystone farm walls are exposed for these few short hours; normal commerce is held in suspension; the archipelago becomes, once again, a little like the single land mass – probably called *Ennor* in Brythonic – that it was during the Roman period and as late as the eighth or ninth centuries.

Ennor's main Roman harbour seems to have been located at the now-flooded inlet called Great English Island Neck, between St Martin's and the small island of Nornour. During those centuries a putative beacon sited at a shrine* on Chapel Down, St Martin's at the eastern edge of the archipelago, was visible from another at Sennen Cove near Land's End on the Cornish mainland nearly 30 miles away, aiding regular navigation between the two.[24] Scilly's advantage was its convenience as a landfall at the southern end of the Irish Sea and as a pilotage and trading gateway to the Insular Atlantic seaboard. That status probably continued even after the end of imperial control over *Britannia* at the beginning of the fifth century.

Whether or not Scilly was the Cassiterides or Tin Islands mentioned in ancient Greek geographies is uncertain; there is no winnable tin here. Instead, *Ennor* may have been the hub for trading with both the tin mines of Cornwall and the copper, gold, silver and lead mines elsewhere around the Irish Sea basin that had drawn the Roman state to Britain in the first century CE. The survival of early chapels in the north of the archipelago on the higher ground of St Helen's and Tean, which escaped the marine inundation at the end of the first millennium, and finds of Mediterranean and Gaulish pottery from excavations on several islands, suggest that *Ennor* played no small part in linking Britain and Ireland with the Late Antique church and the maritime trading world. That network of connections would play a role in

* Charles Thomas inferred a dedication to Vesta, the goddess of hearth, home and family. The fire that always burned would be a suitable symbol for a navigation beacon whose counterpart, *Antivestaeum*, lay on the mainland. Thomas 1985, 165ff.

the early history of Insular Christianity and the Age of Saints. It brings archaeologists face to face with the politics, economics and anthropology of fifth- and sixth-century lordship and territory; and it confronts them directly with Gildas's all too unsaintly tyrants.

Early Medieval lords were required by the reciprocal rules of the food render to feast their dependants and to reward them with gifts. Birdoswald's converted granary, with its hearth, may be the modest material evidence of such bonding behaviour, inextricably tied up as it was with harvest surplus and the oath-swearing, drinking and bragging culture of the warband celebrated in *Beowulf* and *Y Gododdin*. Excavations at the costal trading site at Bantham in south Devon have revealed evidence of both production and craft activities indicative of lordly residence; and of the midden deposits that tell of conspicuous consumption.[25] Amphorae, glass drinking vessels and other fine wares recovered from élite hillfort sites – Dunadd, Cadbury, Congresbury and Dinas Powys, for example – are the solid debris of lordly feasting, perhaps at key festivals during the year.

There is no contemporary British written evidence to prove that such gatherings relied on the acquisition of wine and drinking vessels from Bordeaux and the Mediterranean; but Irish texts from the eighth century onwards are rich in allusions to the trade. They describe a certain type of jar, an *escop fina*, as a vessel for measuring wine among Gaulish and Frankish traders. A contemporary Irish term for a meeting place, or city – *bordgal* – is a proverbial borrowing from Latin *Burdigala*: Bordeaux.[26] Wine was regarded in Ireland as one of the luxuries expected at a great feast,[27] and the presence of very fine glass drinking vessels at a number of sites where imported amphorae and E Ware vessels have been found supports the case for wealthy decadence. In Christian communities wine was necessary for the celebration of the eucharist; olive oil too, perhaps, for anointing. Other valuable commodities – precious purple dyes, spices and gemstones and, in a Christian context, Egyptian papyrus for writing – are likely to have travelled as part of the same mixed, high-value/low-volume cargoes in which lords were particularly interested to assert their rights of first pickings.

Tin from Cornwall, lead from the Mendip hills, copper, silver and gold from mines in Wales and Ireland and salt from Droitwich provided incentives for Atlantic traders to make the long voyage to northern waters. Other commodities peculiar to these latitudes, and potentially highly desirable in more southern lands, included fine hunting dogs, sealskins and walrus ivory, furs and slaves – the latter acquired as payment of debt, as prisoners of war or kidnapped in raids. It was, after all, the appearance of a northern Anglian slave in the markets at Rome that supposedly inspired Pope Gregory the Great's pun on Angles and angels (*non Angli sed Angeli!*) and induced him to despatch Augustine on a proselytizing mission to Kent at the end of the sixth century.[28]

The first Mediterranean pottery imports seem to date from the decade around 475. If Gildas was writing at the end of that century, then his *tyranni* were likely both patrons and consumers of the trade in luxury goods and capable of controlling the resources to pay for them. Constantine, Aurelianus Caninus, Vortipor, Cuneglasus and Maglocunus were all conveniently placed, so far as one can locate them, in coastal territories possessing one or more known importation site. Acquiring and distributing such exotica reinforced ideas about lordly exclusivity, generosity and economic power and allowed the potentates of the old *civitates* to maintain links, albeit tenuously, with the Eastern empire.[29] Whether these lords are worthy of the title 'king' is another matter. Unless the courts of such men are to be found within the walls of late Roman towns – and so far Chester, Exeter and Caerwent have produced little or no imported material – one must suppose that they were the residents of those timber halls built at the newly fortified or re-occupied hillforts of the west. But there is nothing at any of these sites (Tintagel may be a possible exception) on a scale to compete with the early seventh-century princely burial at Sutton Hoo, the royal township of Yeavering in Northumbria or the fortress of Dunadd in Argyll.

It was in the nature of lordship that luxuries and perquisites were distributed among élite clients, collateral family members and dependants, as largesse or reward for services that might include fighting, serving at the lord's table, accompanying hunts or fostering lordly children. But another view is possible: that otherwise invisible entrepreneurs* might have enjoyed independent trading relations with overseas merchants; that they were able to enjoy the fruits of those links but were also forced to pass on to their local and regional lords a proportion of the material profits in the form of render or tribute. Either way, in western Britain, where native settlements of the post-Roman centuries look to archaeologists much like those of the Iron Age and Roman periods, the occasional presence of imported pottery and glassware from excavations otherwise lacking dating evidence brings into focus the lives of what used to be called 'the middling sort' – relatively prosperous families from stable, modestly comfortable communities. In Ireland more than 40,000 of the small, enclosed élite homesteads called raths are known. In Scotland crannogs like that excavated at Buiston in Ayrshire or Loch Glashan in Argyll have yielded imported pottery and glassware. In Cornwall many hundreds of so-called 'rounds' have been identified; just one has been completely excavated and published to modern standards.[30]

Trethurgy† lies some 2 miles north of St Austell Bay in a richly diverse landscape of granite hills and narrow, wooded valleys, set in a picturesque mosaic of odd-shaped hedged fields but blighted by the industrial debris of mines and China clay workings. Arable and dairy farms thrive here and the land, with its mild, moist climate, has supported a relatively large population since the Iron Age. A circular enclosure of about 200 ft across was constructed at Trethurgy sometime in the middle of the second century CE: a narrow, insubstantial ditch surrounding a well-constructed drystone and earth rampart. A generously proportioned, double-gated entrance was flagged and kerbed with stone – scored arcs on the flags show where the gates rubbed as they opened inwards. A central courtyard was flanked by five oval-shaped houses set inside

---

* Like the householders of Trethurgy, see below.
† *Tre-* is the Old Cornish prefix for a farmstead or estate; the qualifier here, *doferghi* means 'otter'; it might also be a personal name.

the rampart. A large byre, granary, outhouses and workshops were squeezed into available spaces, while a curious, compact polygonal structure that opened onto the courtyard has been interpreted as a shrine of some sort. Over more than 400 years the round was maintained through phases of stagnation and rebuilding, while the relative fortunes of its households waxed and waned. Into a midden deposit in the byre, some time during or after the fourth century, a tin ingot was thrown, perhaps as a cache.

Without the presence of glass and pottery from Mediterranean and Gaulish sources to back up a small number of Carbon[14] dates, Trethurgy's abandonment might have been placed conservatively at the end of the fourth century, after which no Roman coins were available to chart its fortunes. But sherds of amphorae, a fragment of a distinctive decorated conical glass beaker probably made in Bordeaux, and a single sherd of Gaulish E Ware (which did not arrive in Britain before about 570) allowed the excavators to stretch the life of the settlement close to 600 CE, after which it seems to have lapsed into terminal decline – perhaps as a result of the famine witnessed by the Alexandrian patriarch's wayward sea captain.

The oval houses so distinctive of this region during more than 1,000 years of pre-Norman history were constructed on drystone walls bearing rafters which probably met at a ridge with rounded gables. Laths strung between the rafters held turves or bundles of thatch. Wide (6 ft) doors at one end allowed light in, and a hearth provided warmth – the smoke filtering through the thatch above. Outside, in lean-to shelters or circular workshops, iron was worked, yarn spun, fabric woven and cattle tended. Surrounding fields provided pasture and ploughland. Pottery known as Gabbroic ware, common to the peninsula, made up the bulk of the objects used to store and cook, from which to drink and eat and in which to ferment ale and strain curds. But pottery also arrived in the area, probably by coastal traders, from south-east Dorset (Black Burnished Ware, which seems to have been produced well into the fifth century). Even the odd pot from Oxfordshire found its way here. Trethurgy was well connected. Grain was milled on saddle and rotary querns and mortaria were used for more refined grinding – of exotic spices, perhaps. A remarkable set of locally made stone bowls – known as Trethurgy bowls – seem to be skeuomorphic* copies of vessels originally fashioned in tin; the details of the handles soldered onto the rims of the tin originals were precisely copied in carving each bowl from a single large stone. Had wet-sieving of soil deposits for the remains of grain, small bones and other environmental debris been standard practice when Trethurgy was excavated in the early 1970s, an even richer picture might have been drawn of its inhabitants' daily lives.

The material gaps in that record are filled, in a general way, by anaerobically preserved organic remains from crannogs in Scotland; but in particular by the 1980s excavation of a comparable site in County Antrim, Northern Ireland. At a beautifully preserved seventh- to tenth-century rath at Deer Park Farms, a wooden mill wheel paddle and axle, details of timber jointing and even the coppiced hazel wattle work of the double-walled roundhouses survived intact. These and other organic materials were preserved in abundance to show the richness of the cultural inventory available in these centuries: diamond twill-woven woollen cloth, dyed red with bedstraw or madder; parts of leather shoes and the lasts used to fashion them; gaming counters; stave-built buckets; any number of small tools and devices and the bones of domestic and wild animals: all are reminders of how much has been lost at most sites.[31] Even the parasites that inhabited the inhabitants' guts are now subject to the scrutiny of palaeobiologists. Early Irish law codes, full of references to the natural world, the farming year and the value of all creatures and objects great and small, reinforce and enrich the testimony of excavation.[32]

The families who lived so comfortably at Trethurgy must stand for the hundreds of others living in similar settlements who managed to survive the end of the empire with little or no adverse

---

* Objects made in a new material but retaining functional or structural elements as decoration: like pottery with basket-weave decoration or stone crosses with pointed bases derived from earlier wooden stakes.

effect. No Roman roads have yet been confirmed this far along the south-west peninsula to indicate military control in the region. If the Roman state established a monopoly over the tin industry, its withdrawal or expulsion may have been entirely liberating. Tin occurs here naturally in pebbles of cassiterite (tin oxide) along what are known as streaming grounds. The ingot found at Trethurgy may have been smelted nearby in a clamp furnace (a hot bonfire) reaching the modest 600° Celsius necessary.* Tin, and the sea, connected the peninsula to a wider world desirous of its precious metal. From small coastal voyages to much more ambitious passages reaching far distant lands, Trethurgy's well-to-do citizens enjoyed broad horizons and the material trappings of an Atlantic-facing world.

Paradoxically, the striking nature of western contact with the Mediterranean and Atlantic worlds, infrequent as it must have been, has attracted disproportionate interest compared to the almost continuous intercourse between eastern and south-eastern Britain and the Continent after the severing of official imperial links. European affinities reflected in the extraordinarily large volume and rich variety of artefacts recovered from furnished burials of the fifth and sixth centuries have concentrated thinking on immigration rather than trade. But even migrating communities had an idea of where and why they would embark on voyages overseas. Like the Irish Sea, the North Sea is a natural basin across and around which vessels plied, sometimes speculatively, throughout the first millennium. Tidal and seasonal currents favoured circular voyages; convenient harbours and river estuaries provided trading, beaching and pilotage opportunities, knowledge of whose advantages and risks were handed down through generations of sailors. Navigation out of sight of land by stars, bird sightings, cloud formations and the characteristic patterns of wave, tide and

---

* By contrast, copper, the other essential metal for the production of bronze, melts at about 1,000°C; an iron furnace demanding much hotter temperatures over 1,500°C, requiring a constructed furnace fired by charcoal.

current allowed canny skippers to map the maritime and riverine world in detail. The Frisian traders of the seventh century and Scandinavian entrepreneurs of the eighth and ninth centuries knew perfectly well what lands and peoples lay on the far side of the North Sea and Channel and where favourable currents would take them at different times of the year.

Boats of this period are very rare finds: the most celebrated of them, the Nydam vessels dating to about 300 CE from Schleswig, southern Jutland, were sleek, clinker-built double-prowed rowing boats with steering oars.* Since they had no true keel they could not bear the mast for a square sail. But it seems likely that very many local shipbuilding traditions, suited to inshore waters, would have generated a variety of vessel types and sizes and it would not be a huge surprise if, one day, the Essex marshes or marine sediments off Ireland yielded a small sailing boat from the early post-Roman centuries. On estuaries and rivers small rowing vessels like the four-oared *faering*, punts, dugout canoes and coracles must surely have been common sights as ferries, fishing boats and short-distance trading vessels. In all waters in all states, detailed local knowledge of conditions, opportunities and hazards was a valuable asset. The well-known tale of St Brendan, so vividly reconstructed by Tim Severin and his crew in the 1970s, shows how intrepid and resilient sailors must have been.[33] The sailor Wallace Clark pioneered experimental voyages in those waters, rowing with his crew from Derry to Iona in 1963 in less than a week, to be met by a throng of supporters, including the archbishop of Canterbury, Michael Ramsey, on the beach below St Columba's abbey.[34]

Pottery is often the most reliable marker for international trade. Black Burnished Ware from south-east Dorset is found on many sites in northern France and if its production continued well into the fifth century, it may bear witness to ongoing cross-Channel trading contacts just as, in return, the Gaulish pottery known as

---

* The word 'starboard' is a contraction of 'steering board', a long paddle flexibly mounted on the aft starboard quarter.

Iona Abbey: the restored medieval complex lies above Columba's
monastic church of the 560s, at the heart of a watery world
connected by trade, culture and politics.

*céramique à l'éponge** came north across the Channel.[35] And if, as
archaeologists now judge, much of the Germanic-style metalwork
so evocative of the Anglo-Saxon colonization of south-east Britain
was, in fact, manufactured in Britain, its inspiration, like that of the
cremation urns and *grubenhäuser*, lay on the far side of the Channel
and North Sea. If one is to argue that large-scale immigration is
unnecessary to explain the rapid adoption of Continental building
and burial styles, material culture and language, one must at least
allow for a continuous and fluid commerce in ideas, trade items
and people in both directions.

The paraphernalia of individual traders – balances and weights
found in graves, especially in east Kent and along the upper Thames,
from the early sixth century onwards – prompts archaeologists to
look for the sorts of commodities passing between Britain and the
Continent.[36] Scandinavian artefacts, particularly decorative wrist

* Fine slipped ware vessels decorated with marbling or sponged patterns.

clasps, found in East Anglian graves, prove ongoing contact across the North Sea. Frankish weapons and jewellery found in Kentish graves might echo immigration or diplomatic contacts, and several scholars have suggested that Frankish kings periodically exercised political and economic *imperium* over Kent.[37] It was probably in the interests of powerful lords on both sides of the Channel to keep the seaways open and free from unsustainable levels of piracy; and it is by no means impossible that some Gallic aristocrats or Frankish lords attempted to maintain or enforce rights to landed estates in southern Britain. A recent survey suggests that the production of iron, from bloomeries in the Forest of Dean and the Weald of Kent, or through the scavenging and recycling of Roman material, might have formed a valuable bulk cargo traded along the Thames and across the Channel.[38] Salt, slaves and woollen products from small British workshops may have helped to sustain the trappings of local lordship and to foster relations further afield. By the late sixth century, we know, Frankish princesses were crossing to Kent as brides for its kings. They cannot have arrived without bearing gifts, and behind their betrothals lurks the toing and froing of diplomats and traders.

In the nineteenth century a particularly rich inhumation cemetery was partially excavated just east of the village of Sarre in the Isle of Thanet, in east Kent. The Wantsum Channel, which separated Thanet from the mainland until the end of the Middle Ages was, in Bede's day, traversable on foot in just two places.[39] Sarre (from the Brythonic word *sarn*, meaning causeway) sits on a bluff looking across low-lying, well-drained fields towards the Canterbury road. When Augustine arrived in 597 on a mission to convert the king of Kent, he was obliged to set up camp on Thanet while King Æðelberht scrutinized his bona fides and considered the embassy's propositions.* The idea that envoys and traders should install themselves at such liminal, perhaps in some way neutral, sites offshore makes sense: after all, it's what made the fortunes of places like Singapore and Hong Kong. The cemetery at Sarre served

* See Chapter 13, p. 416.

A medieval church sits inside the Roman fort at Reculver in North Kent, which overlooked and guarded the entrance to the Thames estuary and the mouth of the Wantsum channel.

a community that included traders. Grave 26 contained both a very rare woodworker's plane and a complete set of balances, with nineteen weights for measuring small, high-value items – coins, in all probability.[40] As a whole, the cemetery reinforces the idea that Kent was well placed to interact with Francia, Frisia and Scandinavia, not just because it lay at the closest crossing point of the Channel, but because its lords benefited from trade along the Thames valley. Skippers wishing to avoid the hazards of the Nore (North Foreland) were able to enter the sheltered shortcut of the Wantsum Channel and pass directly into the Thames estuary at Reculver. Several more sets of traders' balances have been found along the upper Thames.[41] Alternatively, traders at Sarre and at Fordwich on the Stour – the old harbour of Canterbury – provided convenient ports of call.

From the tidal stream of the Wantsum Channel to the drowned landscape of Scilly; from Trethurgy on the Cornish coast to South

Cadbury in the heart of Somerset; from the distinctive names of settlements that told of shelter or of a risky river crossing to the old highways of Roman Britain, the Early Medieval land-scape was known, described and exploited by lords and armies, traders and saints, farmers, potters and boatmen. Most people's lives were lived at the modest scale of field, farm, hill and stream and within the circumscribed social bonds of petty lordship. But alongside such parochial concerns hundreds of communities, with their strong sense of both belonging and identity but also an awareness of a bigger, more exotic and challenging world, were poised in the first quarter of the sixth century to embrace the ideas and institutions that would propel the Atlantic world towards the centre stage of European cultural endeavour.

Chronography II: 500–635

Abbreviations for primary sources

AC	*Annales Cambriae*. Morris 1980.
Adomnán *VC*	*Vita Sancti Colombae*. Sharpe 1995.
Ammianus *RG*	*Res Gestae*. Hamilton 1996.
ASC	*Anglo-Saxon Chronicle*. Garmonsway 1972.
AT	*Annals of Tigernach*. Online edition.
AU	*Annals of Ulster*. Online edition.
Bede *HE*	*Historia Ecclesiastica Gentis Anglorum*. Colgrave and Mynors 1994.
CG452	*Chronica Gallica* of 452. Online edition.
Constantius *VG*	*Vita Germani*. Hoare 1954.
Eddius *VW*	*Vita Wilfridi*. Colgrave 1985.
ELGG	*The Earliest Life of Gregory the Great*, by an anonymous monk of Whitby. Colgrave 1968.
Felix *VG*	*Vita Guthlaci*. Colgrave 1985.
Gildas	*De Excidio*. Winterbottom 1978.
Gregory *HF*	*Historia Francorum* or *Decem Libri Historiarum*. Thorpe 1974.
HSC	*Historia De Sancto Cuthberto*. South 2002.
LLG	*Letters of Gregory the Great*. Schaff and Wace 1895.
Nennius *HB*	*Historia Brittonum*. Morris 1980.
Orosius	*Seven Books of History Against the Pagans*. Fear 2010.
Patrick	*Confessio*. Hood 1978.
Procopius *BG*	*Bellum Gothicum*. Dewing 1914–40.

Prosper *EC*	*Epitoma Chronicon*. Mommsen 1892.
VS	*Vita I Sancti Samsonis*. Taylor 1925.
Zosimus *HN*	*Historia Nova*. Buchanan and Davis 1967.

501	Traditional date for the arrival of a chieftain named Port, at Portchester/Portsmouth with his two sons, Bieda and Magla: he slays a high-ranking Briton (*ASC*).
505	Possible date for baptism of Clovis by St Remigius in Reims.
507	Clovis defeats the Visigothic king Alaric II of Toulouse in the Battle of Vouillé.
508	Cerdic and Cynric fight the Welsh in battle at *Natanleog* (Netley Marsh, Hants), killing their king, Natanleod (*ASC*).
	— Emperor Anastasius confers honorary consulship and patriciate on Clovis; ceremony of the *Adventus* at Tours (Gregory *HF*).
514	Stuf and Wightgar arrive in three ships at *Certicesora* and defeat a British force (*ASC*).
516	The Battle of Badon Hill (*Mons Badonicus*) 'in which Arthur carried the cross on his shoulders and the Britons were the victors' (AC).
519	Traditional date for Cerdic (and Cynric) becoming king(s) in Wessex: Battle of *Cerdicesford* (*ASC*) and founding of the kingdom of Wessex.
520	Birth date of Colm Cille in Donegal (Lacey 2013).
521	Death of St Brigit (AC).
527	Cerdic and Cynric defeat British forces at Battle of *Cerdicesleag* (*ASC*).
	— Justinian becomes Eastern Roman emperor (to 565).
528	Dionysius Exiguus calculates new method of dating Easter (*ASC*); introduces AD dating popularized by Bede in the *HE*.

530	Cerdic and Cynric capture Isle of Wight and slay many men in *Wightgarabyrig* (*ASC*).
531	Procopius records emigration from Britain to Francia (Procopius *BG*).
533–534	Eastern Roman empire recovers Vandal North Africa in campaign under Belisarius.
534	Traditional date of Cerdic's death (*ASC*); he is succeeded by his son Cynric (to 560). They give the Isle of Wight to their two *nefan*,* Stuf and Wightgar.
535	Eastern Roman empire recovers Sicily and Dalmatia in campaign under Belisarius. He makes a triumphant entry into Syracuse, scattering gold coins to the masses (Procopius *BG*).
536	Eastern Roman empire recovers Naples in campaign under Belisarius.
	— Probable start of a series of extreme weather events in the northern hemisphere, believed to be caused by large volcanic eruptions in the tropics which lead to atmospheric veiling. Severe winters and crop failures follow. This may coincide with or precipitate the plague of Justinian. Major global climatic downturn until at least 542, recorded in tree ring sequences.
537	The Battle of Camlann, in which Arthur and Medraut fall; plague in Britain and Ireland (AC).
538	Eastern Roman empire recovers Rome in campaign under Belisarius (lost to Goths in 546; recovered 547).
539	Birth of the Frankish historian Gregory of Tours (died 594).
	— A 'failure of bread' (AU); Described in AT as *Perditio panis* 538.
540	Eastern Roman empire recovers Ravenna in campaign under Belisarius.
	— Traditional floruit of Gildas if the AC dating of the death of Maelgwyn of Gwynedd is correct.

---

* Possibly nephews; possibly grandsons.

	— 'Justinian plague'; first *Mortalitas magna* in Ireland (AT).
544	Wightgar dies (*ASC*); he is buried at *Wightgarasburgh*.
545	The Annals of Ulster record 'the first mortality called *bléfed*' (AU).
546	Founding of *Daire Colm Cille* (Derry) (AU), probably by Fiachra (Lacey 2013, 55).
547	Traditional date of Ida's arrival at Bamburgh (Bede *HE*); but 560 more likely (author's chronology).*
	— Death of Maelgwyn of Gwynedd in plague (AC): 'Then was the yellow plague'.
548	*Cluain Moccu Nóis* (monastery at Clonmacnoise) founded by St Ciarán (AU).
549	Date of *Mortalitas magna* or great plague (AU) – possibly a recurrence of the 'Justinian plague'. A second *Mortalitas magna* is recorded in 550 (AT).
552	Battle of *Seaorburh* (Old Sarum, Wiltshire); Cynric defeats Britons (*ASC*). The same entry includes Cerdic's genealogy.
	— Eastern Roman empire recovers northern Italy and Balkans in campaign under Narses.
554	Outbreak of a pestilence in Ireland called *sámthrosc* – likely to be of leprosy (AU).
556	A battle is fought at *Beranburh* (Barbury Castle, Wiltshire); defeat of British forces by West Saxons under Cynric and Ceawlin.
	— 'A great mortality this year' (AU).
558–560	Eastern imperial authority re-established in Italy.
558	Picts under Bruide mac Maelchon drive Dál Riatan Scots (AU) – ?back to their fortress at Dunadd. Gabrán son of Domangart, king of Dál Riata, killed (558

---

* The author's re-dating of the first few generations of Bernician kings can be found fully in Adams 2013, Appendix A.

in AC and AU; or 560). Succeeded by Conall mac Comgall (to 574).

560 Ælle, son of Yffi, succeeds to kingship of Deira (*ASC*); Ida seizes Bamburgh (author's chronology).

— Ceawlin succeeds in Wessex (to 593) (*ASC*).

— The battle of Cúil Dreimne between the Southern Uí Néill under King Diarmait mac Cerbaill and the Northern Uí Néill. (AU; or 561).

562 Colm Cille is exiled from Ulster and lands in Iona off Scotland's west coast (563 AU; 562 correctly in AC).

565 Founding of monastery on Iona (*ASC*) by Colm Cille.

— Æðelberht succeeds to kingdom of Kent (*ASC*).

— Death of the Byzantine Emperor Justinian (reigned from 527); succeeded by Justin II (to 578).

568 Ceawlin and Cutha fight against Æðelberht and drive him into Kent; they slay Oslac and Cnebba at *Wibbandun* (*ASC*): the first 'English on English' conflict.

570 Death of Gildas, 'wisest of Britons' (AC; AU); but he may have died fifty years earlier.

571 Cutha/Cuthwulf (brother of Ceawlin) fights against Britons in battle at *Biedcanford*. Cutha dies this same year (*ASC*).

— Possible date of death of Ida; succeeded by Glappa in Bernicia (author's chronology).

572 ?Death of Glappa; succeeded by Adda (author's chronology).

573 Battle of Arfderydd (?Arthuret in Cumbria) between British sub-kings in Rheged; legendary madness of Merlin (AC).

574 Death of King Conall mac Comgall (of Dál Riata) who granted the island of Iona to Colm Cille (AU). Succession of Áedán mac Gabrán to Dál Riata after a vision by Colm Cille; he is inaugurated on Iona (Adomnán *VC*).

575	Conference of Druim Cett in Ulster (AU) between Áedán mac Gabrán and Áed mac Ainmirech confirms independence of Scottic Dál Riata from Irish kingdoms and enshrines ownership of tribute and hosting responsibilities; conference is possibly convened by Colm Cille.
577	Battle of Deorham (probably Dyrham, now in South Gloucestershire); Ceawlin of Wessex's victory over the British leads to the capture of the *civitates* of Gloucester, Cirencester and Bath. Three named British kings – Coinmail, Condidan and Farinmail – are killed in the battle (*ASC*).
580	?Death of Adda; succeeded by Æðelric in Bernicia.
580/1	Áedán mac Gabrán of Dál Riata fights sea war against Picts or Irish near Orkney (AU).
582–583	Áedán mac Gabrán fights battle with either Man or the Manau of Gododdin (AU).
584	Death of Bruide mac Maelchon, king of the Picts (AU). — Battle of *Feðanleag* (Stoke Lyne, Oxfordshire): Ceawlin and Cutha fight against the Britons (*ASC*); Cutha slain (but see 571); Ceawlin captures many villages and much booty and departs in anger to his own territories. — ?Deposition of Æðelric in Bernicia; succeeded by Theodoric.
588	Ælle of Deira dies (*ASC*), possibly murdered by Æðelfrið; succeeded by ?Æðelric.
590	Probable date of the Siege of Lindisfarne by Urien of Rheged; Urien betrayed and killed by his ally King Morcant (Nennius *HB*). — Gregory the Great becomes pope, succeeding Pelagius II. — Possible date for Battle of Catraeth; defeat of Rheged and Gododdin warband by Anglian forces; destruction of the last great British warband celebrated in Aneirin's *Y Gododdin* poem.

592   Great slaughter at *Wodnesbeorh* – Adam's Grave (Alton Priors, Wiltshire): Ceol drives out his uncle Ceawlin (*ASC*).

592/3   Succession of Æðelfrið to ?Deira. Takes Bebba as Bernician wife/concubine?

593   Death of Colm Cille at Iona (Lacey 2013); succeeded by Baithne.

     — Death of Ceawlin, Cwichelm and Cridda (*ASC*). Ceawlin succeeded by Ceol (to 597); *imperium* passes to Æðelberht.

596   Death of the Frankish king Childebert II; succeeded by his grandsons Theudebert and Theuderic under the regency of their grandmother Brunhild.

     — Pope Gregory's letters to Theudebert, Theuderic and Brunhild of Austrasia exhorting them to help the mission of Augustine.

     — Augustine departs for Britain; he turns back but is encouraged by Pope Gregory (Bede *HE*).

597   ?Death of Freodwald, king of Bernicia; succeeded by Hussa to 604.

     — Arrival of St Augustine's Christian mission in Kent.

     — Death of Ceol; Ceolwulf succeeds in Wessex (to 611, *ASC*): 'He fought continuously against the Britons, the Anglians, the Picts and the Scots.'

601   Paulinus sent by Pope Gregory to accompany Mellitus to Britain; brings *pallium* for Augustine.

     — Letters from Pope Gregory to Augustine, Bertha and Æðelberht of Kent.

604   ?Death of Hussa, King of Bernicia; succeeded by Æðelfrið (to 617).

     — Æðelfrið, king of ?Deira, defeats Áedán mac Gabrain, king of Dál Riata at the Battle of Degsastan. Deira and Bernicia united as a single kingdom when Æðelfrið marries Acha of Deira. Edwin (son of Ælle and brother of Acha) probably exiled in Gwynedd under Cadfan ap Iago.

— Augustine meets British bishops at Augustine's Oak; they rebut his attempt to integrate them into newly established Kentish church.

— Death of Gregory the Great.

— Death of Augustine (between this year and 610); he is succeeded at Canterbury by Laurence (to 619).

607   Ceolwulf fights against the South Saxons (*ASC*).

611   Death of Ceolwulf of the West Saxons. Cynegils becomes king of Wessex (to 642).

615/16?   Battle of Chester: Æðelfrið defeats British warbands under Solon son of Conan of Powys and possibly a Mercian warband under Cearl.

— Edwin takes refuge with the royal family of East Anglia.

616   Death of Æðelberht of Kent. Eadbald succeeds (to 640). He marries his stepmother and rejects Christianity; but converts *c*.617.

617   Æðelfrið is ambushed and killed by Rædwald of East Anglia at Bawtry (now in South Yorkshire) in the Battle of the River Idle. Oswald, Æðelfrið's son, flees Northumbria and takes refuge at the court of Dál Riata; Edwin becomes king of Deira, having fought beside Rædwald.

619   Edwin conquers the British kingdom of Elmet (AC).

— Construction of a horizontal tidal mill at Nendrum monastery, County Down.

624/5   ?King Rædwald of East Anglia dies and is probably buried in a ship mound at Sutton Hoo (near Woodbridge, Suffolk); he is the fourth of the English kings to claim *imperium*, according to *ASC* (*sub anno* 827, *recte* 829).

625   King Edwin marries a Christian princess, Æðelburh of Kent.

626   Possible early date for the compilation of Tribal Hidage.

— Assassination attempt at Easter on Edwin by an

agent of King Cwichelm of Wessex (Bede *HE*). Edwin recovers from wound and wages campaign against Cwichelm.

— ?Birth of Eanflæd, daughter of Edwin and Æðelburh.

627   King Edwin is baptized in a new wooden church at York by Bishop Paulinus. Mass baptisms follow in the River Swale (*Catraeth*) and at Yeavering.

632   Edwin killed at the Battle of Hatfield Chase by Penda of Mercia.

633   Northumbria fragments into constituent kingdoms; Cadwallon of Gwynedd lays waste to Northumbria.

634   Oswald returns from exile to claim Northumbrian kingdom, ?with brother Oswiu and a retinue including Dál Riatan and Ionan warriors. He defeats and kills King Cadwallon at the Battle of Denisesburn after raising his cross at Heavenfield (Bede *HE*).

635   King Oswald sends for Irish abbot/bishop Aidan from Iona, to establish monastery on the island of Lindisfarne.

PART III

THE FIRST
KINGDOM

Woden begot Beldeg, begot Beornec, begot
Gechbrond, begot Aluson, begot Inguec, begot
Ædibrith, begot Ossa, begot Eobba, begot Ida.
Ida had twelve sons, named Adda, Ædldric,
Decdric, Edric, Deothare, Osmer, and one queen,
Bearnoch. Ealdric begot Ælfret: he is Ædlferd
Flesaur, and he had seven sons...

Historia Brittonum 57[1]

10

Duces bellorum; milites Christi

King Childeric's tomb – Clovis – extensive lordship –
the Yeavering model – the warband – lords of the
cross – the British church – Whithorn

Twelfth-century mosaic from the Duomo di Otranto, Basilica
Cattedrale di Santa Maria Annunziata, Apulia, Italy.

The archaeology of medieval European kingship may be said to begin with the spectacular burial of a Frankish warlord in about the year 481. The chances of uncovering the remains of a real, historical figure of this period, their identity confirmed by the contents of a grave, lie somewhere between slim and none. But in 1653 a mason called Adrien Quinquin, working near the church of Saint-Brice in Tournai,* came upon the spectacular contents of the tomb of King Childeric, progenitor of the Merovingian dynasty – the first rulers of France. Among the treasures he discovered were a fransisca (the Frankish throwing axe), a gold-hilted sword, 200 gold coins, various brooches, buckles and horse harness fittings, a positive swarm of cloisonné bees, a bull's head ornament and the gold seal ring that identified its owner as *Childerici Regis*, portrayed minutely with a clean chin, long hair parted in the centre and holding a spear in his right hand – all very pagan and self-consciously barbarian.† As fate would have it, but for the extraordinarily detailed description of the tomb and its contents recorded in text and drawings at the time, there would now be little proof of the existence of this booty: almost all of it was stolen from the Bibilothèque Nationale in 1831 and melted down by the thieves.[1] The seal ring exists as a lucky contemporary copy of the original; just two of the bees survive.

Childeric's career is known only in its barest outlines, from the *Historia Francorum* written by Gregory of Tours towards the end of the sixth century.‡ Childeric, son of the semi-legendary Merovech – a Frankish equivalent of Hengest – had spent some years in exile from Francia as a result, Gregory says, of a debauched lifestyle and subsequent threats to his life. On his return he made himself useful as one of a number of competing warlords fighting on behalf of the residual commanders of the Western Roman empire against

---

* Close to the modern Franco-Belgian border.
† Guy Halsall thinks it likely that the tomb lay beneath a mound, or barrow. Halsall 2007, 269.
‡ Gregory, born *c*.534, was Bishop of Tours from 573 until his death in 594.

the Visigothic King Theodoric II. His military activities were concentrated along the Loire valley, but his territorial lordship, acquired in all probability by federate treaty, lay further north in the area known to the Romans as *Belgica Secunda*, with Tournai as its capital. Childeric allied his army with the senior commander of imperial forces in Gaul, the *magister militum* Aegidius (died *c*.465) – to whom Gildas made mistaken reference in the historical introduction to *De Excidio*.[2] Aegidius had served under Aëtius, he of the three consulships to whom the Britons supposedly addressed their unanswered begging letter. Between them, Childeric and Aegidius forced Theodoric to withdraw from the Loire.

Little else is known of his career. Exit stage left Childeric to his splendid tomb; enter his son, Clovis. Gregory is vague about the detail of Clovis's thirty-year rule over the Franks; but he is able to portray him, as Bede in his turn would portray Æðelfrið, the Bernician warlord, as a vicarious instrument of God's will. Within five years of his succession in about 481 Clovis inflicted a significant defeat on his northern neighbour Syagrius, the son of Aegidius and ruler of the kingdom of Soissons. Gregory delights in telling how the godless Clovis took Syagrius prisoner and then had him secretly killed; how Clovis's impious armies waged wars, won victories and plundered churches. He records that Clovis married a Burgundian Christian princess, Chlothild, who endeavoured to persuade him of the virtues of conversion and baptism. In Gregory's account, Clovis stubbornly resisted until, fifteen years into his reign in 496, he was confronted with imminent and catastrophic defeat on the battlefield at Tolbiac (in modern North Rhine-Westphalia) and, in that moment of supreme need, prayed successfully to his wife's god for deliverance. The sometimes long-drawn-out process by which such warlords came to embrace the disciplines and opportunities presented by conversion to Christianity is the bridge that spans the worlds of Late Antiquity and the Middle Ages.

Early Medieval royal conversions were rarely simply a matter of personal enlightenment: potential rewards must be balanced against political risks; negotiations with key councillors and commanders might last months or years. Old gods and old ways could not be cast aside lightly. Hearts and minds must be won. Even so, in his *Historia* Gregory was able to portray Clovis's baptism, by the persuasive Bishop Remigius at Reims in about 505, as a triumphant providential ceremony, the Christianization of a whole people: the king stepping forward eagerly to the baptismal font 'like some new Constantine'; the bishop humbling his temporal lord with a portentous admonition to 'worship what you have burned, burn what you have worshipped'.[3]

As conversion narrative Gregory's account is conventional, but it is of towering significance for European history. Underpinning the ceremony lay political processes subtly engineered to align the barbarian Clovis with a Christian, tax-paying, literate Gaulish élite, while drawing his perhaps more truculent warriors towards the virtues of the new faith. In Gregory's eyes the nation of the Franks in Gaul was thus united – a proxy, if you will, for the political and social fusion of a barbarian warrior culture with the late Roman provincial governing class.[4] Conversion brought other benefits, too – not least the legitimizing prayers and political clout of the Gallic church, itself an entrenched landed élite – while subsequent Christian Frankish kings found themselves in a position to be indulged by the far distant emperor in Byzantium, whose immense powers of patronage and political interest, even at so great a remove, might now be tapped.

Two years later, in 507, at Vouillé a few miles west of Poitiers, Clovis led his armies to a great victory against Alaric II, the Visigothic king whose territories encompassed much of what is now southern France and Spain.* Clovis is said, by Gregory, to have killed Alaric himself. Riding triumphantly to Tours, he donated generous gifts to the church founded by St Martin more than 100 years previously.[5]

Historians have always been fascinated by the brief passage in Gregory's *History* that records victory's payoff:

---

* Alaric was the nephew of King Theodoric II, whom Alaric's father, Euric, had murdered. Alaric II's intaglio seal ring also survives and is kept in the Kunsthistorisches Museum, Vienna.

Therefore he received from the Byzantine emperor Anastasius codicils of the consulate and in the basilica of the blessed Martin, placing a diadem on his head, he was clothed in a purple tunic [*tunica blattea*] and the chlamys.* Then, mounted on horseback, he dispensed gold and silver with great generosity along the route that lies between the city gate and the church of the city, scattering it with his own hand to people who were present, and from that day he was addressed as if he were a consul or emperor. Then he departed from Tours and came to Paris, and there he fixed the seat of the kingdom.[6]

In this passage are encoded all sorts of tensions, challenges and opportunities: for those barbarian warlords who would be kings of former Roman provinces, and for emperors who must accommodate new, dangerous realities lying beyond their powers of direct intervention. In such tensions the birth of medieval kingship is crystallized.

Close analysis by Ralph Mathisen, who has made a special study of the Battle of Vouillé and its aftermath, reveals the emperor's subtle hand in bestowing formal honours on this arriviste. Clovis was to be an honorary rather than statutory consul; but he was, in addition, granted patriciate status – formal entry into the highest ranks of Roman nobility.[7] The written codicils, the purple tunic, the self-crowning with a diadem, the mounted procession, acclamation and distribution of largesse were deliberately chosen elements of a coronation ceremony or *adventus*, all with ample precedent in Roman imperial history. With exquisite diplomatic nicety Clovis was granted the formal entitlements of a Roman military governor, while the emperor manifestly sidestepped formal recognition of the kingship that Clovis's pagan father, Childeric, had proclaimed on his seal ring.† Clovis might, by virtue of his military conquest of Gaul, have repudiated such condescension and declared himself king of the Franks in Gaul; that he did not

---

* A ceremonial cloak.
† Kingship carried rather ugly overtones in Roman history.

says much about the ambitions of Early Medieval warlords and their love–hate relations with the empire.

On the face of it, there are neat parallels between the rise of the Merovingians, as cast in Gregory's history of Christian Francia, and the fortunes of the Idings of Bernicia in Bede's portrayal of Northumbria's emergence as a dominant military and political force in Britain force a century later. The legendary progenitor of that line, Ida, was supposed to have established a military bridgehead at the coastal fortress of Bamburgh in the late 540s.* By the early 600s Ida's grandson Æðelfrið had expanded the Idings' territory across the whole of what is now England north of the River Humber and much of Scotland south of the Forth–Clyde isthmus. Bede portrayed him as 'a very brave king, and eager for glory',[8] a latter-day biblical instrument of divine wrath, ravening like a wolf. In Bede's view, when Æðelfrið's pagan army slaughtered more than 1,000 monks in about 616 before a battle against Christian British kings at Chester, he was acting as an instrument of heavenly retribution against the misguided bishops of the British church who had repudiated Augustine's Catholic mission in 604. But Æðelfrið died a year after Chester, cut down in battle by his then pagan brother-in-law Edwin. He, following Clovis's example, was persuaded by his wife and her priest to undergo baptism; but on his death in 632 the Northumbrian nobility apostatized.

It was left to Æðelfrið's son Oswald to take on the role of the convert. Raised from the age of twelve in exile at the Gaelic court of the Dál Riatan kings of Dunadd in Argyll, Oswald was educated and baptized at Colm Cille's monastery on Iona. With the aid of these northern allies, he defeated Cadwallon of Gwynedd to reclaim the Bernician throne in 634. He brought with him an Irish Christian mission to found a daughter church on Lindisfarne, introducing the Northumbrian people to God and the English as a whole to an enduring idea of Christian statehood. Oswald's own rather modest and apparently unplanned *adventus* took place during an Easter feast, at which a multitude of poor people from

* More likely, I think, in about 560. Adams 2013, 395ff.

'every district' came to ask alms of the king. Oswald ordered his dish of choice titbits to be given to them and then instructed that the silver dish itself, on which his feast had been served, should be cut up and distributed among them. His approving Irish bishop, Aidan, held the king's right hand aloft and prayed that it might never wither.[9] For Bede, this was just as significant a moment in the birth of Anglian kingship as Clovis's consular ceremony and scattering of gold to the Frankish people were for Gregory.

In truth, the evolution of Christian kingship in the British Isles was a much more nuanced, complex and obscure process that comes into focus only with Bede's history, looking back on the seventh century as a Golden Age. In the careers of Æðelfrið, Edwin and Oswald modern scholars catch just the final scenes in the story of the first kingdoms; scenes in which former barbarian warlords won God's and their historians' approval and established the lasting relations between church and monarchy on which medieval European kingship was constructed. Only fragments survive to tell of the earlier stages of the action, particularly in British and Irish politics.

In the sorts of lordship and territorial holding that can be reconstructed for the fifth century, in which renders supported a modest élite, there is little to suggest the future fortunes of these great overlords. There is a gulf between the *territoria* of Cadbury hillfort or Great Chesterford and that immense swathe of France over which Clovis's armies could roam, challenging all comers and parleying with the emperor in Byzantium. The careers of Hengest and Horsa, Ambrosius Aurelianus, Vortigern, Gildas's five tyrants and even more obscure figures like Vitalinus, Gwyrangon and Arthur sit somewhere in that gulf. And if the evolution of lordship still has its missing links, then the fortunes of the church, so fundamental to the Early Medieval narrative, are barely more tangible.

Some fifth-century lords may have ruled quite large territories, and the organizational effort required to construct some of the great dyke systems may be their enduring witness. Gildas's five tyrants look as though they inherited or won rights over the lands of former *civitates*. But so little is known about them that it is impossible to say if they possessed extensive allodial* estates of their own or whether, in some senses, their lordship was limited to the functions to which Gildas alludes: warfare, feasting, law, oath-swearing, protection and patronage. If the structures excavated at Dinas Powys, Dinas Emrys, Deganwy and Bryn Euryn are credible reflections of their capital assets, then the economic reach of the *tyranni* may have been quite limited. They may have been chieftains of tribes without necessarily being great landlords; leaders of warbands rather than kings. None can be credited with expanding his territory by conquest. Some few of them may have had their names inscribed on stone memorials – a certain sort of immortality – but their later fame is owed largely to Gildas's fulminations against them; their names are not particularly prominent in the genealogies of later British kings.

Another dozen or so chieftains of former *civitates* or native peoples may have exercised control in parts of western Britain, filling out its geography. Patrick's Coroticus is a good candidate as ruler over the Britons of *Alclut*; so are the unnamed warlords, civil engineers and importers of fine drink who established or re-established hillforts at South Cadbury, Congresbury and elsewhere. Tintagel's rulers – Constantine of *Dumnonia* and his ilk – seem to have exploited opportunities in the Atlantic trade in fine goods to aggrandize themselves.

Vortigern, if he was a genuine historical figure, may have exercised governance over much of the former Roman province. He may, too, have held substantial estates; but there are no means of establishing the geography or nature of his lordship beyond speculation; his tomb and seal ring have never been found. Hengest, Horsa and their antagonists and allies, if real, held land by force or federate treaty. According to the compiler of the *Historia Brittonum*, Hengest was granted Kent, displacing its native King Gwyrangon. The nature of that kingship is as shadowy as its rulers

---

* Allodial – that is to say, under no other lordship; allodial estates could be passed by inheritance, sold or given away without permission from another lord.

although, according to Bede, a monument erected in Horsa's name still stood in the eighth century.[10] The territorial hegemonies of such pirates as Port, Cymen and Wightgar, whose eponymous victories appear so fleetingly in the *Anglo-Saxon Chronicle*, are no more than puffs of smoke in the imagination.

The incipient lordships traced in earlier chapters were broadly of three sorts: either local and centripetal, with immediate control exercised over existing estates by former officials, army officers or élite families; or the land grabs of pirates as, perhaps, at Rendlesham; or they emerged from more communal rights to resources spread disproportionately across weald and fen, dale and moor. The kaleidoscope of political and social geographies that made up what had once been *Britannia* is seen only at second hand through the list that appears in Tribal Hidage. Even so, some of the processes by which petty lords were able to consolidate and expand their horizons, the means by which these larger *regiones* came into being, can be detected through careful scrutiny.

Tensions between lords, their families, their regional rivals, their free and unfree dependants, the vagaries of climate, reproduction and fertility, and the caprices of the fates, allowed some lords to extend their territorial influence at the expense of weaker neighbours. Some territories grew through alliance, marriage and inheritance, processes well-attested in this period. Leaders of federate warbands attendant on their civic superiors took opportunities to marry the boss's daughter; powerful families brokered unions between their children in which rights to draw renders were bartered as dower or dowry.* Vortigern, notoriously, is recorded in the less historical pages of the *Historia Brittonum* as having drunkenly given away the kingdom of Kent (which seems not to have been his to give away) for the sake of a pretty girl.[11]

---

* Dowry is property gifted by the bride's family to the groom; dower property is that given to the bride by the groom's family to protect her in widowhood. Bede's stories about Æðelðrið, the princess of the Gyrwe who married King Ecgfrith of Northumbria and later established a monastery on her own lands at Ely, are instructive examples. Bede *HE* IV.19 etc.

There are striking ecclesiastical parallels: many of the celebrated early saints acted as territorial lords, extending their earthly *paruchiae* through donations of land, either as reward for miracles or battle victories or by virtue of allowing lords and their collateral family members to rule over or take refuge in their monasteries. The records of the community of St Cuthbert of Lindisfarne show very clearly how such entrepreneurial activity on the part of charismatic and successful saints led to the aggrandizement of their churches – sometimes threateningly so, as in the case of Wilfrid, the Northumbrian bishop who must, when he died in 705, have enjoyed a property portfolio the envy of many minor kings.

St Brigit of Kildare, whose life probably spanned the decades between the careers of Patrick and Colm Cille,* enlarged her temporal lordship, as well as her reputation as a provider in times of great hunger, by the application of an apposite miracle. One of two *vitae* purporting to record her deeds and piety tells how once, when she was a guest at the monastery of St Laisre,† Patrick arrived with a great crowd of followers. The community feared that they could not offer so large a number of guests suitable hospitality, having set aside only twelve loaves, some milk and a single sheep to feed Brigit and her attendants. Brigit did not reprise the biblical miracle of the loaves and fishes, but instead called the company to join her in prayer and in reading the Holy Scriptures, whereupon the guests found that they had more than enough food to nourish them: they ate what there was, and no more.[12] The nub of the story, however, is that afterwards St Laisre offered herself and her community to Brigit in perpetuity. Thus, the annalists of Brigit's foundation at Kildare were able to explain, centuries later, how and why they had acquired lordship rights over the monastery of Laisre.

Increasingly, lords must have expanded their territories through military victory although, perhaps surprisingly, historical references

---

* Her death is recorded in the *Annals of Ulster* and the *Annales Cambriae* under various years in the 520s.
† The monastery cannot be identified.

to such events are thin on the ground. The land-grabbing activities of those piratical figures who feature in the *Historia Brittonum* and *Anglo-Saxon Chronicle* may have been the exception rather than the norm. That is, in part, because although warlords might claim possession of territory by conquest, they were unlikely to enjoy, in their new-won lands, the networks of élite client relations on whom secure rule depended. As late as the tenth century very powerful kings of Wessex struggled to engender loyalty among peoples recently 'liberated' from Viking control. There is a fine line, perhaps, between imposing tributary subordination on a weaker neighbour, as in a protection racket, and engineering among relative strangers the reciprocal patronage networks that sustained the institutions of Early Medieval kingship. Even that fine line may be a modern illusion. During the late fifth century it is only possible to detect a more modest process of petty expansionism – the term 'extensification' is employed by scholars. Conquest, the annexation of whole territories and the subjugation or execution of their lords, was more likely an expression of emerging sixth-century overlordship. And then, throughout the much better-recorded seventh century, kingdoms experienced as much fissile fragmentation as they did consolidation. At a smaller scale the possibility that expansion occurred through the voluntary submission of a district, town or *pagus* to a powerful lord in return for protection and the benefits of patronage ought not to be discounted; nor should the likelihood that some landed estates were acquired by purchase, with treasure.

The new economic, social and political powers acquired by lords extending their territorial control over increasingly large estates presented them with fundamental problems of management – not just of the land itself but of dependants wanting access to their *comitatus* – and the responsibilities of administering justice, distributing gifts and maintaining a mobile household. Food renders might only travel so far; the services demanded of dependants could not be stretched over too great a distance.

The solution was for renders to remain tied to their original lordship centre, the *vill* or fort or town, and for the more distant lord to visit each in turn, consuming its surplus on the hoof. The itinerant kings and queens of the Middle Ages enjoyed – or endured – a ritual and economic necessity directly evolved from the necessities of fifth-century lordship. It is true that this 'extensification' of lordly control over adjacent territories cannot be directly observed before the first written records in the seventh century; but by then, as enthusiastic kings began to donate substantial estates to their favoured holy men and women, precious insights reveal an already mature system. Bede, in an almost throwaway line, described how King Edwin and his bishop, Paulinus, spent thirty-six days in the royal township (*villa regia*) at Yeavering in Bernicia in the late 620s, baptizing the Northumbrian élite in the River Glen.[13] Archaeologist Colm O'Brien's insight, in a seminal paper on estate development, was to realize that the number thirty-six is a key that unlocks the system in play: not a random length of stay; not a lunar month; but a tenth part of a year.[14] The royal court stayed at Yeavering in Edwin's day long enough to consume a food and service render that comprised 10 per cent of the king's *feorm* – his income as rendered by the lands subject to his lordship. The estate from which those renders was drawn was reconstructed by O'Brien as Gefrinshire, one of a number of early Northumbrian shires whose extent is traceable through medieval documents.* Logically, a king of Northumbria required a minimum of ten such shire estates in order to provide year-round subsistence for the royal household, its *comitatus* and queenly entourage. In practice, the largest of those shires, centred on the rocky coastal fortress of Bamburgh, may have supplied two or even three months' worth of render – to see the court through the winter months when travel was at its most challenging. At least one other royal township of the Northumbrian kings has been identified by aerial photography at Sprouston, in the historic county of Roxburghshire on the south bank of the River Tweed near Kelso.[15] Others are suggested by later medieval administrative boundaries. Arrangements in Bernicia, then, reveal the internal

* See Chapter 6, p. 262.

workings of a mechanism by which extensive lordship could evolve towards kingship.

Rolling back the process from kingdom to shire* to *vill* allows geographers to reconstruct the building blocks of such lordships in Bernicia: shires – and half-shires – whose component *vills* or townships were grouped in quite consistent bundles of six or twelve. Looking for similar examples further south one might pick out the Rodings in Essex, with its thirteen Domesday manors; or the probable *territorium* of the *Stoppingas* surviving in the eleven medieval parishes centred on Wootton Wawen in Warwickshire.[16] In northern Scotland, thanages in medieval Ross often consisted of multiples of six *dabhachs*.[17] And in medieval Welsh law, in which the memory of *gwestfa* – an obligation to entertain a king and his court when they came to visit twice a year – was enshrined, one 'commote' consisted of twelve 'multiple estates'.[18] If six- and twelve-*vill* units were fundamental to the Insular mechanics of extensive lordship, it is hard to avoid the conclusion that such units may have been ancient even in the fifth century. Travel through Britain today and unless you have an Ordnance Survey map in hand you may not notice yourself passing from one administrative parish, township, *toun* or community to another; but these are fundamental units of the human landscape, evolved over 2,000 years and perhaps more. Their shapes and limits define units of resources from which farmers, craftspeople and warriors have drawn their sustenance and sense of belonging, generation upon generation.

While strong forces drove the extensification of lordship, fissile forces were also at work, fragmenting coagulations of *vills* and shires into their constituent parts and occasionally recombining them. Dynastic failure, uprising and political and military weakness allowed regional rivals to displace each other by violence, alliance and marriage. Elsewhere, the successful defence of communal rights to the land's resources seems to have preserved small territories, like those around the Fenlands, long enough to be listed in Tribal Hidage. Small military fiefdoms of the sort hinted at by traditions

* Or hundred; or lathe in Kent, or *cantref* in the west.

surrounding Hengest and Horsa, and by the archaeology of sites like Rendlesham, remind one of the *longphuirt** of the Viking Age – essentially piratical coastal towns living off a combination of trade, slavery and the resources of their territorial hinterlands. Waterford, Wexford, Dublin, Limerick and Cork owe their origins as county towns to successful Viking entrepreneurs; and the sixth-century archaeology of Britain allows for precedents in the ruins of *Britannia*. Roman towns like Great Chesterford and Alcester might have acted as defensible lowland equivalents of hillforts.

If this mosaic portrait of *civitas* and *pagus*, *vill* and shire, *longphort* and hinterland is broadly right, the sorts of lords who ruled over such territories must have been just as diverse. They are identifiable in Gildas's tyrants, the *Historia Brittonum*'s federate warlords-cum-pirates, the 'chief men of the district' alluded to by Germanus's and the Almsgiver's *vitae* and in entrepreneurial ecclesiasts like Brigit.

That rather begs the question, alluded to in the title of this chapter, of just where an Arthurian *dux bellorum* might be accommodated as a function of lordship. At the core of the meagre Arthurian material purporting to be genuine historical records are a single entry in the *Historia Brittonum* and two in the *Annales Cambriae*, both preserved in the Nennian compilation. The so-called Arthurian section of the *Historia Brittonum* recounts how, after the death of Hengest, the English increased their numbers in Britain and Hengest's son Octha came down from the north to found a royal dynasty in Kent. 'In those days', it continues, Arthur fought against them (who 'they' are is not clear: the rulers of Kent; the English?) with the kings of the British; but he alone was their leader in battle (*dux erat bellorum*). There follows the well-known list of twelve battles[†] over whose locations and military implications historians and fantasists have pored over many generations and not got very far.[19] The last battle, on the unlocated

---

* *Longphort* – the singular form – derives from Latin *longus* (as in Old Norse *Langskip*: longship) and *portus* – port.
† See Chapter 5, p. 150.

Badon Hill, provides a link to both Gildas's narrative and to an entry under the year 516 in the *Annales Cambriae*:

The Battle of Badon, in which Arthur carried the cross of our Lord Jesus Christ for three days and nights on his (?shoulder/ shield) and the Britons were the victors.[20]

A second entry, under the year 537, records:

The strife [or battle – the word used is *gueith*] of Camlann in which Arthur and Medraut fell; and there was plague in Britain and Ireland.

Setting aside the overtly nationalist agenda of the compiler of this history in the first quarter of the ninth century, and leaving discussions of basic source credibility to others,[21] it is worth thinking of a figure like Arthur in terms of the sort of lordship he might have enjoyed. In the *Historia Brittonum* he is explicitly not a king but a leader in war, fighting alongside kings or on their behalf. Conspicuously, while Gildas's tyrants and the piratical warlords of the *Anglo-Saxon Chronicle* and *Irish Annals** are territorial lords, ruling over lands that they have won or inherited, Arthur exists solely as a battle commander, and an apparently wide-roaming commander at that. He lacks both the contextual genealogy and territorial geography that would lend him the dynastic credibility of Gildas's *tyranni*. His career, if real, fits better with that of the military command structure of the terminal decades of the empire than with the types of lordship that come into focus at the turn of the sixth century. He ought, if anywhere, to be found in the Chronography of the Nennian compilation or the *Vita Germani* of Constantius, leading British forces to the Alleluia victory.† An

---

* A collective term for the group of documents that includes the Annals of Ulster, the Annals of Tigernach and the Annals of Clonmacnoise, all variants of a set of records begun on Iona in the early seventh century.
† See Chapter 3, p. 82.

Arthur contemporary with Ambrosius and Vitalinus is more credible than one contemporary with the warlords fighting in the first three decades of the 500s, who combined leadership of warbands and the role of *hlafwearden** – providers of bread to their companions and households. If their role evolved in parallel with the extensification of territorial lordship and with the chieftain's role as head of the *comitatus*, it is hard to see room for a specialist *dux bellorum* in their company. When battles were to be fought, lords fought them as warriors leading their own warbands. In the end, the figure of Arthur disappoints not because he may be fictional but because his career offers no insight into the evolution of Insular lordship.

Lords of extensive territories must manage the opportunities and risks posed by increased numbers of dependants and subordinate lords and the distances over which they needed to be managed. The patronage system thrived because it was reciprocal. Client warrior/farmers sat in attendance on their lord; gave direct service in his household; had their children fostered in his hall; fought as members of his *comitatus*. He feasted and protected them, fed off their produce and crafts, judged their misdemeanours and offered rewards for loyalty. He brought them honour and booty in battle, and glory in death.

In the multi-*vill* or shire system the physical distance between lord and dependent household was stretched. A *vill* would see its lord less often; renders must be adapted to dilations in time and space; distance had social consequences. Archaeologists have seen how the flattish hierarchies of the fifth century, reflected in modest architectural and material displays of rank and wealth in cemeteries and settlements, became more differentiated during the following century. At settlements like Mucking and West Stow, where social rank was at first expressed within households, dominant families began to emerge, perhaps able to successfully exploit new

---

* The Old English word, meaning 'guardian of the loaf' became *hlaford*; then simply 'lord'. The female equivalent, 'lady' derives from *hlæfdige*, 'loaf-eater'.

opportunities under extensive lordship. Physically these are expressed in variations in the sizes of halls, more enclosed space, and the more overt planning seen at multi-period sites like Cowdery's Down in Hampshire and Pennyland in Buckinghamshire.[22] One can only speculate – there are no contemporary diaries, letters or estate accounts to provide the sort of juicy detail of social snobbery seen in medieval families like the Pastons.* But the world that comes into focus in the saints' lives and historical records of the seventh century is a social landscape of mature, hierarchical institutions reinforced by customary law, ceremony and economic necessity, in which transgression was met with extreme physical punishment and the – possibly worse – threat of social exclusion and dishonour: an existence outwith the protection of a lord.

By the seventh century, the sons of senior dependent households† were expected to serve in their lord's *comitatus* (*dryht* in Old English) as military companions – the *comites*. Indeed, their family's status, land holding and enjoyment of favourable relations with their lord depended upon military attendance. Wilfrid, the controversial seventh-century Northumbrian bishop and monastic entrepreneur, was expected as a youth to minister to the needs of visitors to his father's house, 'whether the king's companions or their slaves'.[23] Then, when he was fourteen, he was provided with clothing, a mount and arms suitable to his rank so that he might seek service in the household of Queen Eanflæd. At that time he was, naturally enough, also furnished with the social commendation of his father – a lord in his own right – and began to mix and compete with his social equals. The dual obligations of hospitality and attendance were well understood. A less secure but nevertheless suggestive document, the census known as the *Senchus Fer n'Alban*, which purports to describe the obligations

---

* The collection of letters written by and to the Paston family of Norfolk between about 1420 and 1510 survives in six volumes.
† Logic suggests that these élite households were located at the centres of *vills*, supported by dependant farmers.

owed by households among the disparate *cenéla* of Dál Riata,* tells how each must supply marines to serve in the king's fleet: fourteen (that is, two banks of seven oarsmen) from every twenty households. The other six households must, it seems, have been responsible for the construction and provisioning of vessels.

Lords and their retinues were mobile through necessity and inclination. In the absence of the professional armies of the empire, and by long practice beyond its borders, the warband functioned as a finishing school for warriors, as its lord's personal retinue, as a male feasting and drinking club and as the executive arm of lordship. The warrior culture fed off its own mythologies to exalt martial prowess and the pursuit of war. Its codes are versified in *Beowulf*. Sometimes warbands must have behaved like their reiving descendants in the fifteenth-century Anglo-Scottish borders: as semi-licensed thugs predating on the weak and picking fights with rivals in long-perpetuated blood feuds or turf wars – but as lords, nonetheless. The lord's own household was itself as hierarchical as that of any village squire. The consorts of such lords, poetically exemplified by the figure of Wealþeow in *Beowulf* and by the *Wife's Lament* of the Exeter Book, played critical roles in the management of the *comitatus*, as anthropologist Michael Enright has argued.[24] A noble wife managed the elaborate drinking rituals through which the *comites* were bound into their lord's service as a fictive family. She prophesied on his behalf; cemented rank and status by the carefully controlled presentation of the mead cup and reinforced an order of precedence by naming each drinker in turn. She might incite the warband to arms or calm tensions in the hall. Conscious of the analogy presented by women's role in both brewing and weaving textiles, she wove narratives of past, present and future into the codified brotherhood of the *comitatus*.

Violence, notwithstanding the management of a lord and his consort, was implicit in the institution of the warband. St Guthlac (died 715), who went to live as a troglodytic hermit in an ancient burial mound in the dismal fens of Crowland, cannot have been

* See Chapter 8, p. 259. Bannerman 1974; Anderson 1922, cl.

the only noble Christian youth who began his career with a campaign of mayhem, anticipating the fictional medieval antihero of Herman Hesse's *Narziss and Goldmund*. The eighth-century *Vita sancti Guthlaci* records:

> Now when his youthful strength had increased, and a noble desire for command burned in his young breast, he remembered the valiant deeds of heroes of old, and as though awakening from sleep, he changed his disposition and gathering bands of followers took up arms; [...] when he had devastated the towns and residences of his foes, their villages and fortresses with fire and sword, and, gather[ed] together companions from various races and from all directions, [he]...amassed immense booty.[25]

How big was a warband? The short answer is that it is impossible to know. The circumstantial evidence of the early laws, hints dropped in narrative sources and the logistics of supplying and maintaining an armed retinue offer clues, no more. Augustine, arriving on Thanet in 597, is said to have travelled with forty companions. Wilfrid, another man of God at the head of a band of *milites Christi*, saw off an assault by South Saxon aggressors with 120 companions, although such a biblical number ought to raise an eyebrow of caution.[26] Sidonius's brother-in-law Ecdicius had raised a siege with no more men than he could accommodate in his dining room – a neat, if unconscious, metaphor for the mead hall and its *comitatus*. A much-cited clause in the dooms (laws) of King Ine of Wessex (reigned 689–726) distinguishes the size of an armed party as follows:

> We use the term 'thieves' if the number of men does not exceed seven, 'band of marauders' for a number between seven and thirty-five. Anything beyond this is a raid [*here*].[27]

The size of a lord's *comitatus* must have reflected something like the hidage of land from which he could draw suitable men and arms. The earliest English laws that speak of renders are those

of King Ine,* in which the basic farm unit is a ten-hide holding.†
Assuming that the Wessex tribute listed in Tribal Hidage might be
more realistically set at 30,000, comparable to Mercia, rather than
its punitive listing at 100,000 hides, the number of households in
all the core lands of the former Roman province covered by the
Hidage would give a total in the region of 172,000 or so *familiae*.
If a ten-hide render unit applied, and if one supposes that every such
unit must provide an armed man for its lord's retinue, the Hidage
kingdoms and territories would be able to raise about 17,000 fighting men between them. The nominal strength of a Mercian army
of the seventh century would be 30,000 divided by ten: a force of
about 3,000 men. In 655 King Penda was said, by Bede, to have
commanded thirty *duces* at the battle on the Winwæd. If the entire
theoretical Mercian host went into that disastrous encounter with
the forces of Northumbria's King Oswiu, then each *dux* might
have commanded 100 or so warriors. The more successful *duces*
must also have attracted freelances, perhaps young bloods like
Guthlac, to their banner. To these one might add camp followers,
the *pauperi* whom Imma attempted to impersonate twenty years
later. But these are speculative figures. In the mid-sixth century,
such numbers would probably be at the higher end of possibility.
In the first half of the fifth century, however, a *dux bellorum* like
Ambrosius Aurelianus, Vitalinus or Arthur, supposing they held
some sort of official provincial command and were able to draw
on the services of the sons of men who had fought in the *limitanei*
or in the armies of the *Dux Britanniarum*, may have been able to
draw on more substantial forces.

The military equipment attested by grave goods and narrative
sources allows the archaeologist to picture a warrior with spear,
shield and sword. It is generally agreed that *gesiths* rode to the
battlefield on horses of the fell pony type: not large, but tough
and with high endurance. Some Pictish carvings depict horsemen

* See p. 385 for the food render expected from ten hides of land.
† Leslie Alcock used later Anglo-Saxon evidence to suggest the provision
of an armed warrior from every five hides. Alcock 2003, 156–7.

wielding spears – perhaps in raiding formation; and the *Gododdin* verses imply the existence of light cavalry units among northern British armies; but without stirrups, a later innovation, mounted warriors could not propel a lance with any great power. Horses were ideal for raiding; in a pitched battle between armies most warriors fought on foot. The classic Anglo-Saxon formation of a closely interlocked shield wall, like that which supposedly confronted William of Normandy at Hastings in 1066, expressed solidarity, discipline and power; but sixth- and seventh-century shields as depicted in carvings were small, encouraging a more open formation – perhaps one-to-one combat. When starting formations broke into skirmish, mêlée and rout, chaos might ensue, as it did at the ford on the Winwæd in 655 when more men were drowned in the swollen river than were killed at the point of a sword.[28] Archers may have been deployed in skirmishing and in the defence of fortifications, but seem not to have played a formal role on the battlefield.

The aftermath of conflict saw decapitation and mutilation, trophy hunting and scavenging. Two kings of Northumbria were dismembered on the field of battle. In both cases, some or all of their body parts were later retrieved; Oswald's in a raid by his brother King Oswiu and Edwin's by a devout priestly follower. The Staffordshire hoard offers some clues about how the booty of the battlefield was scavenged for caching, perhaps for redistribution and recycling, to be weighed in as tribute. The victors of the battlefield had a good eye for scrap value, but were temporarily insensitive to aesthetics.

The choice of battle sites – at least of those that can be placed circumstantially – is more than mere happenstance. In the seventh century at least six battles were fought at river crossings on major Roman roads. That is partly a function of the natural movement of armies along routes where they might travel at speed and with baggage; but, as the narrative of the *Táin Bó Cúailnge* implies, fords were regarded as symbolically appropriate sites for confrontation and combat, as being places where gods dwelt and where sacrifices might be made. Roman forts, too, crop up in the geography of warfare; as much, perhaps, for their historical associations and as a suitable stage for the clash of weapons as for any idea that they might provide defensible positions.

It was a lord's obligation to muster his companions for hosting – the cattle raid – or battle. He must enrich his warband by booty won in warfare or by raiding, and enlarge it by the further extension of his lordship. In turn, the *comites* enjoyed a high social status in their communities and patronized lower ranks of householders, craftspeople and attendants. The obligation and right to bear arms and own a mount was enshrined in oaths, accompanied by drinking, of absolute loyalty to one's lord in life and death. His fortune and fate were theirs. When Bishop Wilfrid was expelled from Northumbria after a quarrel with King Aldfrið, his *milites Christi* were expected to follow him into exile, just as if they were members of a *comitatus*.[29] One's lord also embodied the fortunes of a self-identifying *folc*, *pagus*, *civitas* or *tuath*. Settlements, districts and regions that bore the name of a dynastic progenitor – like the Rodings, or the *Cenél nGabrain* of Argyll – invested their social, economic and reproductive capital in the military and political success of their *comitatus*, as display and as a function of lordship and the mechanics of the render.

Wilfrid's experiences, echoed by the careers of St Cuthbert and St Guthlac, St Martin at the end of the fourth century and Germanus in the fifth, as well as many other Early Medieval soldiers of Christ, are a potent reminder that Christianity, lordship, patronage and military power were diverse expressions of a common suite of social and environmental forces. Like the institution of territorial lordship, the church evolved during a period of tensions that stretched the empire to breaking point in the fourth century. Its urban, diocesan institutions acted both as counterweight to social competition in the army, civil service and imperial household and as a focus for spiritual and social needs. From Constantine's conversion in the fourth century to that of Clovis in the sixth, the Christian God promised believers – especially *duces bellorum*, it seemed – both eternal salvation and success on the battlefield. Bishops were masters of social ceremonial and orchestrators of deeply affecting religious celebrations. They also functioned as mediators of theological controversy and rectitude; but in their lordship roles – as protectors of their congregations and often as territorial proprietors in their own right – they behaved, and were recognized as behaving, like the *duces* of *comitates*: hence Æðelberht's treatment of Augustine in 597 and Aldhelm's expectation that Wilfrid's followers would behave like a warband in exile; and hence Germanus's natural presumption of military command on his visit to *Britannia*.

In parallel, there had always been a much more intellectually reflective, subversive thread of Christianity, from the Gnostics of the Dead Sea Scrolls and the supposedly quasi-socialist Pelagians to the inspirational ascetics of the Sinai Desert. Those seeking, in imitation, the contemplative journey of Christ in the desert, craving solitude, knowledge of the divine and simplicity in habit, like Egeria the Gallic pilgrim, St Benedict or St Anthony, were directly inspired by the lives of the apostles, and by more arcane mystics, to live as solitary hermits. In western Europe the exemplar of this movement was the reluctant bishop St Martin, who founded monasteries at Ligugé in Vienne and then at Marmoutier on the Loire opposite Tours at the end of the fourth century. The irony of the eremitic movement was that in living a life of simplicity, virtue and self-denial, such men and women attracted acolytes, supporters, gifts of land and money and wealthy patrons; they morphed into proprietorial lords whether they liked it or not.

The tombs of the Desert Fathers and Mothers became cult centres, famed for the homeopathic virtues of their relics. The churches that grew around those shrines were enriched and very often grew into large communities – by turns both magnificent and corrupt – of a sort that their unknowing founders would have disdained. The cenobitic or communal rule of St Pachomius (died about 348), who had served in the imperial army, had much in common with an idea of soldierly comradeship – a sort of spiritual warband eventually monumentalized in the physical structures of the monastery.[30] In the days of St Jerome (*c*.347–420) the urban church also attracted wealthy patrons and celebrants, including large numbers of women of the sort very likely commemorated in the extravagant plate of the congregation at Water Newton and frowned upon by the misogynist Tertullian. Tensions between the virtuous and gratuitous, between spiritual authority and secular power, were played out in every community, province and tribe where Christians were active and actively engaged in society. It was, ironically, from the unstoppable momentum of the monastic movement that the social contract of Insular Christian kingship would be born in the late sixth century, while the orthodox diocesan church signally failed to exploit its relations with kings.

Holy men and women trod a fine line between spiritual independence, orthodox religious duty and their relations with lords.* Patrick was forced to defend himself against accusations that he had improperly accepted gifts, or taken fees for ordinations, while his relations with kings show that he operated in élite circles.[31] Gildas recalled the biblical corruption of Simon Magus when he accused contemporary clergy of buying priesthoods from his *tyranni*.[32] Those clergy belong to a relatively well-defined ecclesiastical landscape at the end of the fifth century and the beginning of the sixth. Gildas's testimony, stripped of its fulminations against hypocrisy and corruption, paints a lively picture of a dynamic church structure. Bishops, priests, ministers and clerics vie – unworthily – for offices in what seems like a diocesan framework; there are formal church buildings and schools; preachers teach indulgence towards the poor; the shrines of martyrs are objects of veneration. There are hints of communities of male and female religious following a monastic order, and of pilgrims travelling to holy lands for divine inspiration.[33]

Gildas's literary landscape is inhabited by more tangible remains of his dubious office holders and some of their élite followers. Any traveller to the antique lands of Wales, south-west Scotland and the Dumnonian peninsula can read their names, inscribed in Latin and sometimes in Irish Ogham on memorial stones that look for all the world like prehistoric figurative sculptures,

* See Chapter 13.

poetically reminiscent of Shelley's kingly relic, Ozymandias. In St Hywyn's church at Aberdaron, near the tip of the Llŷn peninsula, memorials to VERACIUS PBR HIC IACIT* and SENACUS PRSB HIC IACIT DNEM FRATRUM PRESBYTER can be found.† Among the equally evocative green hills of the Rhinns of Galloway, a collection of memorial stones at Kirkmadrine church includes one with a distinctive broken-shoulder figurative profile, a *chi-rho* symbol in a circle and an inscription to SCI (Sancti) FLORENTIUS. Another, with a similar carved profile, bears a circled *chi-rho* style looped cross and records that HIC IACENT SCI ET PRAECIPUI SACER DOTES IDES VIVENTIUS ET MAVORUS.‡ If the context for these men's lives is literate, Latinate and diocesan, it is also informed by parallels in Gaul and further afield, while the Ogham script that accompanies many such inscriptions tells of strong linguistic and cultural links with Ireland. A multitude of other stones carry simplistically affecting crosses, and a number of possibly early chapels and cemeteries have been identified over the decades.[34] The series of tiny chapels excavated by Charles Thomas on Ardwall Island in Wigtown Bay, Galloway yielded graves, a possible slab shrine and a fragment of a portable stone altar, testifying to itinerant preaching.[35] Similar early shrines are found along the coasts of the Irish Sea basin, as far south as Scilly. The eremitic, not to say self-denyingly harsh, lifestyle attested by these remains is a modest echo of the almost suicidally ascetic lives of the hermits who existed perched on the rock of Skellig Michael, 7 miles off the coast of County Kerry, contemplating mortality and the divine with every salt-laden breath.

A number of memorials recording the names of less explicitly

---

* 'Veracius, presbyter (priest) lies here.'

† 'Senacus, presbyter, lies here with many (*multitudinem*) brethren.' Thomas 1971, 102.

‡ 'Here lie the holy and chief priests Ideas, Viventius and Mavorius.' www.historicenvironment.scot/visit-a-place/places/kirkmadrine-stones/history.

religious individuals who must, nonetheless, have belonged to a landed Christian élite, are found across western and northern Britain. None are earlier than the end of the Western empire. Conspicuously, Latin Christian memorials do not survive in central and eastern Britain.* It seems that by the end of the fifth century an active diocesan church had ceased to function in the heartlands of the former province. That is not to say that Christian congregations and perhaps private cenobitic institutions might not have survived; but archaeologists have so far failed to track them down or at least to verify that some suggestive graves and structures are definitively Christian.[36]

Place names, particularly those bearing the element *ecles* – for Latin *ecclesia* – and, in Wales and the south-west, *Llan-* or *Lan*,† indicate that Christian communities were woven intimately into a landscape of lordship in those areas where British language and sub-Roman culture thrived; perhaps eccentrically so. Candidates for early, organized Christian settlements include Glastonbury Tor, Llandough, Caldey Island and the communities attached to large long cist cemeteries, especially in southern Scotland where, Charles Thomas believed, a diocesan church survived as it may have in Wales and Cornwall.[37] Clusters of Latin inscription stones may also betray the sites of small monastic establishments, at Aberdaron and Llangian on the Llŷn peninsula, at Kirkmadrine and at Llantrisant in Glamorgan.[38] House-monasteries tentatively suggested at late Roman villas such as Frocester, Chedworth and Halstock hint at the private devotions of landed families. The density of small settlements bearing the names of very obscure saints in Cornwall and north Wales, in particular, is suggestive of the idea that élite families were expected to sponsor their own pet holy man or woman.[39] While, in the east, it seems that a rejection of all things Roman, the adoption of a new language,

---

* A collection of rare, probably seventh-century memorials survives at the church of Lady St Mary in Wareham, in Dorset. *An Inventory of the Historical Monuments in Dorset*, 303ff.

† An enclosure, but specifically the circular graveyard around a church.

conspicuous consumption in death and the acquisition of bling were regarded as suitable displays of élite wealth and status, in the west and north possession of a holy man or women or their relics, with a church and its enclosure and overt affiliation with their community, was an appropriate manifestation of lordly patronage. Many of these modest saints are likely, indeed, to have been family members – the ascetics and pilgrims so disdainfully parodied by Gildas. Such displays of spirituality and lordship might have contributed no more than a curious footnote to history had they not played so pivotal a role in the intellectual revolution that defined a new sort of lordship in the late sixth and seventh centuries.*

Few of these sites have given up their secrets to the excavator. The most conspicuous exception is Whithorn in Galloway, which looks across Wigtown Bay towards Ardwall Island and lies a day's hard rowing from Kirkmadrine to the west. Writing in 731, Bede described how a bishop, Ninian, had received orthodox instruction at Rome and converted the Picts of southern Scotland to the faith from his church of St Martin at a place called, in Latin, *Candida Casa* and *Hwitærn* in Old English: 'the white house'.[40] The church, says Bede, was built of stone and there has been much speculation over the years that it was rendered in lime mortar, creating a distinctive whitewashed appearance.[41] By Bede's day Whithorn was a thriving monastic community under the rule of a Northumbrian bishop. But St Ninian is an irretrievably shadowy figure: his *vita*, the *Miracula Nyniae Episcopi*, was written no earlier than the late eighth century and is a conventional, largely unhistorical hagiography.[42] It is likely, however, that a Christian community was active at Whithorn as early as the fifth century. A memorial stone, probably originally located in the churchyard of Whithorn priory, is regarded as the oldest of its type in Scotland. The rather touching inscription reads TE DOMINV(M)/ LAVDAMVS/ LATINVS/ ANNORV(M)/ XXXV ET/ FILIA SVA/ ANN(ORVM) IV/ (H)IC SI(G)NUM/ FECER(V)NT/ NEPVS/

* See Chapter 13.

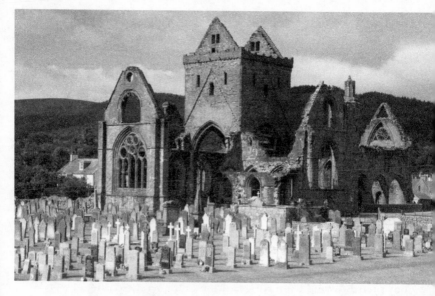

The Early Medieval lordship and/or monastic complex
at Whithorn – Bede's Candida Casa.

BARROVA/ DI: 'We praise the Lord. Latinus aged 35 years and
his daughter aged 4 years. The nephew/grandson of Barrovadus set
up this memorial'.[43]

It is unclear whether the earliest stages of occupation on the
site, which later became a fully developed monastic complex
reminiscent of Armagh in Ireland, were exclusively ecclesiastical.
Excavations south-west of the ruined medieval church yielded evidence of a number of timber and wattle buildings lying, according
to the excavator, just outside an inner precinct enclosed by a shallow
ditch.* The area was characterized by agricultural, industrial and
domestic debris; the buildings were of distinctively consistent
shape: 23–28 ft long with outwardly bowed sides, like those at
Trethurgy in Cornwall. This early phase, ended by the introduction
of the first graves in a closely packed cemetery, probably spanned

---

* A full circular enclosure has been reconstructed on the basis of one very
small fragment of ditch. Hill 1997.

the entire period during which Mediterranean pottery and glass were being traded into western Britain – from 475 to about 550. Whithorn town may lie inland, but it had access to a sheltered port at the Isle of Whithorn, some 4 miles to the south-east, and thence to other Early Medieval sites along the Gallwegian coast and all points beyond. The presence of Gaulish imports of the later sixth century shows that the site functioned as a focus for dwelling, feasting and craft working until it was turned over to burial. The first of several shrines excavated in this area belonged to the phase immediately preceding the development of the cemetery. Much of the site, like most medieval church precincts, is unavailable for excavation.

The Whithorn evidence typifies many of the problems facing archaeologists trying to differentiate the secular functions of lordship and feasting from those of Christian devotion. Was Whithorn a site of lordly consumption? If so, where was its hall? Was it the still-living heart of a bishop's diocese with a developing cult of Ninian, its celebrity holy man, or the busy hub of a monastic community? The distinction may be unnecessary: each was an expression of lordly patronage and display, however distasteful the mixing of sacred and profane may have been to rigidly orthodox men like Gildas and Bede. The wine of the feast and that of the eucharist may have been drawn from the same amphora. Hillforts, episcopal townships and monasteries, with their sense of privilege, exclusivity and defined space, shared many traits. Lordship thrived on the mix.

11

Dynasts

Elements of kingship – royal pedigrees – the *tyranni* – *villae regiae* – Yeavering – hungry kings – a political history – the 536 event – size matters – Rheged

The Pillar of Eliseg, Valle Crucis Abbey near Llangollen, Clwyd, in an etching of 1838.

C lovis's *adventus* and *de facto* coronation in 508 are pivotal moments in the evolution of European statehood. His adoption of orthodox Roman Christianity and formal imperial dignities fused barbarian martial and cultural energy with provincial Gallic sensibility and with ideas of orderly, literate governance. Merovingian Francia emerged as a powerful political force. In Britain that overt choice would not be made before the end of the sixth century; and then tentatively, at first. The decisive events were played out over thirty years and more and with less obviously Roman overtones. Christian kingship in Britain was a hybrid crossed with a hybrid.

At the beginning of the sixth century the components of Insular kingship are barely detectable: there are no contemporary princely burials like that of Childeric, nor of the sort discovered at Sutton Hoo, Snape or Prittlewell, which belong to the cusp of the seventh century. The architecture of royal townships like Yeavering is as yet unknown; recorded political history is virtually non-existent and the supposed progenitors of later dynasties claiming ancient pedigrees are no more than legendary names heading dubious genealogies.

Kings had to be more than mere warlords, as Clovis's investiture shows: they must hold their sceptres and wear their ornamented battle helms as of divine right – whether that divinity was Christian or not. They must be able to claim that their family had *always* been kings; that the territories over which their writ ran had *always* been theirs. They needed to project present realities backwards: to re-imagine the past creatively; to invent tradition. How those key elements of kingship were assembled in Britain reveals much about Early Medieval society, its aspirations and the mechanics of lordship.

Genealogies were held in trust, as oral history, by the bards and scops* of royal households; recited at inaugurations, assemblies, funerals and tributary feasts. Along with such pedigrees, the lengths of reigns were also remembered so that in theory later

* Reciters of poetry.

scholars might, in Bede's memorable phrase, 'compute the dates of kings'.[1] Pedigrees with regnal years attached appear in key sections of the *Historia Brittonum*, allowing modern 'computers' to reconstruct, with care, skeletal frameworks of events assigned to each king's reign. These are supplemented by a series of regnal lists that survive in a collection of Anglian genealogies.[2] The compilers of the *Anglo-Saxon Chronicle* probably had access to such lists, although before the middle of the sixth century these look flimsy, to say the least. In the kingdoms of Wales, the northwest and the south-west, regnal dates might have been inserted as marginalia in contemporary tables used to calculate future dates for the celebration of Easter; and, although none of these survives in an early form it can occasionally be argued that a later source incorporates such material.[3]

In an *Anglo-Saxon Chronicle* entry under the year 552 the West Saxon leader Cynric is said to have fought against 'the Britons' at *Seaorburh* – the hillfort of Old Sarum, just outside Salisbury. The compiler of the 'A' version of the *Chronicle*, picking up his stylus some 340 years later, chose this entry as an appropriate place to interpolate Cynric's pedigree. He was the son of Cerdic, son of Elesa, son of Esla, son of Gewis, son of Wig, son of Freawine, son of Frithugar, son of Brand, son of Bældeg, son of the god Woden. Cerdic was regarded by later generations of West Saxon kings – including Ælfred, who commissioned the *Chronicle* in the 890s – as the progenitor of their line, the natural rulers of the West Saxons. The *Anno Domini* dates of Cerdic's landing on the south coast, his battles and death, were entered confidently by scribes several centuries after the event. From that point they became petrified in written history.

Even setting aside, for the moment, the vexed question of how reliable the *Chronicle*'s dates are for this period, such genealogical material is inherently suspect. Closer inspection of Cynric's pedigree, and those of the other Insular kingdoms, reveals tell-tale repetitions and fabricated names, historical inconsistencies, the dubious motivations of their compilers and the political context in which such dynasts first wrote down their origins.[4] Royal pedigrees established both the antiquity of a lineage and the legitimacy of its claims to the kingship; but kings and their bards were unscrupulous in concocting heroic forebears and their descent from gods, and in their direct theft of the more attractive genealogies of their competitors. The ornately embroidered cloth of royal credentials needs some careful unpicking.

The reliability of the *Chronicle*'s early entries is undermined by stories like the arrival, in the year 477, of Ælle, supposed founder of the ruling dynasty of the South Saxons. He lands at *Cymenesora* with three sons: Cymen, Wlencing and Cissa. Suspicions are immediately raised because all three appear to be folk etymologies* for places – the latter two explaining the origins of Lancing and Chichester respectively. Cerdic, the West Saxon progenitor, is supposed to have arrived from the Germanic homelands with his son Cynric in five ships at a place called *Certicesora* – another folk etymology – in the year 495; 'and the same day they fought against the Welsh' (i.e. the native Britons). Twenty-four years later, after several entries recording battles and the arrivals of other dynastic entrepreneurs on the south coast, Cerdic and Cynric established their rule over the West Saxons in 519 after victory at a place called *Certicesford* – another apparent folk etymology. More battles followed, in which father and son slew various inhabitants of either explicitly or implicitly British territories. Cerdic is recorded as having died in 534, almost forty years after his arrival, and was succeeded by Cynric (until 560). Leaving aside the accuracy of the dates, the folk etymology of two of the battle sites and the credibility or otherwise of Cynric's considerable age at accession, one is inevitably struck by Cerdic's name: it is an anglicized version of the British Caraticos.[5]

One might suggest that Cerdic's arrival with five ships has been

---

* Early Medieval annalists liked to explain the names of places by reference to events and their protagonists: Portsmouth was founded where a legendary or invented pirate named Port landed; *Certicesford* is Cerdic's ford; and so on. Modern scholars have permission to be sceptical about such characters.

manufactured to fit in with expectations of Bede's and Gildas's Continental tribal origins for the English and to avoid politically compromising memories of a native British dynasty. The Cerdic/ Cynric partnership looks rather as though they are the only two names remembered, distantly, from a period when multiple leaders of native and incoming warbands were slugging it out for supremacy over quite modest territories. That suspicion is increased by an alternative foundation account for the West Saxon dynasty, which prefaces the 'A' version of the *Chronicle* and which claims that Cerdic and Cynric landed at *Certicesora* in the year 494; that six years later they conquered the kingdom of Wessex, after which Cerdic ruled for sixteen years (to 516).[6] The obvious discrepancy between this account and the main *Chronicle* entries, in which Cerdic becomes king in 519 and dies in 534 (fifteen years later) suggests to historians that his original landing as recorded in the 'A' version preface, if real, has been placed some nineteen years too early.[7]

It should be obvious from first principles that early dates retrospectively entered in the *Chronicle* and in the *Annales Cambriae* are unlikely to be accurate. In the 520s a Scythian monk called Dionysius Exiguus was the first to calculate the *Anno Domini* dates (as it happens he got his sums wrong) later popularized by Bede; but no contemporary chronicler adopted his method. Marginal entries made by Christian clerics in contemporary Easter tables to the effect that so and so died, or that a battle took place somewhere, might later have been incorporated into the sort of *Anno Domini* records kept on Iona in the 600s and which eventually formed the basis for the collection of Irish annals. It is also possible that some entries in the *Anglo-Saxon Chronicle* and *Annales Cambriae* are derived from such marginalia; but without corroboration from other sources they are at best unreliable. In any case, the *Annales Cambriae* offer just six entries for the first half of the sixth century, while the *Chronicle* gives no more than a dozen. Together, even with imaginative speculation, they frame no sort of political history. The Old English history of the West Saxon kingdom, written in annalistic form by Latin scribes, cannot have been a contemporaneous record much before the middle of the seventh century, when its kings had begun to patronize literate bishops. And the *Chronicle* includes almost none of the detail, found in the Irish Annals, that recorded contemporary preoccupations – portentous events; deaths of notables; feuds between rivals; harsh winters and disease – that would lend them credibility. Where these do appear, they have demonstrably been copied from elsewhere.

The West Saxon picture is further confused by the *Chronicle*'s record of another arrival, in 514, of the 'West Saxons, Stuf and Wightgar'. The latter derives his name from Wight, the *Vectis* of the former Roman province. These two are bequeathed the Isle of Wight by their kin, Cerdic and Cynric, in 534. There appear, then, to be two competing narratives for the foundation of a West Saxon dynasty in the second decade of the sixth century. At some point the favoured creation myth, giving the now-Germanized *Caraticos pride of place, has been brought forward by nearly two decades to give it precedence – but without removing the contradictory entry from 519. The preservation of both legends betrays the paw-print of retrospective tampering. In terms of political history, then, the early West Saxon narrative in the *Chronicle* inspires little confidence. Writing in the eighth century, Bede regarded the West Saxons as being synonymous with a tribe called the *Gewisse*, whose dynastic origins are obscure but whose eponymous founder Gewis was conveniently inserted into the West Saxon genealogy three generations before Cerdic. At the end of the ninth century, it is safe to say, Cerdic and his line were considered to be suitably warlike and heroic Germanic figures from whom to claim royal descent.*

Woden's place at the head of the West Saxon genealogy is paralleled in those of the Bernician and Deiran dynasties of

---

* Just one member of the named West Saxon rulers before the days of King Ælfred's own daughter, Æðelflæd, was a woman: Queen Seaxburgh, who ruled for a single year after the death of her husband Cenwalh and died in 674.

Northumbria and of Lindsey, Mercia, Kent and East Anglia, assembled from various, often inconsistent collections probably drawn up in their surviving form in the ninth century. Only the East Saxon kings, whose pedigree is found in a single document unrelated to other collections, claimed ultimate descent from an alternative member of the Germanic pantheon: the folk-ancestor Seaxneat.[8] The earliest generations of such pedigrees were compiled from a deeply treasured cultural manifest of folk ancestors; but bards and their patrons were not above appropriating ancestors from other, supposedly more auspicious, lines. Several West Saxon ancestors were 'borrowed' from the Bernician list; several Kentish ancestors from that of Deira.[9] The genealogies, as they survive in much later documents, have also been streamlined: they contain no records of parallel claimants, of the well-attested sharing of kingship or evidence of coups d'état.

Compiling family trees for the dynasties that survived and thrived in the seventh century and beyond, through painstaking analysis of a wide body of material, reveals much about the editing processes that lie behind the genealogies. The Oiscingas of Kent traced their lineage, conventionally, back to Woden. Five generations after their godly forebear comes Hengest who, despite historians' doubts about his historicity, has at least the virtue of being named in all the available sources as the leader of an original Germanic warband landing on Thanet in the first half of the fifth century. Even so, the Kentish royal family called themselves not Hengestingas but Oiscingas, after Hengest's supposed grandson; Oisc may justly be regarded as the historical progenitor of the Kentish royal line. Even he lies seven generations before Æðelberht, the king of Kent who first appears as a three-dimensional actor on a solid stage. The highly artificial generations before Hengest, borrowed from the pedigree of Deira, were probably inserted at a time when the two dynasties were linked by marriage, in the days of King Edwin (617–632) and his Kentish queen, Æðelburh.

Many early pedigrees must have been lost in the process of small territories being swallowed by more powerful and aggressive neighbours, because scribal records were never compiled or have been lost. The warlords who followed Ælle and his son Cissa as leaders of the South Saxons are unknown and unrecorded until the end of the seventh century – a gap of 150 years or more.

Some pedigrees contain names of whom not a single figure can be corroborated independently. Lindsey's royal genealogy is short, just eleven generations back to Woden; and the last name on the list, Aldfrið, appears nowhere else in recorded history. Many of the smaller units recorded in Tribal Hidage, if their leaders ever maintained pedigrees in their households, were lost before scrupulous historians like Bede could record them. The *Pecsæte* named in Tribal Hidage did not endure long enough as an independent people for any of their royal pedigrees, if such existed, to survive. Of the kings who inherited the territory of the much better-attested *Wrocansæte* only one can be tentatively named: the 'Cunorix son of Maqui Coline' whose name is recorded on a stone memorial from Wroxeter.* The names of a few individuals are recorded if they witnessed charters as *subreguli* (tributary kings) or *principes* (ealdormen). Tondberht, an ealdorman of South Gyrwa in the Fenlands, is only known because after his death his widow, Æðelðrið, married King Ecgfrið of Bernicia and later became the monastic founder of Ely.[10] The *Hwicce*, whose lands straddled the lower Severn valley, had been conquered by, and absorbed into, greater Mercia by the middle of the eighth century and were already ruled by a series of subordinate ealdormen (the rump of their formerly royal dynasty) from the mid-seventh century. Their pedigree is lost but the names of three otherwise obscure 'British' kings of Hwiccan provinces are recorded under the *Chronicle* entry for the year 577, when a great battle was fought at Dyrham. Ceawlin, king of the West Saxons, killed no fewer than three British kings in the conflict: Coinmail, Condidan and Farinmail, whose territories seem to have been based on the Roman towns of Bath, Gloucester and Cirencester. Whether these men were the last 'native' rulers of the *Hwicce* is unknown.

No fewer than twenty genealogies survive for the ruling houses

* See Chapter 2, p. 64.

of the old west and north, found in the same manuscript, Harleian 3859, that contains standard versions of the *Historia Brittonum* and *Annales Cambriae*. These pedigrees, complete with legendary progenitors and fanciful insertions, are subject to the same sorts of interpretive problems as those of their Anglo-Saxon neighbours. Regnal years are lacking, so their chronology floats uncertainly, or is tied to dubious annal entries. The genealogy of Dyfed, running to some thirty generations up to the early ninth-century King Owain or Ouein,* gives a fascinating insight into the ambitions of its contemporary kings. Eleven generations before Owain one finds the name Arthur; another three generations back brings one to *Guortepir*, the Vortipor of Gildas's day. Seven generations before Vortipor the name *Maxim Guletic* taps into Dyfed's earlier incarnation as the *civitas* of the Demetae, for *Maxim Guletic*, 'Maximus the Great', is none other than the Magnus Maximus who helped suppress the great conspiracy of 367 and who usurped imperial power in *Britannia* at the end of the fourth century. His father is said, in that pedigree, to have been *Protec map* [son of] *Protector*, a reminder of the title recorded for Vortipor on an inscribed stone memorial and a distant memory, perhaps, of provincial power being devolved to the *civitates* when Maximus left on his ultimately fatal Continental expedition. Even Constantine the Great enjoys a mention in the royal pedigree of Dyfed.[11]

Other members of Gildas's tyrannical quintet feature in the Welsh genealogies: *Maglocunus* – Maelgwyn of Gwynedd – is recorded in the fourteenth generation before the ninth-century Owain who tops the list of Venedotian† kings and whose ultimate progenitor was said to have been the Virgin Mary. Maelgwyn's great-grandfather was believed to have been a man named Cunedda.‡ These two are linked by a narrative in the *Historia Brittonum* in which Cunedda

* Died 811, according to the *Annales Cambriae*.
† Venedotian: the adjectival form of Gwynedd – perhaps derived from Old Irish *Feni*.
‡ Cunedda's name is suspected to be a folk-etymological explanation for Gwynedd.

and his eight sons came out of the north, from the country called *Manaw Gododdin*,* 146 years before Maelgwyn reigned. Cunedda was said to have expelled the Irish from what became Gwynedd, with great slaughter.[12] Another of Gildas's tyrants, Cuneglasus, appears as Cinglas in the pedigree of the kings of Rhos. Aurelius Caninus, possibly one of the degenerate grandsons of Ambrosius, may be identified with the Cinnin or Cínan who appears in the otherwise thin Harleian genealogies of Powys. Constantine – his name a faint clue to an imperial past – belonged to a dynasty that can be pieced together only very loosely from fragments contained in a variety of more or less dubious sources, including saints' lives and the much later writings of Geoffrey of Monmouth. The last known king of *Dumnonia* was Geraint, a heroic figure in medieval Welsh poetry, who died early in the seventh century.[13]

The pedigree of the kings of Powys, regarded as inheriting the western part of the territory of the *Cornovii*, is equally fragmentary, inscribed on a tantalizing stone memorial cross close to a ruined abbey, Valle Crucis, just west of Llangollen. The Pillar of Eliseg was erected and inscribed in the ninth century during a period of nationalistic fervour precipitated by Scandinavian raiding and English aggression. A mere phallic remnant of a taller cross, the pillar stands on a prehistoric burial mound, as if tapping into ancient tribal roots. The now impossibly worn inscription once told of the pillar's erection by a king of Powys, Cyngen ap Cadell,† in memory of his great-grandfather Elisedd ap Gwylog. The pillar was vandalized by Parliamentarian soldiers during the seventeenth century but in 1696 the Welsh antiquarian Edward Lhuyd examined and transcribed what was then legible of the inscription. Among the fragmentary Latin lines that he managed to read are 'Maximus... of Britain... Brydw son of Gwerthyrn (Vortigern), whom Germanus blessed, and whom Sevira bore to

---

* The location of *Manau Gododdin* is much debated; but the name may be preserved in Clackmannanshire around the headwaters of the River Forth.

† Died 854; his is the last name in the Harleian genealogy of Powys.

him, daughter of Maximus the king, who killed the king of the Romans...'[14] The ninth-century kings of Powys liked to believe that they were the true inheritors of the traditions recorded in the contemporary *Historia Brittonum*; of the imperial powers of the Roman state and orthodox church, as legitimate rulers of all the Cymry in the fifth century. In that ninth-century context, however, the inscription cannot be used to corroborate fifth-century reality, even if it preserves some dim, genuine memory of actual lineal descent from a Roman usurper.

Gildas's tyrants aside, the first historically credible Insular kings lie several generations along from the original folk ancestors of the royal pedigrees, and almost none can be placed before the second half of the sixth century. Trying to identify the point at which opportunistic warlords were accepted as ruling in a kingly way necessarily invites two questions: what constituted kingship in the sixth century, and what separates those warlords supposed to have landed on the shores of southern Britain from Bede's divinely appointed *reges* or Gildas's *civitas*-inheriting *tyranni*? Were kings defined, tautologically, by ruling over territories that subsequently became kingdoms?

Gildas's *tyranni* – and his use of that particular word may be a pun on the Brythonic word *tigernus*, meaning 'king'[15] – offer a model of tribal leadership, flawed as it was by sin and transgression, as he understood it. He expected that, as inheritors of imperial statesmanship in Britain, they were Christian – or at least nominally so. Maglocunus took monastic vows before renouncing them. Constantine of *Dumnonia* and members of other British dynasties consciously borrowed the name of the emperor who had been acclaimed in Britain and who had encoded the imperial tolerance of Christianity. The Christian kings of Gildas's world swore holy oaths at the altars of churches (even if they subsequently scorned them). When the *tyranni* sinned, they sinned against Christian rules. Among their other crimes are clues to their powers: 'they take their seats as judges' (if amorally); they waged wars (if civil wars); they exalted their military companions, their *comites*. They maintained jails and filled them (unjustly) with political prisoners; they disposed of rival members of 'royal' families. These are universal traits of Machiavellian power, recognizable in the exalted offices of the medieval and modern state and frequently attested by Francia's sixth-century historian, Gregory of Tours.

Kings' legitimacy was earned through a combination of sword-wielding leadership in war and noble bloodline – as the sons or grandsons of men who had been kings (or at least great lords) three or four generations in the past. In Ireland, that birthright was called *rigdomna* – eligibility to rule. In the absence of legitimacy, power was seized by main force. The luckier or more successful a leader was in battle, the more lavishly he rewarded the members of his *comitatus* with booty and feasting, the longer his line lasted and the more legitimate he became.

Clovis came to be regarded by his descendants as the founder of the Merovingian dynasty* because, on the back of impressive military victories and territorial expansion, he had undergone a ceremony, comprehensible to Gaul and Frank alike, of coronation and inauguration, accompanied by the bestowal of imperial titles loaded with symbols of state and the panoply of largesse, purple robe and ecclesiastical blessing. His father's magnificent, accidentally discovered tomb shows that a king – at least a pagan king – was also expected to be buried with symbols of his elevated rank: beneath a mound, with his horse, weapons, helmet, drinking horns, treasures and with great ceremony. Beowulf, dying as a king long in years, receives such a burial. So did the king of East Anglia buried at Sutton Hoo in the early seventh century. But the earliest overtly kingly burials in England – the ship mounds at Taplow and Snape; barrows at Benty Grange in Derbyshire, Ashfield in Oxfordshire and Broomfield in Essex; the sunken chamber at Prittlewell – are not found before the end of the sixth century or the beginning of the seventh.[16] Does this mean that,

* The dynasty ruled all or substantial parts of Francia until the middle of the eighth century.

ceremonially, formal acts of inauguration and the acclamation of warlords as kings of their people were new in late sixth-century Britain, three generations after Clovis in Francia?

In Early Medieval Wales, where kings' ultimate claims to legitimacy derived from imperial or pseudo-imperial credentials unsubtly bolted on to the tails of their pedigrees, no ruler had such a burial, so far as one knows; but a medieval Welsh legend, one of the earlier of the so-called Mabinogion collection of tales, contains an inventory of 'the ceremonial possessions of a traditional ruler: sword, knife, whetstone, drinking horn, cauldron, draughtsboard, mantle and the like'.[17] Feasting, gaming, drinking: these were the pursuits of an élite who did not spend their lives bent double in the fields but specialized in fighting, hunting, touring and feeding off the surplus of their dependants. The conspicuous consumption displayed by kings is typified and symbolized by the drinking horn: a vessel that cannot stand at rest on a table but must be continually passed, and refilled, so long as the participants remain conscious. Unless, as at Sutton Hoo, such artefacts were buried with kings, then the material signs of early kingship are much harder to detect.

How else are historians and archaeologists to detect such signs of incipient kingship? No royal coinage – a key component of political and economic control in Early Medieval statehood – was issued by any king in Britain before the second half of the seventh century, although relict Roman Continental coinage may have been circulating through royal hands during the previous two centuries. The earliest royal laws to survive in written form are those drawn up in Kent by King Æðelberht at the beginning of the seventh century. By then,* the king's status was expressed in terms of his superior *wergild* (head price, or blood-money) – his value in cases of compensation for injury, theft or the breaching of his *mund* or royal protection.[18] It is also expressed by his place at the top of a social and economic pyramid. Below him are his *duces* and *eorls*; the active, unmarried *gesiths* of his warband and older, time-served

---

* Written down, perhaps, with the help of clerics from Augustine's mission; but nevertheless written in Old English, not in Latin.

land-worthy nobles; then various classes or castes of free men and women and three classes of free but dependent '*laets*'. The unfree of these earliest laws include the king's smiths and messengers; various 'maidens', female corn-grinding slaves and married, unmarried and widowed women (each with their own valuation).

Clauses in the early Kentish dooms relating to offences committed at a *cyninges tune* (a king's royal township) and during the course of a feast at the *ham* of one of his subjects reveal some of the underlying mechanisms of peripatetic kingship.[19] Seventh-century kings and their subjects were defined, then, by their kingly behaviour and routine, by different rights to compensation and by their liabilities and legal right to protection and justice; but it is uncertain how far back such distinctions can be projected.

Archaeologists looking for earlier signs of royal activity, and for stages on which kings might act, must try to identify the material remains of these royal townships – Bede's *villae regiae* – in order to corroborate or refute the political narratives of the annals and the tenor of the laws. They look for architectural pretension on a suitably grand scale and for evidence of the economic and political clout required to be able to draw on sufficient materials, labour, surveying skills and craftsmanship to carry their designs through. They look for formal planning and design; for buildings with highly specialized, even ceremonial functions; for the seasonal nature of occupation that would fit the itinerancy of Early Medieval extensified lordship. All these have been found in abundance in what is now an evocatively windswept, desolately beautiful valley close to the Anglo-Scottish border. Yeavering (Figure 4), Bede's royal township of *Ad Gefrin*, lies on the banks of the River Glen, beneath the sensuous twin-domed massif of the Iron Age tribal hillfort on Yeavering Bell. First located by aerial photography in 1949, Yeavering was brilliantly excavated in the 1950s and 1960s by Brian Hope-Taylor, whose technical and narrative skills matched the grandeur of the site. In its earliest incarnation *Gefrin* saw the construction of a large polygonal palisaded enclosure, some 130 yards across, with an imposing entrance flanked by circular terminals – one of them containing a rectangular building

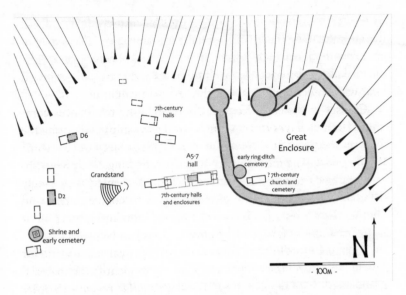

Fig. 4. The Bernician royal township at Yeavering, Northumberland:
excavated structures. Those shaded and outlined in bold belong to
the earliest phases of its development as a royal township.
After Hope-Taylor 1977.

more than 40 ft long.[20] The so-called Great Enclosure seems to
have functioned as a corral for cattle – collected as tribute from
subordinate lords, perhaps – and also as a place of tribal assembly.

A second rectangular building (A5-7) lay immediately to the
west of this enclosure, the first of a series of increasingly large and
elaborate halls constructed on the same site and forming a primary
east–west axial alignment. A further building (D6), constructed
with four opposed entrances, like A5-7, stood 100 yards or so to
the north-west. To the south-west, close to a small natural knoll,
lay a circular shrine in which a single post a foot in diameter
(the size of a tree trunk about forty years old) stood at the
centre. The shrine had once been enclosed by an interrupted ring
ditch which Hope-Taylor believed to have held upright stones,
perhaps the figurative memorials of dynastic ancestors. The
stones were, at some point, dug out, the ditch made redundant

by the superimposition of a square timber fence inside it and the insertion of more than twenty radially oriented graves. Yeavering's élite ring ditch cemetery offers archaeologists a model for kingly burial before the end of the sixth century – materially modest but surely invested with more than trivial power and ceremony. In these early phases at Yeavering one should, perhaps, envisage something like a cross between an annual religious festival, a county show and a rodeo, at which kings sacrificed to their tribal gods and ancestors and paraded the prize cattle and horses brought as tribute by subordinate lords; where warriors showed off their martial and riding prowess and the bragging rivalries of élite warbands were fuelled by an excess of mead and meat.

In these mid- to late sixth-century phases are hints, no more, of Yeavering's magnificent future as a royal residence under Kings Edwin and Oswald, complete with church, great hall and a unique grandstand. But that lack of early architectural pretension may be illusory. If occupation was annual or seasonal, based on a mobile encampment of tents invisible to archaeologists, it might have witnessed grand assemblies, while its evocative setting offered strong tribal associations with the hillfort above. Even so, there is nothing here, before the turn of the seventh century, to match the lavish power of its later kings. Another township complex conceived on the same scale as Yeavering is known close to the River Tweed at Sprouston, detected by aerial photography, but it has not been excavated.[21] Much further south, a similar complex has been detected from the air at Atcham, not far from Wroxeter.

Kingship, with its attendant expressions of consumption and warfare, opens a paradoxical window onto the more humble farming communities that supported it. Across Bernicia very few settlements have been identified, let alone excavated, from the period contemporary with Yeavering's heyday. At Lanton Quarry, across the River Glen to the north, part of a craft and agricultural centre has produced evidence for the semi-free and unfree artisans and farmers whose skills and labour supported the royal township.[22] At Thirlings, overlooking the River Till below its confluence with the Glen, the hall and farm of a minor noble household, whose lord very likely served in the *comitatus* of the Bernician kings, has also been excavated. The buildings are modest, and somewhat later than the first phases at Yeavering; but there is order and structure here: the layout is that of a complex suitable as the centre of a farming estate.[23]

Kingship on the scale that allowed the Bernician kings of the late sixth and early seventh centuries to subdue and reduce to tributary status all of central Britain between the Humber and Forth required a highly productive economy. In the crudest terms, royal households and their attendant warbands were greedy for calories. The larger the outfit, the more bread, ale, meat, honey, fuel, timber, weapons and finery they consumed. On their travels, kings must be sure that, when they stayed for a tenth part of the year at their various *villae regiae*, the lofts and outhouses of their mead halls were stuffed with grain; their smiths amply supplied with charcoal and scrap iron, silver or bronze; their weaving women well-found in wool, flax and dyestuffs, their corrals full of prime beef and swift horses. Yeavering and other *villae regiae* must, in the absence of the king's presence during most of the year, have been managed by a *gerefa*: a king's reeve. Such functionaries and their counterparts at other *vills* managed the farmed and pastoral landscapes of their kingdoms.

Bernicia's landed wealth came from a narrow but fertile coastal plain; from the easily cultivated glacial soils of the Till basin, and from the broad, volcanic uplands of the Cheviot Hills whose pastures fattened horses, sheep and cows alike through long summer days while their bees gorged on heather blossom. Where, then, are the settlements in which all these farmers lived? If Bernicia was comparable in wealth, as it was in size and power, to other first-rank kingdoms, then it ought to have a nominal assessment of 30,000 hides, from which its kings drew the warbands that defeated the thirty *duces* who went to war alongside King Penda of Mercia in 655.

The overwhelming sense among archaeologists is that either we are looking in the wrong places to find, or we are unable to detect, a large majority of the settlements and attendant cemeteries required

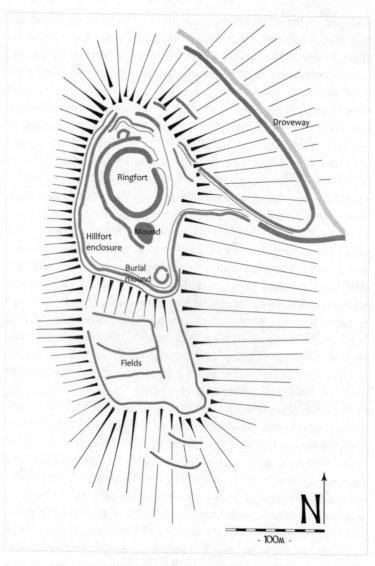

Fig. 5. Plan of earthworks at the Clogher kingship site,
County Tyrone. After Warner 1988.

to support the long-ruling dynasty of the Idings. Northumberland, the most successful of the early Anglo-Saxon kingdoms, must have been a highly productive and organized farming landscape; but only after the establishment of many monastic estates in the seventh century does that human landscape become visible; and then, often, in reflection.[24] The suspicion must be that many of the scores of sites identified as settlements of the Romano-British period – Greave's Ash, Ingram Hill and Haystack Hill in the Breamish valley; Huckoe in central Northumberland; the Wall forts of Tynedale; the villages of the Vale of Pickering in Deira, spring to mind – continued to prosper and render surplus to Bernician kings well into the sixth century, if not beyond.

A broader geography of emerging kingship is provided, across the north of Britain, by defended hilltop sites that have yielded archaeological evidence for the seventh century onwards and, like Yeavering and Bamburgh, can be associated with concrete historical narratives of Early Medieval kingship. Dunadd, rearing fist-like out of the bog of Mòine Mhòr in Kilmartin Glen, was the royal seat and likely inauguration site of Dál Riatan kings (Figure 6). Dumbarton Rock – *Alclut* in Brythonic – was the seat of the kings of Strathclyde for more than 300 years. Like Tintagel, South Cadbury, Bamburgh and Dunadd it dominates its hinterland, the former tidal reach of the Clyde. Further north and east the Pictish heartlands of Fortriu seem to have been ruled from Craig Phadraig overlooking the Beauly Firth, and Burghead on the Moray Firth. Archaeologists are increasingly excited by the evidence of a major kingship site at Rhynie in Aberdeenshire, which bears comparison with both Yeavering and with a defended royal settlement complex at Clogher in County Tyrone.* In southern Pictland Dundurn, where a half-natural, half-carved stone seat or throne sat within an elevated, inner enclosure, seems to dominate the upper reaches of Strathearn. This was, in later centuries, the core territory of the kings of Alba, with their inauguration mound at Scone on the Upper Tay and a royal township at Forteviot. Here, monumental

* See Chapter 12, p. 391.

sculpture reinforces the idea of an extensive, coherent landscape of kingship emerging from an ancient, cultural coreland.

The archaeology of Scottish state formation has been comprehensively mapped in such forts and sculpture, in the presence of early churches and in the historical geography of its shires.[25] In southern Britain, royal residences belonging to well-attested seventh-century kings have been identified more or less confidently at Rendlesham; at Lyminge in Kent; at Cowdery's Down in Hampshire; at Sutton Courtenay in Oxfordshire; at Aberffraw on Anglesey and, tentatively, elsewhere. Canterbury seems as though it must have had a royal residence before the end of the sixth century.

Of the former *civitas* capitals, evidence for continuous lordly, and then kingly, residence is much the strongest at Wroxeter, with its suite of large, architecturally sophisticated and well-planned buildings. Catterick is a promising candidate in Yorkshire, although signs of grand buildings there have so far proved elusive. Of the Roman forts where lordship in some form has been argued for the fifth and sixth centuries – Birdoswald prominent among them – there is no sign at all of regal construction or burial; but a number of forts were given by kings to found churches in the seventh century and later – a hint that they may have functioned as temporary or undeveloped estate centres in royal portfolios.[26]

From about 560 onwards the outline of a continuous political narrative of Early Medieval kingship gradually comes into focus. In that year, according to the *Anglo-Saxon Chronicle*, Ceawlin succeeded Cynric as ruler of the West Saxons. In the north, in Deira, Ælle son of Yffi (no relation to the former South Saxon warlord) gained the kingship. The landing at Lindisfarne under the *Chronicle* entry for 547 of Ida, progenitor of the kings of Bernicia, may be more correctly placed in the same year, if that event is at all historical.[27] Five years later, in 565, Æðelberht succeeded to the kingdom of Kent. The first of the Iclingas of Mercia to play a significant role in political history was Penda, who died some ninety years later in 655; but the Mercian royal progenitor, Icel, comes five generations earlier, from the second half of the sixth century. In East Anglia Rædwald, the king most likely buried in his ship at Sutton Hoo, died in about 625; but the Wuffing who gave his name to the East Anglian dynasty lived two generations before him. Irish annalists ascribe to the 560s the momentous founding of the monastic house on Iona by Colm Cille (himself related to the royal house of the Cenél Conaill) and the establishment of his fateful relationship with the kings of Dál Riata.* If the roots of Early Medieval kingship lie in the lordships of the fifth century, their green shoots first become visible in the second half of the sixth.

One might speculate endlessly on the social and economic drivers and tensions that led to the emergence of recognizable kingdoms and kingship in Britain before the end of the seventh century – almost a hundred years after similar developments in Frankish Gaul. But it is hard to avoid an association between the rise of Insular kingship and what has become known as the '536 event'. All societies reliant on subsistence farming faced the challenge of winters when snow lay on the ground for months at a time; summers when no harvest could be gathered; times of drought, famine, plague and flood. Dire omens warning of such hardship and ill fortune infuse the earliest annals and the lives of saints: lightning, comets and eclipses; fiery dragons in the sky; bizarre plagues of insects; the sky raining fish. The *vita* of St Brigit is played out in a landscape of poverty and hardship where only the divine hand, acting through the saint's miraculous offices, can save the day. Gildas's oddly harmonious portrait of Britain's fertile hills and meadows is set against his own woeful tale of strife and social tension. The fallen warriors of *Y Gododdin* were devoured by hungry wolves and ravens. Gods, auguries, shamanic divinations and propitiatory gifts to springs and wells were implored or deployed to tilt the odds in favour of farmers, warriors, hunters, pregnant women and poorly children; and kings embodied the luck of their *gens* or *cenéla* for good or ill.

The Byzantine historian Procopius, in his exhaustive mid-sixth-

* See Chapter 13, p. 401.

century account of Emperor Justinian's wars against the barbarian kings ruling much of the former Western empire, might have been exaggerating when he wrote of a dreadful portent that marked the tenth year of Justinian's reign in 536:

> The sun gave forth its light without brightness, like the moon, during this whole year, and it seemed exceedingly like the sun in eclipse, for the beams it shed were not clear nor such as it is accustomed to shed. And from the time when this thing happened men were free neither from war nor pestilence nor any other thing leading to death.[28]

Hyperbole, perhaps; but Procopius's grim tidings are echoed in widespread sources. The *Annals of Ulster* report a 'failure of bread' in the same year, and again in 539. A virulent and deadly disease broke out in Egypt four years after the sun's great dimming and spread rapidly along the trade networks of the Mediterranean. The pathogen responsible for what is known as the Justinian plague has been identified as the same flea-carried bacterium, *yersinia pestis*, that caused the Black Death of the fourteenth century. It struck Byzantium in 542:

> Now the disease in Byzantium ran a course of four months, and its greatest virulence lasted about three. And at first the deaths were a little more than the normal, then the mortality rose still higher, and afterwards the tale of dead reached five thousand each day, and again it even came to ten thousand and still more than that. Now in the beginning each man attended to the burial of the dead of his own house, and these they threw even into the tombs of others, either escaping detection or using violence; but afterwards confusion and disorder everywhere became complete. For slaves remained destitute of masters, and men who in former times were very prosperous were deprived of the service of their domestics who were either sick or dead, and many houses became completely destitute of human inhabitants.[29]

The plague arrived in Ireland in the same year, recorded by the *Annals of Tigernach* as a '*mortalitas magna*'. It seems likely that it was carried by traders bringing amphorae of wines and oils and the fine tablewares sought by lords in the West. Further outbreaks are recorded by the Irish annals in 545 and 549, while the *Annales Cambriae*, less reliably, tell of plague in 537 and 547, in which year it was said that Gildas's greatest tyrant, *Maglocunus*, perished.*

The decades immediately following the 536 event have been described as the coldest in the last 2,500 years, evidenced by both ice core samples and contemporary tree rings. The event seems to have been global and, after much debate among scientists over several decades, it has now been ascribed to a sequence of catastrophic volcanic eruptions that threw vast quantities of ash and other sun-masking pollutants into the atmosphere, causing a dust veil in many parts of the world.[30]

Historians are rightly wary of pinning political events onto environmental causes. Neither Gregory of Tours nor the *Anglo-Saxon Chronicle* mention the 536 event or the plague that followed.† But there is no doubting the potential psychological and social effects, personally witnessed by Procopius, of a series of poor harvests exacerbated by disease and, perhaps, depopulation. Empty houses bred crime; empty markets spread hunger. Unfree men and women without masters had no place; no protection. Lords who lost their unfree dependants to famine or plague must fight for their rights or face unrest from more distant and peripheral rivals; territories

---

* The entry recording his death in the *Annales Cambriae* would bolster the traditional mid-sixth-century date for Gildas's *De Excidio*, if it could be relied on.

† Gregory, born in that decade of global cooling, reports a winter so cold that all the rivers froze, and starving birds could be caught by hand. But he seems to be describing the year 548, when he was nine years old. Gregory *HF*: III.37. The failure of the *ASC* to record weather and disease events for the middle of the sixth century may be adduced as evidence that it contains no contemporary entries; or that no such event was sufficiently noteworthy.

without lords, laws or farmers tumbled down to waste or offered opportunities for new lords to try their hand. Physical and social stress induced by the failure not just of a single harvest but of two or more failures within five years, followed by plague, are likely drivers of tensions among and between lordships, of reinforced psychological dependence on credible leadership and religion. The last imports of exotica from the Mediterranean landed on Britain's shores in about 550; maritime trade with Gaul would not resume for another ten or twenty years.

If the dynasties of the great Insular kingdoms first come into focus after the middle of the sixth century, the environmental stresses of those decades may have helped to streamline extensive lordship, to foster the emergence of the most successful – and that may mean most aggressive or competent – warlords, as true kings. A stretched hierarchy of lordship, with a few great chiefs dominating lower tiers of warlords, required that some of them were distinguished by more than martial reputation; that they acquired the aura of god-like beings, inaugurated and legitimized as if by a divine hand.

It is hard to say whether the formal status and paraphernalia of kingship evolved from the realities of enlarged territorial rule, or whether the reverse is true: that kingdoms came to be defined by the nature and extent of ceremonial kingship. It is a nice question. By the time Tribal Hidage was drawn up in the seventh century, a mosaic of polities and peoples co-existed, drawn out across the whole territorial scale. The tiny 300-hide Fenland districts of *Sweodora* and *Wixna*, perhaps retaining lordly independence because of their fiercely defended communal rights, may by then already have been anachronisms in the face of aggressive overlords in Northumbria, Wessex and Mercia. Some formerly indepen- dent territories and peoples had already been swallowed or had coalesced into larger entities. Loosely defined territories, like those of the Middle Angles and Middle Saxons, have left no surviving genealogies and may never have gained kingly status before they were brought into the portfolios of East Anglian or Mercian over-lords.* Mercia's original constituent parts are probably incapable of reconstruction, although three competing dynasties that shared Mercian rule over the next few centuries strongly hint, at the very least, at three core kingdoms based around Winchcombe in Gloucestershire (the heartland of what had once been Hwiccan territory), Breedon on the Hill in Leicestershire, and Tamworth in Staffordshire, the latter with its royal crypt at Repton. In East Anglia the North Folk and South Folk who gave the modern counties of Norfolk and Suffolk their names may mask smaller kingdoms or independent polities already defunct by the seventh century. Rendlesham, closely associated with the royal burial site at nearby Sutton Hoo, can be identified as an early *villa regia* but there have often been suggestions, based on material affinities with both Scandinavia and Francia, that much of East Anglia might have been subject to the imperium of overseas powers from an early date. Kent has been already been proposed as an overseas dominion of Frankish kings.[31]

The constituent territories of what would become the kingdom of the West Saxons are still obscure. The archaeology points to early concentrations of Germanic material along the upper Thames – perhaps the core lands of the *Gewisse* – and to the development of settlement and burial cores around the Solent in Hampshire; and yet, it is hard to avoid the idea that the wealthy *civitates* of the Durotriges based on Dorchester and Ilchester, of the Belgae around Winchester, and the Atrebates whose *civitas* capital lay abandoned at Silchester, were the ancient, stable entities that powered the rise of Wessex from the late seventh century onwards. To their west, native dynasties in *Dumnonia* (Devon and Cornwall) are underplayed by an overtly hostile West Saxon historical record – a *damnatio memoriae* – but they retained both independence and the ability to undertake offensive military campaigns well into

---

* Bede refers to Peada, son of the Mercian King Penda, as *rex* of the Middle Angles (*HE* III.24); but elsewhere calls him merely *princeps* (*HE* III.21; V.24). Campbell 1986, 85.

the eighth century. Earlier in this chapter it was suggested that Cerdic, and the *Gewisse*, may have emerged from 'native' entities. Genealogies also show that the British kingdoms of the west, ruled by Gildas's tyrants at the end of the fifth century, retained their power into later ages. Their kings played no small part in the political evolutions of the seventh and eighth centuries and beyond.

Even in the east of Britain kingdoms and kings with British cultural affinities survived until the first half of the seventh century. The last king of Elmet, more or less encompassing Yorkshire west of York, is named in the *Historia Brittonum* as Ceretic – expelled by King Edwin of Deira as late as the 620s.[32] West of the Pennines lay more shadowy Brythonic-speaking kingdoms: Craven, a polity whose name survives as a modern administrative area around Skipton;[33] and Rheged, perhaps the most elusive and alluring of all Early Medieval realms. Rheged exemplifies the challenges facing geographers hoping to draw neat boundaries around kingdoms whose extent was either never recorded or can only be inferred after later administrators fossilized their boundaries. If some of the earliest territorial lordships are associated with natural cultural corelands such as the drainage basins of fertile plains like *Magh Tóchuir*, the River Arrow, the Tees valley, the Tweed Basin and the lower Severn, one might suppose that many of the earliest kingdoms were similarly delimited by watersheds – circuits of high land whose limits were a topographical and political certainty.

By Bede's day kingdoms were just as likely to be defined by boundaries along major river systems: the Don in South Yorkshire; the Tweed and Thames, for example. This trend away from rivers as cores to rivers as peripheries may owe something to the bellicose proclivities of kings who liked to do battle with their enemies at Roman road crossings of major rivers. The modern desire or need to pin down early kingdoms by drawing speculative boundaries on maps may, in reality, be a wasted exercise if kingship, and the idea and extent of a kingdom, was expressed not by its limits but by a core group of *villae regiae* – centres of itinerant power – allowing for much fluidity or uncertainty at the edges. In the well-documented case of Bernicia, where royal *vills* and their estates have largely been reconstructed for the Early Medieval period and where they may be regarded as genuinely ancient estate centres, it is much easier to say which royal *vills* were claimed by Bede's kings over the course of a century or so than to say where Bernicia ended and Deira, to the immediate south, or Gododdin (to the immediate north, in what would become Lothian), or Rheged in the west, began. Further south, later historical narratives hint that areas outside cultural corelands, like the forests of Selwood, Dean and the Weald, may have constituted *de facto* frontier zones incapable of tighter definition.

All these challenges of identification and extent come together in the problem of Rheged.[34] Neither Bede nor the *Historia Britto-num* records the name. There is a Dunragit, 'Fortress of Rheged', near Glenluce in Galloway, although the only substantial earth-work close to the village is a strange, artificial structure, not unlike Silbury Hill in Wiltshire, called the Mound of Droughdull. It might do very well as a kingly inauguration site, if archaeologists had anything else to go on by way of identifying Rheged's core. Seeking consistency, by analogy with other British kingships of the old west and north, archaeologists have tried to match Rheged with the *civitas* of the *Carvetii*, whose capital lay at *Luguvalium*: Carlisle. Here the valleys of the Eden and Irthing drain into the broad Solway Firth and topographically their drainage basins look like a credible cultural coreland or *magh*, squeezed between the Lake District, the Pennines and the Southern Uplands. But Carlisle and Rheged are nowhere directly associated. Carlisle, *Caer Luel* in Brythonic, became an important estate among the holdings of the Lindisfarne community, donated by Northumbrian kings in the seventh century. It had, then, been a Bernician *villa regia*; but what was the extent of its *territorium*, and to whom did it belong before acquisitive Bernician overlords took it into their possession?

Rheged forces its way into the historical consciousness because the collection of medieval Welsh poetry known as the Book of Taliesin contains several elegies to Urien *Erechwydd*, 'Urien Rheged'. *Erechwydd* has been identified by Andrew Fleming with

Swaledale,* because the name is a Brythonic equivalent to *Catraeth/Cataractonium*, the dashing waters that give Catterick its name.[35] Urien and Catterick are linked in Taliesin's medieval battle poem *Gweith Gwen Ystrat* (Battle of Gwen Ystrat), in which his warriors are 'Men of Catraeth'. Urien himself is here Lord of Rheged, a 'far-famed chieftain who holds kings in check'.[36]

He also appears in the *Historia Brittonum* in the company of Rydderch Hen (king of the Strathclyde Britons), Gwallawg (perhaps a king of Elmet) and Morcant (perhaps a lord of Gododdin), antagonists of the Bernician King Theodoric in a siege of the Island of *Metcaud*: Lindisfarne.[37] A curious but significant interpolation in the same section of the *Historia* relates how King Edwin of Deira (617–632) had been baptized by Rhun, son of Urien – presumably during youthful exile among the British. A later Northumbrian king, Oswiu (642–670), fathered two children with a princess named Rhieinmelth, daughter of Royth, son of Rhun – the result, one infers, of a tributary alliance between Bernicia and Rheged.[38]

The kings of Rheged, then, enjoyed both hostile and more constructive dealings with the Anglian kings of Northumbria; and their dynastic pedigree can be partly reconstructed from a variety of sources, going back to the legendary Coel Hen. Where, then, was Rheged? Did the core lands of *Erechwydd* lie west of Catterick in the Pennine dales, in Dumfries and Galloway or around the Solway Firth? Archaeologist Mike McCarthy, who has studied the archaeology of the Carlisle area in detail, is sceptical of the idea that Rheged could encompass the whole of the Gallwegian coast and Carlisle *and* lands to the east of the Pennines.[39] More recently, claims have been made that an Early Medieval fort, partly excavated at Trusty's Hill near Gatehouse of Fleet, might be a kingship site of Rheged; but the excavated evidence has been oversold.[40] A broader look at the archaeology of the Solway region suggests that Rheged might, in fact, have been a polyfocal kingdom, with key areas of economic productivity, royal centres and ecclesiastical

---

* See Chapter 5, p. 154.

patronage spread from the extreme west of Galloway as far as Carlisle and beyond, united by its seaways rather than as a coherent land unit. Early diocesan markers are found in memorials at Kirkmadrine and Kirkmaiden on the Rhinns of Galloway. The early monastery or *villa regia* at Whithorn – in itself a credible kingship centre – looks across Wigtown Bay to Trusty's Hill and to an early chapel on Ardwall Island; and a seventh-century monastic foundation at Hoddom close to the River Annan has legendary associations with St Mungo or Kentigern. Substantial hilltop enclosures at Burnswark and Tynron Doon, the important, if modestly sized, coastal craft working and importation site at Mote of Mark, further east along the coast, and a possible beach market site across the Solway Firth at Maryport, along with Carlisle's later religious status, hint at a very extensive network of sites and productive landscapes linked by the sea, not just with each other but with Man to the south and Ireland to the west. If Rheged does not sit comfortably within standard models of kingship for this period, it may be the fault of the models.

The first kings of Early Medieval Britain were not off-the-shelf products of a homogeneous history, geography or philosophy; they were experimenting with new forms of power born out of the necessity to rule self-identifying peoples and regions that generated a directly consumable surplus; by the needs of mobile lords and their warbands. In the end, the set of rules by which kingship was held and passed to succeeding generations would be bound by a set of closely defined customary rules. But the first kingdoms rising from this laboratory of social and economic power were also tentative, evolutionary enterprises.

The challenges faced by warlords in first establishing, then defending and expanding, their territorial dominance are traced only at the most superficial level in the surviving sources, where they are often unsubtly portrayed as direct ethnic conflicts between Britons and their enemies – variously Anglians, Saxons, Men of Wessex or, more generically in British sources, as *Lloegr* – Lowlanders. By the end of the sixth century a number of overlords were able to wield *imperium* over other kings by virtue of military superiority, political astuteness and luck. The most powerful of these must find a means to administer the increasing complexities of their domains while providing alternative career paths for an ever-expanding stable of rivals and collateral branches of their dynasties. Like kingship itself, the search for new political tools with which to manage such complexities began with experiments, some more successful than others. Those overlords who managed to engineer or copy such tools and repurpose them for their own needs were unwittingly designing the set of rules for a new sort of historical drama.

12

Overlords

Imperium – *Bretwaldas* – Bernician overlords –
the *Airgíalla Charter Poem* – burying overlords –
Yeavering – Clogher – Rhynie

Reconstruction drawing of the Sutton Hoo whetstone
and stag sceptre, by Kate Batchelor.

Early Medieval kings were required to fight, to defend and expand their territories, and to display their successes appropriately. The *Beowulf* poem provides the model. As Hrothgar, king of the Danes, prospers, so the size of his warband increases:

> Then to Hrothgar was granted glory in battle,
> Mastery of the field; so friends and kinsmen
> gladly obeyed him, and his band increased
> To a great company. It came into his mind
> that he would command the construction
> of a huge mead-hall, a house greater
> than men on earth ever had heard of.[1]

Young bucks and princely exiles from rival kingdoms – those with few prospects at home – were attracted to the households of successful leaders, offering their swords and loyalty in return for the prospect of wealth, glory and the honour of fighting, perhaps dying, for a famous warrior king. An overflowing treasure chest, filled with gold and fine weaponry, was a prerequisite for a king to be able to recruit the best warriors while diminishing the martial pool available to his rivals. Occasionally, as in the Northumbrian King Oswiu's defensive relations with his southern rival Penda of Mercia, such wealth enabled him to buy off his enemy with 'an incalculable and incredible store of royal treasures and gifts as the price of peace'.[2] Penda's eventual defeat in the disastrous encounter on the River Winwæd in 655 ensured that Oswiu became overlord of all the southern kingdoms. Whether or not he got his treasure back is unrecorded; but his powers of patronage and tributary reach were now incomparable.* Overlordship was the magma that drove seismic shifts in royal power and the long-term fates of kingdoms.

* The contents of the Staffordshire hoard, conceivably of the right date for Oswiu, give a good impression of the sort of battlefield scrap that made up such treasure stores. www.staffordshirehoard.org.uk/.

Good kings were 'treasure guardians'; 'ring givers'; 'gold friends'. Bad kings hoarded like dragons.[3] Beowulf, the princely exile who offered, or was incited, to take on Hrothgar's deadly enemy, the monster Grendel, eventually won the right to the kingship for himself. But the risks were immense: kings were either on their way up or on their way down, always one defeat away from disaster and forever at risk from the destructive effects of the feud.* Kings and their sons were frequently killed in battle, sometimes as antagonists. The victor might find himself in a position to impose his own candidate on a kingdom with a young or weak pretender, or force tributary status on a new king too weak to resist by force of arms. Kings forged alliances – often disregarding 'ethnic' or 'national' borders – to defend against or attack a common rival. And, when one king defeated or held political sway over another, the relationship came to be understood in a carefully codified way. No surviving English, Welsh or Scottish document describes such arrangements: the earliest Anglo-Saxon law codes speak of obligations between lords and their followers and dependants, not between kings. Even so, a set of rules can be reconstructed with some confidence through the careers of those who were able to wield *imperium* over others and by looking in detail at the geography of overlordship.

Each victory in the field consolidated political advantage, overthrew an old order, won new territory or maintained a status quo. The small number of battles listed for the second half of the sixth century in the *Anglo-Saxon Chronicle*, remembered from two centuries and more later, probably understates their real frequency, especially of smaller raids, hostings and turf wars. After Cynric's supposed victory against the Britons at *Seaorburh* in 552[†] he fought them again in 556, alongside his son Ceawlin, at *Beranburgh* (Barbury Castle), an imposing hillfort on Wiltshire's Ridgeway. Then, nothing for twelve years, until Ceawlin and his

---

* Grendel may, indeed, be a figurative representation of the insidious effects of feuding, although I have argued elsewhere that he might personify an equally deadly, unseen threat – malaria. Adams 2016, 144.

† See Chapter 11. p. 341.

son Cutha drove Æðelberht into Kent after an engagement at the unknown site of *Wibbandun*, in which two princes were killed. *Wibbandun* is the first recorded conflict between rival 'English' kingdoms. By this time kings with names and pedigrees are known in Bernicia and Deira, in Dál Riata, Gwynedd and Fortriu: the political heavyweights of the next century.

Ceawlin's son Cutha and his brother Cuthwulf are recorded winning a further victory in 571 at *Biedcanford*, probably in what is now Buckinghamshire, while Ceawlin himself led West Saxon forces to a famous victory at Deorham in the West Country in 577 – killing three 'British' kings – and at *Feðanleag* (Oxfordshire) in 584. At *Biedcanford* he took four *tunas*, or *villae regiae*, and after *Feðanleag*, a bloody victory in which Cutha was slain, Ceawlin 'captured many villages and countless booty and departed in anger to his own territories'. The geographical range of these campaigns shows aggressive ambition on Ceawlin's part; but it can be no more than a very partial record: the *Chronicle* fails to note any defeats that the West Saxon king may have suffered during his long martial career. It is no more than a highlights package, and a partisan package at that. The Irish Annals show a fuller and probably more credible account of contemporary conflicts between rival kings on the other side of the Irish Sea, including numerous assassinations, and paints a more nuanced portrait of the waxing and waning of dynastic fortunes than can be found in Insular sources. Gregory's Frankish history reveals similarly bloody political and territorial rivalry across the Channel; and there is no reason to think that Insular kings were any less bellicose or underhand.

Ceawlin's long reign over the West Saxons, from 560 to 592, is, nevertheless, instructive. He was the first of the West Saxon kings whose career is marked by tangible achievements in subduing rivals and poaching their territory. However, looking at the geography of his victories, it becomes clear that his wars were not campaigns of conquest but of subordination. Gloucester, captured after the battle of Deorham, never became a part of Wessex, nor did Bedfordshire or Kent. The spoils of Ceawlin's wars were threefold: the glory and honour of victory; booty with which to enrich himself and reward his followers; and the right to exact tribute from those villages, 'cities' and regions whose lords he had killed or who had submitted to him on the battlefield. In that sense his career provides a significant insight into the ambitions of those who would become overlords in Early Medieval Britain.

The fruits of *imperium* were primarily those of the turf war or protection racket. No king before, perhaps, Constantine II of Alba* or Æðelstan of Wessex in the tenth century, shows any sign of attempting to conquer and unite – or even imagine – a nation entity like 'England' or 'Wales' or 'Scotland'. Their desire was to force submission by any means necessary, in order that they might enjoy lordly rights over other kings and their kingdoms. Only rarely did they seek to annex an inferior territory and subsume it within their own; to rule it as part of an enlarged realm. Such annexations generally became sources of ongoing tension. Northumbria's component kingdoms, Bernicia and Deira, were often ruled by a single dynasty, but their identities remained distinct and mutually hostile for centuries, despite the best efforts of their kings, and of scholars like Bede, to construct a shared ideology and history for their peoples. It is doubtful if Ceawlin believed himself to be king of a such an entity as Wessex, even if he regarded himself as chief among the kings of the tribes of the south. Even so, Bede, drawing on a list probably compiled in Kent in the late seventh century, credited him with being the second of those who had held *imperium* over all the other kingdoms of the south.[4] In the ninth century, the compilers of the *Anglo-Saxon Chronicle* reprised Bede's list and endowed the *imperium*-wielding kings with the title *Bretwalda* – the Old English word means either 'wide ruler' or 'Britain ruler';[5] but historians agree that no such title or office could have existed in Ceawlin's day, even though his is the second name on the list. The first name is that of Ælle, the warlord supposed to have subdued and ruled over the coastal district of the South Saxons at the end of the fifth century. His *imperium* is likely to have been extremely

---

* More properly Causantín mac Áeda, who ruled 900–943 and is regarded as the effective founder of the Scottish kingdom.

limited in extent. In the title *Bretwalda* one hears a distant echo of Gildas's *superbus tyrannus*, Vortigern, and it may be that his contemporary Maelgwyn, king of Gwynedd, whom he calls 'higher than almost all the generals of Britain', was a British exemplar for would-be English overlords to follow.[6]

Ceawlin might certainly have claimed to be the most celebrated king in his generation. A record of victories and territorial expansion over nearly thirty years of the sixth century is no mean achievement, and his warband must have been mighty indeed after the victory at *Feðanleag*. But the loss of his son seems to have weakened him fatally. By the time he was deposed by his nephew, Ceol, in 592, he may have lost bragging rights over any other kings. He is likely, in any case, to have been too old to lead his *comites* to war.

The third king on Bede's list of overlords is Æðelberht, whom Ceawlin was said to have driven into Kent in 568. The *Chronicle* records that Æðelberht began to rule there in 565; Bede's information was that he ruled from 560. Since it is known that he died in 616, historians are sceptical of such an early date for his accession. Either way, his rule was remembered for its length, for the arrival during his reign of Augustine's mission of conversion in 597 and because he married a Frankish princess, Bertha, the daughter of King Charibert (died 567).* In this period, and for many centuries afterwards, the gift of a daughter to another king, as a 'peace weaver', sealed a political alliance between kings, and was a sure sign of political dominance over a son-in-law. If Æðelberht was in some way recognized as overlord of the Southern English, he in turn recognized the Frankish kings as his overlords. Noble and royal daughters and their dowries were the currency of patronage – material and social symbols of alliance reciprocated with at least theoretical loyalty in battle and the tribute of hard cash and mercantile privilege.

---

* Gregory, in a passing reference, recorded that Bertha 'married a man from Kent and went to live there'. *HF* IV.26. Thorpe 1974, 219.

Modern statue of King Æðelberht of Kent outside the city
walls of Canterbury. He was overlord of the Southern English
and the king who received Augustine's mission in 597.

Of all the kings who gained wide *imperium* in the Early Medieval
period, it is hard to think of another who had not gained that
recognition in battle by the defeat of a rival king. No victories, or
indeed battles of any sort, are recorded for Æðelberht's long reign,
by either the *Chronicle* or Bede, whose Kentish correspondents
were nothing if not informative. Since Early Medieval kingship was

predicated on leadership in battle and the primacy of the warrior, that needs some explaining. This may be a trick of the light, since no early Kentish chronicle survives; Æðelberht may have fought battles recorded in sources now lost. But two other explanations come to mind. The first is that, somehow, Kent's traditional status as the first of the Anglo-Saxon kingdoms, its dynasts' claim to descent from Hengest, gave it some sort of mythic primacy among the English. The second is that, by virtue of a long relationship with Gaul and then with Frankish kings,* it had inherited some of the political, even moral authority of the old empire. Indeed, Francia's apparent ability to wield *imperium* across the Channel, borne out by other references in Continental sources,† was never, so far as one can tell, reinforced by a Frankish expeditionary force – not, at least, before 1066. Kent's pre-eminence among the Anglo-Saxon kingdoms was recognized, successively, by the West Saxons (if one may infer negatively from the silence of the *Chronicle* after 584), at least temporarily by Northumbria, to whose King Edwin Æðelberht's successor sent his sister, Æðelburh, in marriage; by East Anglia (whose King Rædwald was baptized at Æðelberht's court)[7] and by the East Saxons (whose King Sæberht, married to Æðelberht's sister Ricule, was also formally converted to Christianity in Kent); and probably, also, by kings in Mercia, if Bede is to be believed.[8]

Aside from Æðelberht's reception of Augustine's papal embassy in 597, little more is known of his record as an overlord. Kentish kings exercised their lordship in at least three locations – at Canterbury itself, where the old Roman theatre provided a suitably

---

* Æðelberht's father is named as Eormenric in the Nennian collection of genealogies. It is a suspiciously Frankish-sounding name. *HB* 57.
† Procopius, in his *Gothic Wars* (VIII.20), says that a Frankish king sent an embassy to Byzantium, accompanied by 'some of the Angli, seeking to establish his claim that this island was ruled by him'. The *Pactus Legis Salicae*, the so-called Salic law first attributed to Clovis, contains a reference (Section XXXIX) to slaves recovered *trans mare*, 'from across the sea', usually interpreted to mean Kent and implying its real or claimed tributary status in the early sixth century. Drew 2012, 101–2.

grand assembly place; at Lyminge, where recent excavations indicate a likely royal presence, and at Rochester, seat of one of the
earliest bishoprics. Æðelberht is likely to have enjoyed royal residences in all six lathes of the kingdom at one time or another.
How and when the king travelled between these sites is obscure;
so too are the details of his relations with subordinate kings. If
Rædwald and Sæberht were baptized at or close to his court, they
must have travelled to him – a tributary act in itself – bringing
gifts and other marks of respect, swearing oaths before the *gesiths*
of both kingdoms and exchanging noble, if not royal, hostages to
ensure continued good relations. At least in theory, their warbands
were obliged to attend his hostings and follow him to war. Since he
does not seem to have prosecuted wars, the nature of his military
alliances is similarly obscure. Nor does his law code, the earliest of
the surviving English dooms, address relations with tributary kings
– even if, in itself, it is evidence of his regal power.

Northumbrian evidence fleshes out this sketchy portrait of early
Anglo-Saxon *imperium*. Bede describes how, in the reign of King
Edwin, fifth on the list of overlords of the southern kingdoms, his
mund – the regal power of imposing peace and protection on his
peoples – was such that a mother with a newborn baby might
proverbially walk throughout the island without coming to any
harm. It had become legendary in Bede's day that Edwin ordered
bronze cups to be set up on stakes where fresh springs rose close to
the highway. Travellers might thus be refreshed and contemplate,
as they drank, the God-like power of their ultimate lord. No one
dared lay their hands on these cups improperly, such was their fear
and love for their king. Furthermore, Bede wrote, 'even in time of
peace, as he rode about among his cities, estates and kingdoms
with his thegns, he always used to be preceded by a standard
bearer', like an emperor.[9]

Edwin's brother-in-law Æðelfrið, his bitter rival and predecessor
as Northumbrian overlord – known to the Nennian compiler as
Flesaur, the 'Twister' – seems not to have concerned himself with
the niceties of political alliance but to have imposed his authority
over all the kingdoms between the Humber and the Forth by

military might and through a ruthless policy of eliminating rivals by murder or proxy. He belonged to the second generation after Ida, the semi-legendary pirate who seized control of Bernicia from a stronghold at Bamburgh on the windswept coast of north Northumberland around 560. Æðelfrið's bloody and impressive career, if the meagre sources can be strung together in something like a coherent narrative, began in exile in the company of his father Æðelric, deposing and killing King Ælle of Deira, their southern rival, in about 588. Perhaps two years later, around 590, they seem to have fought off a concerted alliance of northern British warlords in a furiously bitter siege at *Catraeth* – Catterick – whose tragic glories were celebrated in the *Gododdin* poem. By 592 or 593, it seems, Æðelfrið had succeeded his father in Deira. Twelve years later Æðelfrið was sufficiently powerful to unite Deira and Bernicia under his sole rule, though under what circumstances is unrecorded. His marriage to Ælle's daughter, Acha, was intended to ensure that future heirs might legitimately rule in both kingdoms.

Æðelfrið's *imperium* over all the northern kingdoms south of Pictland was sealed at Degsastan* in 604 by a great victory over Áedán mac Gabrain, himself overlord of Dál Riata – roughly modern Argyll, Kintyre and the Inner Hebrides.† By 616 Æðelfrið was overlord of Deira, Rheged, Gododdin (the Lothians, centred on their fortress of Dun Eidyn – Edinburgh), Dál Riata; probably Lindsey too. He could lead an army through Mercia with impunity. And yet, he does not belong on Bede's or the *Chronicle*'s list of the greatest overlords: Wessex, Kent, East Anglia, Essex and the British kingdoms of Wales lay beyond his control. His ability to secure the north and the future of his dynasty was, even

---

* The battle is unlocated; various suggestions of a site somewhere in the Southern Uplands have been made, with traditional identifications focused on Dalswinton on the River Nith.

† Æðelfrið's children, perhaps counter-intuitively, were able to seek their own protection in exile among Áedán's successors. For a detailed explanation see Moisl 1983.

now, threatened by the existence of a legitimate Deiran rival, his brother-in-law Edwin, whose father he had deposed more than twenty years earlier.

Edwin spent his entire childhood in exile and on the run, notwithstanding any influence that his sister Acha may have had with her husband. Reconstructing his early life from the patchiest references in the *Historia Brittonum*, *Annales Cambriae* and Bede's *Historia*, he can be placed successively at the courts of Rheged and Gwynedd under the protection of Christian British kings.* At some point he married Coenburh, daughter of a Mercian king. He thus found himself under obligation to no fewer than three kings, each of whom would have expected him to fight in their warbands against their enemies and, in return for their having invested in his future success, to have offered himself in alliance as a tributary king, should he fight successfully for the kingdom of Deira. But offering protection and training to such noble exiles set those host kingdoms up as targets for Æðelfrið's wrath. In about 616 he brought his formidable host along the surviving highways of the empire† to the marches of Wales and defeated the army of Selyf ap Cynan, king of Powys, at Chester – a battle remembered for the slaughter of hundreds of monks who made the mistake of overtly praying for a British victory.[10] Within a year of the battle at Chester, whether or not Æðelfrið's campaign had been directed at Edwin or at those who would shelter him, the exiled prince left, or was encouraged to leave, the protection of his British sponsors and seek sanctuary with a king whom he must have believed lay beyond Æðelfrið's reach. Rædwald, he of the Sutton Hoo ship burial and the fourth on Bede's list of *imperium*-wielders, was

---

* By virtue of an interpolation in the *Historia Brittonum* that records his baptism by Rhun son of Urien (*HB* 63 and *Annales Cambriae* under 626); a Welsh triad describes Edwin as having been 'nurtured' on the Isle of Môn (Anglesey, core of the Venedotian kingdom). Kirby 2000, 71.

† The most plausible route would take him south along the Great North Road to Tadcaster, where a direct road led south-west to the former legionary fortress at Chester – a two-week march, more or less, covering 250 miles.

recognized as overlord of the southern English after the death in the same year, 616, of Æðelberht in Kent.

The 350 or so miles separating Æðelfrið's court at Bamburgh from that of Rædwald at Rendlesham in Suffolk may have over-stretched the reach even of Bernician military might. Nevertheless, intelligence reached Bamburgh soon enough that Edwin had now attached himself to Rædwald's banner, a threat that could not be ignored. Now Æðelfrið deployed the diplomatic tools of bribery and coercion. Bede, who had access to reliable source materials regarding Edwin's career, recounts how Æðelfrið sent an embassy to Rædwald, offering him large sums of money to deliver Edwin up.[11] After this first embassy was rejected, Æðelfrið sent further messengers, offering larger amounts of silver and threatening, in the case of a refusal, to make war on Rædwald. The East Anglian king seems now to have been on the point of giving in either to greed or fear; but he changed his mind after what must have been a very intimate and perhaps tense exchange in the royal bed-chamber. Bede's telling account bristles with understatement:

> When he secretly revealed to the queen the plan [...] she dis-suaded him [...] It was in no way fitting for so great a king to sell his best friend for gold when he was in such trouble, still less to sacrifice his own honour.[12]

Just as the *Beowulf* poet has Queen Wealþeow inciting Beowulf to action against Grendel by publicly offering him the mead cup, so Rædwald's unnamed queen, metaphorically if not literally, placed a sword in her husband's lap: a challenge that no warrior might refuse. The queen's own honour was also at stake. Such direct political intervention by royal women in affairs of state is by no means unusual in Early Medieval histories, if rarely so explicit.[13] Now Rædwald mustered his army and, with Edwin and his own followers, perhaps also accompanied by warbands from tributary kingdoms across the south, they marched north, meeting Æðelfrið's forces at Bawtry in what is now South Yorkshire, where the Roman road crossed the River Idle: two mighty overlords slugging it out for ultimate supremacy. The Northumbrian army was resoundingly defeated; Æðelfrið was slain and his *imperium* died with him on the battlefield.

By such strokes of fate Edwin succeeded to the Northumbrian kingdom. In victory, he was obliged to recognize Rædwald's superiority, offering noble hostages to his court, sending gifts reflective of the honour in which he was held and, in theory at least, taking part in his hostings. The beautifully decorated great bronze cauldron found in the Sutton Hoo ship burial, which bears such strong artistic affinities with northern British craftsmanship, may be the product of a Northumbrian master smith. Was this one of Edwin's tributary gifts, sent in gratitude for his former host's loyalty and friendship in war? After Rædwald's death Edwin was recognized in turn as overlord of the southern English.

Rædwald's magnificent grave represents archaeologists' only chance to take stock of the material trappings of such powerful kings. Most archaeologists now accept that the great ship burial beneath its mound on the banks of the River Deben in Suffolk was the tomb of King Rædwald, who died in about 625; but since his mortal remains were not recovered among the treasures of Sutton Hoo it is not entirely certain whether he was interred here or cremated elsewhere. The ship is itself the principal artefact: the ceremonial wave-riding sea chariot of a mighty lord. A later Anglo-Saxon king, Eadgar (943–975), the first to rule over something like a unified England, had his *subreguli* row him in style along the River Dee at Chester – a magnificent display of political superiority. The finest treasures, like the elaborately decorated ceremonial Sutton Hoo helmet, paralleled by at least two others of the same early seventh-century date from York and Benty Grange, must have been the exclusive preserve of the mightiest kings. The carved whetstone, purse, bowls, spoons, great gold buckle and other treasures are the trappings of a powerful and stupendously wealthy lord, to be sure: treasures won in battle or rendered as tribute by subordinate kings. The 2 ft-long whetstone, with its evocative, perhaps totemic mounted stag motif, is reminiscent of a late Roman consular sceptre, likely to have been the exclusive preserve of an over-king. Its echoes of imperial authority are unlikely to have been lost on those who won the right to have it paraded before them.

If Nick Higham is right, and the origins of Tribal Hidage lie in Edwin's court of the 620s, then that list of tributary kingdoms and regions is the first explicit account of how Anglo-Saxon overlords exercised their powers.* The Hidage assessments reflect the political as well as the economic status of their kings, with the fundamental regal unit at 7,000 hides. Mercia and East Anglia, at 30,000, may already have been ruled under overlords drawing their disparate territories together.[14] Kent's assessment at 15,000 hides underpins the long-held belief of historians that it had once been two distinct kingdoms. Higham argues that the enormous Wessex assessment directly reflects Edwin's punitive relations with that kingdom, one of whose rulers, Cwichelm, despatched an assassin in a dramatic but ultimately abortive attempt to murder Edwin in his own hall at Easter 626. A sense of rank, of political importance derived from long-term alliance, recent subjugation and relative political and military clout, is implicit in the Tribal Hidage list. At a great hosting, when subject kings and ealdormen gathered in assembly with their overlord, precedence must have been reflected in seating arrangements, in feasting ceremonies, even in rights to particular camping pitches.

The first of dozens of charters that illuminate diplomatic relations between overlords and their *subreguli* dates from the 670s, two generations after Edwin. In it, Friðuwold, who styles himself 'of the province of the men of Surrey, sub-king of Wulfhere, king of the Mercians' retains the right to donate land from his portfolio to a minster at Chertsey.[15] Bernician kings of the mid-seventh century were wont to install their sons as equivalent *subreguli* in Deira, partly as a policy of devolved dynastic government, partly as training and partly so that they could keep an eye on potential rivals coming up on the rails. By the time detailed itineraries were recorded for West Saxon kings in the ninth and tenth centuries,

* See Chapter 8.

subreguli were often required to attend their overlords in transit as camp followers: witnessing their charters, drinking enthusiastically at their feasts and legitimizing their authority, however reluctantly.

Anglo-Saxon kings played by – and sometimes challenged – a set of customary rules with precedents in Insular tribal lore, in Roman law and in Frankish, Germanic or Scandinavian tradition. There was no need to write these down; historians must therefore carefully unpick the threads of circumstantial evidence. Exemplars drawn from Bede, in particular, make it sound as though the impositions were all one way: *subreguli* owed obligations in marriage, warfare and tribute to their overlords. But in Ireland, where hierarchies of overlordship among its 150 or so small kingdoms had been evolving complex arrangements for centuries, such relations were more nuanced; and one document in particular illuminates those subtleties. The *Airgíalla Charter poem** contains circumstantial evidence for an early eighth-century origin but may embody material from as far back as the sixth century. It describes relations between a confederation of nine peoples settled in central historic Ulster and their overlords, the Northern Uí Néill.[16]

The poem recalls the far-off days when the Airgíalla and their superior neighbours had been kin. According to the partible inheritance rules common among Irish societies, land was divided between sons, whose progeny became neighbours bound in kinship. To avoid disputes that might easily lead to feud, they agreed rules covering compensation, rights of access, the behaviour of their animals and mutual hospitality.[17] Itinerant warrior lordship required additional rules governing the nature and delivery of renders, military service, the judgement of offences and the honours due between lord and dependant. Such relations were generally regarded as honourable because the obligations, such as gift exchange, membership of the *comitatus* and hospitality were essentially those of allies, albeit of different rank, who shared a common ancestor. Relations between lords and dependants who did not share a common or commonly recognized ancestry, such

---

* Pronounced something like 'Aryallia' and anglicized as Oriel.

as those subdued during wars of conquest or blood feud, were less honourable, more punitive, less favourable to the weaker party.

In the *Charter poem* the Airgíalla are keen to stress the honourable nature of their relations with the Uí Néill, some of whose kings sprang from the dynasty of the Cenél nEogain of Inishowen, an exemplar of territorial lordship.* They enjoyed a seat of honour beside the high king of Tara during assemblies held at Tailtiu – Telltown, in County Meath. Their military service was limited to two fortnights every three years and in theory, at least, they did not have to bring their armies into the field during sowing and harvest time. They were entitled to an exceptional level of compensation for their losses in battle and to a generous share of booty won as the spoils of war. Their status gave them immunity from claims made against them during war and peace. Whether all these privileges were acknowledged by their overlords is another matter; but the Airgíalla felt entitled to claim them: they had earned those rights by virtue of historical alliance and through shared kindred.

Airgíalla's lawyers acknowledged, in return, the rights of their overlords. The Uí Néill kings were entitled to 'rising' – that is, they expected that their sub-kings and dependants would rise when they entered hall or chamber. Such diplomatic niceties mattered among allies just as they did between enemies; ignoring or challenging these conventions might lead to a very nasty confrontation. The most dramatic example of such discourtesy is the fateful faux pas committed by the pope's emissary and first archbishop of Canterbury, Augustine, during his meeting with a synod of British bishops in 604.†

More functionally, Uí Néill overlords were entitled to the military services of their under-kings in order to prosecute wars of

---

* See Chapter 8, p. 246. The Cenél nEogain had, over several centuries, expanded successfully from their original cultural coreland, the *Magh Tóchuir*. Before the eighth century the dominant kindred of the Uí Néill high kings had been the Cenél Conaill, to which dynasty the greatest holy man of his age, Colm Cille – St Columba – belonged. See Chapter 13.
† See Chapter 13, p. 419.

expansion against historic antagonists, the Ulaid, in northeast Ulster. As territorial lords they were owed entertainment and hospitality on their progress through dependent territories and to a range of renders, from both their own clients and their under-kings. In practice, this meant that some of the renders collected by the kings of the Airgíalla on their own behalf must be passed on to their Uí Néill overlords, diminishing their potential for accumulating wealth.* Those renders included provisions, the original basis of territorial lordship. The best-known inventory of the food renders expected from a land unit is found in the very comprehensive late seventh-century laws of King Ine of Wessex, which detail annual dues from every ten hides of land and give some idea of the range and quantity of agricultural surplus claimed by lords of their clients:

> Ten vats of honey, 300 loaves, 12 ambers of Welsh ale, 30 ambers of clear ale, 2 full grown cows or 10 wethers, 10 geese, 20 hens, 10 cheeses, a full amber of butter, 5 salmon, 20 pounds of fodder, and 100 eels.[18]

In addition to food renders of this kind, the Uí Néill had the right to requisition 'road calves' – cattle purchased by and for an army on the move through Airgíallan territory. They were able to demand labour for the maintenance of roads and for the construction of houses and fortifications. They might require their dependent lords to fulfil policing duties, including the hunting of pirates and horse thieves. They could even impose a 'madder tax', essentially a render on very valuable red dye. Over-kings also sat in judgement on their client peoples, enforcing rules on the right routes and campsites to use during hosting and compensation for fields damaged on campaign.

If British, Pictish and Anglo-Saxon kings did not often commission such written charters for themselves before the eighth

---

* The same is true of the tributary kings whose lands were listed in Tribal Hidage.

century, it nevertheless seems likely that customary rules governing relations between overlords and their client kingdoms were negotiated in detail, rights and obligations defended zealously, insults bitterly resented, honours repaid with generosity and loyalty. The transfer of a warband's allegiance from one overlord to another would be regarded as a desertion worthy of suitable punishment; of feud prosecuted by war. Tribal Hidage is no more than a hand note of such proceedings.

In death, the overlords of the early English kingdoms are barely visible. There is no record of the ultimate fates of Ceawlin and Ælle. Æðelberht, Bede says, was buried by the side of his queen, Bertha, in the recently completed church of St Peter and St Paul that stood just to the east of the Roman walls of Canterbury. Rædwald may or not have been interred with his ship at Sutton Hoo; but we do not have the body. Æðelfrið, the mightiest warlord of the north, shared the fate of the next three overlords in Bede's list: he was defeated and killed in battle in 617. If his two immediate successors as Northumbrian king are anything to go by, he was probably decapitated and dismembered by his enemies so that his body could not receive burial. King Edwin's body, cut down on the peaty flatlands of Hatfield Chase in Lindsey in 632, is the subject of a curious post-mortem miracle. In the *Earliest Life of Gregory the Great* it is recorded that a priest had a vision in which he was told where to find Edwin's head, lying in a secret place near the battlefield.[19] Miraculously, it was retrieved and interred in the new monastic cemetery at Whitby, where a royal burial cult later developed. The fate of King Oswald's head was to be stuck on a pole at a place that came to be called, in grisly irony, *Croesoswald* or St Oswald's Tree: Oswestry, on the Anglo-Welsh border. It was retrieved by his brother and successor Oswiu, again after a miracle revealed the location, a year after the battle in which he died in 642, and taken to the church at Lindisfarne, while his arms and torso were distributed among other churches. It is possible that the fragments of skull that still lie with the body, coffin and relics of St Cuthbert at Durham Cathedral, and which were once sufficiently complete that three fingers might be inserted into the fatal blade injury, may be Oswald's – if so, it is the only corporeal material to testify to a century of heroic overlordship.

Fortunately for archaeologists, Britain's Early Medieval over-kings invested heavily in the architecture of power. If the skills of the mason and mortar mixer had been lost in the two centuries after Rome's fall, the sweated labour of obliged dependants could still shift earth by the ton, build free-standing walls, frame stout timber joints and contemplate the sublime grandeur of ancient hillforts, Roman walls, theatres, bath complexes and forts. Their mead halls must not merely accommodate their *subreguli* and royal households; they must impress and intimidate them, as Hrothgar's great hall did the *Beowulf* poet. They must own more cattle, collect more treasure, display greater force of arms and be more generous than a mere king. They must invite comparison with now legendary emperors who had (in their minds) progressed with their irresistible armies along the highways of the empire and sat in state at vast tribal assemblies.

King Æðelfrið's ambitions for his royal township at Yeavering (Figure 4) reveal the mindset of, essentially, a cattle baron. In his day, so far as one can tell, the only likely permanent structures on the site were a building where feasts were prepared (D2, with its deposit of ox skulls); two modest halls (D6 and A5-7) and the immense cattle corral where his subordinate kin and *subreguli* are likely to have brought their tributary beasts for his approval and consumption.[20] Yeavering's power lay in its relation to the ancient hillfort that overlooked it and in the cult cemetery – itself a form of social, spiritual and material investment – around whose totem pole Æðelfrið's ancestors (real or appropriated) were buried in ancient ritual. More robust structures are likely to have been constructed on the rocky natural fortress of Bamburgh on the coast; but, so far, they have not been identified beneath the standing medieval and nineteenth-century castle buildings one can see today. Æðelfrið's display at Yeavering seems, in some respects, modest. But anyone who has experienced the sense of awe and of ambivalent belonging and loneliness at a large assembly – a pilgrimage at Mecca, a music festival or cup final – may be able to appreciate the powerful psychological effect of gathering to celebrate, feast and pay tribute to the cult figure of a tribal overlord. Add, in the mind's eye, a few hundred leather or woollen tents, a cluster of chariots, horses, banners and the clank of arms, the smoke and bright flame of camp fires, glint of spear points and mead-soaked song, and you have some idea of the scene. Such figures as Æðelfrið were not only the military and spiritual figureheads of their people; they were the physical embodiment of its identity and fate, bound together in life and death, triumph and disaster.

If Brian Hope-Taylor was right in his mapping of Bede's political narrative onto the ground plan and chronological phasing of *Gefrin*,* the *villa regia* underwent a profound architectural transformation under Æðelfrið's successor, Edwin. During his long exile the Deiran pretender had seen more of Britain's geography than most of his contemporaries. He must have gawped at Chester's walls and amphitheatre, travelled many miles of Rome's highways, camped in its armies' ruined forts. His second wife, Æðelburh, was a Christian raised in Canterbury where a Roman theatre still stood; her mother's cousins were Frankish kings. Edwin's own long-drawn-out conversion to Christianity brought him into contact with men who knew Rome and its faded glories. Edwin knew that Constantine the Great had been proclaimed emperor at York and he was responsible, during his last years, for founding the first post-Roman church there in the ruins of its *principia*. Bede's description of his standard bearer reinforces the idea that Edwin saw himself as an inheritor of both Rome's imperial dignity and its Christian leadership.

It is, then, entirely natural that the unique grandstand feature excavated by Hope-Taylor at Yeavering should be associated with Edwin's rule and, especially, with Bede's story that the king and his priest, Paulinus, spent thirty-six days there baptizing the Northumbrian race in the purifying waters of the River Glen. In Hope-Taylor's scheme, this is the phase during which the hand of an

* Archaeologists have chipped away at the edges and identified a few flaws in Hope-Taylor's sequence; none has seriously challenged his broad thesis.

The reconstructed Viking Age hall at Fyrkat in Jutland shows
how architecturally sophisticated royal halls might be, as
expressions of royal power and wealth.

architect and surveyor can be traced in the axial alignment of new, much more impressive structures lying between the grandstand and the remains of the 'Great Enclosure'.* And if the dull (to the uninitiated) testimony of excavators' post-hole plans evokes little more than the footings of a rustic barn, modern reconstructions of such halls, inspired by and retrospectively applied from the art and architecture of the Viking Age, allow for highly sophisticated and exquisitely embellished superstructures. They are expressions not only of Edwin's wealth and power, but of the resources in timber, labour and craftsmanship on which he was able to draw as lord of Gefrinshire. Edwin's Yeavering was a magnificent palace where ancient British, Anglian, Roman and Christian sensibilities hybridized in an architecture tapping rich aesthetic and symbolic veins in an elemental landscape of sky and earth, water and fire; of beast and mead cup, clashing shield and battle song. That these buildings lay undefended by wall or palisade says much about the self-confidence of its lords. That Yeavering was twice burned to the ground is a reminder of the impermanence of overweening power; even so, Northumbrian kings were able to maintain dominance over their rivals for most of the seventh century, across three generations.†

The geography of Irish overlordship in this period is subtly distinct. More than 100 kingdoms competed and co-operated with one another in a complex, ever-shifting series of alliances. At the base of the pyramid of power lay households inhabiting small, defended ringforts – earthen raths and stone-built cashels, some 40,000 of them – prey to the cattle-raiding pastimes of the junior nobility.[21] They owed obligations to petty dynasts who, in turn, formed alliances with over-kings like the Uí Néill. Kingship

---

* The occupant of Grave AX, buried at the eastern entrance to the great hall of this phase, A4, was interred with a bronze-bound wooden staff and cross piece. It might be a standard; but it also has affinities with Roman surveying equipment. Hope-Taylor 1977, 202.

† After Edwin, Æðelfrið's sons Oswald and Oswiu were both recognized as overlords and their superiority was sustained by Oswiu's son Ecgfrith until his death at the hands of a Pictish king at Nechtansmere in 685.

sites ranged from watery crannogs to modest-looking fortifications perched on rocky promontories. At the peak of the symbolic hierarchy of landscape sat the Hill of Tara complex in County Meath: immemorial seat, spiritual wellspring and inauguration site of the *Ard Rí* or high king of Ireland.[22] Three of its mounds – the *duma nan giall*, 'mound of the hostages', the *forrad*, 'high seat', and the *Ráith na senad*, 'fort of the assembly' – seem to have been the focus for inauguration rituals in the middle centuries of the first millennium.[23] In practice, Early Medieval Irish kings were rarely able to sustain supremacy; the overlords who rode a wave of Christianizing Irish kingship in the sixth century came to prefer the less overtly pagan Tailtiu as their ceremonial focus.

Between Tara and the much less grandiose ringforts of petty kings is a geography of over-kingship that bears comparison to Yeavering. In *Mag Llemna*, the Plain of the Elms in County Tyrone, lies the ancestral seat of the Airgíalla at Clogher, sitting astride one of the principal ancient routes between East and West Ulster (Figure 5). The small town sits on a drumlin* at whose south end lie a cathedral and former monastic precinct and the 'castle': a complex of earthwork fortifications, mounds, barrows, fields and droveways, monumental expressions of the kingship so pragmatically evoked in the *Airgíalla Charter poem*.[24] The first, simple, hillfort rampart at Clogher, enclosing a rectangular plateau about 110 by 185 yards, was constructed close to the end of the first millennium BCE.[25] Around 600 CE, the period on which the charter looked back with retrospective surety, the enclosure at Clogher was rebuilt more modestly as an oval ringfort some 65 yards across. A metalled causeway on the east side crossed a narrow ditch with an ankle-breaking profile, beneath a gate tower constructed on six substantial timber posts. The entrance was revetted with stone. Within the newly constructed bank a huge circular building, some 44 yards in diameter, was identified

---

* A teardrop-shaped hill formed by glacial ice smoothing underlying soil and rock beneath its path.

by its excavator, Richard Warner, as the *rígtech* or royal house.*
That feasting was central to its function is suggested by the
presence of both B-ware amphorae from the Mediterranean and
later Gaulish E Ware, the tell-tales of Continental wine and oil
merchants. Immediately to the south of the enclosure a triangular
mound was 'constructed' by the labour-intensive removal of the
earth and rock around it on all sides. Bronze-working debris
was also found inside the enclosure, indicating the recycling of
metalwork – some of it Roman. In broadly the same period, the
old rectangular bank and ditch that enclosed the hill top, and
which contained the ringfort and its grand house, were remodelled
so that on the east side it formed a funnelled entrance leading
down a slope to the south-east. Here, it morphed into a droveway
leading across the low boggy peatland towards another ringfort
on the other side of the valley. The excavator envisages that the
outer enclosure was, in effect, a cattle corral.[26] One imagines the
intended effect, as the king's entourage looked down on the scene
from above at a seemingly endless trail of beasts stretched across
the bog from one side to the other; and, in later years, stories
being told to wide-eyed visitors: 'In the days of the old king it was
said that here were so many cattle, that the last beast had not left
the fort before the first arrived at the other side...'

Clogher's complex display of overlordship and affinity with
ancient structures of assembly and burial, and in particular its
apparent focus on feasting and livestock corralling, naturally
invites comparisons with Yeavering. So, too, does evidence slowly
emerging from the landscapes of contemporary over-kings in
Fortriu. The careers of Edwin's Pictish contemporaries are obscured
by a lack of written sources, aside from hagiography, sketchy
genealogies and the odd mention in Irish annals. But Pictish, Dál
Riatan, northern British and Anglo-Saxon kings interacted, both

---

* The excavations have never been fully published. But Warner's 1973
plan shows that excavation consisted of several long, narrow trenches – so
a comparative paucity of animal bone and other feasting debris is, perhaps,
unsurprising.

in battle and alliance. Æðelfrið's eldest son, Eanfrið, married a Pictish princess; their son Talorcan succeeded to a kingdom in southern Pictavia.[27] Kings of Dál Riata periodically made war against all their neighbours; and Colm Cille's *vita* tells how, during the late sixth century, the saint travelled from Iona to the fortress of King Bruide mac Maelcon (died *c*.580) in the Great Glen – perhaps Craig Phadraig near Inverness – on a mission of political evangelism. Bruide seems to have enjoyed the overlordship of the northern Pictish kingdoms, including Orkney, from the heartlands of Fortriu around the Moray Firth.

Mag Fortrenn was the cultural coreland of the northern Picts, whose widespread and abundant sculptures were adorned with exuberant, if enigmatic, symbols of rank, nobility, fantasy and warrior prowess. Despite the more visible and robust remains of Early Medieval fortresses at Craig Phadraig – from where sherds of E Ware Gaulish pottery have been retrieved – and Burghead, with its evocative bull carvings, much recent work on Pictish overlordship has concentrated on a site at Rhynie in Strathbogie, Aberdeenshire.[28] Lying at a crossroads of routes between Moray and East Central Scotland, Rhynie is undocumented in written sources; but the name contains the element **rīg*, 'king'. A significant group of what are called Class I Pictish symbol stones* have been found here, including the Crawstane – depicting a salmon riding on the back of a fantastical water beast – that stands close to the crest of a natural knoll, and the grimly determined figure of a bearded warrior with bared teeth wielding a battle axe, carved onto what looks like a prehistoric figurative standing stone.†

Another, poorly preserved human figure carved into a recently discovered stone, Rhynie 3, has been described as a spear-carrying

---

* Stones carved with symbols lacking any obvious Christian iconography and regarded as the earlier strand of the tradition whose genesis can now, perhaps, be dated to the fourth, or even late third century. Noble and Evans 2019.

† Brought to the surface during ploughing in 1978 and now in Woodhill House, Aberdeen.

warrior; but he looks rather as though he were holding a sur-veyor's plumb line.

In the late 1970s aerial photography revealed that the Craw-stane, the only carved stone still *in situ*, stands at the entrance to the buried remains of a palisade enclosing an area 65 yards across, which excavation has since dated to the fifth and sixth centuries. Two concentric enclosures defined by ditches lay within. Close to the centre of the inner enclosure stood a building whose timber post holes form a 30 by 16 ft rectangle but whose footprint, if extended by turf walls and a gable roof, may have been substantially larger. An equally large, 'bag-shaped', building was later built over the demolished enclosure ditches, its entrance immediately adjacent to the Crawstane. From the remnants of a floor layer in another building just to the east of the entrance, fragments of iron horse harness and a late Roman amphora handle were recovered.[29]

Modest though the Rhynie enclosure appears by comparison with Clogher and Yeavering, it sits at a focal point in a landscape busy with prehistoric and Early Medieval burials, forts and stone carvings. As Yeavering has its Bell, so Rhynie has Tap O'Noth hill-fort, enclosing an area of 52 acres, looking down on its dramatic riverside setting from an imperious height of nearly 1,800 ft, a mile to the north-west.* Two other hillforts sit in prominent locations within a mile or so. Metalwork production and the consumption of tributary surplus, betrayed by copious feasting debris, are also significant of Rhynie's lordly, perhaps overlordly, credentials. More than seventy sherds of late Roman amphorae (dramatic outliers from the Insular distribution of such wares), Gaulish glass vessels and large numbers of moulds and crucible fragments from the production of personal jewellery sit alongside more domestic craft items like spindle whorls and quern stones for grinding meal. Only Clogher and South Cadbury, of the major Early Medieval inland sites that have produced such wares, have yielded anything

---

* At the time of writing, fresh evidence is emerging of very significant occu-pation of the hillfort from the third century CE. www.bbc.co.uk/news/uk-scotland-north-east-orkney-shetland-52660032.

like these quantities.[30] Rhynie was connected to a much wider world than its immediate hinterland but, given its decline during the second half of the sixth century, it looks as if the lords who invested so heavily in this landscape were superseded by even more powerful forces emerging in Pictland and beyond.

From the end of the sixth century the narrative of lordship is inextricably bound with an intellectual revolution from which the idea and practice of medieval statehood was wrought. A century after the traditional date for the death of Colm Cille and the arrival of Augustine in Kent in 597, all Britain's kings were Christian, ruling as God's anointed *subreguli* on Earth and sure of an eternal place at his side in heaven. Christian kings and queens and their holy men and women built a new and profoundly affecting model of overlordship, emphatically cemented by the written word.

13

God-given kings

The social contract – Colm Cille – Dunadd – British Christians and their kings – Gregory the Great – royal women – the Augustinian mission – Oswiu and Eanflæd

☧ DEDICATIO BASILICAE
SANCTI PAVLI VIIII KALENDAS MAIAS
ANNO XV ECFRIDI REGIS
CEOLFRIDI ABBATIS EIVSDEM
QVE ECCLESIAE DEO AVCTORE
CONDITORIS ANNO IIII.

'The dedication of the basilica of Saint Paul on the 9th day before the Kalends of May [23 April] in the 15th year of King Ecgfrið in the 4th year of Ceolfrið, abbot and, by the direction of God, founder of the same church.' The Jarrow dedication stone, 685, still *in situ* in St Paul's church.

The rubric of sixth-century overlordship was scrawled in blood on the battlefield, recited in highly coloured poetry and monumentalized in the grand designs of its royal townships. Chief priests interacted on their kings' behalf with a pantheon of gods – of war and the forge, of thunder and fertility. Animist spirits residing in rocks, wells, rivers, caves, in the hearth, in beasts and birds, were to be invoked, placated and nurtured. Cunning-women and -men read runes, interpreted auguries, sacrificed beasts, divined the future, sang incantations and made appropriate offerings, in their secretive arboreal sanctuaries, to ensure the fortunes of their lords and kin.

Victory on the battlefield and political success measured in tribute and booty secured the loyalty of secular élites for their king and his eligible successors; but for a life interest only. Defeat, if not fatal, weakened a king and exposed him to internal coup or external domination. Military disaster might inflict profound trauma on a whole people: Bede recounted how, in the aftermath of many months of anarchy and bloodshed in Northumbria in 632–633, the year had literally been erased from history.[1] The luck of the tribe was invested so heavily in the person of its kings that when they died any *imperium* that they might have exercised over rival kings was void.

As Bede so vividly described it, the pagan supernatural experience was in some sense like the passing of a sparrow into and out of a hall whose warmth and fellowship matched their brief period on Earth while all before and after was cold darkness unknown.[2] If king's lives and legacies were fragile, those of their shamans were more so. The name of just one royal priest, Coifi, survives; and that because he executed a very smart and judicious volteface in support of his lord King Edwin's tortuous conversion.[3]

Pagan kingship was not stupidly irrational. Rulers were bound by conventions of honour, reciprocity and political pragmatism. They calculated odds as coolly – and with about as much reliance on superstition – as any politician or football coach whose tenure might be equally precarious. They, too, had law and custom on their side. But when, in 685, King Ecgfrið's name was chiselled into the foundation stone of a new church at Jarrow on the River Tyne, Abbot Ceolfrið's literate masons were expressing a more subtly coded relationship with their patron, binding him with God and St Paul in an eternal alliance of heavenly sponsors. At the same time they captured the spirit of a novel social, economic and political experiment. The Christian kings of Bede's *Historia* self-consciously reinvented an idea of statehood discarded by the warlords of the fifth century. And just as the forces governing the motions of planets were exquisitely described by Isaac Newton almost exactly a millennium later, so the law makers of the seventh century managed, in a single, brilliant aphorism, to distil the essence of the new world that they were busy constructing:

> *Ðis synd Wihtrædes domas Cantwara cyninges [...] Cirice an freolsdome gafola; ⁊ man for cyning gebidde.*
> These are the dooms of Wihtred, king of Kent [...] The Church shall enjoy immunity from taxation; and the king shall be prayed for.[4]

This apparently simple social contract, in which the church is freed from the burden of the render in return for its prayers – and political support – is the blueprint for the creation of a sort of civil service: intellectual, literate and permanent. It triggered the first injection of capital into the Insular economy for 300 years, and it anticipated the Carolingian Renaissance, the Crusades and the Reformation, Henry II's troubles with his turbulent priest and the *Dei Gratia* embossed on our coins. It also precipitated an ongoing Insular ambivalence towards Europe.

The rapid seventh-century establishment of monastic communities across the Insular kingdoms, supported by extensive, formerly royal estates and nurtured by their relations with kings, parallels the history of secular territorial lordship founded on the right to exact and collect renders from lands and communities, but with a critical difference. The unique brilliance of this new social contract was to convert landed assets otherwise held for a mere life interest – the so-called *folcland* held by thegns and *gesiths* from the king, which returned to the royal portfolio on their death – into the freehold *bocland* of abbots and abbesses. *Bocland* or bookland – what we would call freehold – was fundamental to a relationship meant to last for eternity on Earth and in heaven. It allowed the church to invest physical labour and material wealth in permanent settlements free from the obligations of military service and taxation; to capitalize agriculture and technology. It laid the foundations for a literate, institutional clerical caste and formalized concepts of the obligations owed by kings to their people.

The physical geography of Early Medieval Christian statehood is still tangible. Standing in York's Minster Yard visitors might pose next to a bronze of Emperor Constantine, with the great medieval cathedral church as a backdrop. Somewhere beneath their feet, within the ruins of the *principia* of *Eboracum*, lie the foundations of King Edwin's first church. A short walk along Petergate to King's Square may bring them to the site of Edwin's own secular establishment. Some 150 miles north of York tourists look out from the imposing ramparts of Bamburgh Castle, ancestral fortress of Bernicia's pagan and Christian kings. As the sea fret of a winter's morning lifts they will see, just 4 miles to the north-west, the surf-fringed outline of Lindisfarne, the tidal Holy Island of the abbot/bishops of Northumbria's Golden Age.

One needs a map, or a boat, to comprehend the more liminal but no less potent relationship between Iona, lying off the south-west corner of Mull, and Dunadd, fortress of the Dál Riatan kings in Argyll. The holy men of that island must ply their curraghs across the dangerous open waters of the Firth of Lorn and navigate the treacherous devilry of the Corryvreckan whirlpool between Jura and Scarba to reach the sheltered inlet at Loch Crinan, from where they might approach Dunadd across Mòine Mhòr's boggy reaches.

In Dál Riata and Northumbria a sense of power held at arm's length, of tensions between sacred and secular, eternal and temporal, cross and sword, hint at the dynamics through which these new relations were negotiated. The God-sanctioned kings of Britain and Ireland were both rooted in deep time and astoundingly imaginative in their grasp of the opportunities offered by adopting

Dunadd: fortress of the kings of Dál Riata at the mouth of Kilmartin Glen. Its rocky summit citadel was an expression of temporal and divine power.

Christian kingship. They rode its challenges in the spirit of a new age. Across the Insular landscape stone churches, free-standing crosses and the holy precincts of thriving monasteries stamped an ineradicable Christian mark on the land.

A single figure takes centre stage for the first act of this drama: Colm Cille – St Columba – founding abbot of Iona and charismatic spiritual mentor to Dál Riata's kings. What can be known of his life is filtered through the hagiographic conventions of Adomnán's *Vita Colombae*, the realpolitik of the seventh century when it was written and the demands of a Christian audience who expected their holy men to come with an off-the-shelf suite of miracles, prophecies and a record of devotional excellence. But Colm Cille was a bridge – if not a broker – between multiple worlds and in his career one can reconstruct the founding inspiration for a new concept of kingship.

Colm Cille, Latinized as Columba, 'the Dove', was born in north-west Donegal, traditionally at Gartan, in about 520 – at about the same time as the monastic pioneer St Brigit was dying in

Kildare. His given name was said, by later tradition, to have been Crimthann, 'the Fox'.[5] He was a member of the Cenél Conaill, the ruling dynasty of the Northern Uí Néill, and cousin to King Áed mac Ainmirech (died 598). Colm Cille was fostered by a priest called Cruithnechán and then studied with two teachers: a man called Gemman in Leinster who seems to have been a master of 'divine wisdom' and then with a man variously known as Finnio, Findbarr or Uinniau.[6] In 560, in his fortieth year, Colm Cille was somehow involved in a battle at Cúil Dreimne in County Sligo, between a northern alliance of the Cenél nÉogain, Cenél Conaill and Connachta, and the forces of King Diarmait mac Cerbaill, then high king of Tara. Later legend had it that Colm Cille's prayers for the northern alliance won them a famous victory – and the enduring enmity of the pagan King Diarmait.

Two years later Colm Cille was excommunicated – for the offence, according to later tradition, of having copied a book without permission. Adomnán says that it was for some trivial offence and that Brendan of Birr, a highly respected monastic prior, intervened on Colm Cille's behalf. Much has been read into his precipitate departure from Ireland in 562.[7] In the *Vita* he is said to have gone on pilgrimage to Britain with twelve fellow soldiers,[8] and here to have enjoyed an audience with Conall mac Comgaill, king of Dál Riata (*c*.559–574). Colm Cille's acquisition of the small island of Iona, in the Inner Hebrides, was either a product of that meeting or was confirmed by it. Here he founded a monastery whose fame eventually surpassed that of almost all others. In that marcher land between Irish, Dál Riatan and Pictish interests and centres of power, connected to all parts by the sea, his new church carved out an archipelagic *territorium*.

A multi-faceted personality of immense charisma, endeavour and success emerges from the pages of the *Vita*. Colm Cille was remembered as an exemplary monk and abbot, firm in discipline, compassionate, deeply devout and blessed by visions of great intensity. He saw all and knew all. In the strongly ascetic Irish tradition that led men to set out across the North Atlantic in boats made of hide, and build beehive cells on precipitous, storm-battered rocks, isolating themselves from the material world, Colm Cille and his holy *comites* chose a life apart. Apart, but not passively so. In parallel with many miracles that one can take as conventional or as literal truth, according to taste, there are more than vague hints at the aptitudes of a shaman: seeing events far away; experiencing 'a miraculous enlarging of the grasp of the mind';[9] taking part in staged contests with the *magi* of a Pictish overlord;[10] an apparent astral projection[11] and prophecies, foretelling the deaths of bad men, that are like echoes of the curse tablets tossed into Roman baths.[12]

A much more politically connected image can be constructed from Colm Cille's dealings with kings. In the last book of the *Vita* it is revealed that after Conall's death in 574 Colm Cille was staying in an Ionan daughter house on Hinba* when an angel appeared to him bearing a glass book containing instructions for the ordination of kings.[13] He was told by the angel to give a blessing to Áedán mac Gabrain of Dál Riata (Conall's cousin) and eventually, against his better judgement, carried out the angel's wishes. Colm Cille journeyed, then, to Iona where Áedán was already waiting for him; blessed him and laid his hand on Áedán's head in ordination. Colm Cille, investing both his spiritual power and political capital in Áedán's dynastic heirs, is said to have made a prophecy: that 'until you commit some act of treachery against me or my successors, none of your enemies will have the power to oppose you'.[14] In such terms was the new contract conceived between kings and their spiritual mentors.

In 575, a year after Áedán's ordination, a celebrated conference, convened or precipitated or brokered by Colm Cille, was held at Druim Cett, close to what is now Limavady near Derry. Here two kings, Áedán mac Gabrain and Colm Cille's cousin, Áed mac Ainmirech of the Northern Uí Néill, thrashed out a military alliance against mutual rivals in Ulster, agreed upon the liberation of a royal hostage and resolved to expel the order of bards from

* One of the islands of the Inner Hebrides, not as yet identified despite much effort.

Ireland. Colm Cille is said to have intervened on the latter's behalf;[15] and here also he is believed to have blessed Domnall, the son of Áed, effectively endorsing and legitimizing his succession to the kingship.[16] Colm Cille was playing the part of what would, in later historical dramas, be known as 'kingmaker'. St Cuthbert was encouraged by a Bernician princess to play the same part a century later.[17]

The *Vita Colombae* also contains references to relations with a king of *Alclut* (Strathclyde) and with King Bruide mac Maelchon of Fortriu. In Book II, chapter 35, Colm Cille visits the court of King Bruide for the first time, climbing the steep path to his fortress* only to find its massive gates closed against him – a diplomatic snub, at the very least. Colm Cille's response was to make the sign of the cross on the door and then place his hand on it, whereupon the bars 'were thrust back and the doors opened of themselves'. The king then came to greet the holy man with all due respect and honour.[18] This is political theatre, familiar to anyone who has seen images of Black Rod rapping on the doors of the House of Commons after they have been ceremonially slammed against him in anticipation of the Queen's Speech. In such ceremonials, display is all; and the holy man of Iona was a master of display.

A third strand of Colm Cille's career, rather less prominent in the *Vita*, reveals that he also acted the part of a territorial lord. He founded several daughter houses, including a celebrated monastery at Durrow in County Laois and at least two on islands in the Inner Hebrides. He appointed abbots, intervened in disputes on behalf of clients, and protected exiles.[19] He drew resources, such as building materials, from Iona's hinterland, compensated those who felt hard done by[20] and sought protection for a fellow monk from a *subregulus* of Orkney.[21] Colm Cille was, in one sense, a lineal descendant of the early Desert Father

---

* Perhaps Craig Phadraig, at the very top of the Great Glen, overlooking Inverness and the Beauly and Moray Firths. Excavations here have produced sherds of E Ware from Gaul and a fifth- to sixth-century C^{14} date.

Pachomius.* Colm Cille's monks, too, were soldierly comrades. The monastic community, with its 'great house', was a mirror of the *comitatus* in its mead hall at a royal township, with the additional protection of an enclosing vallum that functioned as both spiritual boundary and amuletic protection.

In his monastic complex on Iona, Colm Cille invested the sweated labour of his lay brethren and monks in buildings, agriculture, metalworking, leather and wood crafts; in boatbuilding and in a *scriptorium*, revealed by finds from various campaigns of excavation.[22] These have also yielded evidence of a water mill – an unthinkable investment in land held for a life interest only – while one of the *Vita*'s episodes implies that Iona was able to develop, or acquire, strains of early ripening barley.[23]

The earliest water-powered mills in the Atlantic islands seem to have been an Irish monastic innovation. Excavation of an outstanding early example, constructed in 619 at Nendrum monastery at the head of Strangford Lough, shows how a sophisticated horizontal paddle turbine was powered by damming the incoming tide, then releasing it through a carefully constructed funnel, or penstock.[24] Investment of expertise, materials and labour on such a scale was only possible with the surety of permanence; it gave the larger monastic complexes a significant economic advantage over their secular rivals.

The core of the monastic complex on Iona lay within a rectangular ditch and bank, or *vallum*, on the sheltered east side of the island, overlooking the sound towards the Ross of Mull. Colm Cille occupied his own, starkly bare cell looking down on the abbey church from a small hill. A 'great house', referred to in the *Vita*, allowed the community to gather en masse. A cemetery, the Reilig Odhráin, lay immediately to the south, eventually attracting the remains of many Scottish monarchs and at least one Northumbrian king. Workshops and grain stores sustained the community's material needs. Bowls turned from alder wood copied the forms of E ware pottery also found on the site, itself a sure sign of

* See Chapter 10, p. 331.

The remains of the tidal mill dam wall at the 7th-century monastery of Nendrum on Strangford Lough, County Down: inalienable property rights fostered capital investment in the technology of food production.

commerce with Gaulish merchants. In later centuries dozens, perhaps hundreds, of carved stone crosses stood in the vicinity.

One of the most remarkable legacies of the Iona community's investment in the technology of literacy was a book written there by Colm Cille's hagiographer Adomnán, called *De Locis Sanctis*. It contains an eye-witness account of the Church of the Holy Sepulchre in Jerusalem, given verbally to the abbot in the 690s by a Frankish bishop, Arculf, whose boat was improbably said to have been driven off course on its return to Francia.[25] Adomnán presented a copy of the book to his friend, the Northumbrian King Aldfrith (whose mother, Fina, was a princess of the Cenél nÉogain), in whose monasteries it was reproduced for redistribution across Europe, becoming something of an Early Medieval standard text.

In acquiring Iona for his community, effectively in perpetuity, Colm Cille was able to invest politically, spiritually and materially in a specialized type of lordship in which the expedient military service and attendance required of secular lords was replaced by a political and spiritual render. The long-term legitimacy of his client dynasts and the effective freehold of his territorial possessions were mutually ensured by the eternal and universal message of the Christian church, backed by Old Testament precedents. When Colm Cille ordained King Áedán on Iona in 574, in what may have been Europe's first explicit anointing of a Christian king, he was consciously evoking Samuel's ordination of Saul.[26] Together, the Dál Riatan overlords and their holy man assembled the key components of Early Medieval Christian kingship: building blocks of statehood that ensured continuity and rationality – in theory – in temporal and spiritual lordship.

There is little in the archaeology of Dunadd, long regarded as the principal seat of Dál Riata's overlords, to suggest their intimate relations with Iona or, indeed, their affinity with Christianity (Figure 6). No church has been discovered on its rocky slopes; no high crosses stand here looking down on a landscape whose monuments are much more profoundly steeped in ancestral, pre-Christian sensibilities. No royal fortress of the sixth or seventh century made space for its own *scriptorium* or sculpture workshop, nor yet the wonders of tide-driven watermills. Dunadd's stone-cut footprint, supposedly employed in inauguration rituals, and the incised Pictish bull carved beside it are decidedly heathen in sensibility.* Dunadd has been only very partially excavated, and much of its stratigraphic sequence was recorded long before modern techniques were employed. There are problems with dating the various phases of its impressive stone enclosures, and evidence for internal structures has been elusive. So Dunadd's archaeological fame rests on its unique location, rising like a behemoth from the bog at the mouth of Kilmartin Glen, and on the richness of its artefacts.[27] Dunadd was busy with highly skilled metalworkers

* An Ogham inscription, carved either side of a fault in the same slab of rock, has Christian affinities only insofar as the language was Irish, probably based on Latin, and is widely found in parallel with Latin memorial inscriptions.

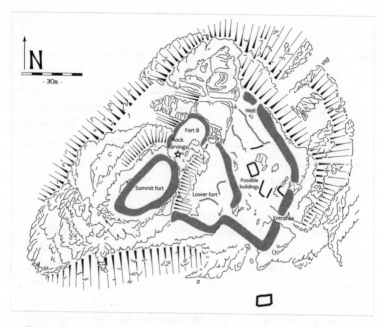

Fig. 6. Dunadd fortress, Argyll. Earthworks and walls, possible hall structures and natural defences. After Lane and Campbell 2000.

in iron, copper alloy, gold and lead, hundreds of whose tools, crucibles and brooch moulds have been recovered. E Ware pottery is present in quantity and variety;* vessel glass suggests feasting. A very unusual mudstone plaque on which animal and interlace motifs had been carved shows the hand of an experimental artist at work. These are all markers for the patronage and investment of very wealthy, highly connected, powerful lords. Two otherwise modest artefacts may hint at the material component of relations between Iona and Dunadd: a quern stone marked with a carved expanded terminal cross, and a small slate disc inscribed with the word *inomine*.[28]

Iona's client kings, the Gaelic overlords of Dál Riata, maintained

---

* One vessel has yielded a residue, analysis of which suggests that it had contained valuable dyer's madder. Lane and Campbell 2000, 100.

and enhanced their influence across the North Channel in Ulster through judicious military intervention* and through the political and dynastic influence of their Iona abbots. It seems, from Adomnán's retrospective testimony, that Colm Cille also acted as a sort of ambassadorial proxy for Conall, and later Áedán, in their relations with Pictish kings and with their close neighbours, the kings of *Alclut* on the Clyde. Despite Bede's belief that Colm Cille went on a mission of conversion to the Picts, there is no sound evidence either for Ionan evangelism on the British mainland before Adomnán's day or that the kings of Dál Riata sought to impose Christian practice on their subdued enemies. But in sheltering the young Bernician exile Oswald Iding, from 617 (when Edwin killed his father Æðelfrið at Bawtry) until he was able to mount a bid for his own kingship in 634, Dál Riata and Iona were investing shrewdly in his political future; an investment whose payoff was more dramatically successful than they can have anticipated. When Oswald returned to Bamburgh to found the monastery at Lindisfarne he was thoroughly Irish; thoroughly Christian.[29]

The works of Gildas and Patrick are proof enough that an institutional church survived in Britain into the late fifth century, but that its relations with kings were at best strained. Memorial stones, crosses, apparently early church dedications, the *vitae* of celebrity holy men and women and place names all testify to the existence of thriving Christian communities enjoying the patronage of secular lords. The few churches that can reasonably be dated to the following century seem to have been founded on good, rather than marginal, land.[30] At the beginning of the seventh century British kings were still nominally Christian and their bishops were able to convene a synod to which many learned religious were invited, in response to Augustine's mission. Bede recorded that more than 1,200 monks assembled to pray for a

* The marine force implied by the renders recorded in the *Senchus Fer n'Alban*.

British victory against a Northumbrian army before the Battle of Chester in 616.[31] King Edwin may have been first baptized by a son of Urien of Rheged during his early exile. So there is a trail of continuity through which an institutional British church can be shown to have survived and interacted with secular powers. But there was no tradition, it seems, of evangelism – no attempt, as Bede recorded with such contempt, to bring God to the English-speaking peoples of the east.

The organization of the Roman church in Britain had been urban and diocesan: bishops sat in *civitas* capitals and held administrative primacy over the religious communities in their *civitates*. In Ireland, where no *civitas* administration, no papal jurisdiction had ever been imposed, the role of bishops was less well defined. The careers of Colm Cille, Brigit and other charismatic religious shows that Irish abbots and abbesses were lords of their *territoriae* and enjoyed direct relations with both God and their patron kings. Sixth-century British bishops also operated outwith papal control, even though they seem to have enjoyed some limited connectivity, via the importation sites of Bantham, Tintagel and elsewhere, with the Christian Latin world beyond.

The geography of the Early British church can be mapped in some detail by the incidence of Welsh *Llan-* names, indicative of an enclosure around a church;* and by Latin and Ogham inscribed memorial stones. In the south-west peninsula equivalent *Lan-* names also survive, vastly outnumbered, particularly in Cornwall and Scilly, by settlements named after local saints whose later obscurity is paradoxically reassuring of their authenticity.[32] Possible early church sites where a circular wall still surrounds a cemetery, especially when it is associated with one or more memorial stones, are the most secure examples.[33] The sort of relationship one finds in the Gaelic church, with the monasteries of principal holy men set deliberately apart, but not too far, from royal secular sites, is much less obvious. The most celebrated saints, like Samson, were

* From Brythonic *lanon: 'cleared or open space; enclosure'. Todd 1987, 241.

SELUS IC IACT: Here lies Selus, perhaps St Seleven, a Cornish
saint of the 6th century. The reverse of the stone carries a
chi-rho cross. St Just parish church.

even more committed to the ascetic life than Colm Cille and
apparently much less inclined to involve themselves with secular
politics or with the conversion of pagans. Even so Samson, whose
remarkable career was beset by tensions between his desire for
an eremitic life and his entrepreneurial, not to say adventurous
spirit, found himself directly involved with royal politics during
a long career in Brittany.* The seventh- to ninth-century *Vita
Sancti Samsonis* describes how, having founded a community at
Dol in Brittany, he petitioned for the excommunication of King
Conomorus and intervened with King Hiltbert (Childebert I) to
promote Conomorus's son, Judual.[34]

---

* Educated by St Illtud at Llantwit Major, Samson was consecrated bishop
in 521; he seems still to have been alive in the 550s and 560s, during which
time he is recorded as having attended a church council in Paris.

David – *Dewi Sant* – the patron saint of Wales, can be said with certainty to belong, like Colm Cille, to the second half of the sixth century – the date of his death is variously given as 601 in the *Annales Cambriae* and 589 in the Irish Annals – but his surviving *Vita* was not written until half a millennium later. His geography is centred on the city that bears his name in Dyfed, although he is said to have founded churches in both *Dumnonia* and Brittany. He enjoyed, if that is the right word, a reputation for extreme severity in the rule of his community; he was known to and revered by Irish ecclesiastics.[35] The subsequent cult of St David has clouded the realities of his career, but his early reputation seems not to have been based on political relations with kings.

It is unclear whether the myriad small religious communities of the British west sustained themselves through their own toil and from gifts, or whether they were also render-gathering lords of very modest *territoria*. One wonders if, in truth, locally powerful lords in *Dumnonia* and in Wales acquired holy men and women as manifestations of lordly display; that landless or displaced members of noble families found such simple but protected lives as priests, ministering to small local flocks of dependants, an agreeable career choice. Like their royal superiors, the lords of the Welsh *cantrefi* valued the presence of ecclesiastics whose intellect and Latinity, like the praise poetry of the bards, was flattering and reminiscent of a dimly remembered Roman past. Endowing churches was good for their souls, as many an Early Medieval charter attests. Their patronage of church offices extended their networks of clients and, therefore, their social and political influence. A career in the church was a useful means of occupying the second sons and unmarried daughters of élite families, especially for those whose aptitudes and tastes disinclined them to life in the testosterone- and drink-fuelled fighting culture of the warband or to an unending cycle of reproduction and cup-bearing in the mead hall. The more cerebral lords and noble women – kings and queens, too – might retire gracefully to a life of enclosed contemplation, taking the tonsure and dressing themselves in the subfusc robes of an ordered life; bringing with them into their communities gifts of land, perhaps books, certainly finery and prestige.

Nonetheless, some of the better-endowed and more populated monasteries cannot have failed to be drawn into their contemporary political orbits. Both *Llan-* names and Latin memorial stones occupy the core lands of the *civitates* of Gildas's tyrants and they commemorate not just the officials of ecclesiastical institutions – presbyters, *medici*, *episcopi* and the like – but also the scions of secular élites. In Môn (Anglesey) the natural fortress of Maelgwyn, Gildas's 'Dragon of the Isle', *Llan-* names and Latin memorial stone inscriptions are widespread. The western and eastern extremities of the island are associated with two contemporary saints, the Cornish Cybi and Seiriol of Rhos. Both were sons of kings; both enjoyed the patronage of the royal house of Gwynedd. Cybi, like many a seventh-century English holy man, was given the ruins of a former Roman fort – at Holyhead (whose native name is *Caer Gybi*) – in which to found his community. One might speculate that he was also granted the right to collect renders from its *territorium*. Seiriol is said to have founded Penmon Priory but wishing, like St Cuthbert, for a more eremitic life, he eventually retired to a small rocky island less than a mile off Penmon Point: Glannauc or *Ynys Seiriol*, later Priestholm.

That Gwynedd's kings tied their own salvation to the faith is indicated by the existence of memorials. At Llangadwaladr, just across the sandy estuary of the Afon Ffraw from the seat of Gwynedd's medieval kings at Aberffraw, a stone commemorating King Cadfan ab Iago (died 635) of Gwynedd survived because it was built into the north wall of the church:

Catamanus rex sapientisimus opinatisimus omnium regum
Cadfan, wisest and most renowned of all kings.[36]

Cadfan must, in his youth, have been something of a foster father to Edwin, who was 'nurtured in the island of Môn', a protected guest at the Venedotian court in return for his future recognition of their *imperium* and the services of his warband in battle against their (and his) enemies. Cadfan succeeded his father, Iago ap Beli, in the year of the Battle of Chester (616), although neither was demonstrably an active participant in the fight against Æðelfrið. Cadfan's son and successor, Cadwallon, was driven into exile on *Ynys Seiriol* by his former foster brother. In turn, Cadwallon was Edwin's slayer in 632, rather suggesting some ongoing and deep-seated animosity between the two princes. By a stroke of the historical fates, Cadwallon's subsequent year-long rampage through Northumbria precipitated the arrival of Edwin's nephew, Oswald, Ionan protégé and champion of Irish Christianity.

While British kings enjoyed an ambivalent relationship with their church, the kings of Dál Riata and their Ionan holy men – Colm Cille's successors – seized the opportunity presented to them by supporting Oswald's military expedition to recover his father's kingdom in 634. Oswald was a known quantity, in whose future Dál Riata and Iona might shrewdly invest their political capital and a small military retinue. Their sponsorship of his bid for the kingdom required in return that he show them honourable loyalty in alliance and Bernicia, once a hostile rival, now became an ally against their antagonists in Pictland, Strathclyde and Ulster. Furthermore, Oswald had acquired something of a reputation during his exile. His Irish nickname *Lamnguin* may mean 'Bright blade' or 'White blade' or even 'Blessed arm'. Iona's abbot (from 623 to 652) Ségéne, who enjoyed a strong personal relationship with the Bernician prince, also saw opportunity in his protégé's prodigal return. Might not a suitable place be found on Oswald's estates for the establishment of an Iona in the east, a daughter house whose bishop/abbots might be recruited from the ranks of the Ionan *paruchia*, mirroring the honourable alliance of its secular rulers? The enthusiasm with which Oswald took up the challenge is a set piece of Bede's *Historia Ecclesiastica*. Oswald sent to Iona for a bishop in 635, within a year of assuming the Bernician throne. He endowed his new bishop, Aidan, with no fewer than three shire estates and personally ensured the success of the Lindisfarne project. From the reign of Oswald, Northumbria's investment in Christian kingship enjoyed unbroken continuity.

A rather different set of relations is recorded in the mission of conversion sent by Pope Gregory the Great* to the *Angli* in the year 596. Gregory is said, by both Bede and the anonymous Whitby author of his earliest *Vita*, to have been inspired by an earlier encounter with some fair, light-skinned youths in Rome. He received them and asked to what race they belonged:

> They answered, 'The people we belong to are called Angles.' 'Angels of God,' he replied. Then he asked further, 'What is the name of the king of that people?' They said, 'Ælle,' whereupon he said, 'Alleluia, God's praise must be heard there.' Then he asked the name of their own tribe, to which they answered, 'Deire,' and he replied, 'They shall flee from the wrath of God [*De ire Dei*] to the faith.'[37]

Bede had access to some of Gregory's letters and cultivated assiduous correspondents in Kent, where many of the mission's narratives were collected. A flurry of genuine contemporary records, together with Bede's partisan but scrutable construction, draws Early Medieval Britain decisively back into European mainstream history. Those records show that Gregory's network of ecclesiastical and royal correspondents enabled him to string together a chain of well-placed agents across Francia by which his principal envoy, Augustine, might be aided in this mission into the unknown. Even so Augustine, who had been prior of the pope's own monastery in Rome, was so daunted by the challenge that he turned back and had to be firmly persuaded to continue by a missive from his master, a copy of which Bede obtained directly from Rome and from which he quoted.[38]

Augustine and his party carried letters of commendation to various bishops, requiring them to render any support necessary. They also bore letters to the courts of Burgundy and Austrasia. The Frankish king of Austrasia, Theudebert II (reigned *c*.595–612) can have been no more than ten or eleven at the time, so Augustine

* He held the papacy between 590 and his death in 604.

also bore a letter from Gregory to Theudebert's grandmother and regent, Brunhild, perhaps then at Tournai or Metz. Neither Frankish kings nor their bishops had previously, so far as one can tell, considered or exploited the political advantages of a sponsored mission to the English. Gregory, appealing primarily to their Christian virtue, asked that they offer support and protection for Augustine's party; he also hinted at temporal rewards, promising that:

> Almighty God, who knows that with devout mind and with all your heart you take an interest in His cause, may propitiously direct your causes, and after earthly dominion bring you to heavenly kingdoms.[39]

If Æðelberht and his Frankish queen, Bertha, were forewarned of the mission or, indeed, if they played a part in its initiation, Bede either did not know or chose to ignore the fact, concentrating instead on a set-piece narrative of initial royal suspicion, countered by virtuous Roman persuasiveness. The king allowed Augustine and his party of forty to set up camp on the Isle of Thanet, where the long-established trading emporium at Sarre may have acted as a caravanserai, or neutral port of entry. Here, their bona fides could be checked. The king, despite his queen's familiarity with church protocols – she, after all, maintained a priest in her household and worshipped in a church just to the east of Canterbury's walls[40] – insisted on an open-air meeting, fearing some magic. Augustine is said to have brandished a panel carrying a silver cross and an image of the lord. The episode may be fanciful, but it is reminiscent of the political theatre enacted between Colm Cille and King Bruide in the Great Glen: the theatre of overlordship.

The king and his councillors, perhaps suitably briefed by Queen Bertha, listened to Augustine's pitch – translated, one imagines, by her priest – and consented to his mission, eventually giving him land 'suitable to his rank'* on which to settle his party. Four years later, the initial success of the mission was confirmed when Pope

---

* Meaning the right to extract renders from an estate.

Gregory sent a party of priestly reinforcements to Kent, along with the books and equipment necessary to expand provision for the faithful. Augustine was sent the *pallium** which conferred on him the status of a metropolitan and the right to consecrate new bishops for sees in Rochester and London. Canterbury had its first archbishop.

The Kentish king's principal concerns may have been less with the immediate prospect of heavenly glory or earthly reward than with the mission's implications for relations with both Frankish kings and with the distant pope, who addressed him in such imperial, portentous terms.† Quite how divine or enthusiastically Christian Æðelberht's rule was after 597 is best left to the imagination. Nor can one say what messages, gifts, orders or requests from the Austrasian court Augustine brought with him to cement the Kentish king's tributary relationship with them. But Æðelberht took advantage of the presence of literate priests to encode his laws in writing – and in Old English, at that. His very first doom addresses compensation for theft of church property on a more or less equal footing with the rights of the king. For his part Gregory was keen, in correspondence with his new *familia* in Kent, to flatter Æðelberht and Bertha by comparison with the greatest of regal entrepreneurs, Constantine the Great and his mother, Helena. And Bede records that Æðelberht built a church at Canterbury, which he endowed with many gifts; that he was eventually buried with his queen in a chapel in the monastery church just outside the city walls.[41] On the other hand, there is little evidence to suggest that the king recognized or exploited the broader benefits to kingship that Iona and Dál Riata had engineered in the north; and in any case, on his death Æðelberht

---

* A ceremonial vestment bestowed upon metropolitans or archbishops.

† Gregory was later to write to Æðelberht, 'this end of the world is approaching, many things are at hand which previously have not been; to wit, changes of the air, terrors from heaven, and seasons contrary to the accustomed order of times, wars, famine, pestilences, earthquakes in various places'. *Letters of Gregory the Great* Book XI, Letter 66.

The medieval remains of St Augustine's Abbey, just outside the city
wall of Canterbury. Here Augustine founded the first church of
Pope Gregory's mission to convert the English.

was succeeded by a son, Eorcenberht, who promptly apostatized.
The same year, 616, King Sæberht of the East Saxons, who had
been baptized in 604, also died. His sons drove Mellitus, the
first bishop of the East Saxons, out of his new church of St Paul
in London.

What can be said with certainty is that Gregory – 2,000 miles
away – believed the mission to have been successful in its first
years. He boasted to the Bishop of Alexandria that Augustine had
baptized no fewer than 10,000 people in Kent, and he credited
the Frankish regent Brunhild with a leading role in the mission's
success:

> As to the great favour and assistance wherewith your Excellence
> aided our most reverend brother and fellow bishop Augustine
> on his progress to the nation of the Angli, fame had already

not been silent; and afterwards certain monks, returning to us from him, gave us a particular account thereof. [...] The succours afforded by you claim to themselves the larger share herein, it having been through your aid, after God, that the word of preaching became widely known in those parts.[42]

Women had been prominent in the institutional church from the fourth century onwards as patrons, active participants and, perhaps, as agents for its spread and acceptance. If the immediate legacy of the Kentish royal conversion, like that of Edwin in Northumbria, was limited by the death of its principal royal sponsor, the longer-term fortunes of the church in Britain were sustained in great measure by a succession of royal women. After Brunhild and Bertha, the latter's daughter Æðelburh was influential in her husband Edwin's acceptance of the faith in about 627 – indeed, it was a condition, long delayed, of their marriage. Their daughter Eanflæd, born perhaps prematurely – even miraculously – on the night of her father's deliverance from the poisoned blade of a West Saxon assassin, played an astute and even visionary part in Northumbria's emergence in the 640s as the first institutionally Christian kingdom and in its exploitation of the church as a tool of statehood. She and her daughter Ælfflæd both became patrons of the royal monastery at Whitby of which Edwin's great-niece, Hild, was the outstanding founder.

The most serious setback to the Augustinian mission during Æðelberht's reign was its failure to reach a harmonious settlement with the British church. After the arrival of reinforcements from Rome, Augustine was concerned to bring the long-isolated bishops of the west into line with orthodox Roman practice – particularly in the critical matters of the timing of Easter and the appropriate baptismal rite. Taking advantage of the king's diplomatic reach, he convened a meeting of British bishops and 'teachers' – Bede's word – on the border between the West Saxon and Hwiccan kingdoms at a place that Bede identified as Augustine's Oak.[43] The papal emissary admonished the British for their failure to preach to the heathen English and urged them to both realign their practices with Roman orthodoxy and join with him in the task ahead: the conversion of the pagan English. They refused. Augustine now effected a miracle, restoring the sight of a blind man of the English race – a very obvious and probably conscious echo of Germanus's allegorical 'healing' of the British Pelagians in 430. In response to this powerful magic, the British acceded to a second conference, to which they would bring seven bishops and many more learned men, chiefly from their most prestigious monastery at *Bancornaburg* (Bangor Iscoed, on the banks of the River Dee south of Chester). In preparation, the British party sought advice from a 'holy and prudent man, a hermit'. This man advised them to test Augustine's humility – the sign of divine authority – before they agreed to abandon such long-held practices.

The intellectual mood is startling in its contrast with the tribal rituals of overlordship by which Dál Riatan and Kentish kings had negotiated their new sets of obligations with Colm Cille and Augustine. The British party did not recognize Kentish overlordship or the spiritual *imperium* of the pope. The outcome was poised delicately on the success of Augustine's diplomacy and on his offer of orthodox integration. A catastrophic failure to rise and greet the British party with due humility at this second conference turned the tide irrevocably against him. Incompatible niceties of Early Medieval political theatre, understood so differently by the two sides, had been lost in translation.

Whatever the personal psychologies of conversion – and there is no doubt that some kings, like Oswald, undertook profound spiritual journeys – the élite adoption of Christianity was a function of lordship. Kings and their consorts, *comites* and households took considerable risks in devolving some of their earthly power to abbots, bishops and distant popes. On the one hand, the Christian contract offered kings the hope of eternal salvation and temporal legitimacy in return for the disciplines of formal instruction and worship; and for cognitive, even emotional investment in a suite of rituals, beliefs, biblical narratives and calendrical observances in which they were coached by enthusiastic priests. Conversion required effort. On the other hand, there was much in the

Christian portfolio that appealed to existing sentiment. Its festivals coincided, more or less, with the quarter days of the year, marking and celebrating natural cycles of fertility, rebirth, hope and sacrifice. The solemn Latin intonation of priests at their liturgies, the wielding of censers and participation in the eucharist induced altered states of consciousness and contemplation, by no means unattractive to those who had invested, and would continue to invest, their fortunes in capricious fates. Ceremonial offerings, promises, sacrifice, immersion in water and the expectation of reward for virtue were comprehensible, familiar even. Priests of any persuasion who successfully wielded magic on behalf of a community or congregation might be safely assured of loyalty. Above all, kings required success in battle; and if the prayers of their Christian holy men brought them victory, who could gainsay their efficacy?

But kings were, primarily, lords of their dependent élite clients; they, in turn, exercised powers of patronage over households. Royal adoption of Christian virtues and ceremonies must be followed by the conversion of the whole *gens*: a much more nuanced affair. In the early summer of 601, Pope Gregory urged his new royal protégé Æðelberht to 'put down the worship of idols, overturn the edifices of their temples'. He soon reflected, however, that such a confrontational approach might not be effective among the *Angli*. Less than a month later he wrote to Mellitus, a member of the mission's second wave of priests sent to support Augustine:

I have long been considering with myself about the case of the Angli; to wit, that the temples of idols in that nation should not be destroyed, but that the idols themselves that are in them should be. Let blessed water be prepared, and sprinkled in these temples, and altars constructed, and relics deposited, since, if these same temples are well built, it is needful that they should be transferred from the worship of idols to the service of the true God; that, when the people themselves see that these temples are not destroyed, they may put away error from their heart, and, knowing and adoring the true God, may have recourse with the more familiarity to the places they have been accustomed to. And, since they are wont to kill many oxen in sacrifice to demons, they should have also some solemnity of this kind in a changed form, so that on the day of dedication, or on the anniversaries of the holy martyrs whose relics are deposited there, they may make for themselves tents of the branches of trees around these temples that have been changed into churches, and celebrate the solemnity with religious feasts. Nor let them any longer sacrifice animals to the devil, but slay animals to the praise of God for their own eating, and return thanks to the Giver of all for their fullness.[44]

The abbots, abbesses, bishops and priests who carried the novel social contract to the emerging kingdoms of the English must finesse their message according to local sensibilities and politics. Their eventual success, from the middle of the seventh century onwards, was ensured by embedding the institution of the church in a model of rational territorial administration: they must be effective lords and, like all successful lords, they must master the rules of landed patronage to maintain and extend networks of followers and dependants; must defend their territory and community from predation by rivals, kings and the powerful forces of secularization. They must make themselves useful – as partners in governance, law making and the judiciary, and as economic drivers towards surplus and investment. They must provide pastoral care, access to the eucharist and to priests who could officiate in birth and marriage rites and, eventually, the formalities of death. Above all, perhaps, they must infuse the landscape with church, monument and sanctity and with competent, not to say progressive, land management. The rise, in the eighth century, of the land charter, the parochial system and universal provision for worship, was their achievement.

The prolonged soul-searching that led to the eventual conversion of King Edwin, as narrated by Bede, was genuine: he must balance political instincts and the sensibilities of his warrior élite against the lever of his immense overlordly capital, his personal spiritual journey and the risks and opportunities presented by new diplomatic relations with the pope – who wrote letters of encouragement to him and to his queen and dangled the offer of an archbishop for York.[45] Edwin, in the end, saw Roman Christian kingship as both a confirmation of his political and military power and as emblematic of his membership of the club of European statehood. But he was uninterested, it seems, in investing the landscape with churches and monasteries. Rædwald, his predecessor as *imperium*-wielder, former host and comrade-in-arms, endured a similar dilemma; but his resolution was to keep a foot in either camp, as Bede and the contents of his ship burial so eloquently testify. The brand of diocesan orthodoxy brought by Augustine and his successors required urban institutions and the support of an active bourgeoisie to succeed. Neither existed in Britain or in Ireland, where the tribally integrated, territorial Christianity of the monastic community had a much greater chance of success in bridging the divide between a *gens* and their king.

Tribal realities were so profoundly ingrained in the practice of Insular kingship that it took a uniquely hybrid circumstance to forge the prototype for an enduring Christian state among the early English kingdoms. After the successive deaths of star overlordly converts – Æðelberht, Rædwald, Edwin and Oswald – both the Irish and Roman projects in Britain were vulnerable to the old rules by which the cult of the king and the king's sponsorship of cult enjoyed currency that dissolved with his almost inevitable death on the battlefield. In the immediate aftermath of Oswald's brutal martyrdom on the Welsh border in 642 at the hands of Penda, an unreconstructed pagan Mercian warlord, the fortunes of the God-given kings hung by a thread.

Enter stage left Oswald's younger brother Oswiu, the first of the Idings to die in his bed: Irish-educated in arms and Christian practice, like his brother, he had taken a lover of Cenél nÉogain stock and fathered a child who would become Northumbria's – and England's – first literate king. Enter stage right Eanflæd, daughter of Edwin and Æðelburh. She had been gifted to the church as a tiny infant, in recognition of her father's deliverance from attempted murder on the day she was born. After her father's death at Hatfield Chase in 632 she was taken to Kent by Bishop Paulinus and brought up in the household of her uncle, King Eadbald, the apostate-turned-convert who, like his father Æðelberht, married a Frankish princess; she also spent time at the Frankish court of Dagobert I. Her education was infused with Continental sensibilities and the sophisticated political culture of Francia. When she and Oswiu were married, to cement a political alliance between the two most powerful English kingdoms in the years immediately after Oswiu's accession in 642, a perhaps improbably effective partnership was founded, lasting nearly thirty years.

Oswiu and Eanflæd succeeded in navigating a series of hazards: the aggression of Penda's emerging Mercian powerbase; fractious relations with the Irish abbots of their mother church at Lindisfarne; tensions with Roman orthodoxy over Easter, monastic rule and the right to appoint a new archbishop of Canterbury; and, not least, competing networks of patronage in Bernicia (Oswiu's homeland) and Deira (Eanflæd's). Political and religious pragmatism set their course at the Synod of Whitby in 664, when they chose Europe and the pope over Ireland and sentiment. A thoughtfully planned and carefully executed policy of founding minster churches on royal estates in both kingdoms, gifted in perpetuity to abbots and abbesses of royal pedigree, ensured an even-handed territorial deployment of royal land and patronage to the church. It set a brilliant precedent. By the time of Oswiu's death in 670 or 671 English kingdoms were set on a path of solidly Christian statehood in which the written word of law and charter took precedence over the ephemeral, the customary. Precedents were set and might be invoked in disputes; evidence produced. Laws were written in the language of the mead hall as well as that of the cloister. Lordship was Christian; Christianity territorial, monumental, rooted in and visible in the landscape of the ancients.

In 410 *Britannia* rejected Rome. The political and theological crisis of the 430s set different parts of the former province on distinct,

In the late 7th-century crypt at Hexham founded by St Wilfrid, decorated monumental stones from the Roman town at Corbridge were deliberately incorporated into the the fabric.

parallel paths of a social and cultural experiment. Whether, looking back, modern sentiment sees the following century and a half as disaster or simply as a fascinating laboratory in which to observe society indulging in an exciting, risky ride towards an unknown future, one cannot help admiring the creativity and richness of the enterprise. The tensions engendered by Britons' sense of regional identity and diversity are still distinctive and productive of creative energy. Whether we would change our judgement, had the meagre written sources that survive from this period been fuller, is another question.

Appendix

Tribal Hidage

British Museum *Harley 3271* folio 6v

Kingdom/ TH entry	Notes	Hidage	Likely or possible *regiones*/districts/ constituent peoples
Myrcna landes is þrittig þusend hyda þær mon ærest Mrycna hæt	*'the area first called Mercia'*	30,000	*Tomsæte* *Gaini* *Pencersæte* *Bilsæte* *Beormingas* *Hrepingas*
W(r)ocen sætna/ Wreocenset is syfan þusend hida	*Centred on Wroxeter*	7,000	*Rhiwsæte* *Scrobsæte* *Temesæte* *Meresæte* *Ercall*
Westerna eac swa		7,000	*Magonsæte* *Dunsæte*
Pecsætna twelf hund hyda	*Peak Saxons*	1,200	
Elmedsætna syx hund hyda	*Elmet, in West Yorkshire*	600	*Loidis* *Burghshire* *Yeadon* *Ribble*

Kingdom/ TH entry	Notes	Hidage	Likely or possible *regiones*/districts/ constituent peoples
Lindes farona syfan þusend hyda mid Hæþ feldlande	*Lindsey (north-east Lincolnshire) with Hatfield Chase*	7,000	*Billingas Winteringas Hæthfelth*
Suþ gyrwa syx hund hyda	*Near Peterborough. Bede's Tondberht was its* princeps	600	
Norþ gyrwa syx hund hyda	*(Near Peterborough)*	600	
East wixna þryu hund hyda	*Possibly Wisbech and area of River Wissey*	300	
West wixna syx hund hyda	*(as above)*	600	
Spalda syx hund hyda	*?Spalding; or Spaldwick (Huntingdon-shire)*	600	
Wigesta nygan hund hyda	*?Wiggenhall in the Norfolk marshlands*	900	
Herefinna twelf hund hyda		1,200	*Hyrstingas*
Sweordora þryu hund hyda	*Associated with Sword Point in Huntingdon-shire*	300	
Gifla þryu hund hyda	*River Ivel (Brythonic; north-east Bedfordshire)*	300	

Kingdom/ TH entry	Notes	Hidage	Likely or possible *regiones*/districts/constituent peoples
Hicca þry hund hyda	*Hitchin (Brythonic; Hertfordshire)*	300	
Wihtgara syx hund hyda	*Wihtware (Isle of Wight)*	600	
Noxgaga fif þusend hyda	*?Suther-ge (Surrey)*	5,000	*Woccingas* *Godhelmingas* *Basingas* *Fullingas* *Meallingas* *Binton* *Eaton* *Sunninges*
Ohtgaga twa þusend hyda	*?Suther-ge (Surrey)*	2,000	
Ðæt is six ond syxtig þusend hyda ond an hund hyda *(Total)*		**66,100**	
Hwinca syfan þusend hyda	Hwicce: *earliest known kings 670s*	7,000	*Husmeræ* *Weorgoran* *Winchcombe* *Eorlingas* *Beansæte* *Stoppingas*
Ciltern sætna feower þusend hyda	*Chiltern 'Saxons' (Brythonic). East Herts down to the Goring gap*	4,000	*Wæclingas* *?Hæmele*
Hendrica þryu þusend hyda ond fif hund hyda	*North Oxfordshire into Buckingham-shire?*	3,500	

Kingdom/ TH entry	Notes	Hidage	Likely or possible *regiones*/districts/ constituent peoples
Unecunga-ga twelf hund hyda	*Buckingham-shire?*	1,200	
Arosætna syx hund hyda	*River Arrow (Warwickshire); ?part of Hwicce*	600	Hahlsæte
Feppinga þreo hund hyda is in Middel-englum Færpinga	*Charlbury, Oxfordshire ?Infeppingurn (Bede HE)*	300	
Bilmiga syx hund hyda	*Northamp-tonshire into Rutland*	600	
Widerigga eac swa	*Wittering and Werrington (Northamp-tonshire)*	600	
Eastwilla syx hund hyda	*?Old Well stream near River Granta*	600	
Westwilla syx hund hyda	*'Stream of the Fen'*	600	
East engle þrittig þusend hida	*East Angles*	30,000	Lodnigas Ickelgas Blythingas ?Wisse Elge
Eastsexena syofon þusend hyda	*East Saxons (Essex)*	7,000	Deningae Uppingas Rodingas Vange Berecingas Haningas Hæferingas ?Wigingas

Kingdom / TH entry	Notes	Hidage	Likely or possible *regiones* / districts / constituent peoples
Cantwarena fiftene þusend hyda	*Kent: formerly two kingdoms*	15,000	Weoware Limenware Burhware Eastorege ? Wester-ge Cæsterware ?Ruminingsæte Stursæte Mercsware
Suþsexena syufan þusend hyda	*South Saxons (Sussex)*	7,000	Meallingas Hastingas Stæningas Chiltin Ondred Peppering
Westsexena hund þusend hyda	*West Saxons (Wessex)*	100,000	Wilsæte Sumorsæte Dornsæte Meanware Readingas Basingas Gewisse Sunningas Wihtwara Lyminge
Ðis ealles twa hund þusend ond twa ond feowertig þusend hyda ond syuan hund hyda *(Total, correctly 244,100)*		242,700	

Kingdom / TH entry	Notes	Hidage	Likely or possible *regiones* / districts / constituent peoples
Other Early Medieval kingdoms and regions not included in Tribal Hidage			
Middle Saxons	*?Hertford-shire and parts of Middlesex. Possibly assessed as part of the East Saxons in Tribal Hidage*		Brahingas Beningas Geddingas Mimmas Gummeningas Lullingas Wixan Hæmele (or in Cilternsæte) Stæningas Gillingas Tottenhale ?Wæppingas
?Middle Angles	*(First bishopric established at Leicester in 737). Peada becomes their king 653–5*		Snotingas Inundulum
Fen territories: *North and South Gyrwe; East and West Wixna; Spalda, Wigesta, Herefinna, Sweordora, Gifla, Hicca and East and West Willa*			Bilsingge Beorningas Terrington Islington Hæferingas Leverington Clencwara Grantesæte Hæslingas Wisse Meahala Ælm Gruntifen

Kingdom/ TH entry	Notes	Hidage	Likely or possible *regiones*/districts/ constituent peoples
Magonsæte	*Herefordshire based on Roman town at Kentchester (Magnis)*		*Stepelsæte*
Ercing/ Archenfield	*South-west Herefordshire: centred on Ariconium, River Wye*		.
Durosæte	Durotriges/ *Durnovaria: centred on Dorchester*		
Sumorsæte	*Durotriges: possibly associated with Somerton close to Ilchester*		
Deira	*East Yorkshire centred on Malton/Derventio*		*Incuneningum*
Bernicia/Bryneich	*Tyne valley and Northumberland*		Coria Bromic Gefrin Bamburgh Yetholm Ahse Kintis

Kingdom/ TH entry	Notes	Hidage	Likely or possible *regiones*/districts/ constituent peoples
Rheged	*?Solway/Eden; Dumfries and Galloway*		*Dunutunga/Dent Swar/Erechwydd Llwyfenydd Swar/ Catraeth Craven/ Cravescire Ribble Catlow*
Westmoringa	*Westmorland; possibly part of Alclud or Rheged*		
Dyfnas	Dumnonia		*Penwith Kerrier Pydar Powder Trigg West Wivel East Wivel*
West Wealas	*Cornwall*		
Dyfed	Demetae		*Cantref Gwatharf Ystrad Tywi Cedweli Gwŷr*
Powys	*North central Wales, Latin* Pagenses		*?Ceri Maelienydd Elfael Gwerthrynion Buellt*
Rhos	= *?Tegeingle, north-east Wales*		
Gwynedd	*North-west Wales and Anglesey; the* civitas *of the Ordovices*		*Môn Gangani*

Kingdom/ TH entry	Notes	Hidage	Likely or possible *regiones*/districts/ constituent peoples
Gwent	*From the* Silures, *via Caerwent*		
Brycheiniog	*Originally part of* *the* Silures		
Aeron	*Ayrshire*		*Cunningham* *Kyle* *Carrick*
Alclud	*Strathclyde:* *Dumbarton Rock* *and the Clyde* *valley*		*Lemnaig*
Gododdin	Votadini: *based* *on Dun Eidyn:* *Edinburgh*		
Manau	*Upper Forth* *valley: ?Clack-* *mannanshire*		
Dál Riata	*Argyll and the* *Inner Hebrides*		*Kindreds: Cenél* *Loiarn* *Cenél nŒngusa* *Cenél Comgaill*
Kintyre/*Corcu* *Reti*			*Cenél nGabrain*
Waerteras	*Fortriu – Moray* *Firth*		
Athfotla	*Atholl*		
Fib	*Fife*		
Cait	*Caithness*		
Sci	*Skye*		

Notes

Part I: The End of History

1 Quoted by Millett 1990, 130.

Chapter 1: Late Romans

1 Curse tablet no. 80. http://curses.csad.ox.ac.uk/4DLINK2/4DACTION/ WebRequestCurseTabletSearch?searchType=latin-index&search Field=CSAD_ID&thisListPosition=0&displayImage=1&displayLatin =1&displayEnglish=1&searchTerm=uley-80.

2 Sawyer 765. King Edgar to Romsey Abbey; grant of land at Edington, Wilts. Latin with English bounds.

3 McOmish 2002.

4 Perring 2002.

5 Jerome, *Epistles* 133.9 to Ctesiphon. Jerome was writing in about 415 CE.

6 Le Roy Ladurie 1980.

7 Tomlin 1996. The district of *Hæmele* (around modern Hemel Hempstead in Hertfordshire) is referred to as a *pagus* in a Charter of the early eighth century (Bailey 1989, 111).

8 Wild 1967. The two other candidates, *Venta Icenorum* (Caistor-by-Norwich) and *Venta Silurum* (Caerwent) are also considered by Wild in this fascinating paper.

9 Mattingly 2013, 312–14.

10 Millett 1990, 181ff.

11 The most detailed critique is to be found in Lapidge and Dumville (eds) 1984.

12 Rippon et al. 2015.

13 Oosthuizen 2019, 106ff; but see Williamson 2013 for a more cautious approach.

14 See Roberts 2010 for the key theoretical statement on cultural corelands.

15 Adams 1999; O'Brien and Adams 2016.

16 An idea proposed by Professor Brian Roberts, to whom I owe grateful thanks for conversations on this and many other matters.
17 Hope-Taylor 1977.
18 *HSC*, section 4. South 2002, 4, 79; Adams 1999; O'Brien 2002.
19 Jackson and Potter 1996, 677ff.

Chapter 2: The ruin

1   Bede, *Prose Life of Cuthbert*, 27. Webb and Farmer 1983, 77.
2   Speed 2014, 92.
3   Millett 1990, 221.
4   Thomas 1981, 214ff; Speed 2014, 67.
5   Darling 1987.
6   The hints are contained in an ovation by Libanius (59: 139 and 141) that contains little detail. Ireland 2008, 142.
7   Ammianus *RG* XIV, 5. Hamilton 1986, 43–5.
8   Jerome, *Epistles* 133.9 to Ctesiphon.
9   There are several Continental references to this initiative. Ireland 2008, 144–5.
10 Hopkins 1980.
11 For a full discussion of the social and structural aspects of Roman housing, see Perring 2002.
12 Perring 2002, 111; see also the British Museum's website entry: www.britishmuseum.org/research/collection_online/collection_object_details.aspx?assetId=463871001&objectId=1362696&partId=1.
13 Ammianus *RG* XXVI, 4. Hamilton 1986, 318.
14 Ammianus *RG* XXVII, 8. Hamilton 1986, 342.
15 Ammianus *RG* XXVIII, 3. Hamilton 1986, 356.
16 Ammianus *RG* XXVIII, 3. Hamilton 1986, 357.
17 Gerrard 2013, 53.
18 Ammianus *RG* XXVIXI, 4,7. Ireland 2008, 150–1.
19 Zosimus, *HN* IV, 35, 2–6 and 37, 1–3. Ireland 2008, 151–2. Zosimus has *Singidunum* (Belgrade) as the place of Gratian's capture; other sources offer *Lugudunum* (Lyon).
20 This is a brief note by Sozomenus in his *Ecclesiastical History*. Ireland 2008, 153.
21 Gibbon, *Decline and Fall of the Roman Empire*, Chapter 30.
22 Zosimus VI 3,1. Ireland 2008, 157.
23 Kulikowski 2000, 333–4.
24 Jones and Casey 1988, 379. *Britanniae* is a plural: the Britains, meaning the four provinces of the diocese.

25 Zosimus *HN* VI, 5, 2–3. Translation anonymous, published by Green and Chaplin 1814.

26 Zosimus *HN* VI, 10, 2. Ireland 2008, 160.

27 For a useful discussion of the problem see Higham 1992, 73.

28 Gildas *De Excidio* 19. Winterbottom 1978, 23.

29 Dark 2002, 60.

30 Bede *HE* II.16.

31 Speed 2014, 84–92.

32 Speed 2014, 155–60 for a table summary of the evidence.

33 Speed 2014, 74.

34 Speed 2014, 94. The only certain chartered municipium in Roman Britain was *Verulamium*.

35 Barker et al. 1997. Barker himself suggested the reuse of the frigidarium as a centre for collecting the *annona* (p. 168).

Chapter 3: Signs of life

1   Thomas 1981, 115.

2   Madigan and Osiek 2005; Dunn 2003.

3   Thomas 1981, 221–4.

4   Wilkinson 2006.

5   Petts 2014, 79–80; Dark 2002, 80ff.

6   Gelling 2011, 992ff.

7   Surveys of the evidence can be found in Thomas 1981, Watts 1991 and Petts 2011.

8   The evidence is reviewed in the surveys by Thomas 1981, Watts 1991 and Petts 2011.

9   Upex 2011.

10 Upex 2011, 97.

11 *Acta Concilii Arelatensis*. Petts 2006.

12 Athanasius *Historia Arianorum* 28. Frend 2003.

13 Sulpicius Severus *Chronicorum* XLI. Schaff and Wace 1894.

14 The *Vita Martini* was written by his contemporary Sulpicius Severus around 397, the year of Martin's death. Hoare 1954.

15 *De Laude Sanctorum*. Clark 1999.

16 See Barrett 2009, 200.

17 Morris 1995, 121.

18 Prosper *EC* 1301. Muhlberger 1981, 84. Barrett (2009, 200) suggests that Agricola may have been in exile in Britain.

19 Constantius *VG* XII. Hoare 1954, 294.

20 Constantius *VG* XIV. Hoare 1954, 298.

21 Higham 2014, 124.

22 Wood 2009.

23 Gildas *De Excidio* 10.2. Winterbottom 1978, 19.

24 Niblett 2006.

25 In a charter of Athelstan. Howe 2008, 41.

26 Bede *HE* I.vii. Colgrave and Mynors 1969, 19.

27 Constantius *VG* XVII. Hoare 1954, 300–1.

28 Wood 2009.

29 Thompson 1984.

30 Woodward and Leach 1993.

31 Croxford 2003.

32 Powlesland, D. J. *25 Years of Archaeological Research on the Sands and Gravels of Heslerton*. www.landscaperesearchcentre.org/html/25_years_digging.html.

33 Roberts 2010, 127.

34 Wilmott 2010, 13–14.

35 Hood 1978, 41, 56. The first section of the *Confessio* describes Calpornius as a deacon; in the tenth section of the *Letter to Coroticus* he is a decurion.

36 Thomas 1981, 310ff.

Chapter 4: Of grub huts, urns and isotopes

1   Blinkhorn 1997.

2   Perry 2013.

3   Lines 3110 onwards in the Penguin Classics edition. Alexander 1973.

4   Williams 2011, 249.

5   Paul Blinkhorn, personal communication.

6   E.g. Adams 2018, 105ff.

7   Hills 2006, 107.

8   Owen-Crocker 2017.

9   Carver, Hills and Scheschkewitz 2009.

10 Carver, Hills and Scheschkewitz 2009, 48–9.

11 Hills and Lucy 2013, 297.

12 Arnold 1988, 4.

13 Leyser 1995, 151.

14 Hamerow 2012, 1.

15 Tipper 2003, 35ff, believes that few, if any, post-hole buildings were missed by excavators in the southern half of the settlement, suggesting that the earliest settlement phase comprised *grubenhäuser* almost exclusively.

16 Lucy 2016.
17 Tipper 2004.
18 Pliny, *Natural History* XIX.9, quoted by Hamerow 1993, 17.
19 Hamerow 1993, 15–17.
20 Hamerow 1993, 14ff; Tipper 2004, 106.
21 Tipper 2004, 147ff, 106.
22 West 1985 volumes 1 and 2.
23 Walton Rogers 2007.
24 The historical evidence for women's role in cloth making, and for what amount to textile ateliers, is collected and discussed by Herlihy 1999.
25 Powlesland 1999.
26 Montgomery et al. 2005.
27 Budd et al. 2004, 135.
28 Adams 2018, 14.
29 See Oosthuizen 2019 for a recent, compact summary of the standard model.
30 Myres 1986.
31 Pryor 2005.
32 Oosthuizen 2019.
33 Gildas *De Excidio* 25.2.
34 Enright 1996.

Chapter 5: Of famine, sword and fire

1 The definitive Latin edition with parallel English translation is that of Winterbottom 1978; the most comprehensive volume of critique is that edited by Lapidge and Dumville 1984. The manuscript source is Cotton MS Vitellius A VI, copied in the late ninth or early tenth century.
2 Gildas *De Excidio*, chapter 19.
3 Gildas *De Excidio* 20.1 Winterbottom 1978, 23–4.
4 Gildas *De Excidio* 22.2 Winterbottom 1978, 25–6.
5 Gildas *De Excidio* 23.1 Winterbottom 1978, 26.
6 Gildas *De Excidio* 24.4 Winterbottom 1978, 27.
7 Gildas *De Excidio* 26.1.
8 See, for example, Higham 1994, 120ff.
9 Higham 1994, 137.
10 From a letter written to Namatius by Sidonius Apollinaris in about 480. *Letters* Book VIII.6: 13–15. Dalton 1915.
11 Higham 1994, 40.
12 Note especially the sequence known as the Tale of Emrys in the *Historia*

Brittonum 40–2. He also features in the Nennian Chronography under a year which equates to 437.

13 Higham 1994 presents the case for Gildas writing before the end of the fifth century. His arguments have not gained universal acceptance, but offer a serious challenge to the Gildas of the mid-sixth century. See also Chapter 6.

14 See Wood 1984 for a discussion of problems in accepting these entries at face value.

15 From the *ASC* 'E' version. Garmonsway 1972.

16 Bede, *HE* III.1.

17 The standard English edition is that of Hood 1978. Surviving but much later hagiographies of Patrick compiled in the ninth-century *Book of Armagh*, in which the *Confessio* and *Letter to Coroticus* are also preserved, have been treated at great length by Hanson 1968 and Dumville 1993. Thomas 1981 distils the Patrician material in so far as it illuminates British Christianity in the fifth century.

18 Morris 1980 is still the standard English edition, although Morris has been much criticized for his editorial hand.

19 Nennius *HB* 31. Morris 1980, 26. But Thanet is, correctly, Brythonic **Tanneton*. The name was known, in a variant, to Ptolemy in his second-century CE *Geographia*.

20 Nennius *HB* 38. Morris 1980, 29.

21 Nennius *HB* 43–4.

22 Nennius *HB* 46.

23 Nennius *HB* 66.

24 Adams 2015, 259.

25 Nennius *HB* 56. Morris 1980, 35.

26 For a generous and fascinating interpretation see Alcock 2001; for the most up-to-date and impressive analysis of the myth see Higham 2018.

27 Alcock 1972.

28 Adams 2015, 258ff.

29 Rahtz et al. 1992. Excavations at Dinas Powys were published by Alcock 1963.

30 Wilson et al. 1996.

31 For a discussion of the arguments surrounding the place name *Cat-raeth* and its identification with the battle site of *Y Gododdin*, see Wilson et al. 1996, 6.

32 Bede *HE* II.14.

33 Wilson 1996, 1–2.

34 Fleming 1994.

35 Fleming 2010, 139ff.
36 Fleming 1994, 25.
37 Rippon 2018, 322ff.

Part II: After History

1   Bede *HE* V.24. Colgrave and Mynors 1994, 291.

Chapter 6: Private enterprise

1   Penn and Brugmann 2007, 94–5.
2   Gildas *De Excidio* 1.14.
3   Gerrard 2004.
4   Higham 1992, 45–6, 146–7.
5   Wilmott 2010; and see the papers collected in the same volume, *Finds From the Frontier*. Collins and Allason-Jones 2010. A recent contribution to the debate sees the nascent Early Medieval kingdom of Bernicia being founded along the Wall line in the fifth to sixth century. Wood 2018.
6   Hopkins 1980, 104.
7   Tony Wilmott, 'Buried at Birdoswald'. *Current Archaeology* 353, August 2019.
8   Petts 2013, 328.
9   Petts 2013.
10 Petts 2013, 319.
11 Speed 2014, 104.
12 Thomas 1981, 51.
13 Speed 2014.
14 Gerrard 2013, 164–5.
15 John 1961, 12.
16 Gerrard 2013, 164–5; 199; 258.
17 Oosthuizen 2019.
18 Rippon 2018.
19 Evison 1994; Medlycott 2011.
20 Medlycott 2011, 124.
21 Bassett 1989, 25.
22 Gerrard 2013, 234.
23 Alcock 1995, 151. The pottery dates from between about 475 and about 550. See Chapter 9.
24 Alcock 1995.
25 Powlesland et al. 2006.

26 Gerrard 2013.

27 Gelling 2011.

28 Dyer 2007.

29 Smith 1985; response in Webster and Smith 1987.

30 Dark 2002, 113.

31 For both Melania and the Dumnonian landlady see Applebaum 1958, 80, fn. 2.

32 Adams 2015, 75, 210.

33 Sidonius Apollinaris to his friend Domitius. ?461–7 *Letters* Book II.2: Dalton 1915.

34 Gildas *De Excidio* 27. Winterbottom 1978, 29.

35 Sidonius Apollinaris to his friend Hypatius. c473 *Letters* Book III.5: Dalton 1915.

36 Sidonius Apollinaris to his brother-in-law Ecdicius. C4743 *Letters* Book III.3: Dalton 1915.

37 Jordanes *Getica*, XLV, 237–8.

38 Sidonius Apollinaris to his friend Riothamus. c472 *Letters* Book III.9: Dalton 1915.

39 For a comprehensive and definitive consideration, see Higham 2018.

40 Oosthuizen 2019; see also Chapter 7.

41 Alcock 1963; Alcock 1972; Rahtz et al. 1992; Savory 1960.

42 See Higham 1994, 108–11.

43 Percy Bysshe Shelley, *Sonnet: Ode to England in 1819.*

44 Gildas *De Excidio* 30. Winterbottom 1978, 30.

45 Higham 1994; EGLWC/1. From the excellent website Ogham Stones of Wales: www.babelstone.co.uk/Blog/2010/03/ogham-stones-of-wales.html.

46 *De Excidio* 31. Winterbottom 1978, 31.

47 *Habet Britannia rectores, habet speculatores.* Winterbottom 1978, 15, 89.

48 Simms-Williams 2003, 346–7.

49 The genealogies are preserved in Harleian 3859, which also contains the standard manuscript of the Nennian compilation. Bodleian Library, Jesus College MS 20, folios 33r–41r. See also www.kmatthews.org.uk/history/harleian_genealogies/index.html.

50 Gildas *De Excidio* 32. Winterbottom 1978, 31.

51 *British Archaeology* 29, November 1997: News.

52 Gildas *De Excidio* 33–6.

53 Alcock 1968; Alcock 2001, 160–1.

54 See, for example, Higham 1994, 118–41; Dumville 1984; see also Chapter 5.

55 Bede *HE* III.22.
56 Scull et al. 1990.

Chapter 7: Belongings

1 Carson 2007.
2 The collection known as the *Mabinogion*. Davies 2007.
3 Jackson 1969.
4 Alexander 1973.
5 Anthony 2007.
6 Kelly 2000.
7 From the collection known as *Anglo-Saxon Maxims II*. British Library Cotton MS Tiberius B.i ff. 115r–v. The translations are adapted from Tom Shippey's *Poems of Learning and Wisdom in Old English*. Cambridge: DS Brewer, 1976.
8 Bede *HE* I.1.
9 Bede *HE* I.22 for his comments on Gildas and the Britons' failure to preach to the Angles or Saxons.
10 Bede *HE* IV.22.
11 Bede *HE* I.25.
12 Bede *HE* I.26.
13 Attenborough 1922, 31; see Chapter 9 for the law in full.
14 Gerrard 2013, 204; and see material relating to the analysis of the body and grave in the 'Meet the Ancestors' BBC TV series: www.springfieldspringfield.co.uk/view_episode_scripts.php?tv-show=stories-from-the-dark-earth-meet-the-ancestors-revisited-2013&episode=s01e04.
15 See, for example, Penn and Brugmann 2007.
16 'Meet the Ancestors', www.springfieldspringfield.co.uk/view_episode_scripts.php?tv-show=stories-from-the-dark-earth-meet-the-ancestors-revisited-2013&episode=s01e04.
17 Härke 1990.
18 Gerrard 2013, 65.
19 The inscribed stone can be found inside the church.
20 Charles-Edwards 2014, 176; see also Chapter 8.
21 Charles-Edwards 2014, 105.
22 Gerrard 2015.
23 Wright et al. 2000.
24 Thomas et al. 2006.
25 For example, Pryor 2005.
26 The principal arguments are summarized in Higham 1992, 189ff; in

the chapters by Schrijver, Coates and Tristam in Higham 2007; and by Oosthuizen 2019, 41ff.

27 Coates 2007.

28 Schrijver 2014, 43.

29 Schrijver 2014, 18.

30 Gelling 1979, 111; Schrijver 2014, 20.

31 Schrijver 2014.

32 Oosthuizen 2019, 67ff.

33 For general references to these issues, see Adams 2018. Lisa M. Bitel's outstanding 1996 essay on Ireland, 'Land of Women', is a key text. The standard work on *Women in Anglo-Saxon England* is Fell 1986.

34 Chadwick 1964 for an assessment of the various Welsh traditions about Edwin. The Rheged connection is alluded to in Nenius *HB* 63.

35 Bede *HE* II.20.

36 Dickinson 1993; Hope-Taylor 1977, 67ff, 200.

37 Williams 2002.

Chapter 8: Territories

1 Davis and Vierck 1974; Higham 1995.

2 See Higham 1995, 74ff for the argument that King Edwin of Northumbria had the list drawn up in about 627 by Bishop Paulinus in the aftermath of his war against Wessex. The perceived crime was an assassination attempt on Edwin by a Wessex ambassador in 626, vividly described by Bede in *HE* II.9. Higham also summarizes the arguments for Tribal Hidage being compiled in Mercia.

3 Hart 1971; Davis and Vierck 1974.

4 For the Northumbrian argument, see Higham 1995; for the Mercian argument see Davies and Vierck 1974.

5 Gelling 1979, 115–17.

6 Bassett 1989, 18.

7 Bassett 1989, 21ff.

8 In Dál Riata, for example. Bannerman 1974.

9 For Bernicia see Roberts and Wilmott in Collins and Allason-Jones 2010; for the *Hwicce* see Bassett 1989.

10 Gelling 1989, 201.

11 Roberts 2010.

12 Charles-Edwards 1989, 34.

13 Tírechán 47.4, 48. Bieler 1979, 160.

14 O'Brien and Adams 2016.

15 Pretty 1989; see also the Appendix.

16 Eddius *VW* 42. Colgrave 1985.
17 Brooks 1989, 70.
18 Bailey 1989, 111.
19 Harrington and Welch 2014.
20 Bede *HE* IV.6; Blair 2005, 254 n. 31.
21 Bede *HE* IV.19.
22 Colgrave 1985, 169, 195.
23 Oosthuizen 2017, 69.
24 Oosthuizen 2017, 65.
25 Bede *HE* V.19.
26 Cox 1976, 41.
27 Cox 1976 lists all the place names known to have been in existence before about 730.
28 Oosthuizen 2017, Chapter 4.
29 McOmish 2002, 110.
30 Bede *HE* III.24.
31 Charles-Edwards 2013, 18.
32 Grigg 2015, 201.
33 Charles-Edwards 2013, 278.
34 Charles-Edwards 2013, 278.
35 Charles-Edwards 2013, 289.
36 Bannerman 1974.
37 Foster 2014.
38 Foster 2014, 62–3.
39 Driscoll 1991.
40 O'Brien 2003.

Chapter 9: Horizons

1 Cole 2013; Gelling and Cole 2014.
2 Gelling 1967.
3 Cox 1976.
4 Bede often tells his readers which language a name belongs to – for example Cnobheresburg (Burgh Castle: *HE* III.19); and he often translates, as in Hreutford, 'that is, the ford of the reed' (modern Redbridge) – *HE* IV.16. He gives English Heavenfield in both its contemporary form and in Latin: *Caelestis campus* (*HE* III.2).
5 Songlines are mnemonic lyrics describing the dreamtime and 'real' landscapes inhabited by Australian aborigines. *The Songlines* is the title of a 1987 book by Bruce Chatwin in which he explores them.
6 Cole 2013, 10; Cox 1976, 63.

7   Worcestershire County Council: Minerals Local Plan Background Document September 2018: Salt and brine in Worcestershire.

8   Watt 2004, 195.

9   Morris 1980, section 68.

10 Hooke 1985, 122ff.

11 See for example, Gerrard 2004, 67 and his references; Whyman 2001, 253.

12 Hooke 1985, 122ff.

13 Cole 2013, 9.

14 Cole 2013, 54; Hooke 1985, map on p. 125.

15 Gildas *De Excidio* 10.

16 Cole (2013) has assembled all the currently available evidence using place names and the supporting evidence of coins and pottery.

17 Bede *HE* II.2. The meeting was convened 'at a place which is still called in English *Augustinaes Ac*'. Colgrave and Mynors 1994, 71. See also Chapter 13.

18 Wihtred cap. 28. Attenborough 1922, 31.

19 Griffiths et al. 2008.

20 The Life of St John the Almsgiver from *Three Byzantine Saints*, translated by Elizabeth Dawes with notes and an introduction by Norman H. Baynes, London 1949. https://sourcebooks.fordham.edu/basis/john-almsgiver.asp.

21 Duggan 2018, 7. Campbell 2007 offers a very comprehensive view of post-Roman trade linking the Atlantic seaboard of Britain and Ireland with the Mediterranean and Frankish Gaul.

22 Quinnell 2004, 75.

23 Campbell 2007; Duggan 2018; Wooding 1996.

24 Thomas 1985, 165ff.

25 Duggan 2018, 71–3.

26 Kelly 2000, 319.

27 Kelly 2000, 359.

28 Colgrave 1968; see also Chapter 13.

29 Harris (2003) proposes semi-formal diplomatic links with Byzantium.

30 Quinnell 2004.

31 Lynn and McDowell 2011.

32 Kelly 2000.

33 Severin 2005.

34 Barry 1964.

35 Petts 2014.

36 Scull 1990.

37 Brooks 1989; Harrington and Welch 2014; Wood 1992.

38 Welch and Harrington 2014: Chapter 7.
39 Bede *HE* I.25.
40 See the Kent Archaeology online inventory of the graves: www.kentarchaeology.org.uk/11/04/03/026.htm#026e%20Anglo-Saxon%20Plane. See also the discussion by Scull 1990.
41 Arnold 1988, 60ff.

Part III: The First Kingdom

1 Morris 1980, 36.

Chapter 10: *Duces bellorum; milites Christi*

1 The account of the tomb's discovery was published in 1655 as *Anastasis Childerici I. Francorvm Regis, sive Thesavrvs Sepvlchralis Tornaci Neruiorum* under the authorship of Jean Jacques Chifflet.
2 Gildas *De Excidio* 20. The 'Agidius' of the original is usually transliterated as 'Aëtius'.
3 Gregory *HF* II.31.
4 Halsall 2007, 305.
5 Gregory *HF* II.37.
6 Gregory *HF* II.38. Translation from Mathisen 2012, 79.
7 The patriciate is not mentioned in II.38 but in Gregory's own chapter index. Mathisen 2012, 79.
8 Bede *HE* I.34.
9 Bede *HE* III.6.
10 Bede *HE* I.15.
11 *Historia Brittonum* 37.
12 *Vita Prima Sanctae Brigitae* 42. Connolly 1989.
13 Bede *HE* II.14.
14 O'Brien 2002, 66.
15 Smith 1991.
16 Bassett 1989, 22, 19.
17 Noble and Evans 2019, 25.
18 Jones 1979; Campbell 1986, 97. Jones's multiple estate model has been much criticized over the years; but the arithmetical element of his scheme is sound.
19 *Historia Brittonum* 57.
20 *Annales Cambriae sub anno* 516. Morris 1980, 45.
21 The classic case for a historical Arthur was made by John Morris in *The Age of Arthur* (1973) and by Leslie Alcock in his 1971 book *Arthur's*

Britain. A second edition of the latter carries a more sceptical note. The most recent and definitive treatment of the legendary Arthur is Nick Higham's *King Arthur: the Making of the Legend* (2018).

22 Hamerow 2012.

23 Eddius *VW* 2.

24 Enright 1996.

25 Felix *VG* XVI; XVII. Colgrave 1956, 81.

26 Eddius *VW* 13.

27 Ine cap. 13.1. Attenborough 1922, 40–41.

28 Bede *HE* III.24.

29 In a letter to them from Aldhelm. Abels 1988, 16–17.

30 Dunn 2003, 26.

31 Patrick *Confessio* 49, 50.

32 Gildas *De Excidio* 67.

33 Gildas *De Excidio* 66.1 for references to priests, ministers, clerics; 69.1 for bishops; 66.3 for hints of cenobitic life; 67.5 for overseas pilgrimage; 10.2 for the holy martyrs.

34 The standard work on the *Early Christian Archaeology of North Britain* is still Charles Thomas's superb, if dated, 1971 study of that name. More recent analysis of much of the material can be found in Dark 2002.

35 Thomas 1971, 72–3, 196.

36 Dark 2002, 80ff.

37 Dark 2002, 122; Thomas 1971, 16, 48ff.

38 Dark 2002, 177.

39 See Adams 2015, Chapter 6.

40 Bede *HE* III.4.

41 Perhaps the small structure at the east end of the later monastic enclosure excavated by Raleigh Radford in the late 1940s and early 1950s. Thomas 1971, 14; Hill 1997, 9, 28–9.

42 Hill 1997, 1ff; 11ff.

43 Translation from Thomas 1971, 98. For a detailed consideration of the history of the stone, and a possible Constantinian *chi-rho* symbol once traceable above the inscription, see Hill 1997, 614.

Chapter 11: Dynasts

1 Bede *HE* III.1. Bede was writing of an infamous year in Northumbrian history, after the death of King Edwin in 633, when all was anarchy and apostasy. Those who computed the dates of kings had erased the year from their mnemonic lists.

2 Dumville 1976.

3 See Alcock 2001 for both the optimistic view on Easter table material and Alcock's own more reductionist musing two decades on from the original publication of *Arthur's Britain*.

4 For a clear exposition of the problems encountered in interpreting the early centuries of the *Chronicle* and the various collections of genealogies see Simms-Williams 1983 and Dumville 1976.

5 Simms-Williams 1983, 30. Cynric may also be a Brythonic name, according to Simms-Williams.

6 Garmonsway 1972, 2.

7 Simms-Williams 1983 explains the likely causes of discrepancy.

8 The East Saxon genealogy is found in British Library Add. MS 23211.

9 Detailed discussion of the Anglian collections of royal genealogies is found in Dumville 1976.

10 Bede *HE* IV.19.

11 The website www.kmatthews.org.uk/history/harleian_genealogies/2. html contains useful transcriptions of the Northern and Western genealogies from Harleian 3859.

12 *Historia Brittonum* 62.

13 Todd 1987, 236ff.

14 Charles-Edwards 2013, 417–19.

15 Dark 2002, 177.

16 Burch 2015.

17 Alcock 1988, 37, quoting a paper by Doris Edel (1983) 'The Catalogues in Culhwch ac Olwen and Insular Celtic. Learning', *Bulletin of the Board of Celtic Studies* 30, 253–73.

18 Attenborough 1922.

19 Æðelberht cap. 1. Attenborough 1922, 4; Brooks 1989, 67.

20 Hope-Taylor 1977, 70ff.

21 Smith 1991.

22 Johnson and Waddington 2009.

23 O'Brien and Miket 1991.

24 O'Brien and Adams 2016b.

25 Driscoll 1991.

26 For a full discussion of royal residence sites at this period, see Burch 2015.

27 Adams 2013, 395, Appendix A: The Bernician kinglist problem.

28 Procopius *BG* IV.15. AD536.

29 Procopius *BG*: II.23.

30 Dark 2009, 24–5. Articles accessed online: www.historicalclimatology. com/blog/something-cooled-the-world-in-the-sixth-century-what-was-

it); www.sciencemag.org/news/2018/11/why-536-was-worst-year-be-alive?et_rid=377269358&et_cid=2490907.

31 By Harrington and Welch 2014, for example.

32 *Historia Brittonum* 63.

33 Wood 1996.

34 McCarthy 2002, McCarthy 2011.

35 Fleming 1994, Fleming 2010.

36 Lewis and Williams 2019, 6–7.

37 *Historia Brittonum* 63.

38 *Historia Brittonum* 57.

39 McCarthy 2002, McCarthy 2011.

40 See, for example, 'Rheged rediscovered: Uncovering a Lost British kingdom in Galloway', *Current Archaeology* 327. The excavation report is by Toolis and Bowles 2017.

Chapter 12: Overlords

1 *Beowulf* lines 64–70. Alexander 1973, 53.

2 Bede *HE* III.24.

3 Campbell 1986, 92–3.

4 Bede *HE* II.5.

5 *ASC* 827, correctly 829.

6 Gildas *De Excidio* 33. Winterbottom 1978, 32.

7 Bede *HE* II.15.

8 Bede *HE* II.3. Bede says that Sæberht was Æðelberht's nephew. In the same chapter he says that Æðelberht held sway over all the kingdoms south of the Humber.

9 Bede *HE* II.16. Colgrave and Mynors 1994, 100.

10 *Annales Cambriae* under the year 613 (for 616); Bede *HE* II.2.

11 Bede *HE* II.12.

12 Bede *HE* II.12 Colgrave and Mynors 1994, 93–4.

13 Enright 1996.

14 Bede counts North and South Mercia separately as having been assessed at 7,000 and 5,000 hides respectively. *HE* III.24.

15 Whitelock 1979, 478.

16 O'Daly 1952; Bhreathnach 2005, 98–9; Bhreathnach 2014, 67; Charles-Edwards 2005.

17 Kelly 2000.

18 Ine cap. 70. Attenborough 1922, 59.

19 *ELGG* XVIII. Colgrave 1968.

20 See O'Brien 2005 for the most significant and apposite recent analysis

of the 'great enclosure' and of Hope-Taylor's sequence.

21 Warner 1988, 51.

22 Bhreathnach 2014, 56ff.

23 Warner 1988, 57.

24 See figure 2 in Warner 1988 for a plan of the site's principal features.

25 Warner 1973.

26 Warner 1988, 62.

27 Talorcan is named as Eanfrið's son in an entry for 654 in the *Annals of Tigernach*. Anderson 1922, 172.

28 Noble and Evans 2019.

29 Noble and Evans 2019, 66.

30 Noble et al. 2019, 76.

Chapter 13: God-given kings

1 Bede *HE* III.1.

2 Bede *HE* II.13.

3 Bede *HE* II.13.

4 Wihtred cap. 1 and 1.1. Attenborough 1922, 24, 25. Wihtred was king of Kent from 690 to 725.

5 Lacey 2013, 29.

6 Adomnán *VC* II.1; II.25.

7 Adomnán *VC* I.7.

8 Adomnán *VC* III.3.

9 Adomnán *VC* I.1 Sharpe 1995, 109ff.

10 Adomnán *VC* I.37, II.34.

11 Adomnán *VC* I.42.

12 Adomnán *VC* I.36; I.39; II.20, for example.

13 Adomnán *VC* III.5.

14 Sharpe 1995, 209. The passage is believed to have been directly copied from an earlier *Vita* of Colm Cille dating to about 640: the *Liber de vertutibus sancti Colombae* by his nephew Cumméne Find (seventh abbot, from 656). Lacey 2013, 96; and Sharpe 1995, n. 360.

15 Lacey 2013, 52.

16 Adomnán *VC* I.10.

17 Chapter 24 of Bede, *Prose Life of Cuthbert*.

18 Sharpe 1995, 184.

19 See, for example, Adomnán *VC* I.45 for the appointment of his uncle as prior on Hinba; II.22 for his intervention on behalf of a client; and II.23 for his protection of a Pictish exile.

20 Adomnán *VC* II.3.

21 Adomnán *VC* II.42.

22 Iona has produced a huge bibliography, from the first antiquarian interest in Columba to various, not always judicious, campaigns of excavations. See www.scottishheritagehub.com/rarfa/cs9 for a full list.

23 Adomnán *VC* II.3.

24 McErlean and Crothers 2007.

25 Bede *HE* V.15.

26 See Adams 2013, 62 for a brief discussion of the academic arguments for and against Áedán's ordination as a precedent.

27 Lane and Campbell 2000.

28 Campbell 1987.

29 For Oswald's story see Adams 2013. I am grateful to Dr Hermann Moisl for many enlightening discussions on Oswald and related Irish matters.

30 Turner 2003.

31 Bede *HE* II.2.

32 Todd 1987, 240ff.

33 Thomas 1971, 68.

34 *VS* I.59.

35 Wooding 2007.

36 Charles-Edwards 2013, 133.

37 Anonymous *ELGG* IX. Colgrave 1968, 90, 91.

38 Bede *HE* I.23.

39 Pope Gregory to King Theudebert, 596. *Letters of Gregory the Great* book VI, letter 51.

40 Bede *HE* I.25, I.26.

41 Bede *HE* II.3, II.5.

42 Pope Gregory to Eulogius. *Letters of Gregory the Great* book VIII, letter 30; Pope Gregory to Brunhild, book XI, letter 62.

43 Bede *HE* II.2 contains an account of the meeting and its aftermath. The site has not been identified.

44 Pope Gregory to Mellitus. *Letters of Gregory the Great* book XI, letter 76.

45 Bede *HE* II.17. York did not acquire metropolitan status, in the end, until 735.

Bibliography

Abels, R.P. 1988 *Lordship and Military Obligation in Anglo-Saxon England*. London: British Museum Publications

Adams, M. 1994 *Linear Earthworks of Land Division on the Yorkshire Wolds*. Unpublished BA thesis, University of York

Adams, M. 1999 Beyond the Pale: Some Thoughts on the Later Prehistory of the Breamish Valley. In Bevan, B. (ed.) *Northern Exposure: Interpretive Devolution and the Iron Ages in Britain*. Leicester Archaeology Monographs 4, 111–22. University of Leicester

Adams, M. 2013 *The King in the North: The Life and Times of Oswald of Northumbria*. London: Head of Zeus

Adams, M. 2015 *In the Land of Giants* London: Head of Zeus

Adams, M. 2018 *Unquiet Women: From the Dusk of the Roman Empire to the Dawn of the Enlightenment*. London: Head of Zeus

Adams, M. and O'Brien, C. 2020 A Sparrow in the Temple? The Ephemeral and the Eternal in Bede's Northumbria. In Hüglin, S. and Gramsch, A. (forthcoming 2020) *Petrification Processes in Matter and Society*

Alcock, L. 1963 *Dinas Powys: An Iron Age, Dark Age and Early Medieval Settlement in Glamorgan*. Cardiff: University of Wales Press

Alcock, L. 1968 Excavations at Deganwy Castle, Caernarfonshire, 1961–6. *The Archaeological Journal* 124, 190–201

Alcock, L. 1972 *'By South Cadbury is that Camelot...' Excavations at Cadbury Castle 1966–70*. London: Thames and Hudson

Alcock, L. 1995 *Cadbury Castle, Somerset: The Early Medieval Archaeology*. Cardiff: University of Wales Press

Alcock, L. 2001 *Arthur's Britain*. 2nd ed. London: Penguin

Alcock, L. 2003 *Kings and Warriors, Craftsmen and Priests in Northern Britain AD 550–850*. Edinburgh: Society of Antiquaries of Scotland

Alexander, M. (ed. and trans.) 1973 *Beowulf*. London: Penguin

Anderson, A.O. 1922 *Early Sources of Scottish History AD 500 to 1286*. Edinburgh: Oliver and Boyd

Anthony, D.W. 2007 *The Horse, the Wheel and Language: How Bronze-Age Riders from the Eurasian Steppes Shaped the Modern World.* Princeton: Princeton University Press

Applebaum, S. 1958 Agriculture in Roman Britain. *The Agricultural History Review* 6:2, 66–86

Arnold, C.J. 1988 *An Archaeology of the Early Anglo-Saxon Kingdoms.* London: Routledge

Attenborough, F.L. 1922 *The Laws of the Earliest English kings.* Cambridge: Cambridge University Press

Bailey, K. 1989 The Middle Saxons. In Bassett (ed.) 1989, 108–22

Baker, J. 2017 Old English *Sæte* and the Historical Significance of 'Folk' Names. *Early Medieval Europe* 25:4, 417–42

Bannerman, J. 1974 *Studies in the History of Dalriada.* Edinburgh: Scottish Academic Press

Barker, P., White, R., Pretty, K., Bird, H. and Corbishley, M. 1997 *The Baths Basilica, Wroxeter: Excavations 1966–90.* English Heritage Archaeological Reports 8

Barrett, A.A. 2009 Saint Germanus and the British Missions. *Britannia* 40, 197–217

Barry, J. 1964 *Joyful Pilgrimage: The Voyage of the Iona Curragh.* Donegal: Company of the Iona Curragh

Bassett, S. 1989 In Search of the Origins of Early Anglo-Saxon Kingdoms. In Bassett (ed.) 1989, 3–27

Bassett, S. 1997 Continuity and Fission in the Anglo-Saxon Landscape: The Origins of the Rodings (Essex). *Landscape History* 19:1, 25–42

Bassett, S. (ed.) 1989 *The Origins of Anglo-Saxon Kingdoms.* London: Leicester University Press

Bell, M. 2012 *The Archaeology of the Dykes.* Stroud: Amberley

Bhreathnach, E. 2005 The Airgíalla Charter Poem: the Political Context. In Bhreathnach (ed.) 2005, 95–9

Bhreathnach, E. 2014 *Ireland in the Medieval World AD 400–1000.* Dublin: Four Courts Press

Bhreathnach, E. 2005 (ed) *The Kingship and Landscape of Tara.* Dublin: Four Courts Press

Bieler, L. 1979 *The Patrician Texts in the Book of Armagh. Scriptores Latini Hiberniae.* Dublin: Dublin Institute for Advanced Studies.

Bitel, L.M. 1996 *Land of Women.* Ithaca: Cornell University Press

Blair, J. 2005 *The Church in Anglo-Saxon Society.* Oxford: Oxford University Press

Blinkhorn, P.W. 1997 Habitus, Social Identity and Anglo-Saxon Pottery. In Blinkhorn, P.W. and Cumberpatch, C.G. (eds) *Not So Much a Pot,*

More a Way of Life: Current Approaches to Artefact Analysis in Archaeology, 113–124. Oxford: Oxbow

Brooks, N. 1989a The Creation and Early Structure of the Kingdom of Kent. In Bassett (ed.) 1989, 55–74

Brooks, N. 1989b The Formation of the Mercian Kingdom. In Bassett (ed.) 1989, 159–70

Brugman, B. Migration and Endogenous Change. In Hamerow et al (eds) 2011, 30–45

Buchanan, J.J. and Davis, H.T. (ed. and trans.) 1967 *Zosimus, Historia Nova: The Decline of Rome.* San Antonio: Trinity University Press

Budd, P., Millard, A., Chenery, C., Lucy, S. and Roberts, C. 2004 Investigating Population Movement by Stable Isotope Analysis: A Report from Britain. *Antiquity* 78, 127–41

Burch, P.J.W. 2015 *The Origins of Anglo-Saxon Kingship.* Unpublished PhD thesis, University of Manchester

Campbell, E. 1987 A Cross-marked Quern from Dunadd and Other Evidence for Relations between Dunadd and Iona. *Proceedings of the Society of Antiquaries of Scotland* 117, 105–17

Campbell, E. 2007 *Continental and Mediterranean Imports to Atlantic Britain and Ireland, AD 400–800.* Council for British Archaeology Research Report 157

Campbell, J. 1986a Bede's Reges and Principes. In Campbell 1986b, 85–98

Campbell, J. 1986b *Essays in Anglo-Saxon History.* London: Hambledon Press

Carson, C. 2007 *The Táin: A New Translation of the Táin Bó Cúailnge.* London: Penguin

Carver, M. (ed.) 1992 *The Age of Sutton Hoo.* Bury St Edmunds: Boydell Press

Carver, M. (ed.) 2003 *The Cross Goes North: Processes of Conversion in Northern Europe, AD 300–1300.* Woodbridge: Boydell Press

Carver, M., Hills, C. and Scheschkewitz, J. 2009 *Wasperton: A Roman, British and Anglo-Saxon Community in Central England.* Anglo-Saxon Studies 11. Woodbridge: Boydell Press

Carver, M., Sanmark, A. and Semple, S. (eds) 2010 *Signals of Belief in Early England: Anglo-Saxon Paganism Revisited.* Oxford: Oxbow Books

Chadwick, N.K. 1964 The Conversion of Northumbria: A Comparison of Sources. In Chadwick (ed.) 1964, 138–66

Chadwick, N.K. (ed.) 1964 *Celt and Saxon: Studies in the Early British Border.* Cambridge: Cambridge University Press

Charles-Edwards, T.M. 1989 Early Medieval Kingship in the British Isles. In Bassett (ed.) 1989, 28–39

Charles-Edwards, T.M. 2000 *Early Christian Ireland*. Cambridge: Cambridge University Press

Charles-Edwards, T.M. 2005 The Airgíalla Charter Poem: the Legal Content. In Bhreathnach (ed.) 2005, 100–24

Charles-Edwards, T.M. 2014 *Wales and the Britons 350–1064*. Oxford: Oxford University Press

Clark, G. 1999 Victricius of Rouen: Praising the Saints. *Journal of Early Christian Studies* 7:3, 365–99

Clark, K. 1969. *Civilisation: A Personal View*. London: BBC

Coates, R. 2007 Invisible Britons: The View from Linguistics. In Higham (ed.) 2007, 172–91

Cole, A. 2013 *The Place-name Evidence for a Routeway Network in Early Medieval England*. BAR British Series 589. Oxford: Archaeopress

Colgrave, B. (ed. and trans.) 1968 *The Earliest Life of Gregory the Great by an Anonymous Monk of Whitby*. Cambridge: Cambridge University Press

Colgrave, B. (ed. and trans.) 1985 *Felix's Life of Saint Guthlac*. Cambridge: Cambridge University Press

Colgrave, B. (ed. and trans.) 1985 *The Life of Bishop Wilfrid by Eddius Stephanus*. Cambridge: Cambridge University Press

Colgrave, B. and Mynors, R.A.B. (eds and trans) 1994 *Bede: The Ecclesiastical History of the English People*. Oxford World Classics. Oxford: Oxford University Press

Collins, R. and Allason-Jones, L. (eds) 2010 *Finds from the Frontier: Material Culture in the 4th–5th Centuries*. Council for British Archaeology Research Report 162

Collins, R. and Gerrard, J. (eds) 2004 *Debating Late Antiquity in Britain AD 300–700*. British Archaeological Reports British Series 365

Connolly, S. 1989 *Vita Prima Sanctae Brigitae*: Background and Historical Value. *Journal of the Royal Society of Antiquaries of Ireland* 119, 5–49

Cox, B. 1976 The Place Names of the Earliest English Records. *The Journal of the English Place Name Society* 8, 12–66

Crossley-Holland, K. 1999 *The Anglo-Saxon World: An Anthology*. Oxford World's Classics. Oxford: Oxford University Press

Croxford, B. 2003 Iconoclasm in Roman Britain? *Britannia* 34, 81–95

Dalton, O.M. (ed. and trans.) 1915 *The Letters of Sidonius*. 2 vols. Oxford: Clarendon Press

Darling, M.J. and Keith, A. 1987 The Caistor-by-Norwich 'Massacre' Reconsidered. *Britannia* 18, 263–72

Dark, K. 2002 *Britain and the End of the Roman Empire*. Stroud: The History Press

Dark, P. 2009 *The Environment of Britain in the First Millennium* AD. London: Duckworth

Davies, S. (ed.) 2007 *The Mabinogion: A New Translation by Sioned Davies.* Oxford World Classics. Oxford: Oxford University Press

Davis, W. and Vierck, H. 1974 The Contexts of Tribal Hidage: Social Aggregates and Settlement Patterns. *Frühmittelalterliche Studien* 8, 223–93

Dewing, H.B. (ed. and trans.) 1914–40 *Procopius.* 7 vols. Cambridge, MA: Loeb Classical Library

Dickinson, T.M. 1993 An Anglo-Saxon 'Cunning Woman' from Bidford-on-Avon. In Carver, M. (ed.) 1993 *In Search of Cult: Archaeological Investigations in Honour of Philip Rahtz.* University of York Archaeological Papers. Woodbridge: Boydell Press, 45–54

Dickinson, T.M. 2011 Overview: Mortuary Ritual. In Hamerow et al. (eds) 2011, 221–37

Dillon, M. 2006 Lebor na Cert. *Corpus of Electronic texts.* University College, Cork. https://celt.ucc.ie/published/T102900.html

Drew, K.F. (trans) 2012 The Laws of the Salian Franks. *The Middle Ages.* Philadelphia: University of Pennsylvania Press

Driscoll, S.T. 1991 The Archaeology of State Formation in Scotland. In Hanson, W.S. and Slater, E.A. (eds) 1991 *Archaeology: New Perceptions*, 81–111. Aberdeen: Aberdeen University Press

Driscoll, S.T. and Nieke, M.R. (eds) 1988 *Power and Politics in Early Medieval Britain and Ireland.* Edinburgh: Edinburgh University Press

Duggan, M. 2016 Ceramic Imports to Britain and the Atlantic Seaboard in the Fifth Century and Beyond. *Internet Archaeology* 41. https://doi.org/10.11141/ia.41.3

Duggan, M. 2018 *Links to Late Antiquity: Ceramic Exchange and Contacts on the Atlantic Seaboard in the 5th to 7th centuries* AD. British Archaeological Reports British Series 639

Dumville, D.N. 1975 *The Textual History of the Welsh-Latin* Historia Brittonum. Unpublished PhD Thesis, University of Edinburgh

Dumville, D.N. 1976 The Anglian Collection of Royal Genealogies. *Anglo-Saxon England* 5, 23–50

Dumville, D.N. 1984 The Chronology of *De Excidio Britanniae*, Book 1. In Lapidge and Dumville (eds) 1984, 61–84

Dumville, D.N. 1989 The Origins of Northumbria: Some Aspects of the British Background. In Bassett (ed.) 1989, 213–22

Dumville, D.N. 1993 (ed.) *Saint Patrick* AD *493–1993*. Studies in Celtic History XIII. Woodbridge: Boydell Press

Dunn, M. 2003 *The Emergence of Monasticism: From the Desert Fathers to the Early Middle Ages.* Oxford: Blackwell

Dyer, C. 2007 Landscape and Society at Bibury, Gloucestershire, to 1540. In Bettery, J. (ed.) 2007 *Archives and Local History in Bristol and Gloucestershire, 126–139*. Bettey: The Bristol and Gloucestershire Archaeological Society

Eagles, B. 1989 Lindsey. In Basset (ed.) 1989, 202–12

Enright, M. J. 1996 *Lady with a Mead Cup: Ritual, Prophecy and Lordship in the European Warband from La Tène to the Viking Age*. Dublin: Four Courts Press

Esmonde Cleary, S. 2011 The Ending(s) of Roman Britain. In Hamerow et al. (eds) 2011, 13–29

Evison, V. I. 1994 *An Anglo-Saxon Cemetery at Great Chesterford, Essex*. CBA Research Report 91. York: Council for British Archaeology

Fear, A. T. (trans) 2010 *Orosius, Seven Books of History Against the Pagans*. Liverpool: Liverpool University Press

Findell, M. and Kopár, L. 2017 Runes and Commemoration in Anglo-Saxon England. *Fragments* 7. http://hdl.handle.net/2027/spo.9772151. 0006.004

Fitzpatrick-Matthews, K. J. and Fleming, R. 2016 The Perils of Periodization: Roman Ceramics in Britain after 400 CE. *Fragments* 5. http://hdl. handle.net/2027/spo.9772151.0005.001

Fleming, A. 1994 Swadal, Swar (and Erechwydd?): Early Medieval Polities in Upper Swaledale. *Landscape History* 16, 17–30

Fleming, A. 2010 *Swaledale: Valley of the Wild River*. Oxford: Windgather Press

Foster, S. M. 2014 *Picts, Gaels and Scots: Early Historic Scotland*. Edinburgh: Birlinn

Fowler, P. J. 2002 *Farming in the First Millennium AD*. Cambridge: Cambridge University Press

Fraser, J. E. 2009 Caledonia to Pictland: Scotland to 795. *The New Edinburgh History of Scotland*. Edinburgh: Edinburgh University Press

Frend, W. H. C. 2003 Roman Britain, A Failed Promise. In Carver (ed.) 2003, 79–91

Frodsham, P. and O'Brien, C. F. (eds) 2005 *Yeavering: People, Power and Place*. Stroud: Tempus

Fulford, M., Handley, M. and Clarke, A. 2000 An Early Date for Ogham: The Silchester Ogham Stone Rehabilitated. *Medieval Archaeology* 44, 1–23

Gardiner, M. 2012 An Early Medieval Tradition of Building in Britain. *Arqueologia de la Arquitectura* 9, 231–46

Garmonsway, G. N. (ed.) 1972 *The Anglo-Saxon Chronicle*. London: J. M. Dent

Gelling, M. 1967 English Place-names Derived from the Compound *Wicham. Medieval Archaeology* 11, 87–104

Gelling, M. 1979 The Evidence of Place-names 1. In Sawyer (ed.) 1979, 110–21

Gelling, M. 1989 The Early History of Western Mercia. In Bassett (ed.) 1989, 184–201

Gelling, M. 2011 Place-names and Archaeology. In Hamerow et al. (eds) 2011, 986–1003

Gelling, M. and Cole, A. 2014 *The Landscape of Place-names.* 2nd ed. Donington: Shaun Tyas

Gerrard, J. 2004 How Late is Late? Pottery and the Fifth Century in Southwest Britain. In Collins and Gerrard (eds) 2004, 65–75

Gerrard, J. 2013 *The Ruin of Roman Britain.* Cambridge: Cambridge University Press

Gerrard, J. 2015 Synthesis, Chronology and 'Late Roman' Cemeteries in Britain. *American Journal of Archaeology* 119:4, 565–72

Gerrard, J. 2016 Romano-British Pottery in the Fifth Century. *Internet Archaeology* 41. https://doi.org/10.11141/ia.41.9

Griffiths, D., Philpott, R.A. and Egan, G., 2008 *Meols: The Archaeology of the North Wirral Coast: Discoveries and Observations in the 19th and 20th Centuries, with a Catalogue of Collections.* Oxford University School of Archaeology Monograph 68

Grigg, E. 2015 *Early Medieval Dykes (400 to 850AD).* Unpublished PhD thesis, University of Manchester

Hall, A. 2010 Interlinguistic Communication in Bede's *Historia Ecclesiastica Gentis Anglorum.* In Hall, A., Kiricsi, A. and Timofeeva, O. (eds) 2010 *Interfaces between Language and Culture in Medieval England: A Festschrift for Matti Kilpiö. The Northern World* 48, 37–80

Hall, A. 2011 *A gente Anglorum appellatur*: The Evidence of Bede's Historia Ecclesiastica Gentis Anglorum for the Replacement of Roman Names by English Ones During the Early Anglo-Saxon Period. In Timofeeva, O. and Säily, T. (eds) 2011 *Words in Dictionaries and History: Essays in Honour of R.W. McConchie. Amsterdam:* John Benjamins, 219–31

Hall, D. and Coles, J. 1994 *Fenland Survey: An Essay in Landscape and Persistence.* English Heritage Archaeological Report 1

Halsall, G. 2007 *Barbarian Migrations and the Roman West 376–568.* Cambridge Medieval Textbooks. Cambridge: Cambridge University Press

Halsall, G. 2013 *Worlds of Arthur: Facts and Fictions of the Dark Ages.* Oxford: Oxford University Press

Hamerow, H. 1993 *Excavations at Mucking Volume 2: The Anglo-Saxon Settlement.* English Heritage Archaeological Reports 21. British Museum Press

Hamerow, H. 2012 *Rural Settlements and Society in Anglo-Saxon England.* Medieval History and Archaeology. Oxford: Oxford University Press

Hamerow, H., Hinton, D.A. and Crawford, S. (eds) 2011. *The Oxford Handbook of Anglo-Saxon Archaeology.* Oxford: Oxford University Press

Hamilton, W. 1996. *Ammianus Marcellinus: the Later Roman Empire (AD 354–378).* Penguin Classics. Harmondsworth: Penguin

Hanson, R.P.C. 1968 *Saint Patrick: His Origins and Career.* Oxford: Oxford University Press

Härke, H. 1990 'Warrior Graves'? The Background of the Anglo-Saxon Weapon Burial Rite. *Past & Present* 126, 22–43

Härke, H. 1997 Early Anglo-Saxon Social Structure. In Hines (ed.) 1997, 125–70

Härke, H. 2011 Anglo-Saxon Immigration and Ethnogenesis. *Medieval Archaeology* 55, 1–28

Harland, J.M. 2019 Memories of Migration? The 'Anglo-Saxon' Burial Costume in the Fifth Century AD. *Antiquity* 93:370, 954–69

Harrington, S. and Welch, M. 2014 *The Early Anglo-Saxon Kingdoms of Southern Britain AD 450–650: Beneath the Tribal Hidage.* Oxford: Oxbow Books

Harris, A. 2003 *Byzantium, Britain and the West: The Archaeology of Cultural Identity AD 400–650.* Charleston: Tempus

Hart, C. 1971 The Tribal Hidage. *Transactions of the Royal Historical Society* 21, 133–57

Hawkes, J. and Mills, S. 1999 *Northumbria's Golden Age.* Stroud: Sutton

Hedges, R. 2011 Anglo-Saxon Migration and the Molecular Evidence. In Hamerow et al. (eds) 2011, 79–90

Henig, M. 2011 The Fate of Late Roman towns. In Hinton, Crawford and Hamerow (eds) 2011, 515–33

Herlihy, D. 1999 Opera Muliebria: *Women and Work in Medieval Europe.* Philadelphia: Temple University Press

Higham, N.J. 1986 *The Northern Counties to AD 1000.* Harlow: Longman

Higham, N.J. 1992 *Rome, Britain and the Anglo-Saxons.* London: Seaby

Higham, N.J. 1993 *The Kingdom of Northumbria AD 350–1100.* Stroud: Sutton

Higham, N.J. 1994 *The English Conquest: Gildas and Britain in the Fifth Century.* Manchester: Manchester University Press.

Higham, N.J. 1995 *An English Empire: Bede and the Early Anglo-Saxon Kings*. Manchester: Manchester University Press.

Higham, N.J. 2014 Constantius, St Germanus and Fifth-century Britain. *Early Medieval Europe* 22:2, 113–37

Higham, N.J. 2018 *King Arthur: The Making of the Legend*. Newhaven: Yale University Press

Higham, N.J. (ed.) 2007 *Britons in Anglo-Saxon England*. Publications of the Manchester Centre for Anglo-Saxon Studies 7. Woodbridge: Boydell Press

Hill, D. 1984 *An Atlas of Anglo-Saxon England*. Oxford: Blackwell

Hill, P. 1997 *Whithorn and St Ninian: the Excavation of a Monastic Town 1984–91*. Stroud: Sutton

Hills, C. 2006 *Origins of the English*. Duckworth Debates in Archaeology. London: Duckworth

Hills, C. 2011 Overview: Anglo-Saxon Identity. In Hamerow et al. (eds) 2011, 3–12

Hills, C. and Lucy, S. 2013 *Spong Hill Part IX: Chronology and Synthesis*. McDonald Institute Monographs. Cambridge: Cambridge University Press

Hines, J. (ed) 1997 *The Anglo-Saxons from the Migration Period to the Eighth Century: An Ethnographic Perspective*. San Marino: Boydell Press

Hoare, F.R. 1954 *The Western Fathers. The Makers of Christendom*. London: Sheen and Ward

Hodges, R. 1982 *Dark Age Economics*. London: Duckworth

Hood, A.B.E. 1978 *St Patrick: His Writings and Muirchu's Life*. Arthurian Period Sources 9. London: Phillimore

Hooke, D. 1985 *The Anglo-Saxon Landscape: The Kingdom of the Hwicce*. Manchester: Manchester University Press

Hooke, D. 1997 The Anglo-Saxons in England in the Seventh and Eighth Centuries: Aspects of Location in Space. In Hines (ed.) 1997, 65–100

Hope-Taylor, B. 1977 *Yeavering: An Anglo-British Centre of Early Northumbria*. London: HMSO

Hopkins, K. 1980 Taxes and Trade in the Roman Empire 200 BC–AD 400. *Journal of Roman Studies* 70, 101–25

Howe, N. 2008 *Writing the Map of Anglo-Saxon England: Essays in Cultural Geography*. Newhaven: Yale University Press

Hyer, M.C. and Owen-Crocker, G.R. 2011 *The Material Culture of Daily Living in the Anglo-Saxon World*. Liverpool: Liverpool University Press

An Inventory of the Historical Monuments in Dorset, Vol. 2, Southeast 1970. London: HMSO

Ireland, S. 2008 *Roman Britain: A Sourcebook.* 3rd ed. London: Routledge

Jackson, K.H. 1969 *The Gododdin: The Oldest Scottish Poem.* Edinburgh: Edinburgh University Press

Jackson, R.P.J. and Potter, T.W. 1996 *Excavations at Stonea, Cambridge-shire 1980–85.* London: British Museum Press

James, E. 1989 The Origins of Barbarian Kingdoms. In Bassett (ed.) 1989, 40–52

John, E. 1964 *Land Tenure in Early England.* Studies in Early English History 1. Leicester: Leicester University Press

Johnson, B. and Waddington, C. 2009 Prehistoric and Dark Age Settlement Remains from Cheviot Quarry, Milfield Basin, Northumberland. *Archaeological Journal 165,* 107–26

Jones, G.R.J. 1979 Multiple Estates and Early Settlement. In Sawyer (ed.) 1979, 9–34

Jones, M.E. and Casey, J. 1988 The Gallic Chronicle Restored: A Chronology for the Anglo-Saxon Invasions and the End of Roman Britain. *Britannia* 19, 367–98

Kelly, F. 2000 *Early Irish Farming.* Early Irish Law Series IV. Dublin: Dublin Institute for Advanced Studies

Kirby, D.P. 1966 The Anglo-Saxon Bishops of Leicester, Lindsey (Syddensis) and Dorchester. *Transactions of the Leicestershire Archaeological and Historical Society* 41, 1–8

Kirby, D.P. 2000 *The Earliest English Kings.* London: Routledge

Koch, J.T. (ed.) 1997 *The* Gododdin *of Aneirin: Text and Context from Dark Age North Britain.* Cardiff: University of Wales Press

Kulikowski, M. 2000 Barbarians in Gaul, Usurpers in Britain. *Britannia* 31, 325–45

Lacey, B. 2013 *Saint Columba: His Life and Legacy.* Dublin: Columba Press

Lane, A. and Campbell, E. 2000 *Dunadd: An Early Dalriadic Capital.* Oxford: Oxbow Books

Lapidge, M. 1984 Gildas's Education and the Latin Culture of Sub-Roman Britain. In Lapidge and Dumville (eds) 1984, 27–50

Lapidge, M. and Dumville, D. (eds) 1984 *Gildas: New Approaches.* Studies in Celtic History V. Woodbridge: Boydell Press

Le Roy Ladurie, E. 1980 *Montaillou.* Harmondsworth: Penguin

Lewis, G. and Williams, R. (trans) 2019 *The Book of Taliesin: Poems of Warfare and Praise in an Enchanted Britain.* London: Penguin

Leyser, H. 1995 *Medieval Women: A Social History of Women in England 450–1500.* London: Phoenix

Lucy, S. 2016 Odd Goings-on at Mucking: Interpreting the Latest

Romano-British Pottery Horizon. *Internet Archaeology* 41. https://doi. org/10.11141/ia.41.6

Lynn, C.J. and McDowell, J.A. 2011 *Deer Park Farms: The Excavation of a Raised Rath in the Glenarm Valley, Co. Antrim*. Northern Ireland Archaeological Monographs 9. Belfast: Northern Ireland Stationery Office

Mackreth, D.F. 1996 Orton Hall Farm: A Roman and Early Saxon Farmstead. *East Anglian Archaeology* 76. Nene Valley Archaeological Trust

Madigan, K. and Osiek, C. 2005 *Ordained Women in the Early Church: A Documentary History*. Baltimore: Johns Hopkins University Press

Manco, J. 2018 *The Origins of the Anglo-Saxons: Decoding the Ancestry of the English*. London: Thames and Hudson

Mason, A. and Williamson, T. 2017 Ritual Landscapes in Pagan and Early Christian England. *Fragments* 6, 80–109

Mathisen, R.W. 2012 Clovis, Anastasius, and Political Status in 508 CE: *The Frankish Aftermath of the Battle of Vouillé*. In Mathisen and Shanza (eds) 2012, 79–110

Mathisen, R.W. and Shanza, D. (eds) 2012 *The Battle of Vouillé, 507 CE: Where France Began*. Millennium Studies 33. Boston: De Gruyter

Mattingly, D. 2006 An Imperial Possession: Britain in the Roman Empire. *The Penguin History of Britain*. London: Penguin

McCarthy, M. 2002 Rheged: an Early Historic Kingdom near the Solway. *Proceedings of the Society of Antiquaries of Scotland* 132, 357–81

McCarthy, M. 2011 The Kingdom of Rheged: A Landscape Perspective. *Northern History* 48:1, 9–22

McErlean, T. and Crothers, N. 2007 *Harnessing the Tides: The Early Medieval Tide Mills at Nendrum Monastery, Strangford Lough*. Northern Ireland Archaeological Monographs 7. Belfast: The Stationery Office

McGrail, S. 1990 *Maritime Celts, Frisians and Anglo-Saxons*. CBA Research Report 71. York: Council for British Archaeology

McOmish, D., Field, D. and Brown, G. 2002 *The Field Archaeology of the Salisbury Training Area*. Swindon: English Heritage

Medlycott, M. 2011 *The Roman Town of Great Chesterford*. East Anglian Archaeology Report 137. Essex County Council

Millett, M. 1990 *The Romanization of Britain: An Essay in Archaeological Interpretation*. Cambridge: Cambridge University Press

Millett, M., Revell, L. and Moore, A. (eds) 2011 *The Oxford Handbook of Roman Britain*. Oxford: Oxford University Press

Moisl, H.L. 1983 The Bernician Royal Dynasty and the Irish in the Seventh Century. *Peritia* 2, 103–26

Mommsen, T. (ed.) 1892 Prosperi Tironis epitoma chronicon ed. primum a. CCCCXXXIII, continuata ad a. CCCLV. In Mommsen, T. (ed.) *Chronica minora saec. IV, V, VI, VII*, vol. 1, MGH Scriptores. Auctores antiquissimi 9. Berlin: Weidmann, 341–499

Montgomery, J., Evans, J.A., Powlesland, D. and Roberts, C.A. 2005 Continuity or Colonisation in Anglo-Saxon England? Isotope Evidence for Mobility, Subsistence Practice, and Status at West Heslerton. *American Journal of Physical Anthropology* 126, 123–38

Morris, J. 1973 *The Age of Arthur*. London: Weidenfeld & Nicolson

Morris, J. (ed) 1980 *Nennius. British History and the Welsh Annals*. Arthurian Period Sources 8. London: Phillimore

Morris, J. (ed) 1995 *Arthurian Period Sources 3: Persons*. London: Phillimore

Morris, R.K. 1989 *Churches in the Landscape*. London: Phoenix

Muhlberger, S. 1981 *The Fifth-Century Chroniclers: Prosper, Hydatius, and the Gallic Chronicler of 452*. ARCA Classical and Medieval Texts, Papers and Monographs 27. Cambridge: Francis Cairns

Myres, J.N.L. 1986 *The English Settlements*. Oxford: Clarendon Press

Natal, D. 2018 Putting the Roman Periphery on the Map: the Geography of Romanness, Orthodoxy and Legitimacy in Victricius of Rouen's *De Laude Sanctorum*. *Early Medieval Europe* 26:3, 304–26

Niblett, R. 2006 Verulamium: Excavations within the Roman Town 1986–88. *Britannia* 37, 53–188

Nieke, M.R. and Duncan, H.B. 1988 Dalriada: the Establishment and Maintenance of an Early Historic Kingdom in Northern Britain. In Driscoll and Nieke (eds) 1988, 6–21

Noble, E. and Evans, N. (eds) 2019 *The King in the North: The Pictish Realms of Fortriu and Ce*. Edinburgh: Birlinn

Noble, E., Gondek, M., Campbell, E., Evans, N., Hamilton, D. and Taylor, S. 2019 A Powerful Place of Pictland: Interdisciplinary Perspectives on a Power Centre of the 4th to 6th Centuries AD. *Medieval Archaeology* 63:1, 56–94

Nugent, R. and Williams, H. 2012 Sighted Surfaces: Ocular Agency in Early Anglo-Saxon Cremation Burials. In Danielsson, I-M., Fahlander, F. and Sjöstrand, Y. (eds) 2012 *Encountering Imagery. Materialities, Perceptions, Relations*, 187–208 Stockholm Studies in Archaeology 57. Stockholm

O'Brien, C. 2002 The Early Medieval Shires of Yeavering, Breamish and Bamburgh. *Archaeologia Aeliana* Series 5, 30: 53–73

O'Brien, C. 2005 The Great Enclosure. In Frodsham and O'Brien (eds) 2005, 145–52

O'Brien, C. 2010 The Emergence of Northumbria: Artefacts, Archaeology and Models. In Collins and Allason-Jones (eds) 2010, 110–19

O'Brien, C. and Adams, M. 2016a Early Ecclesiastical Precincts and Landscapes of Inishowen, Donegal. In O'Carragain, T. and Turner, S. (eds) *Making Christian Landscapes in Atlantic Europe*. Cork: University of Cork Press, 159–76

O'Brien, C. and Adams, M. 2016b The Identification of Early Medieval Monastic Estates in Northumbria. *Medieval Settlement Research* 31, 15–27

O'Brien, C., Adams, M., Haycock, D., O'Meara. D., and Pennie, J. 2016 The Early Ecclesiastical Complexes of Carrowmore and Clonca and their Landscape Context in Inishowen, County Donegal. *Ulster Archaeological Journal* 72, 142–60

O'Brien, C.F. and Miket, R.F. 1991 The Early Medieval Settlement of Thirlings, Northumberland. *Durham Archaeological Journal* 7:7, 57–91

O'Daly, M. 1952 A Poem on the Airgíalla. Contributions in Memory of Osborn Bergin. *Ériu* 16, 179–88

Oosthuizen, S. 2017 *The Anglo-Saxon Fenland*. Oxford: Oxbow Books

Oosthuizen, S. 2019 *The Emergence of the English*. Leeds: ARC Humanities Press

Owen-Crocker, G.R. 2007 British Wives and Slaves? Possible Romano-British Techniques in 'Women's Work'. In Higham (ed.) 2007, 80–90

Owen-Crocker, G.R. 2017 Furnishing Heorot. In Cambridge, E. and Hawkes, J. (eds) 2017 *Crossing Boundaries: Interdisciplinary Approaches to the Art, Material Culture, Language and Literature of the Early Medieval World*, Oxford: Oxbow Books, 232–42

Pattison, J.E. 2008 Is it Necessary to Assume an Apartheid-like Social Structure in Early Anglo-Saxon England? *Proceedings of the Royal Society of Biological Sciences* 275, 2423–19

Penn, K. and Brugmann, B. 2007 Aspects of Anglo-Saxon Inhumation Burial: Morning Thorpe, Spong Hill, Bergh Apton and Westgarth Gardens. *East Anglian Archaeology* 119. Dereham: Norfolk Museums and Archaeology Service

Perring, D. 2002 *The Roman House in Britain*. London: Routledge

Perry, J.P. 2013 *United in Death: The Pre-Burial Origins of Anglo-Saxon Cremation Urns*. Unpublished PhD thesis, University of Sheffield

Petts, D. 2011 Christianity in Roman Britain. In Millet, Revell and Moore (eds) 2016, 660–80

Petts, D. 2013 Military and Civilian: Reconfiguring the End of Roman Britain in the North. *European Journal of Archaeology* 16:2, 314–35

Petts, D. 2014 Christianity and Cross-Channel Connectivity in Late and Sub-Roman Britain. In Haarer, F.K. and Collins, R. (eds) 2014 *AD 410: The History and Archaeology of Late Roman and Sub-Roman Britain*. London: Society for the Promotion of Roman Studies, 73–88

Pohl, W. 1997 Ethnic Names and Identities in the British Isles: A Comparative Perspective. In Hines (ed.) 1997, 7–40

Powlesland, D. 1997 Early Anglo-Saxon Settlements, Structures, Form and Layout. In Hines (ed.) 1997, 101–24

Powlesland, D. 1999 The Anglo-Saxon Settlement at West Heslerton, North Yorkshire. In Hawkes and Mills (eds) 1999, 55–65

Powlesland, D., Lyall, J., Hopkinson, G., Donoghue, D., Beck, M., Harte, A. and Stott, D., 2006 Beneath the Sand – Remote Sensing, Archaeology, Aggregates and Sustainability: a Case Study from Heslerton, the Vale of Pickering, North Yorkshire, UK. *Archaeological Prospection* 13:4, 291–9

Pretty, K. 1989 Defining the Magonsaete. In Bassett (ed.) 1989, 171–83

Pryor, F. 2005 *Britain AD: A Quest for Arthur, England and the Anglo-Saxons*. London: Harper Perennial

Quinnell, H. 2004 *Trethurgy. Excavations at Trethurgy Round, St Austell: Community and Status in Roman and Post-Roman Cornwall*. Truro: Cornwall County Council

Rahtz, P.A., Woodward, A., Burrow, I., Everton, A., Watts, L., Leach, P., Hirst, S., Fowler, P. and Gardiner, K. 1992 *Cadbury Congresbury 1968–73: A Late Post-Roman Hilltop Settlement in Somerset*. British Archaeological Reports British Series 223. Oxford: Tempus Reparatum

Rippon, S. 2018 *Kingdom, Civitas and County: The Evolution of Territorial Identity in the English Landscape*. Oxford: Oxford University Press

Rippon, S., Smart, C. and Pears, B. (eds) 2015 *The Fields of Britannia: Continuity and Change in the Late Roman and Early Medieval Landscape*. Oxford: Oxford University Press

Roberts, B.K. 2008 The Land of Werhale – Landscapes of Bede. *Archaeologia Aeliana* Series 5:37, 127–61

Roberts, B.K. 2010 Northumbrian Origins and Post-Roman Continuity: An Exploration. In Collins and Allason-Jones (eds) 2010, 119–32

Savory, H.N. 1960 Excavations at Dinas Emrys. *Archaeologia Cambrensis* 109, 13–77

Sawyer, P.H. (ed.) 1979 *English Medieval Settlement*. London: Edward Arnold

Schaff, P. and Wace, H. (eds) 1894 *The Nicene and Post-Nicene Fathers* Second Series, Volume 11. Sulpicius Severus, Vincent of Lerins, John Cassian. Buffalo: Christian Literature Company. Revised and edited for

New Advent by Kevin Knight. www.newadvent.org/fathers/360206058. htm

Schrijver, P. 2014 *Language Contact and the Origins of the Germanic Languages*. Routledge Studies in Linguistics. London: Routledge

Scull, C. 1990 Scales and Weights in Early Anglo-Saxon England. *Archaeological Journal* 147, 183–215

Scull, C., Minter, F. and Plouviez, J. 1990 Social and Economic Complexity in Early Medieval England: A Central Place Complex of the East Anglian Kingdom at Rendlesham, Suffolk. *Antiquity* 90:354, 1594–612

Severin, T. 2005 *The Brendan Voyage: Across the Atlantic in a Leather Boat*. Dublin: Gill Books

Sharpe, R. (ed. and trans.) 1995 *Adomnán of Iona: Life of Saint Columba*. London: Penguin

Simms-Williams, P. 1983. The Settlement of England in Bede and the Chronicle. *Anglo-Saxon England* 12, 1–41

Simms-Williams, P. 2003 *The Celtic Inscriptions of Britain: Phonology and Chronology, c.400–1200*. Oxford: Palaeological Society

Smith, I.M. 1991 Sprouston, Roxburghshire: An Early Anglian Centre of the Eastern Tweed Basin. *Proceedings of the Society of Antiquaries of Scotland* 121, 261–94

Smith, J.T. 1985 Barnsley Park Villa: Its Interpretation and Implications. *Oxford Journal of Archaeology* 4:3, 341–51

Snyder, C.A. 1998 *An Age of Tyrants*. Stroud: Sutton

Sparey-Green, C. 2003 Where are the Christians? Late Roman Cemeteries in Britain. In Carver (ed.) 2003, 93–108

Speed, G. 2014 *Towns in the Dark? Urban Transformations from Late Roman Britain to Anglo-Saxon England*. Oxford: Archaeopress

Taylor, J. 2007 *An Atlas of Roman Rural Settlement in England*. CBA Research Report 151. York: Council for British Archaeology

Taylor, T. (ed. and trans.) 1925 *The Life of St. Samson of Dol*. London: Society for Promoting Christian Knowledge

Thomas, C. 1971 *The Early Christian Archaeology of North Britain*. Oxford: Oxford University Press

Thomas, C. 1981 *Christianity in Roman Britain to AD 500*. London: Batsford

Thomas, C. 1985 *Exploration of a Drowned Landscape: Archaeology and History of the Isles of Scilly*. London: Batsford

Thomas, M., Stumpf, M.P.H. and Härke, H. 2006 Evidence for an Apartheid-like Social Structure in Early Anglo-Saxon England. *Proceedings of the Royal Society of Biological Sciences* 273, 2651–7

Thompson, E.A. 1980 Procopius on Brittia and Britannia. *The Classical Quarterly* 30:2, 498–507

Thompson, E.A. 1984 *Saint Germanus of Auxerre and the End of Roman Britain*. Woodbridge: Boydell Press

Thorpe, L. 1974 *Gregory of Tours: The History of the Franks*. Harmondsworth: Penguin

Tipper, J. *The* Grubenhaus *in Anglo-Saxon England*. Yedingham: The Landscape Research Centre

Todd, M. 1987 *The South-west to AD 1000*. London: Longman

Tomlin, R. 1996 A Five-acre Wood in Roman Kent. In Bird, J., Hassall, M.W.C. and Sheldon, H. (eds) 1996 *Interpreting Roman London: Papers in Memory of Hugh Chapman*. Oxford: Oxbow Monograph 58, 209ff

Toolis, R. and Bowles, C. 2017 *The Lost Dark Age Kingdom of Rheged: the Discovery of a Royal Stronghold at Trusty's Hill, Galloway*. Oxford: Oxbow

Turner, S. 2003 Making a Christian Landscape: Early Medieval Cornwall. In Carver (ed.) 2003, 171–94

Udolf, J. 2012 The Colonisation of England by Germanic Tribes on the Basis of Place-names. In Stenroos, M., Mäkinen, M. and Særheim, I. (eds) 2012 *Language Contact and Development Around the North Sea. Current Issues in Linguistic Theory* 321, 23–52. Amsterdam: John Benjamin

Ulmschneider, K. 2011 Settlement Hierarchy. In Hamerow et al. (eds) 2011, 156–71

Upex, S.G. 2011 The *Praetorium* of Edmund Artis: A Summary of Excavations and Surveys of the Palatial Roman Structure at Castor, Cambridgeshire 1828–2010. *Britannia* 42, 23–112

Walker, R.F. 1976 *The Origins of Newcastle upon Tyne*. Newcastle upon Tyne: Thorne's Student Bookshop

Walton Rogers, P. 2007 *Cloth and Clothing in Early Anglo-Saxon England, AD 450–700*. York: Council for British Archaeology

Walton Rogers, P. 2018 From Farm to Town: The Changing Pattern of Textile Production in Anglo-Saxon England. In Ulanowska, A., Siennicka, M. and Grupa, M. (eds) 2018 *Dynamics and Organisation of Textile Production in Past Societies in Europe and the Mediterranean*. Fasiculi Archaeologiae Historiciae Fasiculus XXXI, 115–24 Łódź: Polish Academy of Sciences

Warner, R.B. 1973 The Excavations at Clogher and their Context. *Clogher Record* 8:1, 5–12

Warner, R.B. 1988 The Archaeology of Early Historic Irish Kingship. In Driscoll and Nieke (eds) 1988, 47–68

Warner, R.B. 2000 Clogher: An Archaeological Window on Early Medieval Tyrone and Mid Ulster. In Dillon, C. and Jefferies, H. (eds) 2000 *Tyrone, History and Society*, 39–54 Dublin: Geography Publications

Watts, D. 1991 *Christians and Pagans in Roman Britain*. London: Routledge

Watts, V. 2004 *The Cambridge Dictionary of English Place-Names*. Cambridge: Cambridge University Press

Webb, J.F. and Farmer, D.H. (ed. and trans.) 1983 *The Age of Bede*. Harmondsworth: Penguin

Webster, G. and Smith, L. 1987 Reply to J.T. Smith's Suggested Reinterpretation of Barnsley Park Villa. *Oxford Journal of Archaeology* 6:1, 69–89

West, S. 1985a *West Stow. The Anglo-Saxon Village Volume 1: The Text*. East Anglian Archaeology Report 24. Suffolk County Planning Department

West, S. 1985b *West Stow. The Anglo-Saxon Village Volume 2: Figures and Plates*. East Anglian Archaeology Report 24. Suffolk County Planning Department

Whitelock, D. (ed.) 1979 *English Historical Documents c.500–1042*. 2nd ed. London: Eyre and Spottiswoode

Whyman, M. 2001 *Late Roman Britain in Transition: A Ceramic Perspective*. Unpublished PhD Thesis, University of York

Wild, J.P. 1967 The *Gynaeceum* at *Venta* and its Context. *Latomus* 26:3, 648–76

Wilkinson, J. 2006 *Egeria's Travels*. London: Society for the Promotion of Christian Knowledge

Williams, H. 2002 Cemeteries as Central Places: Place and Identity in Migration Period Eastern England. In Hårdh, B. and Larsson, L. (eds) 2002 *Central Places in the Migration and Merovingian Periods: Papers from the 52nd Sachsensymposium Lund, August 2001*. Acta Archaeologica Lundensia Series 8:39, 341–62

Williams, H. 2005a Cremation in Early Anglo-Saxon England – Past, Present and Future Research. In H-J. Häßler (ed) *Studien zur Sachsenforschung* 15: 533–49. Oldenberg: Isensee

Williams, H. 2005b Keeping the Dead at Arm's Length: Memory, Weaponry and Early Medieval Mortuary Technologies. *Journal of Social Archaeology* 5:2, 253–75

Williams, H. 2011 Mortuary Practices in Early Anglo-Saxon England. In Hamerow et al. (eds) 2011, 238–59

Williamson, T. 2013 *Environment, Society and Landscape in Early Medieval England*. Anglo-Saxon Studies 19. Woodbridge: Boydell Press

Wilmott, T. 2010 The Late Roman Frontier: the Structural Background. In Collins and Allason-Jones (eds) 2010, 10–19

Wilson, D.M. (ed) 1976 *Archaeology in Anglo-Saxon England*. Cambridge: Cambridge University Press

Wilson, P., Cardwell, P., Cramp, R.J., Evans, J., Taylor-Wilson, R.H., Thompson, A. and Wacher, J.S. 1996 Early Anglian Catterick and *Catraeth*. *Medieval Archaeology* 40, 1–61

Winterbottom, M. 1978 *Gildas: The Ruin of Britain and Other Works*. Arthurian Period Sources Volume 7. London: Phillimore

Wood, I. 1984 The End of Roman Britain: Continental Evidence and Parallels. In Lapidge and Dumville (eds) 1994, 1–26

Wood, I. 1987 The Fall of the Western Empire and the End of Roman Britain. *Britannia* 18, 251–62

Wood, I. 1990 Before and After the Migration to Britain. In Hines (ed.) 1997, 41–64

Wood, I. 1992 Frankish Hegemony in England. In Carver (ed.) 1992, 235–42

Wood, I. 1994 The Mission of Augustine of Canterbury to the English. *Speculum* 69:1, 1–17

Wood, I. 1997 The Channel from the 4th to the 7th Centuries AD. In McGrail (ed.) 1997, 93–7

Wood, I. 2009 Germanus, Alban and Auxerre. *Bulletin du Centre d'Études Médiévales d'Auxerre* 13, 123–9

Wood, I. 2018 The Roman Origins of the Northumbrian Kingdom. In Balzaretti, R., Barrow, J. and Skinner, P. (eds) 2018 *Italy and Early Medieval Europe: Papers for Chris Wickham*. Oxford: Oxford University Press, 39–49

Wood, P.N. 1996 On the Little British Kingdom of Craven. *Northern History* 32:1, 1–20

Wooding, J. 1996 *Communication and Commerce along the Western Sealanes AD 400–800*. British Archaeological Reports International Series 654

Wooding, J.M. 2007 The Figure of David. In Evans, J.W. and Wooding, J.M. (eds) *St David of Wales: Cult, Church and Nation*. Studies in Celtic History XXIV. Woodbridge: Boydell Press

Woodward, A. and Leach, P. 1993 *The Uley Shrines: Excavation of a Ritual Complex on West Hill, Uley, Gloucestershire 1977–9*. Swindon: English Heritage

Woolf, A. 2007 From Pictland to Alba 789–1070. *The New Edinburgh History of Scotland*. Edinburgh: Edinburgh University Press

Wright, S.M., Rahtz, P.A. and Hirst, S. 2000. *Cannington Cemetery*. Malet Street: Society for the Promotion of Roman Studies.

Yorke, B. 2003 The Adaptation of the Anglo-Saxon Royal Courts to Christianity. In Carver (ed.) 2003, 243–57

Yorke, B. 2013 *Kings and Kingdoms of Early Anglo-Saxon England*. Abingdon: Routledge

Online primary sources

Annals of Tigernach. https://celt.ucc.ie//published/G100002/index.html

Annals of Ulster. https://celt.ucc.ie//published/T100001A

Chronica Gallica of 452. Translated by Aymenn Jawad Al-Tamimi www.aymennjawad.org/23320/the-gallic-chronicle-of-452-translation

Image credits

Sources of the chapter-opening images

Chapter 1, p. 3: www.beastcoins.com/RomanImperial/X/ValentinianIII/
ValentinianIII.htm.

Chapter 2, p. 35: www.beastcoins.com/RomanImperial/X/ValentinianIII/
ValentinianIII.htm.

Chapter 3, p. 69: British Museum, www.britishmuseum.org/research/
collection_online/collection_object_details/collection_image_gallery.as
px?assetId=1274315001&objectId=1358236&partId=1. Cf. Thomas
1981, 116.

Chapter 4, p. 99: www.bl.uk/anglo-saxons/articles/women-in-anglo-
saxon-england

Chapter 5, p. 135: British Museum, www.britannica.com/topic/
bracteate-coin/media/76736/7904.

Chapter 6, p. 171: Thomas 1971, 103 and 110.

Chapter 7, p. 205: Williamson (2009) after Roach Smith (1852).
For more information see https://webapps.kent.gov.uk/
KCC.ExploringKentsPast.Web.Sites.Public/SingleResult.
aspx?uid=%27mke7638%27.

Chapter 8, p. 237: British Library MS *Harley* 3271 folio 6v.

Chapter 9, p. 265: Glasgow Museums Collection.

Chapter 10, p. 309: Duomo di Otranto, Basilica Cattedrale di Santa
Maria Annunziata, Apulia, Italy.

Chapter 11, p. 339: https://research.britishmuseum.org/research/collection_online/collection_object_details/collection_image_gallery.aspx?assetId=354692001&objectId=1571525&partId=1.

Chapter 12, p. 369: www.kate-batchelor.co.uk/uncategorized/day-174-2016-sketch-day-challenge.

Chapter 13, p. 397: Church of St Paul, Jarrow.

Sources of the images within the text

Photographs and settlement plans within the text are by Max Adams.

Index

Page references in *italics* indicate images.